JEREMY BENTHAM'S ECONOMIC WRITINGS

JEREMY BENTHAM'S ECONOMIC WRITINGS

Critical edition based on his printed works and unprinted manuscripts

by W. Stark

VOLUME II

LONDON AND NEW YORK

First published 1952
by Routledge

Published 2014 by Routledge

2 Park Square, Milton Park, Abingdon, Oxfordshire OX14 4RN

Simultaneously published in the USA and Canada
by Routledge

711 Third Avenue, New York, NY 10017

First issued in paperback 2014

Routledge is an imprint of the Taylor & Francis Group, an informa business

Transferred to Digital Printing 2008

Typeset in Times by Keystroke, Jacaranda Lodge, Wolverhampton

British Library Cataloguing in Publication Data
A catalogue record for this book is available from the British Library

ISBN 978-0-415-31868-6 (hbk)
ISBN 978-1-138-86166-4 (pbk)
ISBN 978-0-415-31866-2 (set)

Publisher's Note

The publisher has gone to great lengths to ensure the quality of this reprint but points out that some imperfections in the original may be apparent

JEREMY BENTHAM'S ECONOMIC WRITINGS

CRITICAL EDITION
BASED ON HIS PRINTED WORKS AND
UNPRINTED MANUSCRIPTS

BY

W. STARK

VOLUME TWO

LONDON AND NEW YORK

CONTENTS

INTRODUCTION

THE three years from the beginning of 1796 to the end of 1798 mark a certain deviation from the main direction of Bentham's economic studies. The various financial plans which he had just elaborated were, to use his own phrase, laid upon the shelf, and he turned his attention for a while to one of the most eagerly debated topics of the day—the subject of poor relief. Closely related though it is to political economy proper, we have no choice but to pass it over here: space and time alike forbid us to follow Bentham along this secondary road. His plan for the poor was an outgrowth of his plan for a model prison, the Panopticon, and it goes without saying that a consideration of that famous and ill-fated project would take us much too far afield.

But the discussion of the problems of poverty did not monopolize Bentham's mind for very long. When the war clouds began to gather over France, and when the storm began to break over Europe, the preoccupations of the general public rapidly changed, and Bentham's attention was radically redirected. Now the main question was how to provide the money that was needed to defeat Napoleon and his legions: for Bentham, as for everybody else, the task of the hour seemed to lie in the field of finance. The national emergency did not find Bentham altogether unprepared. In 1794 and '95 he had, by slow degrees, made his way towards a grand plan for the relief of the Exchequer, and in particular for the reduction of the national debt. The papers prepared then could now be taken down from the shelf where three years' dust had accumulated upon them, reconsidered and rearranged, and launched, in a perfected form, out into the world. Circumstances had changed: the men at the Treasury, in their dire straits, would perhaps not be quite so haughty as they had been four years before. So at any rate Bentham was inclined to hope. The reawakening of his interest in matters of finance was undoubtedly due to a revival of his faith in practical success.

What was it that Bentham had to offer to the men of Whitehall? To understand his new plan of financial salvation, we must first of all consider two proposals which were drafted at the same time as *Escheat vice Taxation* and *Tax with Monopoly*, but which show still more boldness and imagination than even those bold and imaginative proposals which had, after all, still been conceived and couched in terms of taxation. As we shall see, the idea elaborated by Bentham in the year 1800 and propagated in 1801 was the recommendation of an interest-bearing government currency or circulating annuity. This proposal had grown out of two earlier suggestions of which one was that the government should take up the insurance business, annuity-dealing as Bentham called it, and the other that the Treasury should issue a paper money of its own, Exchequer Notes. Both these inspirations were laid down in concise pamphlets between 1794 and 1796, and we shall now investigate them in turn. Their study will prepare us for the understanding of Bentham's master-scheme, the Annuity Note proposal, which will occupy the better part of the present volume.

"A PLAN FOR AUGMENTATION OF THE REVENUE"

In a *résumé* of his financial projects, said by Bowring to have been prepared by Bentham for Charles Long (*Works* X, 303 seq.), there is mention of a "Proposal for an unburthensome augmentation of the Revenue, by an extension of the traffic in money on Government account, to divers modifications of demand, in addition to those to which it has already been extended, on the part either of Government, corporate bodies, or individuals: whereunto might be added a tax on such as cannot be carried on with so much advantage on Government account, as on account of individuals" (ib.). Some branches of "money traffic", Bentham seems to argue, such as the sale of perpetual redeemable annuities, or the sale of chances of large sums for small—the lottery business—are already acknowledged and established fields of government activity: why should not others which are at present in the hands of corporate bodies, or even of individuals, also be undertaken by the state? It is difficult to withstand the temptation to characterize this proposal as an early and primitive nationalization scheme. Its aim was plainly to transfer a complex of lucrative transactions from private hands into the hands of the public.

A proposal of this sort had, of course, as an essential and indispensable presupposition a clear proof that the interest of the public would not suffer under the suggested transfer of business to the government. Being, in his heart of hearts, a confirmed votary of *laissez-faire,* Bentham felt it incumbent on him to give this proof in unequivocal and incontrovertible arguments, and he promised to prefix to his pamphlet "an Inquiry, in answer to the question,—What lucrative occupations are capable of being carried on with advantage on the account of the Government?" He pledged himself in particular to furnish "1. reasons for apprehending that the *Friendly* Societies will, in general, scarce be able to make good the *half* of what they are likely to undertake for; 2. reasons why the honour of Government is concerned in procuring a complete stock of the requisite *data,* without which all calculations, relative to the values of Life Annuities in general, and in the instance of the Friendly Societies in particular, must be fallacious—viz. a complete and authentic set of statistical Returns, showing the proportion of deaths to inhabitants in the several parishes throughout the kingdom; 3. reasons why it would be of advantage as well to the individuals particularly concerned as to the public in general, that Government should take the business of the Friendly Societies into its own hands, that part which concerns the insurance against sickness only excepted." (*Works,* X, 304.)

To whet Long's appetite, Bentham included in his *résumé* a sample computation which, he hoped, would prove what a gold mine, what a god-send, this economic activity would be for an empty treasury. He gives as his example the "profit by the conjunction of the business of buying life annuities for the lives of sellers, with that of selling life annuities for the lives of purchasers":—

"Receipt:

For £50,000 a year, sold for the lives of purchasers, at fourteen years' purchase ... £700,000

Disbursement:

For ditto, bought for the lives of sellers, at eight years' purchase (lives of equal goodness) ... ... [£]400,000." (ib.)

The profit of this type of business alone would amount to £300,000—not a bad contribution to the income of the state!

This alluring proposal was subsequently embodied in a pamphlet, though it is more than doubtful if Charles Long ever came to read it: as far as we know, it was never set up for print. It is just possible that Bentham did not even finish his manuscript. From a table of "heads" contained in box III of the University College collection (sheet 286[1]) we see that three major chapters are missing: one on the "modifications of demand" for annuities; one on the corresponding "modifications of ability to purchase"; and one on the "Equitable Society's business". Furthermore, there were to be two minor chapters which were probably never written, the one to be entitled "exchange of annuities", and the other "power of redemption". In spite of these

[1]Cf. the text in the survey of the excluded material, below, vol. III, end, and also *sub* CLXVI, 54-57.

gaps, however, we are in a position to arrange the materials which we have in a way that yields a coherent and fairly convincing text, and displays the main outlines of this revolutionary proposal.

Bentham starts from an assertion which is not likely to be challenged: namely, that the national debt, for all its intrinsic disadvantages, has at least one decided advantage for the public—to allow individuals to invest money in a comparatively sound and safe way—an advantage which is particularly important where the property of orphans is concerned. In view of this outstanding merit, it would almost be a pity to see the debt paid off. But the opportunities which it offers are too narrow. There are "other modifications of demand in this line" which are not provided for, and so Bentham suggests that the dealings of government should be extended to all "modifications of money-traffic"—a term which he takes good care clearly to define.

After this general introduction, the various fields of government activity in the money market are systematically surveyed. There is first of all government borrowing (ch. I). The government could borrow more cheaply than it actually does, Bentham claims, but why and how is not explained, and we are referred to a further pamphlet which we shall come to consider in due course. Next there is government lending (ch. II). This possibility, too, does not detain Bentham for long. The Treasury has not much to lend out—it is usually all too empty; nor could it conceivably borrow cheaply and lend at a profit. Pawnbroking is a special case, but none the more attractive for that. Bentham asserts that a government monopoly in this branch of business would be obnoxious, and that individual pawnbrokers, under the lash of competition, serve the people better than the public could ever do. His arguments sound convincing enough, but they have hardly been borne out by subsequent experience.

As we turn to banking, the subject of chapter III, we enter upon a more promising path. "Banking in the way of deposit"—i.e. keeping cash for the owner, or running a "ware-house" or "lodging-house" for money—is a branch of business in which the government could and would outdo all other bankers because it would offer much better security. The money, it is true, would lie idle in the vaults: but the depositors would willingly pay a fee for having it guarded, which would, to a large extent, be clear gain. "Banking on the ordinary terms"—i.e. accepting money from one part of the public, in order to lend it out to another—is likewise a service which the state could well undertake to offer. Bentham is fully aware of the economic advantages of banking and speaks about them in a rather amusing way. It is with some surprise, therefore, that we read his contention that "there can not well be a . . . branch . . . more within the competence of government to exercise". The borrowing, certainly, is simple enough: but the same cannot be said of the lending. Could a civil servant know better which new enterprises to finance, and which demands to reject, than a private banker actuated by personal interest, the source and mainstay of all true application? It goes without saying that Bentham suggests no such thing. If he says that government should take up "banking on the ordinary terms", he does not think, however surprising that may be, of the main economic function of all banks, to direct the stream of productive credit. He is only concerned with the fiscal aspect. Government, he submits, should lend the monies it would collect only to itself, or at most to such semi-public bodies as the East India Company whose financial soundness is obvious and notorious. The cash deposited would thus in effect be an interest-free loan to the state.

After a short chapter entitled "Life Insurance" which in reality deals only with a very small corner of that wide field, Bentham comes to his main subject—what he calls "annuity dealing" (ch. V). He discusses first the *sale* of life annuities, the case where the government accepts a lump sum, or several successive sums, against the obligation to make certain periodical payments during the annuity-purchaser's life (or, in the case of Tontines, several stated lives). This contract is suitable as a case of government dealing because of the government's incomparable security and longevity, both boons to the intending purchaser and investor. Special attention is given to the sale of life annuities for a man's own life "to commence at the end of a certain period, if he be then alive"—the method by which a man can make provision for his own old age. This case covers the activity of the Friendly Societies, of which Bentham was a genuine admirer. "The businesses of the Friendly Societies, of the Amicable Society, and of the Equitable Society" he says in a disjointed note, "have their origin in the two best principles of human nature: that of the Friendly Societies in prudence: and that branch of prudence which is stiled providence: the business of the other two societies in benevolence. All are the fruit of modern times: of modern security, of modern ingenuity, of modern wisdom, of modern virtue. It ought to be known to whom we are indebted for these admirable inventions. Their statues ought to be with Howard's in St. Paul's." (U.C. CLXVI, 33.)

Yet in spite of this unstinted admiration for the Friendly Societies, Bentham believed that their essential function could be still better performed by the state. He wants the government to take over and to adapt the business to the circumstances of the poorest classes, of the men in the most inferior situations. What he is driving at is quite clearly a public system of social insurance on a voluntary basis. Let the reader study points 1-10 enumerated as desiderata under this sub-heading, and he will see how true this contention is. There is even a suggestion that the "annuities to commence at the end of a certain period, if the purchaser be then alive"—the contributory old age pensions as we call them—should be paid out "through the medium of the Post-Office establishment".

After discussing the sale, Bentham considers the purchase of life annuities by the government, the case where government pays out a certain lump sum and in exchange draws periodical payments from the seller as long as he is alive. This particular branch of the insurance business, Bentham admits, is somewhat risky, but, he insists, not unduly so. A specially important *species* of this *genus* is the "purchase of life annuities for a man's own life against the payment of a principal sum on his death"—the method by which a man can make provision for his dear ones in case of his demise. The Amicable Society cultivates this field, just as the Friendly Societies do the other, but again Bentham claims (not unreasonably) that the government could offer more in this field than any private body, however well-run and well-intentioned.

It is obvious from the text that there is a serious gap in this discussion of the purchase of life annuities from individuals. A few pages seem to have been lost: it is rather unlikely that they were never written. What is missing is a consideration of the purchase of life annuities—to express it in Bentham's manner—"for a man's own life, against the payment of a life-annuity to a third person after his death": the case where a man secures, by periodical payments, a life-long pension for someone dependent on him, say, his widow or some other "antient female". No doubt, Bentham would have claimed this branch for the government, as he does the others, and perhaps with even more alacrity.

In his concluding observations on annuity dealing, Bentham sounds a note of caution. The whole insurance business, he claims, rests as yet on very frail foundations because the mortality tables available and in use are not reliable. He calls for a parliamentary inquiry into the matter which alone could lead to the information the actuary needs, and which alone would yield it in a form that would be above all doubt and suspicion.

The salient feature of the whole plan, as far at any rate as the fiscal side of it is concerned, is the fact that it would bring money into the Treasury without any taxation whatsoever. *Supply without Burthen* had still been the suggestion of a special tax, a death duty, however unwilling Bentham may have been to give it that name. *Tax with Monopoly* had advocated another special tax, a licensing fee, however much it was supposed to be overbalanced by an indemnity. But here there is no suggestion of any tax whatever: the income to be gained by the state is to be a business profit pure and simple. This at once raises the question whether government should not extend its activities in the open market still further: whether it should not nationalize further branches of economic enterprise. To make it quite clear that he did not wish to go very far in that respect, Bentham appended to his pamphlet a chapter on the "limitations of government traffic". He discusses "what can not be done". In general, he points out, the state is unfit for the exercise of lucrative occupations: civil servants want the spur of personal interest, and they are addicted to board management, the clumsiest way of doing business. But that does not exclude the possibility—and indeed the reality—of governmental superiority in special fields, such as those of annuity dealing and money traffic. Superior security and superior longevity guarantee the nation advantages when such services are transferred from the hands of private individuals into the hands of the public.

The last passages of the pamphlet indicate in a more concrete and practical way how government should proceed when it came to the realization of the project—what organization should be set up, what procedures followed, etc. What Bentham says here is only a small fragment of what he could have said. With the typical passion of the utopian for detailed regulations he thought out an "establishment" that was to manage this new department of governmental activity. On a sheet of preliminary notes (U.C. CLXVI, 27) we read of "commissioners for buying annuities": there were to be two sets of them, one " to approve of the security", the other "to approve of the life": the former consisting exclusively of lawyers sitting under a judge, the latter composed of both legal and medical practitioners. In either case "responsibility and number of the *quorum* the greater as there can be no publicity, out of tenderness to the candidate"; and, as a further safeguard, "right of appeal to a rejected candidate". "Certain diseases or habits of body to be made grounds of abatement in price, instead of rejection *in toto*"—"punishment in case of [a] false answer to examination [to be an] encrease of [the] annuity [owed and payable], and publication of the answer and the disproof of it at the expence of the seller". In this style Bentham would have worked out his whole project if the Treasury had been interested in it: he was ready to obey the call, but that call never came.

THE "PROPOSAL FOR THE CIRCULATION OF A [NEW] SPECIES OF PAPER CURRENCY"

Apart from the three pamphlets of 1794-96 which we have already reviewed—*Escheat vice Taxation, Tax with Monopoly,* and *A Plan for Augmentation of the Revenue*—Bentham drafted in this period yet another proposal which, it seems, was never mentioned to Charles Long, but which struck deeper roots in his own mind than any of the others and was based on an idea destined to loom large later on, in 1800 and 1801, when it was fully elaborated and pressed on Long's successors. We do not know exactly when it was written, but it is likely that it came later than its companions, perhaps in the second half of 1795, perhaps even early in 1796. It is one more attempt to achieve "supply without burthen", to fill the Treasury without taxing the population.

The very first paragraph clearly expresses the obervation on which this particular proposal is based. If government issues paper money (the word must here be taken in a very wide sense), if it issues for instance Exchequer Bills, it has to pay 5% to its creditors: but if private bodies, like the Bank of England, or private individuals, like the country bankers, issue paper money, they can circulate it on credit without interest. Hence if the government could take over this fiduciary circulation, it would save each year 5% on the whole amount of it—in the given circumstances 5% of 20 millions, i.e. one million pounds, a sum considerable enough not to be despised. And why should the government not monopolize the emission of paper money? The coinage is an acknowledged prerogative of the Crown: when it was instituted, it comprised all money-making in the country, paper money being unknown in the Middle Ages: to extend the prerogative from minting to printing would be re-establishing an old right of government rather than usurping a new one. There can be no valid argument, utilitarian or legalistic, against the institution of a state-managed system of paper currency.

So far chapter I. Chapter II has a more theoretical complexion.[1] It starts the question *why* bank and bankers' notes circulate at more favourable terms than government paper? The disadvantage of the latter, Bentham urges, cannot be due to inferior credit: whose credit could be more complete and more undoubted than that of the community itself? The explanation of the phenomenon must be sought, not in the essentials, but in accidental traits. Bank paper is *technically* more efficient as a means of circulation than government paper in its given form: that is the secret of its success. Bentham enumerates five concrete features which make up its strength: it is payable on demand; it is transferable without formality, just like coin; the sums involved are small, which meets the exigencies of everyday economic intercourse; the notes are handy; and the public is thoroughly used to them. The existing types of government paper (Exchequer Bills and Navy Bills) have four corresponding disabilities: they are for high and sometimes uneven sums, so that not many people can have any use for them in day-to-day traffic; they are payable only after the lapse of half a year; the terms and the mode of payment are unduly complicated; and the appearance of the notes, of the actual pieces of paper, is unattractive and unprepossessing. There is a thorough discussion of what—in Bentham's English—could be called *circulability*. The upshot of it is that Exchequer Bills are "a paper fitter to constitute a source of income than for general circulation". This is a statement of more than theoretical value: it indicates the direction in which a remedy and a reform has to be sought.

In chapter III Bentham comes to grips with these practical problems. The suggestion that Navy Bills, as a type, should be scrapped and replaced by Exchequer Bills, because they are at a still greater discount, is comparatively uninteresting: it could promise only a very minor economy. The main proposal is much more imaginative and enterprising: it aims at the introduction of a government currency. Bentham calls for an experimental issue of £1,000,000, the notes to be either interest-free, or interest-bearing, the rate in the latter case to be as low as 2% or thereabouts. An interest-free emission should consist, in good part at any rate, of £2 10s. and £1 5s. notes,

[1]Bowring printed these first two chapters, in a somewhat castrated form, as appendices to a later work. Cf. *Works* III, pp. 148-153.

so as to be in units which would be small enough for daily circulation, and so as not to interfere with the notes of the Old Lady, of which the smallest was at that time for £5. An interest-bearing emission, on the other hand, should and could enter into competition with the notes coming out of Threadneedle Street: Bentham suggests £20, £10, and £5 notes, the most widely current units of the Bank.

Bentham expressly says that he entrusts the "determination in respect of eligibility to those to whom it appertains"—that is, of course, to the men at the Treasury. But he leaves no doubt whatever that he regards the interest-free variety as by far the more preferable. No interest-payment is needed: so why throw money away? In fact, an interest-bearing paper, being more awkward, might be more difficult to circulate than the simple interest-free variety—a truth which he was later thoroughly to forget.

In view of this decided preference for an interest-free type of paper, it is perhaps surprising that the concrete plan for the institution of a government currency contained in chapter IV now following reckons throughout with a rate of interest of 2%, or rather a farthing a day on a principal of £20. But the puzzle is quickly solved, and we can easily close the gap in the text. It is obvious from the very first sentence of chapter IV itself that Bentham regarded the financial sacrifice involved in a small interest-payment as a sort of bait for the public, to get them to accept the new paper. He saw clearly that the promise to pay interest would really be an encumbrance in circulation and, *pro tanto,* a handicap in the effort to dislodge Bank Notes: but he felt, on the other hand, that Bank Notes were so well established in the market that a decisive attraction would have to be added to the intrinsic qualities of the proposed Exchequer Notes, "at least at the outset of the experiment", to make them part and parcel of the national currency, and that attraction, he thought, could best be given in the tangible form of hard cash. If Exchequer Notes did all Bank Notes could possibly do, and yielded a farthing a day to boot, they would carry the day: once their victory was assured, it was time enough to change from an interest-bearing to an interest-free government currency, the theoretical ideal. Most probably it was Bentham's secret hope that the *promise* of interest would be quite sufficient to gain "these new creatures of finance" a foothold in the country, and that performance of the promise would not often be demanded.

As practical models for this currency-to-be Bentham takes the Notes of the Bank of England, a type of paper preferable on many accounts to cash itself, and, to a lesser extent, the Bonds of the East India Company. Yet there are to be differences: Exchequer Notes are to be payable, principal and interest, only once a year; and they are to be payable not only in cash but (at the option of the issuer) also in bonds conveying the right to a perpetual annuity. The latter stipulation Bentham thought it necessary to introduce in order to guard against the dangers of a run when metal might not be available in sufficient quantities and something else ought to be at hand to take its place. In an age in which gold was still the money *par excellence,* this was a serious stipulation, but Bentham was convinced that it would not be prejudicial to the circulation of the proposed Government Notes. In fact, he expected a "very considerable" premium on his Exchequer Notes. A short consideration is inserted here to show the reason why. If government enjoyed full trust and credit, if the Exchequer Notes were payable on demand at the option of the noteholder, and if they were payable in gold, then, Bentham argues, the premium in comparison to Bank of England Notes would be—would naturally be—2%, or rather exactly the interest promised and paid. But even with the drawbacks proposed, even if not payable on demand and in cash, but annually and, if need be, in annuities, Bentham claims there would soon be a similar premium, as these modifications are too slight to make much difference in public estimation.

An important sub-heading of chapter IV is sub-heading C, on "advantages to individuals". It is important, not so much in the context in which it stands, but with reference to Bentham's later thought: the ideas here expressed were destined to develop and to inspire the work on "Circulating Annuities". Bentham explains that the proposed Exchequer Notes would have a double nature: they would be "running cash" and invested capital at the same time: "by keeping his own, a man will be lending it to government and getting paid for it"—"a man puts his money out at interest, without parting with it out of his hands"—in short, "these Notes would, to a poor man, be like buying a little fortune into the funds". Every man could in this way be his own banker.

At the moment, this "advantage to individuals" did not interest Bentham as much as it did later on: he was too preoccupied with the advantage offered to government. We see this in the very next sub-heading, D, which shows that he regarded the payment of interest, on which the double nature of the Notes depended, as a purely temporary affair. If an agio develops (as he was sure it would), this is a sign that more of the new money can safely be issued: and if the agio is considerable (as he was sure it would be), an issue at lower interest can be placed in the market. If the agio reaches the full amount of the interest, interest-free rates can be substituted without much difficulty for the interest-bearing ones with which the experiment was to start. This event Bentham calls "no unreasonable expectation". Once it has come about, it is clear that Exchequer Notes will just be cash, or cash-substitutes, but no longer a means of "buying a little fortune into the funds". It is here that Bentham later modified his great idea in the interest of the saving poor. Compared to this essential point, the rest of D is rather dull: it discusses the possibility of a temporary discount due to the trouble of cashing in the interest when it has become payable.

An obvious objection to the scheme, which Bentham takes up at this stage, is the fact that the Bank of England and all other banking houses in the country would necessarily suffer from the realization of the proposed plan. Bentham freely admits that profits would be diminished (a prospect which, not unnaturally, causes him very little concern): but he is anxious to emphasize that the credit of the banks would be strengthened rather than weakened by the operation. If the circulation of promissory notes were reduced through the issue of the new government money, the relation of bankers' liabilities to their cash reserves would be improved, and the whole banking trade and every participant in it would be much sounder than before. Corresponding to the agio on Exchequer Notes, Bentham expected a disagio on Bank Notes, but he points out that, in accordance with the smallness of the interest allowed, it could never be anything but inconsiderable.

A set of problems which excited Bentham as much as it leaves us cold today, concerns the prevention of forgery. It appealed to the inventor in him, and also to the law-reformer, for executions for forgery were then a rather frequent occurrence. The sub-heading F on this topic reads rather amusingly at this distance of time. Here at any rate is a problem which seems to have been solved quite satisfactorily since Bentham's day.

Sub-heading G is decidedly disappointing. To the question what limits there would be to the emission of Exchequer Notes, Bentham gives the Salomonic answer that the maximum would obviously be "the amount of the paper currency of the country". It is like saying "the sky is the limit" when we do not know how high the sky may be. It is true that Bentham has mentioned £20 millions as the probable amount of all interest-free paper current in the country. But from this estimate, or rather guess, it does not in any way follow that the proposed government currency would, should, or could be confined to this particular volume. There is a much deeper economic problem involved which Bentham does not care to face.

Bentham makes again somewhat short work of the difficulties involved in his proposal when he discusses by what method the government could secure a monopoly of the issue of paper money. He simply suggests that private notes payable to the bearer and promising interest should be prohibited. By acting in this way, he felt, Parliament would simply reassert an old prerogative of the Crown which should never have lapsed. There is a link here between the Exchequer Note proposal and the proposal contained in *Escheat vice Taxation:* both aim at the revival of mediæval institutions for the benefit of the modern state. Bentham scholars will once again note his decided interest in history. There is a historical strain, too, in the sub-chapter which closes this pamphlet—"Why not before?" A governmental paper currency has never been attempted, partly for historical and partly for administrative reasons: historically, the Bank of England has got a start over the government in the building-up of a stock of financial credit: and the administration has always been too clumsy and too lazy to seize the opportunities open to it. But there is no reason why either of these facts should be a bar to future action in this field.

Taken as a whole, the pamphlet under discussion is fairly complete. There is little in the preliminary notes which would yield further information worth having. Only one single point deserves to be mentioned: Bentham drafted the text of the proposed Exchequer Note itself. As we shall see, he severely criticized a similar proposal later on because its author had failed to indicate the "tenor" of the "instrument". The "tenor" of the Exchequer Note is set out in the following sketch: it was meant to be connected with the table of interest contained, as will be seen, in the text of the pamphlet printed below.[1]

"This note bears interest at the rate of a farthing a day, the 5 last days and the odd day in a leap year excepted, being nearly two per Cent per annum for ever, omitting fractions as by table annexed.

[1]Cf. p. 179 seq.

"Days of payment any day, Sunday excepted, between the 1st day of Jan[uary] and the [ ] day of Feb[ruary].

"Hours from [ ] to [ ] o'[clock].

"Place of payment.

"The holder may within the time for payment of the interest claim payment of the principal: which will be paid him accordingly, unless the office by order should in lieu thereof deliver to him a perpetual warrant for an annuity of £1 per annum: payable at the office of the annuities and not transferable otherwise than in the manner of the said annuities.

"N.B. This note will be received at all his Majesty's offices: to wit for the amount of the principal together with the interest up to the day when the same shall be paid in, exclusive." (U.C. CLXVI, 33.)

THE TWO "LETTERS ON THE STOCK NOTE PLAN" AND THE ESSAY "ON THE FORM OF THE SUPPLY TO THE SINKING FUNDS"

This, in general outline, was Bentham's idea of a new government-sponsored means of circulation which, he was sure, would greatly benefit the Exchequer. In 1795/96 when it was worked out, Bentham did not bother to press his plan: Mr. Long's response to his suggestion that the ancient prerogative of escheat should be revived, had been all too disappointing. But if Bentham laid the Exchequer Note proposal aside, he certainly did not give it up: he was convinced that he had discovered a sound and promising measure of finance, and he continued to hope that it would some day come into its own. The idea sprang to his mind again when, in the winter of 1798/99, an accidental event turned his imagination anew to the possibilities of currency reform.

Among Bentham's personal friends was Sir Reginald Pole Carew, a country gentleman from Cornwall who, like many of his forebears, sat in the House of Commons and took a vivid interest in the affairs of the community. Now, Pole Carew was, about this time, much preoccupied with the financial plight of the country, and his meditations on that dismal topic at last matured into a manuscript to which he gave the title "Ideas on Financial Reform". He sent it to Bentham, and Bentham, in his answer, gave clear proof that he was not at all disinclined to return to the consideration of economic problems in the narrower sense of the word, and to close his investigations of the subject of poverty and poor relief. "My Dear Sir," he writes to Pole Carew on August 16, 1798, "Your Finance Papers are now sprawling out before me in form, and have already afforded me very important information, which, I am satisfied, I could not have obtained from any other source. In testimony of the respect I feel for the work, as well as my wish not to be regarded as ungrateful by its author, behold, without further preface, the following offer: Say you will print it, together with my observations, and my observations shall be written: as to *names*, whether *both* shall appear or *neither*, or *one* and *which*, without the other, that shall be exactly as you please; but I must know before I write, whether my own part will appear or no, because, if it does, I must suppress a good deal of what I might otherwise insert: for example, what concerns your great man[1], of whom my sentiments are such as it would be neither prudent nor even decent to exhibit with my name. (Upon second thoughts, no use in any such personalities; they being all beside the purpose.) My observations might likewise be either in the form of a *perpetual commentary*, like Barbeyrac's on Puffendorf, or in a separate work: and this should also be as you pleased. Moreover, where we don't agree, I give you the last word. You engage not to leave out anything either of the text or of the observations on it: but you reply to the observations what you please, and it rests with you to put or not to put your own name." (*Works* X, 323-324.)

After these preliminaries, and a short lecture on tact and tactics in pamphleteering, Bentham proceeds to discuss the merits of Pole Carew's central idea. "The proposition is, that if the portion of revenue at present appropriated to the buying up a proportionable part of the annuities which have been sold by Government, and which Government would otherwise have been bound to pay to individuals, was to be disappropriated and made applicable to the discharge of a further mass of annuities, which, it is proposed, should be sold by Government, and the payment charged upon this fund, the monied man would be as ready to lend his money upon the fund thus proposed to be *re*mortgaged, as he is at present upon new and clear funds. Making the experiment on myself, this readiness is what I must confess I do not feel. So far from it, that were I to think of becoming a subscriber to what is called a new *loan*, i.e. a fresh mass of annuities offered to be granted, payable as usual, nominally, out of the produce of taxes to be imposed on the occasion and for the purpose, my view would be directed slightly, or rather not at all, toward that *particular* fund, but exclusively to the *general* fund at present standing *behind*

[1]Probably Pitt.

them: satisfied as I am, and should be, that Government would never do any such unjust and impolitic thing as to stop payment of one part of the mass of annuities it has granted, for the mere purpose of buying up another. In this point of view, every portion of the mass of annuities which the Government buys up, seems to me an additional security for the payment of the rest. While this *general* fund subsists, every *fresh* and successive mass of annuity, as well as every old and already existing one, has *two* securities to stand upon, viz. the *general* fund, which, in the case of a fresh annuity, a man thinks about, I suppose, more or less, and some *particular* one which, in the case of an old annuity, no man, I am sure, ever thinks anything about at all. Were it to be proposed to me to buy a fresh mass of annuities, and by way of security, were this general fund proposed to me and nothing more, my answer would be—*what you now offer me is a second mortgage upon an estate already in mortgage.* Whether I might not look upon the estate as capable of bearing this second charge is another question: but certainly I could never look upon the security offered to me on these *new* terms as equally ample with, much less as being more ample than, the security offered, upon the hitherto *usual* terms: I could never look upon any *one* security by *itself*, as equally ample with that same security and another put together.

"You understand already, that as to the selling over again the annuities Government has bought up (subject to the above *lien*), it is what I cannot agree with you in: what concerns the suspending of further purchases of the same kind during the war (leaving accordingly the funds allotted to that purpose to be applied to the current services of the year), that is a question that remains for consideration. You have shown, and shown most clearly and effectually, to how great a disadvantage, in point of profit and loss, all such purchases are made. I am sorry to see that what we are obliged to raise in *present* money, we must pay so dearly for, if ever we do pay for it, in *future* money: but, heavy as the expence is, I really do not see how it can be avoided. The security, such as it is, is not by any means too great: many are the people who as it is (so I hear from auctioneers) sell out of the funds, where a man makes above 6 per Cent, for the purpose of buying land that does not afford 3½ per Cent; and the very remarkably high price of land, in comparison of Government annuities at the present period, as compared with the close of the American war, seems to prove at once two things—viz.

the superior plenty of money, and the superior want of confidence in the solvency of Government. In this view of the matter, I must confess, I cannot so far join with you as to say of the *buying-up plan* that from the first, *fieri non debuit:* but if I did, I could not forbear adding, *factum valet:* for if what has been thus bought up, were to be attempted to be resold, I can not forbear thinking, that (though I myself should not), yet people in general would, regard the attempt as the first scene of an act of bankruptcy: to produce the contrary impression, does not appear to me to lie within the competence of the united powers of human reason and human eloquence. What you say about the monies being employed to more advantage in the hands of individuals than in those of Government, is true *to a certain extent*: but the extent to which it *is* true you have not as yet defined; though the defining it is a task that seems not only well worthy of your powers of investigation, but altogether indispensable for the purpose of your argument. For my own part I must confess I do not much expect to find it true to the extent in which it is necessary it should be true, for the purpose of that argument. The one thing needful is £10 every year in the Exchequer for every annuity of £10 sold. This Mr Pitt and you join in providing: but he adds £1 or £2 over, to provide against contingent deficiencies; and *that* increasing, to provide against the increasing *danger* of deficiency. This surplus you, instead of gathering it into the Exchequer, prefer leaving in the hands of the individual: concluding that, if left there, it will, somehow or other, go farther towards the payment of the annuities in question, or towards the satisfying the other demands of Government, than if taken into the hands of Government. But to produce this effect, I am afraid to say (for fear of your being angry with me, and saying I have misrepresented you) what requisites are necessary: the individual, instead of employing the greatest part of the labour in question (I should be apt to say, at random, *nine-tenths* at least), in ministering to the purpose of present gratification (extra eatables and drinkables, for example), (in other words, *spending so much of the money*), must employ the whole, or the greatest part, at least, in giving birth to instruments of future and durable gratification or use (on *building*, for example, or *draining land*), (in other words, *laying by so much of the money*); and this stock of wealth, with its increase (the house-rent, or additional land-rent, thus produced), instead of employing on his own account, he must (I am afraid to say it, but the purpose of the argument, I think, requires it), he must pay into the Exchequer: and this track of unrelaxing good economy (not to add *generosity*), every individual in question must go on persevering in for the forty or forty-five years which you speak of, with a regularity as inviolate as that with which the portion of wealth in question would, if received into the Exchequer, have been applied to the buying up of the annuities granted by Government. What a man would be saved, by your system, from paying to the new taxes in question, he would (it is true), in the course of his expenditure (whether *consumptive* or *productive*), he *would* pay in *part* towards the *already existing* taxes: but this happily is but a *small* part: you yourself have stated it somewhere at about a *tenth.*" (*Works* X, 325-326.)

The final passages of the letter are again significant as showing Bentham's keen—not to say vital—interest in the subject. "Is there any other way," he asks, "in which I could contribute more towards the dissemination of your ideas, and the extraction of that truth which would alike be the object of us both? Shall I, too, sit down to inquire what is best to be done? Write an essay accordingly, and you a *critique* upon it? Writing more at leisure, and being arrived at a sort of method by hard labour, I should abstain from treading upon collateral topics with more rigour than you have done: but perhaps your wish is to make this work a vehicle for your sentiments upon other subjects: if so, strict unity of design would be unfavourable to your purpose. Society, especially society like yours, would animate me, and *might* inspire me with the exertion necessary: but without you I shall not meddle with a subject so remote from any of my former views: for I have neither heart to write nor money to publish of myself.

"Neither of these plans need supersede the other: except the having the same subject, nothing could be more different than the two works. The greater part of the topics you have introduced in your work would not appear in mine: mine, on the other hand, would present others, which do not occur in yours. But whichever may come out first would be referred to in the other; or if they come out together, then, by the help of cross references, each might serve to procure readers for the other. Your method would certainly be more agreeable to *some* readers (I do believe to *most* readers); mine, perhaps, to others: and what is odd enough, to yourself perhaps in the number.

"My aim in all this is neither more nor less than to second what

I understand to be your wishes, as far as can be done, without prejudice to that sincerity, any departure from which would be more repugnant to them than any other part I could take. Those wishes are—to attract readers to the subject, by all lawful and honourable means. Among these means, *debate* is an article of approved efficacy, according to the notions current among booksellers: what distinguishes the proposed debate from ordinary ones is, its being so purely amicable, and published — not the two sides of it by the respective parties, each with opposite views, but by one of them, for the furtherance of his own views, and yet with the consent and concurrence of his opponent. But this singularity, whether the parties be or be not known (a point which I finish by leaving entirely to your choice), would contribute (I imagine) rather to strengthen than weaken the attraction; rather to increase than diminish the number of readers. Converts I could neither promise you without breach of that sincerity, nor endeavour to procure for you without a breach of that probity, neither of which you would wish to see impaired in any man whom you honour with such a place in your friendship as you have given me. To do what may be in my power without any such breach—to help find you *readers*, has been *my* concern: to make them *converts* will be *yours*. In the *transport inspired by the idea* of a severe labour ended, and a great work achieved, you *'did not conceive it possible that he* (the author) *should be convicted of error in the conclusion'*. Should that persuasion have preserved itself, to the present period, in unabated force, it may inspire you with some apprehension for a friend whose temerity prompts him thus to raise his head against demonstration: but your friendship will suggest, on the other hand, that his address, though in a bad cause, may be trusted to for saving him from gross ignominy in his defeat: and, at the worst, the maxim, *volenti non fit injuria,* may serve to tranquillize your conscience. Whatever there may be of *badinage* in all this, there is not a syllable of *persiflage* which, from me to you, would be abominable. Whimsical as the offer may appear to you, gratitude was the source of it; and in *dropping* it, the golden rule, which is the foundation of Christian morality, as been my constant guide." (*Works* X, 327.)

Pole Carew, it appears, was not quite so keen on the subject as Bentham, and his answer (dated Sept. 3) is in a much lighter vein. "Ranks by threes! to the right about, wheel! Not one wet day in four weeks! The hours which have not been dedicated to my Troop, have been bestowed in giving shape and form to my garden—to increasing the grass of my fields, that we may be able to go on in paying the one per Cents, over and above all the five, six and seven per Cents, that are, and must be required of us. It is not ingratitude, nor a want of a full sense of the value of your correspondence; but real fatigue of body, and incapacity of mind, which has been at grass with the body, that has prevented me from thanking you for two sheets and half of well-covered, I wished I could say *well-written* paper. Do not mistake me, however; I have been digging in this mine from time to time ever since, and find nothing in it but gold; but the labour of digging even for such metal is so great, that I have no difficulty in saying *imprimatur* to this, though I shudder at the very sound of the word when applied to any scrawl of mine. But to the point. When I took the liberty of requesting you to peruse my ill-digested labours, I relied upon your friendship, as well as upon your ability, to point out all their errors and imperfections, as well in point of matter as in style and management, being fully conscious, that in the present state of the work, it was wholly unfit to see the light; and being really unwilling to bestow any more labour of my own upon it, unless I could find a friend upon whose judgment I could rely, who would fairly tell me whether there was anything in it worthy of the light, and who, in the next place, would assist me in giving it that shape and form, which would best introduce it into the world. Many parts, I know full well, are extremely imperfect, and were merely thrown on paper to discharge my mind of them. Other parts are probably too obscurely treated, and require further elucidation. Some are, I believe, reflections of what has preceded. There is a want of arrangement throughout, and no pretension to style in any part. But the subject has appeared to me to be of that importance, that I could not, with the opinions I entertained, help endeavouring to express them; but I am so tired of the work, that I should find great difficulty in any attempt to express them better, and I was in hopes, therefore, that your acuteness and taste would, if you thought the paper worthy of any attention, point out the defects and apply the remedy, that, if it was its fate to appear at all, it might appear in the best dress which I and my friend could give it. But having never yet exposed myself to public criticism, I should not for the first time wish to show myself like a bear, with a leader to point out the awkwardness of my gambols.

"I am persuaded that your object is to investigate the truth, and to render it triumphant, and not to expose your friend by the sallies of your wit; but I should very much fear, that as I have treated a very dry subject very drily, that the commentary alone would be read, and truth and the text be entirely hidden by your more attractive mantle.

"If the party were more equal, I agree with you that there would be piquancy in the exhibition of single combat. But you must first give me a better spear and shield, and a complete suit of armour, before I can descend into the arena with you. First render me invulnerable like yourself, and, for the amusement of bystanders, I should have no objection to breaking a lance with you; but even then I should never lift the beaver, but wish the inexperienced to remain the unknown knight.

"The first question with me, is, whether it is possible for any friendly aid to render my labours worthy of the public eye; and whether, when put into a better shape, they could be of any public use.

"Sure I am, that they are not fitting to appear without much of this aid; and I should despair of their making any useful impression, unless time were given for its being made previous to what the playfulness of your wit might successfully urge against the dryness of my argument.

"Louis the Fifteenth was so fond of play, that he would often give his courtiers money, to have the pleasure of winning it back again. Many a sturdy coal-heaver has given a man a guinea to fight him, for the satisfaction he took in threshing; but *you* must bribe higher, and give me a better opinion of my own dexterity, before I consent to be baited.

"Make me worthy of you—let it be Bentham *versus* Bentham, and we will then see what is to be done. I wish to be corrected before I am exposed; you wish me to be exposed before I am corrected. But as I have never yet been accustomed to being *fleayed* (is that English?) I should wince under the knife." (*Works* X, 328-329.)

This new proposal of Pole Carew was not to Bentham's taste. A real fight, yes, however friendly the combat; a mock tournament, no. Hence the invitation to write a book together is changed into an invitation to spend a week together. "Now then," Bentham says,[1] "I will try another experiment upon you, and at the risk of another

[1]This text is taken from a draft in the University College collection (CVIII, 1), for no reason attributed to the year 1776 in the Catalogue (cf. p. 36). Inner evidence, as the reader can see, shows beyond the shadow of a doubt that it is the concluding part of this correspondence.

misimputation, substitute to my offer an invitation which will be received according as the statesman and the author on the one hand, or the fine gentleman and man of the world on the other happen to predominate. Quit Antony a week earlier than you would otherwise; plant, as before, your amiable incumbrances as their father and grandfathers; come and abscond with me at this my absconding-place. Now redemption system shall be the order of the day, and the sole order of the day the whole time. The 140 pages shall be discussed, paragraph by paragraph, with all their relations and dependencies. *Et nato natorum, et qui nascentur ab illis.* We will take a conjunct survey of the whole field of political economy, for nothing less is necessary to determine in *connoissance de cause* whether *stet* or *dele* shall be respectively affixed to the aforesaid paragraphs. We will take a joint observation of political and especially financial futurity under the several contingencies which present themselves as its phases. It will be the first week of your life that you will have applied yourself without interruption to the sort of business which God Almighty, and your ancestors have joined in qualifying you for, and the electors of I don't know what place have made your duty: and the ice being broke, I think it would not be the last. Whether your papers see the light or continue upon the shelf, the instruction you have gained by them (for there is no learning well without teaching) have already afforded you rich payment for your trouble. They have led you to exercise yourself with vigour and address in the field of analysis, the only track in which genius is displayed and truth discovered." (U.C. CVIII, 1.)

Whether Bentham and Pole Carew met, we do not know, nor is it much to our purpose. The fact is that the literary project dissolved into thin air. But Bentham had not long to wait for another opportunity to discuss the matter.

About this time, an anonymous author printed and privately circulated a small pamphlet entitled *A Method of Increasing the Quantity of Circulating Money.*[1] A copy of it came into Bentham's

[1]This is the title quoted on p. 87, University College collection, box XVII. It seems, however, that Bentham based his comments on an enlarged version entitled *Two Letters describing a Method of Increasing the Quantity of Circulating Money upon a New and Solid Principle*, of which the introduction is dated April 23, 1799, while the earlier simpler version of only 12 pp. is dated Sept. 27, 1798. Bentham, on p. 83, obviously refers to Sect. VI of Letter II—the letter added in 1799 to the original first letter of the fall before. This would date Bentham's discussion of the pamphlet: he must have read and pondered it between April and July, 1799. The pamphlet, incidentally, was not published until 1818 when it appeared in the *Pamphleteer*, still without indication of the name of its author.

hands and he was asked to express an opinion about it, either by the author himself, who hid behind a common friend,[1] or by Mr. George Rose, then Secretary to the Treasury. We do not know who it was that wished to hear Bentham's estimate of the proposal: we have two drafts of his critical account, one of which would seem to indicate that it was the bashful author's "anxious desire" to know Bentham's reaction to it, while the other would lead us to believe that it was the minister who sought Bentham's advice (cf. U.C. XVII, 87 as against 83). However that may be, Bentham decided not to write to the author, but to Rose,[2] assuming that Rose was interested in the idea and perhaps a friend of its originator, and arguing that the paper would not be worth discussing anyway if those in authority were unwilling to give it their serious consideration. It is perhaps not unfair to suggest that Bentham preferred this mode of procedure for purely selfish reasons. Could a "Letter on the Stock Note Plan" not be made a vehicle for his own Exchequer or Annuity Note proposal? Was not here a heaven-sent opportunity to approach the seat of power with a hope of success? Mr. Long had not been inclined to listen, it is true, but Mr. Long was out of office and Mr. Rose, being a new man, was at the same time a new possibility, a new chance, a new expectation.

Bentham seized the opportunity with vigour. He wrote two letters on the proposal. The second (dated July, 1799) has come down to us with the Vansittart papers now in the British Museum:[3] the first also left Bentham's hand, but we do not know whether it was ever received at the Treasury: it seems that it was first indirectly lent to the author —as we now know, a Mr. Ambrose Weston—who failed to return it. "Letter I is neither very material nor recoverable," reads a N.B. on the second letter, "applications for the return of it (concomitant as well as subsequent to the delivery) having remained unnoticed."[4] Fortunately we are able to reconstruct this earlier epistle, or at any rate to indicate its general drift. from the drafts which are contained in the University College collection (XVII, 83-89). If Mr. Weston kept it back and suppressed it, we cannot be surprised: though polite in

[1]It may be that this "common friend" was Sir Samuel Romilly, but we cannot be certain. Cf. the evidence in *Works* X, 341.

[2]The University College collection contains even a rough draft of a letter to Pitt on this subject (IIa, 22), but it is virtually certain that it was never sent.

[3]Nicholas Vansittart was Secretary to the Treasury under Addington.

[4]Cf. also the letter to Sir Francis Baring, *Works* X, 341.

form and even appreciative, it is obviously the product of a rival, and he could not expect that it would in any way promote his designs.

The argument of Ambrose Weston's pamphlet is rather simple. He begins by stating that "permanent loans of money are now, and for a long time have been, difficult to be obtained; and this difficulty must, from obvious causes, continue to increase so long as the war lasts". Hence "there would be found great convenience in the establishment of a good, solid, circulating medium, upon a more enlarged scale than any that exists at present, and adapted to the extended and extending state of our national commerce". Such a new circulating medium could be based on the existing national debt which nominally amounts to £400 millions (or more) of 3% annuities, and at a marketable value of 50% represents an actual available capital of £200 millions. Part of this inert mass could be mobilised and directed into the money market. "Let any stock-holder, who would wish to circulate some part of his stock, without selling it, transfer a certain quantity of it, suppose £20,000 3 per Cents, to the governors and directors of the Bank. The Bank is then to deliver to him fifty certificates, or notes of the transfer . . . the whole together to be of the amount of £5,000. By this means every particular quantity of stock might produce a fourth part of its nominal amount for the purposes of circulation," as "the mercantile world, who now take bank-notes in payment, would, with equal confidence, receive and circulate these stock-notes". There is no reason why they should not, "the security being fully equal to that upon which the credit of bank-notes is founded". While the capital and other effects of the Bank are not quite twice the amount of its liabilities, here the stock deposited would be fully double the value of the notes based upon it, assuming it to be saleable at 50% of its nominal amount; 3 per Cents would thus be circulated at 25—"a supposition low enough, for those who give any degree of credit whatever to the public funds". The creation of these new stock-certificates would at once relieve the money market because "the notes . . . might be used for loans or for capitals to trade upon; their use in trade, and for other purposes, being supposed the same as specie or bank-notes". (Sect. I-III.)

Bentham allows that the idea is *prima facie* attractive. There seems, he says, "a good deal of ingenuity and contrivance in it" (l.c. 83[1]). But he is critical all the same, and his criticism concerns a

[1]As above indicated, we do not possess the version of Bentham's first letter which left his hand. The following quotations are taken from the draft which definitely seems the maturer one. There is no reason to assume that it does not fully represent Bentham's considered judgment on the Stock Note proposal.

rather essential point—the question whether an increased circulation of paper money is really wanted. This is how he puts his point: "What [the author] appears to assume without discrimination is that *any* extension, as he calls it, of the circulating medium, any accession to the existing quantity of paper received as money, would be conducive to the public good. In this general point of view the proposition seems to be erroneous. The articles of which the existing quantity of '*circulating medium*' is composed are either metallic money or paper money. To the quantity of metallic money, the plan does not profess to afford any addition: but only to that of paper money. But as far as paper money is concerned, every modification as yet existing in this country agrees in this, viz. that it consists of an undertaking to deliver metallic money. But of the quantity of such promises there neither is, nor is at all likely to be, any deficiency, if compared, as it ought to be, with the capacity of performance. The great complaint is that an excess exists already: witness the case of Bank paper: and a great apprehension is lest that excess should go on encreasing more and more" (84). For this reason, the proposed stock-note paper will only be a safe and sound and solid expedient, if it is unlike the existing paper money whose circulation is based on a promise to deliver cash for it: but if it carries no such promise, whereon will its circulation be based? Why should people accept it in lieu of cash? The salient question then is, "what is the thing proposed to be undertaken for—the act promised to be done in and by a Stock Note? A Bank Note, an India Bond, the Navy Bills, an Exchequer Bill, an accepted bill of exchange—every existing species of paper money that occurs to me is a promise". The element of promise seemed to Bentham essential in any definition of a circulable paper or cash-substitute, and he felt that here lay the Achilles heel of the Weston plan. "A Stock Note is called in one place a Certificate. But a certificate neither is itself a promise, nor of itself implies any such thing as a promise. Each Certificate is supposed to be worth £100: but whence is it to derive that, or any other value? A Promise to pay £100 may be worth any sum not exceeding £100. A certificate relative to £100 is an attestation that somewhere or other, at some time or other, there did exist that money: but what can be the value (I mean the transferable value) of such an attestation to the holder of it?" (83).

To clear up this preliminary but essential point, and to determine the true nature of the suggested Stock Note, as well as its chances of success in the market, it would be necessary to give its text "*in terminis*"—to draft the engagement or undertaking which would have to be printed on it, and on which its acceptability to the public would have to rest. It would then appear "1. who the *promiser* is; 2. what is the *act* promised to be done; 3. *at whose instance* it is promised to be done; 4. in what *event,* i.e. on what conditions; 5. at what point of *time*" (ib.). As the author has not given any information on these all-important details, it is impossible to see whether his new circulating medium would be a practical proposition or not—whether or not it would be likely to gain currency and thus to become active and effective. Bentham leaves it at that. But, clearly, he is sceptical. He seems to imply, or at any rate slyly to hint, that there are only two alternatives, both equally fatal to the plan: *either* the Stock Note would be based on gold, in which case it would not be a novelty and, what is worse, would be pernicious because it would still further increase the relative excess of circulating paper; *or* it would *not* be based on gold; but then, Bentham suggests (at least *insinuando*) it would not be likely to capture the confidence of the public and thus fail to circulate. It would be a still-born child.

This criticism seemed to Bentham fairly decisive. But he has not done with Weston yet: on the next page, he has a further telling argument against him ready to put forward: the assumption that there is in the country a want of circulating medium, he points out, is false in a second respect. It is not only erroneous in point of fact, but also betrays a faulty diagnosis of the prevailing economic malaise. "The article with reference to which the supposed want is real, is—not paper money as compared with metallic money; not promise as compared with the means of performance—but *present money* as compared with *future*: principal, ready money, capital, as compared with interest, annuities, or whatever be the word. In a time like the present, in a time of war, the demand for present money [i.e. loans] is continually encreasing: encreasing on the part of government, and thence on the part of individuals. But for obtaining present money, and with consent of the proprietors, there is but one possible means, which is the making over future money (i.e. *promises* of future money, or, at any rate, a right to future money) instead of it. If in any instance where at present a man will accept of nothing but present money, an expedient can be employed by which he may be brought to accept of future money instead of it, without adding to the quantity of future money brought to market [i.e. bonds or debentures], the advantage is therefore manifest and indubitable" (84).

Is Mr. Weston's proposed Stock Note such an expedient? Bentham concedes that—in intention at least—it is. "This," he says, "is what appears to be aimed at by the gentleman's plan: and this it is that forms the apparently meritorious as well as characteristic feature of it. Without adding to the quantity of future money, he renders a portion of it capable of being given in exchange for present money. Without adding to the quantity of future money, and at the same time without adding to the quantity of fallible [?] promise (viz. promise of present, or almost present, say *ready* money) as compared with the quantity of performance. I see: for promise of ready money is *every instant* exposed to failure: promise of future money as above defined, *never*. Promise of ready money always: for the time of performance is come already; promise of future money never: for the time for performance is never come" (ib.). The underlying *intention* of the Stock Note plan is thus quite sound: but it is another question whether the *means* suggested and relied on to produce the desired end is adequate: and on this point Bentham expresses serious doubts. "As to the precise mode in and by which the general idea as above delineated is proposed to be carried into effect and applied to practice, it is more than I have been able to discover" (ib.).

Having thus dealt the Weston plan a double knock-out blow (not the less effective for being administered in such a gentlemanly way) Bentham proceeds to offer Mr. Rose his own substitute. "Among the effects of the communication thus made to me from a stranger was the bringing back to my mind an old idea of my own which, though not the same, stands on contiguous, if not on precisely the same ground. His plan goes to the transfer of future money in the way of mortgage, and consequently without addition to the existing mass: mine goes to the transfer of future money as at present in the way of sale, but with such circumstances of additional convenience as shall enable it to be disposed of by government on better terms" (85). Would Mr. Rose be interested in this proposal? Bentham indicates that he would not be disinclined to elaborate and elucidate his idea—under one condition: anterior promise of serious official consideration. "In this case as in others, the completion of the labour depends, as is natural, upon the prospect of its being of use. Discussions of this sort require leisure: the wit of man when drawn upon every day by the business of the day, does not afford a residuum of solvency equal to the task. Suggestions from me have sometimes been thought worth attending to, at other times not. The latter appeared the case three years ago, when the ideas in question first presented themselves to me: and it was for that reason, and that only, they were laid by. They have sometimes been more fortunate, when presented in other names and by other hands. At the present, as at all times, if it be worth your while, and Mr Pitt's, to say to me that Mr Pitt and you will read, it will be worth my while to write, otherwise at present not . . . .. I allow a month for the experiment: after which, if no commands from you on the subject reach me, the plan will be laid on the shelf or committed to the press as chance may dictate" (86).

As already explained, we do not know whether this gentle ultimatum was ever delivered; or if delivered, whether it drew any favourable response. All we do know is that Bentham did not lay the subject aside, but followed up his first by a second critical examination of the Stock Note proposal. This later essay certainly did reach the Treasury as it has come down to us with the Vansittart papers—the papers of Nicholas Vansittart who succeeded George Rose in the position of Secretary to the Treasury when Pitt was dismissed early in 1801. Rose, it seems, must have handed the new Bentham epistle to his successor when he left Whitehall for the wilderness. Now, Bentham's second letter deals with the Stock Note idea in a still more decided fashion than the first. "In my former Letter on the Stock Note Plan, I confessed myself not to understand it," he says. "On further consideration, I am sorry to add, that, if my optics do not deceive me, I descry the impracticability of it even before I understand it" (British Museum, Add. MSS 31235, 1). But the new attack is not so direct as the first was. It does not at once go to the core of the matter: it approaches it by way of discussing a special feature of Weston's plan. Weston's conception was that Stock Notes, being money, would be capital as well. He says: "These notes being, by supposition, of the same value, and passing with the same facility as bank-notes do, will be considered as cash, and consequently, if lent by the original holders, or by any others, who may become the holders of them, would entitle the lender to receive interest on the loan, in like manner as the lender of bank-notes now receives interest on the loan of those notes." Assuming the new currency to circulate as expected, "every particular quantity of stock, transferred in the manner . . . . stated, would yield a profit to the stock-transferrer equal to 5 per Cent on the amount of stock-notes obtained by him". Hence on £20,000 stock deposited, he would receive £600 dividends and in addition £250 interest, the latter through the medium of the £5,000

Stock Notes based on the stock deposited. "Thus £850 would be gained annually, instead of £600, by every proprietor of £20,000 stock, who should avail himself of the opportunity of procuring stock-notes" (Sect. III). For a theoretical consideration it is immaterial that Weston suggests that the extra profit should, in part at any rate, be diverted to the government and the Bank of England.

This contention that the plan would succeed in "making the same parcel of stock bear twice over" and "produce a dividend to one man, and, without a diminution (or at least without a proportionable diminution) of this dividend, interest to another" aroused Bentham's most determined opposition, and, contemptuously, he calls it "a contrivance for creating value out of nothing". The thing cannot be done: it is a sheer impossibility. "By these Stock Notes" he explains, "stock is, in some way or other, proposed to be *mortgaged*. But what cannot be done in this way by mortgaging land, cannot be done by mortgaging stock" (ib.). The matter is very simple: "If, on a landed estate that would sell for £2,000, and that produces you £100 a year neat money, you wish to borrow £1,000 in the way of mortgage, say at 5 per Cent, you can no otherwise obtain this £1,000 than by engaging to pay £50 a year for such time as the £1,000 remains unpaid" (2). It is not so that you get £100 without deduction, and your creditor an additional £50 out of the blue: you have to *split* your £100 with him, and that is all. If the pledge is a government annuity, and not a piece of land, the same holds good. "It is no more possible for you to make the same subject matter produce twice over in this case than in the other. Without receiving interest, a man will no more lend the money upon a government annuity than he will upon land: nor will a man lend his money for less interest upon the annuity than upon the land" (3).

There is only one contingency in which the matter would assume a different complexion: "If you could get the moneyed man to lend [you] his £1,000 *without* interest, while *you* are *making* interest by lending it to another, you might, on that supposition indeed, make £150 a year out of your estate, instead of the £100 a year which it is worth." This would in fact be making money out of nothing—on your part at least. But, Bentham implies, your additional £50 would then be a free gift to you from your creditor, and creditors are not the people to make free gifts. In any case, as far as Mr. Weston's pamphlet is concerned, "this is not what is supposed" (2).

It seems that at this juncture Bentham is less than fair to his opponent. Surely, this is *precisely* what is supposed. He does not for a minute suggest that the stock should be mortgaged in the ordinary way, but rather that it should be deposited in the Bank of England (not a typical creditor!) against the issue of interest-free Stock Notes which would be tantamount to a gratis loan in ordinary Bank Notes. If the stock-holder would lend this interest-free money out against interest, he would clearly be in a position to draw 3% from the Treasury on the face value of his stock, and a further 5% on the amount of his outstanding loan. He would in fact trade upon capital that has come to him out of the blue: he would be "making money out of nothing". Did Bentham miss the salient point of the Weston plan, namely, that he proposed a public note issue, and not a private credit transaction?

It looks for a moment as if he did. But as we read on, we see that the argument returns to a safe track. For, even if we allow that Mr. Weston thinks of a public issue of *interest-free notes*, we must not forget that these notes, devoid as they are of metallic backing, must *circulate* if they are to be of any use, and their acceptance in circulation, Bentham seems to urge, would be a proper private credit transaction which would not come off without the essential inducement of an appropriate payment of interest. "Take one of the proposed £100 notes," Bentham says, "call it what you please, call it a 'Certificate', call it a 'Stock Note', a man will not receive it for £100—a man will not receive it as an equivalent for £100 metallic money in hand—unless he sees clearly some person or other, who, being able, stands bound to give him £100 worth of metallic money for it: viz. on demand, if he is *not* prepared to wait for it a certain time, or if he *is*, £100 of such money at the end of that time, whatever it be, with interest in proportion to the time. If this interest is not to be paid out of the stock in question, i.e. out of a sufficient and determinate portion of the general mass of government annuities, it is not secured to be paid out of any thing." But, surely, "if no specific and adequate pledge be given as a security for the payment of that sum, or no interest, or any thing less than the full interest, be allowed, and secured, for the money expected to be received in exchange for it, it will not be circulated, because people will not be found to circulate it: if any specific and adequate pledge *be* given for the payment, and at the same interest, and that full interest, be allowed and secured for the money received in exchange for it, it will not be so much as created, because nothing will be to be got by the creation of it." With this damning either/or—which is, in essence, a more pointed reformulation of the central argument of the first letter—Bentham brings this train of reasoning to an end: "Such is the dilemma to which the plan in question appears to me to stand exposed: if any means of escaping from it can be discovered, the discovery will afford the country much benefit, and myself in particular real pleasure" (6, 7).

With this rhetorical flourish Bentham could have brought his epistle to a close. But he was not satisfied with showing that the Weston plan was based on a delusion: he felt it incumbent on him to discuss and expose the source of that delusion, and he sets about this task in a thoroughly characteristic way. The root of the evil, he says, is, as so often, a faulty use of language. "There are two sorts of names by which this species of property is indiscriminately denominated. The one proper, determinate, and clear of fiction—an annuity, a government annuity: the other (which has many synonyms) improper, figurative, and derived from fiction, viz. stock, property in the funds, money in the funds, whence the phrases *to buy stock, to buy into the funds, to invest money in the funds.* Unfortunately the obscure and hence delusive mode of denomination is of the two (as is but too natural) by much the most common and familiar." Out of these ill-conceived words grow ill-conceived ideas. "The funds, according to this notion (a notion which appears to have occupied the writer's mind, not only while [one particular] sentence was penning, but as often and long as the project occupied its place in the same quarter) are a set of immense reservoirs, in which the wealth of individuals—of as many individuals as have been said to have invested money in these funds—(in plain truth to have parted with their money in exchange for government annuities) has all along been collected, and in which so much, as has thus been collected, has always remained, and even now remains . . . . In a word, what is it he must have been thinking of while writing and talking about these English funds? Neither more nor less than a bank of deposit, such as that of Amsterdam was once, and by Adam Smith has been described to be" (7-9).

Needless to say, this is a crude misconception. "Is it then true," Bentham asks, "that government, as often as it receives money by borrowing on annuities, undertakes to keep, in a place called *the Funds,* or in any other place, whatever money it thus receives? To keep it under lock and key, as in the Bank of Amsterdam, ready to be restored at any time on demand? By no means. That which government, in thus creating a mass of annuities, undertakes to deliver is—not *ready*—not *present*—but *future* money: money to be delivered in a long chain, and perhaps an endless one, of periodical transfers. For this future money, for these successive transfers, provision it does make, and I hope and dare believe, it ever will continue to make: for the aggregate mass of these transfers, as the respective periods occurr, but for nothing more." Here, in a nutshell, we have the point which Ambrose Weston has missed, and, Bentham concludes, "in this misconception you may see the foundation of the whole of this project" and with it the proof of its "impracticability" (9, 10, 7).

The point thus made seemed to Bentham of the utmost importance as it involved the whole theory of public borrowing. Weston—for Bentham not so much a stray individual as the representative of a whole host of mistaken reasoners—had put forward in his pamphlet an "axiom" which Bentham regarded as the very epitome of economic error: "In a commercial country there should be as little dead or unproductive capital as possible, but the wealth of individuals collected in the funds is dead to trade and general use, except only so far as the dividends are spent and circulated, and not invested in the same funds by way of farther accumulation" (Sect. XI). As if money lent to the state were capital immobilised! As if a public loan were not simply a shift of the capacity to consume from the individual to the community! "What becomes of the money so made over? Is it kept in the Exchequer? waiting there the influx of other moneys without efflux, destined continually to '*accumulate*'? Alas! no such thing. No sooner does it get there, than it is disposed of: disposed of exactly as the projector himself would wish to see it disposed of, viz. '*spent and circulated*': spent and (for one move at least) pushed on, with a degree of celerity and certainty not only equal to, but exceeding that, with which even '*the dividends*' are '*spent and circulated*'." This is so plainly true that it cannot reasonably be doubted. Weston and those who think like him do not see what is yet so obvious, namely, that a government loan is an inter-temporal exchange, arranged for a consideration, of government expenditure at once for delayed expenditure on the part of individuals. "What is a government annuity? Future money given in return for present money—the money made over [now] to government" (9).

Yet not only Weston's definition of stock—of "future money", as

Bentham calls it—but even his idea of present, or paper money, is at fault. That can be seen from his "second and concluding axiom" which Bentham takes up for criticism before he finally lays down his pen. "There ought to be no such thing known as want of money," Weston says. "And, in my opinion, no such want could be known in a perfectly well-regulated commercial state: I mean no want of that kind should be known or felt by those who possess property of any kind, whether it consists of lands, merchandize, or credits well secured. All such property should enable the owner to procure a representative sign capable of general circu[l]ation" (Sect. XI). In other words, according to Weston, every material value whatsoever should be acknowledged as a possible basis for the issue of paper money.

This postulate, like the former, seems to Bentham completely devoid of all common sense, and again he breaks into a string of indignant invective. "Property of *every* kind capable of answering the purpose of coined metal, and of constituting a fund to draw upon like coined metal! Yes, if selling were an operation that, in the instance of every species of property, could be performed with as much dispatch, as well as certainty, as buying. Yes, if property of every kind were as portable, as readily divisible, as imperishable, as easy of estimation, as the precious metals. That land, for one, is not quite so portable, so readily divisible, nor so easy of estimation, our projector might have learnt at the Air Bank: that butcher's meat is neither quite so portable, nor by a good deal so imperishable, he may learn at any time at the butcher's. When in this way he has gone the rounds of the different species of property which the inventory of national wealth contains, he may perhaps see reason to substitute to his pair of axioms, a single one not quite so brilliant, but rather more consistent with sound reason, as well as with good faith: viz. *that a promise to deliver hard money ought to have hard money ready to make it good*" (13, 14).

With this opinion Bentham seems to have fairly expressed what was generally felt about the matter at the time. On Dec. 27, 1799, he laid his criticism of the Weston proposal before Sir Francis Baring and asked him for his expert view. "As these things are *work* to your humble servant, though *play* to *you*," he writes to the banker, "it has come into my head this moment to bore you with the said second letter, for the chance of taking the benefit of your opinion[s] on the subject, and learning whether my own are fortunate enough to stand confirmed by yours, and to receive any correction which you may have the charity to give me." Sir Francis Baring's reply must have been music in Bentham's ears: "I thank you very much for the perusal of your letter, and agree entirely with you in opinion on the subject. I must, however, in candour, point out to you an error you have committed in saying, *you do not understand, &c.* Now it is evident that your assertions and observations are decidedly at variance. I have heard of the plan for about twelve months, perhaps it may accompany the union, for it is much too sublime for an English head: and your ideas about the tenor of the note are just, as I think it impossible to frame a note founded on so visionary a basis, as would inspire confidence: you should recollect that when Mandats were established, they were combined in a degree with Assignats: the consequence was, that in fourteen days Mandats were at 30 per Cent discount, and in six months both Mandats and Assignats were swallowed up in the same bottomless pit. I have marked with a pencil a short observation which cannot be answered, and therefore *satis est.*" (*Works* X, 341.)

Highly encouraged by this generous praise from an outstanding expert on financial affairs, Bentham at once decided to use his *Letters on the Stock Note Plan* as an open sesame to the Treasury door. As George Rose, who held the decisive post of Secretary of the Treasury, was not precisely his friend, Bentham tried to by-pass him and to thrust his letters right under the Prime Minister's eyes. But this could only be done if a very influential personage consented to carry them with his own hands to Mr. Pitt. Bentham looked round for a promising mediator, and chose Lord Auckland, joint Postmaster-General and an *intimus* of the Prime Minister. "My Lord," he writes to Lord Auckland on Jan. 6, 1800, "I take the liberty of submitting to your Lordship's notice, a short paper, with no other introduction or pretence than the reception which a very voluminous unpublished work (*Panopticon*) from the same quarter, was honoured with in its day.

"Of the paper in question, the *direct* object is, to save to Mr Pitt (if practicable and necessary) the expenditure of any more of his attention, on a project which assumes the having occupied some share of it.

"A collateral object is, that it may be seen, whether a pen that has given birth to *another* plan, which might be in some danger of being confounded with that in question, and which is nearly in a state to be submitted, has not been sufficiently on its guard, against the delusions to which the ground stands so much exposed, and in which *that* project took its rise.

"Another channel which I am by no means unacquainted with (not to speak of personal friends) would have been more regular: but it is because I am so well acquainted with it, that I am unwilling to rely upon it exclusively, or in the first instance: one danger amongst others being, lest the proper view of the subject should be eclipsed by the irrelative [*sic*] idea of some miserable personal interest, as being at the bottom of the proposal; an idea which, besides being groundless, would (it can scarce be necessary to observe to your Lordship) be nothing to the purpose.[1]

"From the quarter alluded to, the alternative would be—approbation with insult, or insult pure: either would be borne, and borne with cheerfullness, for the public service: but the misfortune is, that the attention requisite would be so apt to be called off altogether from the proper points to these irrelevent ones [*sic*].

"From *that* channel I hope I shall stand excused in thus seeking refuge in *another,* in which the qualities, requisite to the trying the question on its own merits, are united with those, by which disapprobation is divested of its harshness, and approbation rendered doubly valuable.

"The labour of revising copies hanging heavy on a time more than fully occupied, it would be a particular favour, if, after making any use of the paper which it may be thought worth while to make of it, in the way of communication, copy, or extract, and without thinking it necessary to say a syllable on the subject of it, your Lordship would have the goodness to let it be returned in the compass of about a week.

"P.S. On recollection, I may possibly have occasion to wish for information on certain points relative to the course of business at the Post Office.—Another apology, as well as reason, for pitching upon your Lordship to undergo the trouble of this address." (U.C. IX, 21.)

On Jan. 10, Lord Auckland replied as follows: "I return your papers with sincere thanks. The perusal of them has been both amusing and instructive to me, and yet I did not want the aid of your acuteness and abilities to enable me to see that the project in question is a fallacy. The statement, however, both in its original and corrected publication, carries with it an air of such earnestness and right mean-

[1]The allusions are obviously to George Rose and the Panopticon project, the financial fate of which depended more or less on George Rose's decision.

ing, that its author appears to me to have deceived himself before he exerted his ingenuity to deceive others.

"If the notes proposed to be issued are payable on demand, I do not see how they differ from any other circulating paper, dependent partly on confidence, and partly on a lodged security. If they are not to be payable on demand, it is evident that they cannot obtain a circulation, and the project of course will be abortive.

"I have reason to believe that there exists no doubt in the quarter to which you appear to have sent your first letter. If any occasion should occur, I will not fail to mention your subsequent letter. But I am afraid to charge myself with the transmission, as it is probable that, without any intentional disregard, they might be sent [?] under the pressure of other businesses." (ib.)

The last clauses of this epistle must have been very disappointing for Bentham. Auckland obviously did not want to be his messenger. But Bentham thought the game was not yet lost. Perhaps Auckland's interest could be stimulated by bringing in the Exchequer or Annuity Note idea which, Bentham was convinced, had a very strong moral claim to the earnest attention of every public man. So another letter went (on Jan. 11) from Queen's Square Place to Eden Farm: "Excuse my troubling your Lordship once more for the purpose of rectifying a misconception to which some obscurities of expression on my part (I see) have given birth. The *supposition* is, that my first letter on the *Stock Note* Plan had been sent or communicated to somebody in office. The *fact* is, that it never was sent to any person but the private friend to whom it was addressed in compliance with his own request, made to me on behalf of the author who had expressed much anxiety (he said) to submit his project to the author of the *Defence of Usury*—and of projectors.

"The detection of the tinsel in question—an operation which was play to your Lordship—was hard work to me whom it found raw and new to it. Will your Lordship allow me to submit to you another composition, similar in name, opposite, or rather *disparate,* in every thing else? Should it bear the crucible, your Lordship will find no difficulty, but a real pleasure in reporting as much to those, who, on that supposition, will be equally happy to make use of it.

"P.S. Your Lordship is pleased to speak of *amusement.* Will you forgive my proposing to you a Rebus or two?—too much (you will think) in the *Marquis of Worcester* stile.

"Problem 1. How to frame a government paper that, though

universally current, shall not be susceptible either of rise or fall? This problem I look upon as solved.

"Problem 2. How to order matters so, that under the most extensive and sudden demand for ready money possible (bating fear of invasion or civil war) government annuities (though they be all of one kind) shall be convertible into ready money in any quantity without loss. Solution still more incontrovertible.

"[Problem] 3. How to render it impossible for executors, assignees of bankrupts, prize-agents &c and other trustees of all sorts, to avoid making interest of their respective trust-monies to the uttermost farthing, or giving the benefit of it to their respective trust, so long as they refrain from parting with it out of their hands?

"[Problem] 4. How to render it impossible for the *Globe-Insurance Company's Frugality Bank* ever to receive a single farthing, and this without any legal obstacle?

"What will my friend Sir Fred[erick] Eden say to me for thus treating a deserted child of mine which he took to nurse![1]

"[Problem] 5. How to frame a security against forgery, which, to appearance, shall be but a toy, but which shall demonstrably be more effectual than any other that can be devised?

"If your Lordship has a mind for any more amusement, desire him to hand over these problems to his illustrious colleague, to review and report upon, *en attendant* till time comes for adding them to his *History of the Revenue*."[2] (ib.)

Auckland replied once again to this effusion, but his answer of Jan. 15 is icy cold and decisively negative: "I write merely to acknowledge your obliging attention in correcting a misconstruction given by me to some expressions in your second paper on the Stock Note project. I certainly had supposed that your first paper on that subject was remaining in the hands of some official friend, to whom it had been communicated. Happening to be a little occupied at present, I cannot attempt to discuss the ingenious problems which you offer to me, on government paper, governmental securities &c." (ib.)

Thus another attempt to gain the ear of the cabinet went astray. But Bentham was not easily discouraged. If this approach failed to bring results, perhaps another would be more successful. After only

---

[1]The meaning of this sentence will become clear later on when Sir Frederick Eden himself appears upon the scene. Cf. p. 85 seq.

[2]Sir John Sinclair, author of a *History of the Public Revenue*, 1784.

half a year, we find him returning to the attack. On July 23, 1800,[1] he sent to Pitt and to Rose copies of a short essay[2] called *On the Form of the Supply to the Sinking Fund*, or "Hints respecting the mode of feeding the old Sinking Fund in war-time: proposing, that it be by interest, as in the case of the new Sinking Fund: not by principal; that being a mere fiction, which neither is, nor ever can be, realized". Here are his opening paragraphs which clearly indicate the problem at issue: "By the Act establishing the *first* Sinking Fund (26 G.3. c. 31) it being a year of *peace*, an appropriation was made of a million a year in money, to be applied annually to the buying in of Stock: the mass of annuities 'thereon attendant' to be applied to the purchase of more Stock, and so on, upon the principle of interest upon interest.

"By the Act establishing the *second* permanent Sinking Fund (32 G.3. c. 55 par. 2) *war* being then in contemplation, the form given to the contribution destined for the redemption of the expected debt of the expected war, was adapted to a year of *war*: the provision made accordingly is—that upon the first loan that shall thereafter be made, a perpetual annuity, to the amount of one per Cent, upon the Stock created by that loan, shall be created, payable in quarterly payments (the first payment to be made, on the quarter day next after the passing of the Act authorizing that loan), and be put into the hands of the commissioners, to be employed in buying in the capital of such first loan, and of all such further loans as shall come to be made in the course of the war: and so in general to all succeeding loans. But the war-mode designed for the establishing a fresh fund for the redemption of the debt about to be created in such *war-years* (or as they may be termed *no-surplus years*) as might thereafter ensue, was not extended and applied to the administering, during such future war years or *no-surplus* years, the masses of supply allotted to the then already-existing fund established in a *year of surplus*. The consequence was—that, during all such *no-surplus* years, the old part of the debt was left to be supplied in *one* way, the *new* part, in another: the new part, in a mode suited to the time; the old part, in a mode *not* suited to the time: in a mode so far from being suited to the time, as to be in *effect* not *practicable*, though by the

[1]The date appears on p. 64 of box IIIa, University College collection. BM Add. MSS 31235, p. 27, only has "1800".

[2]It is possible, of course, not to say probable, that "Letter II" *On the Stock Note Plan* was forwarded on the same occasion.

continuance of the same *forms,* the impracticability of it is screened from view." (B.M. Add. MSS 31235, 23-24.)

It must be borne in mind, Bentham seems to urge, that a year of war is, in the nature of things, a year when it is difficult, not to say impossible, to raise such a considerable sum as £1,000,000: that it is necessarily "a year in which, there being an extra demand for money to a greater amount than the million in question, and no expectation of a surplus sufficient to answer that extra demand, the deficiency requires to be supplied in the way of a loan, that is by creating and selling fresh masses of annuity". In other words—to make the matter quite plain—the £1,000,000 redemption money has to be *borrowed* in war-time, and would not be available otherwise. Hence "by the supposition the very sum you pay with *one* hand, you either have borrowed already, or immediately after will have to borrow, on that account, with the *other*: which, to the amount of that sum, comes to exactly the same thing, as if you had neither paid nor borrowed". What is the only practical effect? That a parcel of *old* debt is replaced by a parcel of *new* debt: that the new fund fed by an annual supply of 1% of the amount of debt outstanding is burdened to the same extent to which the old fund fed by fixed and round sums annually paid in is relieved. What can be the point of such a curious *quid pro quo*? Bentham suggests that it should be dropped. "This," he says, after showing, rather clumsily, in some detail, what is going on, "being what is done at present, but in a roundabout, indirect, fictitious, and obscure way, what is proposed is, that in future the same thing should be done, but in a direct, true, and perspicuous way; as is actually done in the other case—in the case of that portion of the grants of a war-year, which is made for the redemption of the debt created in that same war-year". The proposed reform, to be enacted for the duration of the national emergency, could be summed up as "the substitution of an annuity to the principal sum; of the £60,000, £50,000, £40,000 *a year,* &c (as the case may be), to the million *once paid*". On the return of peace, "it being supposed a year actually affording a surplus to the amount in question, the mode suited to the season might, and naturally would, be resumed".

Bentham proposes this war-time measure as a piece of common sense. He does not claim for it outstanding merits or startling effects. Yet he always knows how to show his ideas in a favourable light, and so he appends three "heads of argument suggesting the inconveniences resulting from the present mode, and consequently the advantages derivable from the proposed change". Here they are:

"I. Pecuniary losses, *capable* of being liquidated—

£ s. d.

"1. By *subscribers profit,* every year, upon so much money raised, or so much Stock created ... ...

"2. By expence of *Bank management,* commencing upon the creation of the Stock, ceasing as soon as an equal quantity has been bought in ... ...

"3. By difference (if any) in point of *interest,* between the day on which the first dividend in the Stock thus *created* is *paid,* and the day on which the first dividend in the Stock *bought in* with the money is *received* ...

"4. By allowance (if any) to the Bank for *receiving* subscription money upon this part of the loan ... ...

"II. Pecuniary loss, *scarce* capable of being liquidated—

"5. Extra *load* on the market; viz. at the time of the contracting for the loan: thence extra *price* paid in *annuities* for the *money* produced by the rest of the loan ... ...

"The load (it may be said) is removed afterwards, and the removal is capable of being foreseen and argued upon at the making of the contract. True: but still the state of things is not altogether the same as if there was no such load. The gross—the *erroneous conception*—presents itself to a certainty, and at all times: the presence of the *corrective observation,* is but occasional and precarious.

"III. *Inappretiable* inconveniences: but of a kind commonly adduced in argument.

"6. *Finances,* exhibited as so much *worse* than they are, by the addition made to the loan: *people,* less in heart, &c.

"7. The war represented as by so much more *expensive* than it *is*:—administration, the less popular: *people,* the less contented. What if the new Sinking Fund had been fed in the same way? the *apparent* load would have been *apparently* intolerable. (*Per contra* the apparent amplitude of the old Sinking Fund would be so much the *less,* upon the *proposed* plan:—unless explained, for which a line or two in a preamble would suffice).

"8. *Inconsistency*, as compared with the *new* Sinking Fund: *fiction, complication*, and *obscurity*." (B.M. Add. MSS 31235, 25-26.)

After this imposing array of arguments, the paper ends with a typical *argumentum ad hominem*: "The unprecedented clearness of the financial picture is among the characteristic glories of the present administration. Should any thing be left that can obscure it?"

Once again we are without a clue to the question whether Bentham's suggestion was taken seriously and discussed. There is nothing to indicate that it was. Bentham may well have wondered if the big-wigs at the Treasury would ever take notice. Another man would surely have begun to despair: he did not, because he had the fanatical self-confidence of all men with a mission. So the rest of the year 1800 slipped by. But it did not slip by unused. The Annuity Note proposal which had all the time been taking shape in Bentham's mind, had meanwhile ripened and reached the stage of printability, if not of publicability. The first three chapters of a concise exposition of it, and part of its fourth chapter, were set up: the remainder was clean-copied by busy amanuenses. Presently, in January 1801, Bentham was to try to bring it to Pitt's notice, or at any rate to induce Rose to have a look at it. But before we open this new chapter in the painful history of Bentham's disappointments and frustrations, we must try to understand what the proposal was, and what it meant.

THE "ANNUITY NOTE" PROPOSAL AND ITS FATE

I. THE PROPOSAL ITSELF

If the time spent on an idea is any measure of the importance attributed to it by its author, the Annuity Note proposal must rank as the suggestion on which Bentham pinned his highest hopes. He worked at it for upwards of a year, an exceptionally long time measured by Bentham's standards. The first sketch of the first chapter of the intended work may have been written as early as August 1799, or even before, though the matter is not quite clear (cf. University College collection IIIa, 46): what is certain is, that in October of 1799, the work was in full swing (ib. 31 et seq.). The day on which the subject was laid aside can be pinned down with more exactitude, for, as a kind of good resolution for the new century, Bentham seems to have made up his mind in January 1800 to be more careful about dating his manuscripts. On October 19, 1800, we still find him working on the book which was to contain this proposal, though he is ominously speaking of a "delusion which had exercised its delusive power in his own instance" (U.C. Ia, 15): but on October 22 he is already drafting a "brouillon" for an entirely different work (destined never to be written) on "National Prospects or a Picture of Futurity".[1] Finally, on October 30, we see that the pamphlet on *Paper Mischief* is engrossing all his attention, and the Annuity Note idea has faded out.

A whole year is a long time in which a steady and conscientious worker like Bentham is bound to produce a vast mass of manuscripts. We possess in fact no less than four boxes of Annuity Note material (U.C. Ia, Ib, IIa and IIb) comprising roughly 1,400 sheets. Up to July or August 1800, Bentham worked away without considering whether anybody would be willing to read so voluminous a work as the one which was growing up under his hands. But then he seems to have stopped to consider the question, and decided that probably nobody would. So he began to recast his material in order to bring it down to a manageable size. In September and October he drafted the *Abstract or Compressed View of a Tract intituled Circulating Annuities* which Bowring included in his *Works,* and which is printed below. There seems no point whatever in publishing the chapters of the "body of the work" which run parallel to the chapters of the "compressed view": the contents are to all intents and purposes the same. The only exception is the heading under which the relation of monetary circulation and national wealth is considered, and this particular chapter is given in the present edition in all its successive shapes.

We have just said that Bowring included the *Abstract or Compressed View* in his *Works.* Those who know the *Works* may well be surprised about this contention. There is no item which actually bears this title, but the text is none the less contained in vol. III and fills pages 106-148. What has happened is that Bowring manufactured a new name for the manuscript which runs as follows: "A plan for saving all trouble and expense in the transfer of stock, and for enabling the proprietors to receive their dividends without powers of attorney, or attendance at the Bank of England, by the conversion of stock into note annuities" (*Works* III, 105). It is easy to guess why Bowring discarded Bentham's title and substituted for it another: his own was sure to have a stronger appeal in 1843 when vol. III of the *Works* came out, and he was anxious to prove that Bentham's ideas were still "useful to humanity", even though they had been written

[1]Cf. University College collection IIIa, 83, and the summary below, vol. III, end.

up some forty years before. The same desire to "modernize" the work is visible in the text itself. Wherever there is any reference to contemporary conditions, for instance, wherever Bentham quotes concrete figures relating to the actual state of the national debt, Bowring mercilessly cuts them out: while Bentham had produced a tract for the times, Bowring tried to convince his readers that the fundamental idea of the Annuity Note proposal was timeless wisdom. Apart from this rather important point, and a less important change in the numeration of the chapters, Bowring followed the original text fairly well, although there are the usual misinterpretations, misreadings, and misprints.

As has already been mentioned, a small part of the *Abstract or Compressed View* (three-and-a-half chapters, or 48 pages) was set up for print in 1800/1801 and a few copies actually run off. These offprints obviously contained the final version of the beginning of the pamphlet, in the form in which Bentham wished to give it to the world, and it would have been highly desirable to base the text of the present critical edition directly on their text. Unfortunately, the most assiduous research has failed to produce a single copy. The British Museum originally possessed the one copy which Bentham had given to Francis Place, but enemy action destroyed it prior to 1945, and it had not been photostated. Bowring noted on p. 106 that he "has been able to discover only a single copy of those chapters" and does not tell us whether he himself printed from it or not. But, for once, his very negligence comes to our help. Page 107, where the pamphlet actually begins,[1] is headed "Circulating Annuities, &c": it gives the very title which Bowring had decided to suppress, and this is clear proof that the twelve or fourteen pages that follow are in fact taken from the pamphlet Bentham had begun to print. For this reason our text follows that of Bowring until we come to chapter IV where we turn to those original manuscripts which he is using, too. In the circumstances, we get nearest to the authentic text if we treat chapters I-III in Bowring's edition as we would a copyist's copy of Bentham's autograph.

Written at a time when Bentham had already thoroughly considered the whole complex of problems involved, the *Abstract or Compressed View* makes, on the whole, fairly good reading. Chapter I, it is true, is somewhat tiring, because it goes in some detail into the administrative apparatus necessary for the actual issue and pay-

[1]Bowring's faked title-page is on p. 105.

ment of the proposed circulating annuities: but this is the very chapter which Bentham shortened most. The "body of the work" enters much deeper still into the various aspects of practical management. The rest of the explanation is brisk and to the point, and has benefited greatly by the pruning and abridgement.

With the proposal set forth in these pages, Bentham attempted to secure two great improvements at one stroke: to reduce the burden of the public debt on the finances of the country; and to induce the lower classes to save and thus to make provision for old age and against sickness and unemployment. At first sight it may seem difficult, if not impossible, to couple two aims so utterly alien to each other: but Bentham flattered himself that his ingenuity and inventiveness had found a means to encompass them both. If the Exchequer would issue a circulating annuity, i.e. a paper of small nominal value expressing and representing a debt of the government to the bearer and yielding some yearly or half-yearly interest just like stock, but at a rate inferior to that paid on stock, and this paper could be made to circulate in the way Bank Notes do, the poorer people would be able to make some interest on their day-to-day holdings and on their "petty hoards" by using these notes in lieu of cash, which would evoke and foster a spirit of frugality in their minds; and the government would be enabled to pay off the existing national debt with its comparatively high rate of interest, or rather convert it into a set of obligations much less burdensome to the Treasury. The reader can find the gist of the proposal well set out in a condensed form in the "Introduction" to the pamphlet, and so no more need be said about the general idea of it here. The fatal weakness of the whole suggestion (which Bentham either did not fully grasp, or else did not care openly to discuss) is rather obvious: surely, the two aims would not, in practice, harmonize after all. If the rate of interest on the proposed Annuity Notes were comparatively high, the burden on the Treasury would not be sensibly reduced: but if, on the other hand, it were possible to set it rather low, the inducement to save would be practically nil. It is only at the end of chapter XVI that Bentham faces up to this dilemma, and he seems to suggest there that the conflict should be solved by sacrificing the "moral advantages" of the "measure" to its financial advantages. In fact, the whole pamphlet lays more stress on the fiscal aspect than on the social: but it is possible that this is simply due to the natural desire on the part of Bentham to impress the Treasury who, he feared, would be little interested in, and perhaps little sympathetic to, his endeavour to turn the small man into a petty capitalist.

The first chapter develops the plan in concrete terms, and the footnotes which run along the main text descend to the level of the minutest detail. It is not difficult to see that Bentham meant these 23 articles to be the raw material of an Annuity Note Bill, and ultimately of an Annuity Note Act. H.M. Exchequer, he explains, is to issue, with the technical help of the Post Office, promissory notes which would be Bank Notes and Exchequer Bills at the same time. The standard note (at roughly 3% p.a.) would give a farthing a day interest, and would consequently have to bear the nominal value of £12 16s. Bentham knew that this must seem odd, but he was convinced that it would be better to give the daily increase in value in a round sum because in the currency he wanted to create it would be the constant appreciation that would be its distinguishing feature and its main attraction, and not the figure printed on the face of it. The Notes were to show a table clearly indicating their concrete value for each particular day. Without such a table there would, quite obviously, have been no hope whatever of making the paper circulate, because every transaction would then have presupposed a complicated mathematical computation. Bentham thought that his table would counterbalance the awkward fact that this type of money was to have a different purchasing power every day. It is clear that he much underestimated the need in economic intercourse for a means of circulation that is supremely simple and utterly unproblematic.

For every note annuity created, Bentham demanded that an existing stock annuity should be wiped out. At first, as long as stock was yet under par, stock annuities were to be bought in, the profit of the operation going to the Sinking Fund; as soon as the powerfully increased demand had raised stock to par or above it, the remainder was naturally to be paid off at par, rather than to be bought up in the open market at a higher price. The issue of Annuity Notes was to remain open as long as there was still any stock as yet unredeemed, but it was to be closed as soon as the last particle of it had been cleared away.

Once all stock annuities were replaced by the new note annuities, Bentham suggested that a further conversion should take place. A new issue of Annuity Notes bearing a reduced rate of interest—2⅜% —was then to be launched, and with the proceeds of it the old issue promising nearly 3% to be redeemed, in the same way in which the first issue had expelled the original stock. Nor did he think that $2\frac{3}{8}\%$ need be the final level of interest on the public debt. He envisaged a third issue at $1\frac{1}{2}\%$, and indeed yet further issues at even lower rates of interest "*toties quoties*, in so far as any such further reduction may be deemed eligible". In this way the national debt would progressively cease to be a worry for the Chancellor of the Exchequer.

In lieu of a chapter II, Bentham presents us with the "form of the proposed Annuity Note", complete with a portrait of the King crowned on its face, and a portrait of the Auditor of the Exchequer on its back—"for security against forgery". Chapter III gives a comparison of the intended new creation with the existing and familiar government securities. Bentham finds that eight features of it are "already exemplified", while twelve others are "altogether new". In a way, this chapter is nothing but a reiteration of the claims Bentham has put forward in his "introduction", especially of the claim that his Annuity Notes would be completely "depretiation-proof". Very much the same can be said of chapter IV—"Grounds of expectation in regard to the proposed measure". Here, too, the aim is to demonstrate all the benefits that the suggested Annuity Note currency would bestow upon the country, and to dispel the fears which such an experiment could conceivably call up in a timid mind. Bentham here makes an attempt to enumerate the probable customers for the new-fangled paper in order to prove its general usefulness as well as its attractiveness to vast classes of individuals. Characteristically, he mentions "provision for widowhood or superannuation" in the first place. After surveying the prospective customers Bentham tries to assess the comparative advantages offered by Annuity Notes to these customers by holding the new type of investment against investment in government stock and Exchequer Bills and the placing of money in the form of private loans.

Chapters V-X are all taken up by a discussion of the expected financial advantages, i.e. the profits that are likely to accrue to the Treasury. These chapters are largely self-explanatory. Chapter IX, headed "Concluding Period", is the most interesting. It undertakes to provide "a picture of the last moments of the expiring debt". Is it likely, Bentham asks, that it will be possible to reduce the rate of interest below $1\frac{1}{6}\%$? This, he answers, will depend on the general rate of interest current in the country, and hence in good part on the influence on that general rate of the reductions of the special rate paid for stock. This influence is bound to be considerable; it will be in keeping with the size of the national debt that is being redeemed, and its proportion to the general volume of capital in the national economy. Now, as "the general mass of national capital" is increasing spontaneously, there is a spontaneous tendency of the general rate of interest to fall; and with this tendency the proposed measure is expected to join up, reinforcing it and being in turn reinforced by it, so that even 1⅙% need not be regarded as the *non plus ultra* of reduction. Certainly a very bold view!

The whole note annuity operation will come to an end by the elimination of the customers who have taken Annuity Note paper "as a source of permanent income"—the hoarders or investors in the narrower sense of the word. They will lose interest in it because it will no longer pay well; and/or they will be paid off. Annuity Notes will, however, remain as a simple means of circulation. The small interest that will still be payable on them will, as far as it goes, be welcome to people who use them in lieu of cash; whatever they get is, after all, more than they get out of cash. But, being "users in the way of circulation", they will cash in the amount of interest due from other users and not come for it to the Annuity Note Offices. Thus the national debt will practically cease to be a burden, and there is no point in going on with the redemption of it which would, after all, presuppose taxation (which *is* a burden) to finance it; quite apart from the fact that the withdrawal of the Notes might have unwelcome deflationary effects.

In chapter XI Bentham turns away from the fiscal aspects and takes up the more definitely economic implications of his proposal. He claims that the measure would bring about a calculable increase in national capital. His general thesis is that every pound paid in discharge of the national debt is a pound added to productive capital. Why? Simply because it is taken from the taxpayer, a typical spender, and transferred to the public creditor, a typical investor. Now, the proposed measure will speed up the redemption of the national debt and thus advance this addition to national capital. The benefit it will secure will be in proportion to the number of years by which the repayment of the debt is brought forward. If total redemption is advanced by five years, and if the national capital accumulates at the rate of 5% in every year, the advantage in question will be exactly £110,512,624—i.e. 5%, for five years, at compound interest, on the debt, due to creditors at home, of £400,000,000. Not every pound seized by taxation and transferred would, it is true, have been spent unproductively if it had remained in the pockets of the taxpayers. But even if we assume that an eighth of it would have been saved and invested productively, there remains an increase in national capital to the tune of £96,698,546 which could be reaped from the realization of the Annuity Note proposal.

Chapter XII, dealing with "commercial security", claims that the new currency would guard the country against the danger of economic crises due to purely monetary causes, such as runs on and failures of paper-emitting banks. Bentham presupposes that his reader is familiar with the evils of inflation, but he strongly insists on the less obvious, though not less real evils of a "shortage of money". Were the suggested Annuity Notes to be introduced, Bentham argues, there could henceforth be neither a deficiency nor a glut in circulation: the new type of paper money would act as a sort of regulator because it could be used either as a means of payment or as an investment—either as currency or as capital. Annuity Note paper, he says, has two natures and is at all times either the one thing or the other, whichever is wanted more in the given situation. It is easy to see how Annuity Notes would help in times of deficiency: they would simply stream out of hoards into circulation and thus close the gap. But it is not so easy to make out what use they could possibly be during a spell of inflation. Inflation, however, is a problem in itself which Bentham tries to tackle in chapter XIV. Here he thinks more of the danger of a general run on the banks. Should such a run develop, Bentham contends, the very existence of Annuity Notes would steady everybody's nerves by presenting to the public the image of a species of paper money which *cannot* fail. Annuity Notes do not pretend to be covered by metal; they only promise a half-yearly payment of interest which will always be easy to fulfil, and so there would never be any rational ground for mistrust against this type of currency. On the other hand, there will always be sound reasons for mistrusting bank notes, especially private ones, which are never covered in full by gold reserves as they pretend to be, and whose weakness in that respect is the main cause of all monetary crises and runs. Bentham obviously takes a much too formalistic and legalistic view of the problem. It is true that his note annuities would not have promised more than the Exchequer could always fulfil, but that would have been no guarantee at all against the general desire to get rid of paper altogether and to seek refuge in goods which is so characteristic of most crises of confidence.

What social classes or groupings would be adversely affected by the introduction of the recommended Annuity Note currency? This problem is investigated in the next following chapter, chapter XIII. Bentham thinks mainly of two categories: 1. The stockholders of the "paying-off season". They stand to lose because they will be deprived of a convenient and comparatively secure and lucrative investment. But these people cannot be surprised, and consequently cannot really complain, because they have always had to reckon with the fact that the government would get rid of the national debt as soon as it is humanly possible. 2. The banking interest. Bentham considers in turn the Bank of England, the issuing country bankers, and the non-issuing London banking houses. For none of them does he show any sympathy or solicitude. In any event, the bankers would gain the same advantage as Annuity Notes would be bringing to everybody in the community: they would be enabled to make interest on their hoards, i.e. their cash reserves, by keeping them in the form of circulating annuities, instead of being forced, as hitherto, to fill their coffers with unproductive metal.

Chapter XIV is entitled "Rise of prices—how to obviate". Would the mobilization of the national debt in the proposed form, its transfiguration into state notes ready to circulate alongside the existing bank notes, not bring about a terrific inflation that would mar the whole measure? Would it not, by this effect, create much more confusion, and indeed misery, than it could ever hope to counterbalance by all its advantages, financial, economic, moral and political taken together? Bentham well knew that here lay the theoretical crux of the matter. It took him many months of sustained thought to come to a clear vision and assured solution of this problem. The stages through which he went before he reached clarity are so interesting that we propose to print below an extract from the papers in which he formulated his ideas at certain intervals (cf. pp. 301-342). At the present moment we are only concerned with the final position which is mirrored in the chapter under review.

Already at the end of the "Introduction" and at the end of chapter XI Bentham had hinted that in its possible effect on the price level lay the doubtful element of the proposal he was putting forward; here he begins by frankly admitting that it would probably lead to an "extra rise" of prices, i.e. to inflationary results. Should this fear prove justified, Bentham suggests that the issue of some types of Annuity Notes should be stopped forthwith, e.g. the issue of those below the

£102 8s. mark. He does not say that such a step would make nonsense of the whole measure: surely, Annuity Notes for more than £100 would simply have been Exchequer Bills re-christened and made out for an awkward uneven sum, instead of circulating, as before, under their well-accustomed name and with a sensible round figure on their face.

However, it is not this desperate check that Bentham wants to see applied. He hopes and expects that his Annuity Notes would drive the other types of paper money out of the market and hence not constitute "a neat addition" to the total means of circulation in use. Should, against expectation, bank and bankers' notes maintain themselves in economic life, he urges that their expulsion should be artificially engineered. The government could, for instance, refuse to accept Bank of England Notes at its offices; and paper issued by country bankers could be taxed and thus weakened and killed off. Bentham endeavours to show that the loss thus caused to the banking profession would be incomparably smaller than the loss to the community at large, if an inflation were allowed to develop.

The last two paragraphs of the chapter present Bentham's final opinion on the effect of inflationary measures on national welfare. If there are, before the influx of the additional money, unemployed resources, human or material, and the influx brings them into play, inflationary measures *do* increase the standard of living in the country. But if, at the beginning of the operation, all resources are fully employed, no more can possibly be produced, and the only effect of an attempt to pump fresh money into the circulation is bound to be a rise of prices.

After these considerations it is somewhat surprising to find that in chapter XV Bentham returns to a discussion of the financial aspects of the proposal, and there is little doubt that it would have been better to insert this heading after chapter X where it would have had a more appropriate place. The special contention here is that the conversion of the national debt from the form of stock into that of note annuities would be more profitable to government than the conversion carried out under Pelham in 1749.

The last two chapters, XVI and XVII, though both comparatively short, contain ideas which, one cannot help feeling, carried much more weight in Bentham's mind than appears from what he put down in black and white. Chapter XVI claims two great "moral advantages" for the measure: 1. prevention of improbity, and 2.

promotion of frugality. Once Annuity Notes exist, a good deal of improbity could and should be prevented if all trustees were put under a statutory obligation to invest their trust monies in these annuities. Frugality would be promoted, and insobriety checked, if a positive premium for saving were offered to all small earners to counterbalance their all-too-natural tendency to spend at once what they have got. In the present state of affairs, Bentham urges, rich people make interest on their savings, but poor people do not: the proposed currency reform would remove this economic iniquity and thus mitigate, at an essential point, the cleavage between the social classes. He only forgets that the daily interest on a Sixpenny Annuity Note of, say, the third issue at 1½% p.a., would hardly have been a strong incentive to frugality!

The "constitutional advantage" of the measure, finally, would consist in turning the "little monied interest" away from subversive ideas, and injecting into them a more conservative spirit. Bentham obviously believed in the Gospel words that where one's treasure is, there is one's heart also, and he saw before his eyes the example of the Glorious Revolution in which the creditors of the state had played a by no means unimportant role. The chapter, brief as it is, is of considerable interest to students of Bentham's mental development. It shows him poised between conservative and progressive sentiments: the aim is still to give society stability and peace, but his sympathies are already turned towards the masses from whom he expected, in his later days, that reform of public life which the upper classes were manifestly unwilling to accept at his hands.

Looking back over the *Abstract or Compressed View* as a whole, it is clear that chapters XI and XIV are by far the most interesting for the theoretical economist. Originally these two headings had formed a single one under the title "Annuity Notes and National Wealth". It was only at the end of September or begining of October that Bentham decided to divide the subject matter of the one (addition to national capital) from the subject matter of the other (rise of prices) —the advantage from the difficulty. It seems well worth while to follow the development of Bentham's thought on these topics in more detail, and accordingly this edition contains four excerpts from the papers which lead up to the final position as contained in the pamphlet which we have just been studying. Naturally, these materials show many imperfections and are sometimes ill-worded and often repetitive, but, such as they are, they show us the picture of a great mind grappling with a great problem. Bentham made his task much more difficult by completely disregarding contemporary economic writing which could have told him quite a lot about the process of inflation, but he was not inclined to accept other people's ideas on any subject that he felt he could tackle himself: this sense of independence is, for better or worse, one of his outstanding characteristics as a man, a thinker, and an economist. It explains to a certain extent why he had to re-formulate his discussion of the connection between "Annuity Notes and National Wealth" four times before he could feel assured that he had properly understood the matter and mastered its difficulties.

The first version of this important chapter was written in March 1800. At that time Bentham had as yet only a dim and partial view of the inflationary effects his Annuity Notes were likely to produce, and he clearly does not regard them as a major drawback of the proposed operation. The net addition which the new currency would make to the existing mass of paper money in circulation, he says, would add as much to national wealth as would an equal amount of hard cash; the only difference would be that Annuity Notes, unlike coin, cannot be made into goblets and trinkets and gold teeth. Now, extra cash adds to national wealth by dint of the extra quantity of labour which it draws into the process of production: the addition is, in fact, measured by that newly mobilized quantity of labour, or rather by the mass of goods which that labour brings into the world.

Following up this fundamental assertion, Bentham then endeavours to show in which ways extra money can call forth extra labour and increased productivity. He enumerates ten important points which speak for themselves. In point 4 we have a faint echo of the physiocratic doctrine which had been so prominent in the pamphlet against Pitt (cf. vol. I, pp. 38 and 47); in points 7-9, and even in point 10, there is still recognizable the old mercantilistic outlook and attitude. But what follows now is really much more interesting, for Bentham begins at this point to face up to the problem of inflation. The influx of Annuity Note money into circulation, he admits, would have two undesirable consequences: it would 1. increase the rent of land, and 2. raise the wages of labour. Both effects would be due to increased competition among the buyers of these factors of production who would have more to offer in the market than before. Only the second, the wages problem, is discussed in some detail. If the new mass of money were transposed exclusively into offers of employment to unemployed workmen, there would of course be no upward swing of wages; if, on the other hand, it were transposed exclusively into a demand for labour of the sorts that are at the moment in full employment, there would be a strong upward swing of wages; but neither limiting case is ever likely to be realized. It is in particular well-nigh impossible to direct the newly financed demand exclusively to the unemployed: an influx of money will in practice always create an increased all-round demand for labour, and, because of the competition among employers, a rise of wages.

A rise of wages, then, would be likely to follow upon, and arise from, the realization of the Annuity Note proposal. Goods would become dearer, and the receivers of fixed incomes would be hurt. But though this is an obvious inconvenience, Bentham is not disturbed. *Any* increase of national wealth, he argues, would have this result, and it would be ridiculous to oppose an advancement in general well-being just because it is bound to have some less desirable by-products. Moreover, Annuity Notes will, to a considerable degree, be hoarded for investment purposes, and thus they will not inflate the circulation to the same extent as cash or bank notes of equal amount. Finally, he seems to ask in conclusion (though the text is not very explicit at this point)—is it really true to say that an inflationary rise of prices is a pure evil? Granted that it depresses those who draw fixed incomes, does it not at the same time bring higher prosperity to the workers, "the bulk and great majority of the whole community"? At this stage of his thought, Bentham seems to have been under the impression that the main effect, or at any rate one of the main effects, of an inflationary development is an increase in the real wages of labour.

This argument is conspicuously absent from the second version of the chapter drafted during the summer months of the year. The starting point is indeed the same—the contention that circulating annuities would increase national wealth in the same way, and to the same extent, as so much hard cash; but otherwise the train of thought is rather different. We can see that Bentham's mind is somewhat unsettled; he is hesitant; and there is more emphasis on the "bad effects to be apprehended". He speaks of a "plethora" of the body social, a state of fullness or even over-fullness, a high degree of liquidity on the money market which would tend to reduce the rate of interest and thus hit the moneyed man. The case of the moneyed men—of the "possessors of unencreasable incomes"—is regarded with much more sympathy than before; they are called "victims of the change", and the reduction of the interest-rate is described outright as "an evil". Indeed, there is at one point an implicit admission, or half-admission, that the final effect of the introduction of the proposed Annuity Notes would be an uncontrollable inflation.

But Bentham tries to argue himself out of this unfavourable position into which his own thought on the subject has manœuvred him. First of all, he consoles himself by saying that "in political economy, as in chemistry, results are scarce ever obtained pure": a certain price must be paid for every improvement. Then he does his best (for himself as well as for his prospective readers) to play down the probable amount of the influx of money into the market which would be caused by the advocated mobilization of the national debt; and, finally, he brings in the problem of "peace and war" to save his project. Let us not forget, he urges, that Annuity Notes have a double nature, that they are cash and capital at the same time. This "unexampled ductility" will ensure that they will never really glut the money market. In war time they will act mainly as currency—but then money is scarce, because government has to collect it in its coffers to finance its high expenditure, and so Annuity Notes will be welcome to prevent an acute shortage. In peace time they will become predominantly means of investment—but then their withdrawal from circulation will be all to the good, because money will tend to be too abundant, to be accumulated "faster than a correspondent portion of dormant labour can be found to be put in action by it", and there would be a sensible surplus if the interest promised by the Annuity Notes did not induce people to hoard them up and thus withdraw them from current use. It must remain an open question whether Bentham really believed in the efficacy of this mechanism, even while he was writing these pages. It was in any case a bold statement to say that "it followed from the convertibility" of the Annuity Note currency from cash into capital, and from capital into cash, "that it can not on any supposition be ever existing in excess".

In the third version of the chapter, written in the month of September, an entirely new idea is seen to emerge. Bentham now suggests that the addition to the sum-total of national wealth produced by an additional quantity of money introduced into the economic system, depends on the *use* made of that money. In so far as the new Annuity Notes would provide the means for the redemption of the national debt, they would add, to their full amount, to national capital and hence to national wealth, because the public creditors into whose hands the additional money would flow, are typical investors and sure to employ whatever they get in a productive way. But in so far as the annuity currency would flow into and swell the general stream of circulation, it would effect an augmentation of national wealth only in the proportion in which it would be divided between current expenditure and saving, i.e. between consumption and capital investment. The specific problem of inflation—depreciation of the currency and general rise of prices—is not properly discussed in this version: but it rather looks as if the pages just reviewed were no more than a fragment.

The idea that the redemption of the national debt, by giving capital to capitalists, will increase the real wealth of the nation, is preserved in the final version of the chapter of October 1800 and carried over into chapter XI of the *Abstract or Compressed View*. But there is nevertheless a great difference between Bentham's state of mind in September and in October. It is only in October that he has reached a firm point of view with regard to the influence of monetary operations on the advancement of real wealth. He sees now that economic progress depends on the rate of capital formation, i.e. on the prevalent relation between saving and spending; and he rightly concludes that money as such is simply irrelevant. If new means of circulation are introduced "by hands of the productive class" and used "at the first step" for investment purposes, the additional money will help to make an addition to fixed capital, and hence to prosperity, —but this is the *only* way in which it can make *any* contribution to the growth of material wealth. At the second step already, when it has left the investor's hands, it will begin to cause an inflationary depreciation of the circulation into which it flows, and this is the *only* effect it can ever have if it is not, at its first introduction, employed to finance some tangible improvement of the apparatus of production. Bentham has come to realize—not for the first time perhaps, but more clearly than ever before—that the price level depends on the relation between vendible commodities—"the stock of goods"—on the one hand, and the volume and velocity of circulation—"the stock of money"—on the other.

This realization must have come as something of a shock. As we have seen, Bentham had always feared that the launching of his Annuity Notes would interfere with the stability of the price system, but that apprehension had been a vague feeling rather than a clear expectation: now it stared him in the face as an unavoidable fact. The pages printed below (325-342) show him grappling with this most unwelcome difficulty. He is supremely honest about it. A rise of prices, he now admits, can only be avoided if the proposed Annuity Notes either produce a flood of goods big enough to counterbalance and absorb the incoming flood of paper, or expel other paper money and cash to their own amount. He does not stay here to investigate the first possibility: he seems to have realized that money can be pumped in very quickly, while the commodity market can never be filled up otherwise than very slowly. As far as the expulsion of the competing paper and cash is concerned, he suggests that it would be all to the good; but he is not certain that it would be altogether easy to get rid of the cash. The whole investigation comes to an abrupt termination without any very tangible result. But in the penultimate paragraph there is talk of "proposing the quantity of money of all sorts already in circulation as the standard of reference, in respect of the quantity to be suffered to exist after and in consequence of the introduction of the proposed paper", and that leads us directly to the position taken up in chapter XIV—headed "Rise of prices—how to obviate"—of the *Abstract and Compressed View*. There, it will be recalled, the suggestion is that, should the Annuity Note currency threaten to swamp the circulation, "it would be necessary to apply the check to the proposed paper itself . . . . by stopping the issue of all Annuity Notes below a certain magnitude", for instance £102 8s. But this expedient, to which the fear of inflation has forced Bentham, means in effect the virtual abandonment of the whole Annuity Note idea which was, as he had told us in the very first sentences of his pamphlet, "the affording to the least opulent and most numerous class of individuals the means of placing out *small hoards,* however minute"—a description hardly applicable to a sum of more than £100, and in his day still less than in our own. There can be no doubt that the discovery of the mechanism of inflation greatly weakened Bentham's faith in the grand scheme which had held him spell-bound for so many months. It is true that he tried to press it on the government in the following year, as we shall see presently, but it is somewhat difficult to believe that his heart was still fully engaged in the affair after the autumn of the year 1800 when these pages were thought out and written down.

2. THE FATE OF THE PROPOSAL

If Bentham did not drop the Annuity Note proposal altogether, but on the contrary began to take active steps for its adoption, the reason was that a new motive had come to operate in his mind. True, Annuity Note paper, like all paper money, brought with it, as he now saw, the danger of upsetting the price level: but was that danger not much greater in the actual state of things than it could ever be after the introduction of Annuity Notes? In the actual state of things, the amount of paper money thrown into circulation was beyond anybody's control: who could know what the numerous country bankers up and down the country were doing? Who could hope to impose limits on their issues? Were they not, without perhaps suspecting it, inflating the circulation and raising the price-level day after day, week after week, and year after year? Did there not lie here a great danger for the community which ought to be energetically tackled by the government, and which could best be tackled by replacing private paper by a public currency? Such considerations, as we shall see in due course, occupied Bentham from October 1800 onwards well into 1801 and drew another vast amount of manuscript material from his pen. Here we are only mentioning the matter in order to throw light on his motives and to justify his conduct. Annuity Notes, he told himself in November and December 1800, whatever else they might or might not be, would in any case be a government-controlled kind of currency, and as such they would be decidedly preferable to the uncontrolled and uncontrollable currency that was actually dominating the country. Thus there was, after all, every reason to press the Annuity Note idea, and none for hanging back.

After having first prepared the ground through a reliable and faithful friend (Evan Nepean, at that time Secretary of the Admiralty—a well-connected man whose voice seems to have counted in the inner circles) Bentham launched this proposal (tentatively, it is true, but all the same ambitiously and courageously) in the first days of the new year. On Jan. 3, 1801, he writes to George Rose[1]: "Of the plan of which the accompanying MS contains the two last chapters, the three sheets that have been printed, together with the two tables, have

[1]Bentham at one time considered writing to Pitt directly. The University College collection (II, 15-17) preserves a rough draft which, as it refers to "Mr. Pelham's reduction of interest", seems to have been penned in connection with the Annuity Note scheme.

been recommended to your notice (I understand) by Mr Nepean. These two last chapters being so short, I could not resist the temptation of adding them in this way to such part of the work as I have been able to submit to you in a more commodious form. Any other part might be brought forward in the same way; and had it not been for the apprehension of overloading you, I should have added, even now, another chapter (Ch. XV)[1] in which is displayed the peculiar facility afforded by the proposed plan for the performance of that operation (the reduction of interest), which, in some way or other—at some time or other—will be to be performed at any rate; a facility which, I think, would be found to amount in value to some millions.

"There are some documents which, perhaps, you might have no objection to my being furnished with, and which would enable me to carry on the investigation in some points with increased advantage.

"The quantity of letter-press that has been kept standing is so great—a considerable part of it for these five or six months—that I am under continual apprehension of being obliged to break it up; at the same time, how many copies to print, or *whether to go on* with the impression at all, are points, in relation to which I should be extremely sorry to come to a determination, while thus in the dark as to all particulars I stand in need of for my guidance.

"Under these circumstances, if your time admitted of your obliging me with some *general* communication of your sentiments, from which I might judge whether any further labours of mine on this ground presented any chance of being of use, it would be no inconsiderable addition to those testimonies of your regard with which I have been honoured in former days.

"Decision on the affirmative side, at least, is, in the present stage of the business, altogether out of the question; but if I were fortunate enough to know that the plan were so far thought deserving of attention, as to be set down for serious *consideration*, no exertions, past or future, on my part, would be grudged, whatsoever might be the result.

"I cannot help thinking but that, if taken up with spirit, it might, by the prospect it would bring to view, have some influence, perhaps, on the terms even of the *next* loan; at least, if the proposed paper

[1]Bowring prints "Ch. XX" (*Works X*, 360) but this seems to be a misprint or a slip of the pen. When the same material was later put before Rose's successor, Bentham added a clear copy of "Ch. XV. Reduction of Interest—proposed mode compared with Mr Pelham's" (B.M. Add. MSS 31235 ff. 27-30).

were, from the outset, made receivable all over the country in payment of taxes. As to the quantum of the profit, it were too much to regard it otherwise than as uncertain in the extreme; on the other hand, it requires neither sacrifice nor risk to purchase it. At the present price of stocks, if you sold but £100,000 of the proposed paper the first year, you would gain between £37,000 and £38,000 by it." (*Works* X, 359-360.)

Once again Bentham is seen angling for official encouragement, not to say official recognition. But George Rose was more than careful. Was it the traditional Whitehall reticence? Or did he regard Bentham as a hopeless crank? The reply, as it stands, is certainly not unfriendly. Indeed, it contains half a promise. "Mr. Nepean put into my hands, some time ago, the proofs and some MS notes of your intended publications, which I really had no leisure to look at while I was in town, owing to a more than usual pressure of business upon me, from the circumstances arising from our present difficulties in various respects; I really intended to have brought the whole with me here, in order to have bestowed the attention upon them which the importance of the subject, and the application of your talents and labour, entitle them to; but, unfortunately, in the hurry in which I left London, I left them there secured, where no one could find them in my absence. I will, however, on my return, before the meeting of Parliament, look carefully through what you have written, and endeavour to get Mr Pitt's attention to it, which would be a thousandfold more useful than mine.

"I should be unpardonable if I were to allow you to lay aside any publication by a judgement of mine." (*Works* X, 360.)

Bentham's feelings on the receipt of this letter cannot have been altogether unmixed. But it is a good guess that hope prevailed in his breast. His answer (dated January 10, 1801) is pressing but not dissatisfied: "Foreseeing as not altogether improbable, the accident which in the letter I was honoured with, dated the 5th instant, you speak of as having actually taken place, Mr Nepean, I understand from him, had addressed to you (on what precise day I know not) another copy, which, from your silence in relation to it, he supposes to have been prevented by some accident from reaching your hands. It is on this account that, at his suggestion, I take the liberty of troubling you with the enclosed. In consequence of some typographical arrangements that have intervened, this third copy has the advantage of carrying the thread of the argument a little further than either of the two preceding ones; and comprising an account, by which it is shown how much more eligible a property the proposed Note Annuities would be to the holder in comparison of the existing Stock Annuities, for the investment of even large sums, if for a short or uncertain length of time, or of small sums for any length of time, though the burthen to Government would be less than 3 per Cent, by which, at this time, little less than 3 per Cent would be saved. The intention you have the goodness to express, of recommending the plan to the notice of Mr Pitt, cannot but be highly flattering to me. In the same state in which you receive this, I could, to save time, send him one before your return; but this will be as you think best." (*Works* X, 360-361.)

Did Pitt go into the matter? Most probably not. Those were the last days of his first ministry, and he must have been preoccupied with graver affairs. Within two months he was out of office, and the mind of a political leader, when he feels the power slipping from his hands, is rarely calm enough to ponder schemes of world improvement and proposals of economic reform, especially if they are full of puzzling technicalities. Bentham, as it seems, never heard from either Pitt or Rose. He writes to Lord St. Helens on April 4: "Mr Rose promised, three or four months ago—and even in writing—to place [the project] with his own secretarial hands—and that right soon—on that great theatre of oscitancy and procrastination—the table of Mr Pitt" (*Works* X, 362)—indicating that it had become the victim of that very "oscitancy and procrastination". Pitt had never been Bentham's favourite, as we have noted before, and it is humanly understandable that he saw him go without regret, perhaps even with secret satisfaction. Had he and his lieutenant, Mr. Rose, ever taken an intelligent interest in the benefits which his plans were promising the nation? In fact, had these two men not been the very roadblock on his way to success? The change at the top inspired Bentham with new hopes: at any rate, it presented him with new opportunities, and, as always, he was determined to use them to the uttermost.

Of Bentham's dealings with Rose's successor we have a detailed account from his own pen which is well worth quoting in full, even though it is somewhat lengthy (University College collection II, 1-12). It was written many years later, in 1818, when continental developments drew his attention once more to currency problems and there was a passing flicker of a hope that his economic experiments might be tried out, say, in Spain. It will be interesting to contrast this description of what went on in 1801 with the immediate sources, and to see how far Bentham's memory deceived him and played him false—why he thought he had been unsuccessful, and why he actually was.

"It was in the year 1801,[1] soon after the accession of Mr Addington, upon the close of the first reign of Pitt the second, that the ensuing plan for a supposed improvement in the currency was submitted by me to the constituted authorities. It was more immediately addressed to Mr Vansittart, at that time, in conjunction with Mr Hiley Addington, one of the Secretaries to the Treasury. The notice taken of it was prompt. A business of another kind had brought me for a few minutes, and, if I misrecollect not, without any application on my part, into the official chamber and presence of Mr. Vansittart. [2]I was received with that urbanity, which, according to every thing that I have ever understood, is among the generally conspicuous features of his character.[3]

"After the receipt of the printed papers, [4](for, for greater facility of perusal, the first and most essential parts of the plan had been passed through the press, constituting besides the two Tables that will be seen, three sheets of letter-press) not many days, I believe, had elapsed when, in pursuance to appointment, I repaired to his official chamber, and found with him another official gentleman of subordinate rank, to whose Department a plan of the sort in question was regarded as more particularly belonging.

"Some discussion ensued. Nothing could exceed the good humour with which on all sides it was accompanied. For the renewal of it, another day, and that a short one, was appointed. On my arrival, I was told, and in a tone and manner which, from my unhappy experience in that quarter, I knew could not have originated in the messenger himself, that Mr Vansittart could not see me: no expression of regret accompanied the information, no intimation that at any succeeding time I might hope to be more fortunate. Of a letter in which these circumstances were brought to view, no notice in any shape was then or has ever since been taken. The original urbanity was ascribed by me of course to the character of the

[1]The MS reads "1800", but the mistake is obvious. Pitt resigned as Prime Minister and Chancellor of the Exchequer on March 14, 1801, and was succeeded by Addington in both these functions.

[2] [3]Later put into brackets.

[4]By mistake the MS places this bracket after the word "for".

individual: of the final inurbanity which formed so striking a contrast with it, long and disastrous experience soon pointed out to me the source. It lay in those exalted region[s] which are so constantly and so providently wrapt in clouds. It will be manifest enough on reflection that by a person in the Right Honourable Gentleman's situation a less exceptionable course could not have been taken than that which was chosen as above: at no higher expence than that of the meaner [?] and common place virtue of urbanity, the higher and rarer virtue of sincerity was saved from violation.

"The expence incurred in printing had already amounted to between £30 and £40. [1]In the course of the discussion,[2] by[3] myself no such petty object had been so much as hinted at, [but] by a spontaneous offer a proposal was made to exonerate me from it. The kindness which could not but have dictated such an offer produced correspondent thankfulness. But even economy would, without other motives, have sufficed to preclude acceptance.

"Aware of the manner in which, to a degree beyond my powers of estimation, the scheme could not but be prejudicial to the interests of the Bank of England, never had the ultimate adoption of the scheme presented itself to me as standing in the scale of probability much above the point of hopelessness. Not so much as one guinea would I have given to receive a hundred in case of success. But in comparison of the advantage which presented itself to my eyes, the offering cast, as above, into the Treasury was but a mite!

"Supposing the establishment of this currency, what use or demand there could be for Bank paper I neither saw, nor found any reason for being anxious to enquire.

"But the particular interest of that corporation is, in a way which is not now a secret to any body, subservient to the most insatiable of all lusts, the lust of power, and in that way inseparably linked and interwoven, not only with the sinister interest of any administration, but thence with every the minutest fibre of the sinister interest of the ruling few.

"To have supposed the Bank would leave any imaginable stone unturned that could present a possibility of crushing it, would have been among the most unpardonable of all weaknesses.

"Among the advantages that might have been attendant on the proposed plan, one was the saving of no inconsiderable proportion

[1] [2]Crossed out in the MS.
[3]Written with a capital "B".

of the number of crimes of which Bank of England paper as hitherto constituted has been the source: of crimes, together with the slaughter, of which in the seat of power and impunity they are productive.

"To no new currency could these means of security against forgery have been refused which, to their own paper, the gentlemen in the Bank Direction have, amidst groans and hisses—and denuntiations and exposures, with such imperturbable serenity persevered in refusing, and, as far as appears, by a law borrowed from the Medes and Persians, determined for ever to refuse.

"Of this steadfastness, the cause lies not at any great depth beneath the surface of the case. Keeping the subject of the crime, without men of their property, whatever be the loss by the forgery, they thus ment of their property, whatever be the loss by the forgery, they thus shift it off from themselves. So far from loss, gain, it will be seen on a nearer inspection, is actually the result.

"In every body of which men are the members, the most concentrated will, in the ordinary course of things, dissolve and swallow up the more dilute [?] interest. The interest of the few prevails over the interest of the many, the interest of the one over the interest of the few. [1]Scarcely will you see that empire that has not in the heart of it one still more powerful by which, in a manner still more irresistible, the universal interest, the common interest of the governors and governed, is overborn[e] and sacrificed.[2] In the vast East India monopoly, the millions of subjects are preyed upon by the thousands of proprietors, the thousands of proprietors by the confederacy of Directors, and controuling Ministers.

"Solicitor to the Bank is to me the name of a species, not of an individual. Of the individual I know absolutely nothing: I know nothing of his character. I know not so much as his name. I have not the least need of any such knowledge. What I do know is his situation and the sources from whence the profit of that situation is derived. Knowing this I know, and with an assurance altogether sufficient for every practical purpose, that in his eyes no encrease in the number of such forgeries can fail of being a source of self-complacency, no decrease of being a source of regret. A Solicitor of the Bank, suffer, if he could help it, a decrease to be made in the number[3] of forgeries of Bank paper? As well could I believe that a Chancellor receiving

[1] [2]Put into brackets at a later date.

[3]The MS reads "numbers".

fees on Bankruptcies would suffer, if he could help it, a decrease in the number of Bankruptcies, or a Chief Justice of the King's Bench receiving fees on suits to the King's Bench, in the number of those suits. Should any one of these official persons come forward and say: In my office, in those offices which are at my disposal, substitute salary to fees (for as to abolition without equivalent I would as soon expect to hear him say: Cut my throat or hang me), then, and not till then, shall I be able to believe that he will cease to nurse to his utmost the miseries out of which, under the system of misrule, his comforts are extracted. To know this, what else can it be of any the smallest use to know of an individual so posted, of the individual by whom any such situation is occupied? whether he makes himself sick with the money, or starves himself while he is grasping it? Let him call his maker to witness that his own nature has nothing in it that is common with that of other men, let him heap protestations upon protestations, let him follow them up with volleys of curses, or with streams of crocodile tears, shall I believe him any thing the more for any such display? As soon while I heard him speak, could I believe he was not speaking.

"For the sake of a few pounds of what is called blood money, two or three men of low degree, at the risk of their own necks, add now and then to the number of individuals convicted of highway robbery in the course of the year, and all mouths are filled with exclamations at the thought of such unheard of and inconceivable atrocity. By prosecuting for forgery, two men, without any the smallest risk, have for these last thirteen years gained upon each of 200 of their fellow men a sum much more likely to be greater than to be less than any sum that, as above, was ever earned or grasped at in the shape of blood money.

"Good heavens, what calumny! Suppose, though it were but for the purpose of argument, that a gentleman, a member of so honourable a profession, and, above all, so high in the scale of opulence, should have in his mind any one spring of action in common with such low and needy miscreants? Dare [you] thus to put all characters upon a level? What is this but a part of that scheme which you, and those who think and act as you, never cease to pursue, for applying your levelling instruments to all fortunes?

"Mean time, what human being in the highest of all ranks ever existed who, so it were but in the regular way of warfare—in the way of destruction, waste, depredation, rapine, and murder—so it were but committed upon the largest scale, ever hesitated to sacrifice lives by hundreds of thousands, and pounds of money by millions, so that in his view, with or without [the conquest of][1] an uninhabited island or a desert village, honour and glory was to be got by it?

"A plan for prevention of forgery is presented to a Director[2] of the Bank. How is he to deal with it? Unless for shortness it seems good to him to suppress [it], one course alone, and the best course that can happen to it, can he take with it: it is to be submitted to the Honourable Board. When Honourable Board has got it, what does Honourable Board do with it? There stands, or there sits, Mr Solicitor to whom, in virtue of his office, it belongs to consider and report upon it. See here, Mr Solicitor, here is a scheme for diminishing the number of forgeries, take it with you and let us have your report upon it. Report upon a plan, the effect of which, if it produces its effect, is to take so many thousands a year out of his pocket! Who is there who from these data could not give the substance of such a report as well as the person by whom it was made?

"This answer given, then let him form his estimate of the quantity of reproach due to that most troublesome of all theorists whose aim is to destroy the confidence of the public in all public men, ascribing all effects to their unquestioned and unquestionable causes!

"Destroy all confidence in all public men! as if any useful confidence could be destroyed by holding up to the view of politicians the A.B.C. of politics! as if the possessors of power ever failed, or ever could fail, to join all over the world in the pursuit of one common end, one common scheme of division, by which impunity and honour is endeavoured to be heaped upon the misdeeds by which they profit, while the monopoly of punishment and disgrace is secured to those from which, without adequate prospect of gain, they apprehend loss and sufferance to themselves.

"Sir Samuel Romilly, whose want of confidence in public men has been so flagrantly and so repeatedly manifested by his attempts to rob so many Honourable Gentlemen of the privilege of improving their fortunes by legalized and established swindling, let him declare whether he has found those inflexible supports to legitimacy, styled Country Gentlemen, less strenuous in their determination to secure to themselves the faculty of obtaining by false pretences money to an

[1]A short sign in the MS between "without" and "an" is undecipherable.
[2]The MS reads "Directors". The first version was "the Directors".

unlimited amount without disgorging any part of it. Let him say whether he has found them less strenuous in these their high endeavours than in their solicitude to heap punishment upon the heads of the rabble who, without any such licence as is attached to the possession of fee tail or fee simple, scruple not to ape in this audacious manner the example set them by their superiors.

"The document shewing the number of the prosecutions for counterfeiting the metallic part of the currency we have: and in no slight degree is it instructive.

"But for compleating the body of instruction afforded by it, three other documents are requisite.

"One is, the amount of the Solicitors' bills of costs in the several prosecutions: including a tabular view in which, under the several appropriate heads, shall have been distinguished the profit made not only by the Solicitor, but by the several learned gentlemen of the several superior ranks, rising one above another, in the scale of dignity, and thence of profit, distinguishing moreover the profit made by those who have done something, from the profit made by those who have done nothing, for their fees.

"Another is a document on the same plan as the one above mentioned as having been made public, shewing the numbers of the prosecutions for counterfeiting the paper part of the currency, distinguishing those of which the Bank of England paper has been the subject, from those of which the paper of all other paper banks put together has been the subject.

"Of those of which the Bank of England paper has been the subject, the number might, by House of Commons Order sent to the seat of that vast corporation, be obtained with as much facility as that of those of which the metallic part of the currency was the subject, as above.

"Of those of which the paper of the several country banks was the subject, the number might, with the same facility, be obtained by means of the same investigational instrument sent to the respective banks.

"The third and last of the desiderated documents is a synoptic table, exhibiting the state of learned profits by that destruction of human life of which the paper part of the currency has been made the instrument: a document constructed upon the plan herein proposed, as above, with reference to the metallic part.

"On one of the sides of the proposed sort of note, called an Annuity

Note, the reader will observe a place marked out for a portrait. A portrait of the human face had presented itself to me as that sort of ornament, in the framing of which the work of an ordinary artist might, as it appeared to me, be most generally and promptly distinguished from that of a superior one.

"This idea had formed a principal feature in a plan which, some twenty years ago or thereabouts, I caused to be presented to the hands of one of the Bank Directors. It had furnished handwork for some days, and head-work for some days more. All expectation of personal advantage in any shape being out of the question, it seemed to me that a line acknowledging the receipt would not, even though a word of thanks had been returned for the intention, have been too liberal a requital for it. No such requital, either in black and white, or so much as by word of mouth, ever came to hand. If, for so obscure a person as I have ever been, and shall ever continue to be, so high a token of regard would have been too great an honour, there was my illustrious friend Mr Colquhoun, whose favourable opinion of me was not concealed from any body, and whose hand I took the liberty of borrowing for the conveyance. The gentleman's name was Bosanquet. Whether his place be still in the Direction, whether his place be still in this sublunary world, I, who know nobody, and am known to nobody, do not know."

As far as the very last point is concerned, Bentham's memory did not deceive him. We have a letter from Patrick Colquhoun to Bentham of May 21, 1800, which is full of indignation of Mr Bosanquet: "I mean to go to the Bank on purpose to-day, to see Mr Bosanquet on the subject of your paper on forgery, &c. The conduct of the gentlemen appears to me to be very strange. They are morally bound to protect individuals against frauds, and they ought to be roundly told of it.

"I really want to converse with them on the subject, particularly with Mr Bosanquet. I am very much hurt; and were I not accustomed to neglect of this sort, I should be in a considerable degree enraged; but this answers no purpose." (*Works* X, 357-358.)

The paper on forgery referred to by Colquhoun is contained in the University College collection (IIIb, 303-340 and 341-357); it is a highly technical affair which bears no direct relation to economic problems. Bentham intended to print it in "some of the periodical publications", but, as so often, let the matter drift and drop. This was a point on which he was sceptical, not to say embittered, even in

1800. "Individuals are plundered," he writes to Colquhoun, "and every now and then a caitiff swings. But what is that to the gentlemen of the Bank? They are never the poorer, and their friend, the solicitor, is the richer." (*Works* X, 357.)

Still, though the anti-forgery ideas were incorporated with the Annuity Note plan (cf. notes 14, 22, 24 to Table II), and there may have been some resistance on the part of the Bank of England to Bentham's ideas on the subject, this was not the rock upon which the whole proposal split and foundered. The reasons were different in kind and more honourable in nature; they bore upon the merits of the scheme. We can follow its progress in some detail since the Vansittart papers have become available, and a short sketch of what happened follows here. The curtain rises as the fall of the Ministry in March 1801 brought new men into the seats of power at Whitehall.

Confident that Vansittart and Addington would be more approachable and more reasonable than Rose and Pitt had proved to be, Bentham at once decided to submit his Annuity Note scheme to them. As he had first asked Nepean to establish some sort of personal contact, however indirect, with the late Secretary of the Treasury, so he now used Romilly to open the door for him (cf. *Works* X, 362). Perhaps Romilly was the carrier of the following letter[1] which Bentham wrote to Vansittart on April 20, 1801: "Enclosed are a few printed sheets, the impression of which I had brought on thus far, for the purpose of the communication I accordingly made of them to Mr Rose, who, in a letter from the country, dated the 5th of January last, was pleased to say: 'I will, on my return, before the meeting of Parliament, look carefully through what you have written, and endeavour to get Mr Pitt's attention to it'.

"From that time to this, I have neither addressed him by letter, nor made any attempt to obtain an interview—circumstances sufficiently obvious presenting to my mind the requisite share of attention, as altogether hopeless.

"Knowing, as I had occasion to do, how insufficient his time was to the demands continually made upon it—this, added to some other considerations, better omitted than expressed, had concurred (as I had mentioned more than once to several friends) in determining me,

[1]The letters to Vansittart of April 20 and 24, and Aug. 10, 1801, are contained in the British Museum collection, Add. MSS. 31235, 9—15 and 33—35. Their text tallies on the whole with the text given by Bowring. The only material deviations are noted below.

in the event of my being favoured with an interview on the subject, to have proposed a request on his part, to the defender of British prosperity, against Jasper Wilson and Mr Morgan,[1] to give the plan a perusal, and report to him how far, if at all, it might be worth his notice.

"At that time I little suspected how near we were to that period (a joyful one to me on more accounts than one) at which official was about to be added to personal competence. The immediate object of the present address is—to take this chance for learning any wish or opinion which Mr Addington, upon your statement, might possibly entertain in regard to the publication of a plan of the nature of that which is now before you. My reason is that should it happen to be regarded as possessing any claim to notice with a view to practice, circumstances occur to me, which might perhaps be productive of regret, were it to have been previously divulged in the way of ordinary publication. Some temporary reserve might possibly be deemed advisable, in respect of the particular interests that might be affected, or supposed to be affected.

"The French Government, in the event of their regarding it as beneficial and applicable to the circumstances of that country (an application to which I see no conclusive obstacle), might chance to take it up: in which event, at the comparative rate of progress as between the two Administrations, meaning of course the late for one of them, the measure might have produced its fruit in *that* country some years before a glance had been found for it in this. The surmise about France will already have brought a smile upon your countenance, when, on turning to the name at the end of this paper, you find it too obscure to have ever met your notice; scarce, indeed, would the idea have passed the limits of my own breast, had it not been for some proofs that unexpectedly enough have just fallen into my hands, of the anxiety with which everything that bears that name is sought after at this moment with a view to immediate practice. Whether to suppress altogether, or, if to print, whether to print for publication, or only for private distribution (50 or 100 copies, for example); whether there be any other commands which Mr Addington might

[1]This "defender of British prosperity" is Vansittart himself who had written *A Reply to the Letter addressed to Mr Pitt by Jasper Wilson* in 1794 and *An Inquiry into the State of the Finances of Great Britain, in Answer to Mr Morgan's Facts respecting the State of the War and the Actual Debt* in 1796. Cf. also his *Reflections on the Propriety of an Immediate Conclusion of Peace,* 1793.

be disposed to honour me with on the subject, or assistance to afford me upon occasion in the way of information: such are the points in regard to which I should be glad to be informed.

"The produce of the tax on country bank paper, for example, distinguishing the magnitude of the notes. The returns that have been printed—such, at least, as have reached me—go little, if at all, beyond the produce of the first quarter, and without any distinction. You might, perhaps, see no objection to my being furnished with any such information on that head as could be come at without too much trouble. For these six or seven months (I think it is that) the press of all, or most of these pages has been kept standing for the chance of hearing from Mr Rose—the patience of the printer has been beyond all expectation; but I cannot depend upon the being allowed to trespass upon it much longer. The expence *thus far,* according to his account, has been uncommonly great, though he has not given me any information of the amount of it. The further expence of completing for publication would, I believe, hardly come within a hundred pounds. The assurance of what, in lawyers' language is called *a fair hearing,* would be accepted as a good and valuable consideration for any such expence, whatever might be the result; but without some such consideration, it would be rather too great a sacrifice for a man whose property has already suffered a defalcation to about a hundred times the amount, from the confidence he was unfortunate enough to place on the good faith of some of your predecessors.

"In dismissing the topic of money, allow me, Sir, to add—unknown to you as I am—since it may help to put both of us at our ease, that there is no trouble on the occasion of this business that I would not gladly take upon me, nor any pecuniary indemnification, not to speak of remuneration, that I would accept for it.

"The second of the two copies is sent under the notion that, in the event of your not having at present any time at command to bestow upon the plan, you might, perhaps, find a relief in consigning it to the scrutiny of so able a pen as that of Dr. Beeke,[1] whose assistance, were he to favour me with it, would eventually be of the greatest use. Any objections or doubts that might occur to him, I should hope to be favoured with the communication of, and in a form specific enough to admit of discussion." (*Works X,* 363-364.)[2]

[1]Dr. Henry Beeke, author of *Observations on the Produce of the Income Tax.*

[2]One paragraph of the letter is omitted here and quoted in the introduction to vol. III.

In a way, this letter is a psychological masterpiece. It is subtle in its flattery and just as subtle in the still more delicate task of self-advertisement. Vansittart acknowledged it at once, though, it seems, only formally, for we find among Bentham's letters, as reprinted in Bowring's *Works,* the following epistle which is quite obviously Bentham's answer to a short note he had received: "Dear Sir,—I have to thank you for the favour of your obliging letter of yesterday.

"If it would in any degree facilitate a decision on the subject, to place it in the clearer point of view, or lessen the labour of taking a survey of it, I could, and very readily would, give an abridged sketch of the argument contained in the long paper, leaving out what I look upon, and from the first did, in this as in all other cases, look upon as a surplussage, viz. everything that savours of personality. By confining one's self to a bare indication of the topics, it might be brought perhaps into the compass of a single sheet, written on one side. But as there might be a great deal of it lost labour, proving what was already clear and settled, if it were agreeable to you to send it me back with short marginal notes, just to say, relative to each point, whether you agreed with me—whether you definitely and positively disagreed with me; or whether the question appeared at the moment remaining in doubt, and requiring further elucidation. In short, where the shoe pinched, and where it did not pinch.

"If, in a subject so involved in obscurity, and, consequently, exposed to error, you will repose so much confidence in me, as to trust me with the first runnings of your thoughts, at the hazard of their appearing erroneous to your own maturer consideration, you may depend on my not making any ill use of your confidence; or, if you lay your injunction on me to that effect, so far as trusting your memoranda to any other eye. The idea may strike you as a presumptuous one. Of all the persons whose opinions on the subject have passed under my review, I know not of one to whom errors may not in any view of the matter be imputed; and there is scarce any erroneous opinion, which, when the erroneousness of it comes to be pointed out, and placed in a clear light, may not appear absurd to a degree of ridicule. In my own instance, this has happened to me many and many times. Yes—many times have I caught myself in harbouring ideas—in making suppositions, which, when compared with one another, turned out to be repugnant to one another, and incompatible. At this moment, I have before me a point on which Mr Pitt, Mr Fox, and Mr Boyd, present themselves in my view, as concurring in one error, such as, when once pointed out, appears so palpable, that a man would wonder how anybody could have fallen into it.[1]

"On every new point, what errors remain to be discovered, the event only can show; but with very moderate and inferior faculties, there will be nothing wonderful, if a man, who for these two and a half years has thought of scarce anything else, should not have hit upon some truths which have escaped the notice of those who have not had leisure to bestow upon this subject, amidst the crowd of so many other more pressing ones, more than here and there a momentary glance." (*Works* X, 365-366.)

After this exchange of letters, Vansittart kept the ball flying. He writes to Bentham "Thursday morning"—i.e. April 23: "Sir,—I feel very sensibly the mark of confidence and esteem which you have offered me in the communication of your unpublished work. I have not yet had time to give it the attention which everything which comes from your pen must merit, and therefore can give no opinion as to the plan itself. Dr Beeke, I have no doubt, will be happy to contribute his assistance in any way which can be useful; and you will find that he has paid much attention to such subjects.

"I cannot help thinking (at first sight at least) that any subdivision of the *unit* or *standard* note would be unadvisable. In the first place, any interest note seems to me ill calculated to supply the place of metallic money in small payments, as the variation of value would render it perplexing and unintelligible to the common people, and expose them to imposition, notwithstanding any contrivance of tables, &c. In the next, I am afraid we have already a larger proportion of paper circulation than is consistent with our security in times of public alarm; and in the third, it would be very difficult at any office to make an actual payment of interest on the small notes on account of their dispersion and multiplicity. But these, and any other observations which may occur to me, I shall be glad to talk over with you, when I have better considered the subject." (*Works* X, 366).

Critical though this letter was, Bentham was pleased. The objections seemed unexceptionable: they had about them the air of a positive attitude: and, what was best, there was the prospect of a personal meeting which must have attracted Bentham very much. His reply of April 24 reflects a more hopeful mood than he had felt

[1]This allusion refers to the subject of country bankers' paper money as discussed in *The True Alarm, q.v.* in vol. III.

for many a day: "Sir,—I was not more flattered than surprised by the attention you have in so very short a space of time found means to bestow upon my plan, amidst occupations so urgent as yours must be: and in the account of 'confidence', I must acknowledge myself richly overpaid by receiving so much from an office from which so little was to be expected: I mean by the communication made of the first runnings of your mind in black and white, which, as far as time can be afforded for it, is, according to my experience, a much more effectual mode than *viva voce* conversation for the discovery of truth, though, unquestionably, on occasion, both modes may have their use.

"In looking over your extempore list of objections, it was no small satisfaction to find them grounded, as far as appeared to me, on a momentary misconception in regard to the purport[1] of the plan itself, and so far (whatever further objections may come to be suggested by a closer scrutiny) not indicative of any ultimate difference between us. Misconceptions of this kind, I, in whose brain the plan originated, have too frequently caught myself falling into, not to regard them as more or less inevitable on the part of anybody else.

"Not to overload this letter, I dismiss my answers to a separate paper, in which form you may either throw them aside definitely, or postpone them for future consideration; and, in the meantime, hand them over to any third person—for example, Dr Beeke.

"I will not attempt to nail *your* attention any closer to a subject which has no necessary claim to it, and may never pay for it; but, in case the Doctor should amuse himself with it, I should hope to find, that any objections he may think worth communicating, had been minuted down opposite the particular articles to which they respectively applied; and that, if, in any note, or any explanatory chapter, he found an answer which appeared to him insufficient, he had expressly referred to it as such, rather than pass it by without reference—not forgetting, that out of seventeen chapters you have yet but three, with the commencement of the fourth.

"For the *statesman*, it was necessary to present the plan under all its possible extensions and modifications, for the purpose of enabling him to take a view of whatever effects might follow, or be derivable from it. But to suppose that, in any such complicated form, it is proposed to be presented to the uninformed minds of the experimental set of expected customers, is a supposition on which the most

[1] Bowring, p. 364, prints "prospect".

express negative is put at the very outset of the Introduction, besides other places." (*Works* X, 364-365.)

The "separate paper" containing Bentham's replies to Vansittart's objections, is printed below (pp. 343-350). It tells us as much about Bentham's coming works as about the work under discussion, but here we must keep to the problems of the Annuity Note scheme. Bentham is particularly bold in this defensive argument: he recommends his currency proposal as a positive safeguard against inflation, and makes a braver attempt than ever before to demonstrate that his Annuity Notes would be a very nearly automatic regulator of circulation, that they would flow in when other money streamed out, that they would stream out whenever a "plethora" developed. Whether his arguments are convincing (especially point 2 in the answer to objection 1) is, of course, a totally different matter.

As Bentham had suggested, or rather requested, the proposal was submitted to Dr. Henry Beeke, an expert whom Bentham thought of highly, and whose *Observations on the Produce of the Income Tax* he much used. Dr. Beeke's reaction reveals why Bentham had been so anxious to see him consulted: it is rather obvious that he knew that here was a kindred spirit. "I have read Mr Bentham's plan with much interest and attention," Dr. Beeke writes on May 6, "and am flattered not only by the manner in which he expresses himself respecting me in his letter to you, but also by the very near agreement of his leading proposition with the different projects which I communicated to you some years ago for *Interest Notes*, and also with the principle of that respecting *Provincial Banks*, which I communicated two years ago, to you and to Mr. Addington.

"Mr Bentham has studied the subject very profoundly and very accurately: but I am sure he will forgive the freedom I take in saying, that I fear the minuteness of detail in the printed sheets with which I have been favoured (though of infinite use to those who might wish to carry his plan into execution) is not altogether well calculated for a first publication, and might even be an impediment to its favourable reception. The impatience of modern readers is so great, and, I may add, the inattention to the minutiæ of all questions of Political Economy is so general, that such propositions as this of Mr Bentham's have, I think, but little chance of being well received, unless they are, first of all, enunciated in the simplest form of which they are capable. and are, as much as possible, divested of practical detail.

"With respect to the plan itself, the important circumstance in which it differs from any of mine, and in which it greatly excels them, is in the *manner* of converting the public debt into circulating annuities. But, in some other respects, I could wish to submit to Mr Bentham's judgment, whether his plan may not be liable to serious objections. My proposition was made when the funds were at a much lower value than at present (3 per Cents below 50), but I still am inclined to think it, in some respects, preferable. I think the *standard note* should bear a *weekly interest.* Mine you know was at the rate of 3d per week for £20, or £3 5s per Cent per annum. There are various reasons which induce me to think that too great a facility of circulating wealth is really a very great evil; and, therefore, I should by no means wish that such a plan should at first be recommended on too *extensive* a scale: and the more so because I think a near approximation to the requisite quantity of circulating money in any country is a problem of no very difficult solution. The more I have considered the subject, the more I have become persuaded that the disadvantages resulting from the use of paper money of so small value as to be commensurate with any convenient metallic coins very greatly preponderate over the advantages. Of course, I am convinced that *one pound notes* are really much more injurious than useful; and at any rate, in the first publication of such a plan as Mr Bentham's, I should greatly wish to suppress any mention of silver or copper notes for two reasons:—First, if such notes could be substituted for metallic money, yet the value wanted for circulation would be too inconsiderable to make such a substitution an object of national importance. Of the aliquot parts of any piece of money, for instance of a sixpence, no more can ever be wanted for all the purposes of circulation than at the rate of about fourpence or, at most, fourpence-halfpenny per head of the population, exclusive of infants. Say at most, in the whole United Kingdom, fourteen or fifteen millions of groats—or about £250,000 sterling. In the same manner, where (as in this country) the policy adopted has been such as to make *gold* the only species of metallic treasure — if only guineas were coined, I doubt whether even then more circulating silver money would be wanted, than at the rate of at most about 21s per family, or a little more than three millions sterling. But, with a sufficient supply of seven-shilling pieces, hardly half this value would be wanted in silver money. Now, I think Mr Bentham will agree with me, that the smaller denominations of paper money would never be *hoarded* in any considerable quantity.

"A second reason why I would avoid any mention of small paper money *bearing interest,* is from a recollection, that many more really useful plans have been rendered unpopular by the ridicule of ignorance than by grave opposition to them.

"I am most clearly of opinion, that if such a plan should be adopted no aliquot parts of a standard note of £20 ought, on any account, and even at any future time, to be allowed, excepting notes for £10, £5, and perhaps £13 6s 8d, and £6 13s 4d—if the interest were taken at £3 5s. per Cent per annum, which rate, for many reasons, I should at present prefer. I also think that the aliquot parts of the standard note should only bear a monthly interest.

"I had intended to give my reasons for these remarks more at length, and the intrinsic value of Mr Bentham's plan would require it from me, if I could find time to do it with any convenience: but a detailed explanation of the circumstances which have induced me to adopt the opinions that I have stated, would fill not a letter only, but a volume. If accident or choice should lead Mr Bentham into Bond Street, I shall be glad if this letter should lead to our better acquaintance." (*Works* X, 370-371.)

Bentham must have been *beaming* when he received and read this communication! It gave him a lever, so he thought, to set things going, and his next letter to Vansittart (May 11) marks the apex of his hopes and dreams: "Sir,—I plume myself not a little at the thought of the two reviewers I have been fortunate enough to obtain for my plan: and the finding in one of them a concurrent—and such a concurrent—is a source of the purest satisfaction to *me;* as, from what I see of the turn of his mind, I am sure the correspondent discovery is to *him*: for approbation has no evidence comparable to such coincidence.

"At the sight of the observations you had favoured me with, I had ventured to say already, that I saw in them no indications of any ultimate difference between us: at the sight of *his,* I can venture so much further as to say, as to everything *material,* I see very satisfactory indications to the contrary. Whether there would be any difference at all, remains to be ascertained, when the considerations that have respectively operated on our minds come to be displayed on both sides. In the meantime the utmost possible difference is not so great in my eyes, but that I would compound most gladly for the seeing the plan carried into execution, simply and absolutely according to the ideas already manifested by Dr Beeke.

"As to *publication,* and the mode of it—*close* or *open* (as you say of committees)—the first point seems to be to ascertain what the leaning of Mr Addington's mind is, as to such parts of the plan in respect of which the Doctor's ideas and mine are found already to coincide: in which description is already included all that presents itself as worth contending about in my eyes: and so far, at least, as the Doctor's ideas went, at the period he alludes to, Mr Addington is already (I conclude) no stranger to it.

"On the assurance, even in that shape, that his opinion was sufficiently in favour of it to induce a wish on his part to see us set to work upon it in concert: what I should then be disposed to submit in that view would be this:—

"1. That I should go on with the impression of my plan (for the whole of it *is,* or at least *was,* ready for the press), printing fifty or a hundred copies or so, for the use of any such persons as you might have the goodness to point out as proper to be consulted in relation to it.

"2. That Dr Beeke's original plans, as alluded to in his letter, should be printed, in the same view, either in the state in which they were originally communicated, or with such amendments, if any, as he might now see reason to make in them: or if, in the meantime, before the copies were thus multiplied, he were disposed to favour me with the communication of them, I could take the liberty of submitting my observations on them without reserve. The probability appears to me to be much in favour of an exact agreement, as between him and me: but it by no means follows, that that agreement would be adopted by those to whom it belongs to judge. To him (such is his liberality and strength of mind), the plan—that part of it, for instance, that relates to *'conversion'*—is regarded as an improvement —and that a considerable one—upon those parts that belong to us in common: but it does not absolutely follow that it should be regarded in the same light by others.

"3. If, then, the opinion of those to whom it belonged to judge, were found to lean to the adoption of the plan—either according to the Doctor's modification of it, or according to mine—or according to a *tertium quid,* which should have been pitched upon in preference to both—then would be the time to decide, whether *anything* on the subject should be laid before *the public at large,* and, if anything, *what,* and by *whom*: if by me, then again would be the time for the Doctor to use the *pruning-knife,* which, with respectful gratitude, I would put into his hand—then, when the prunable matter would be completed, and swelled from the three sheets to, perhaps, eight or ten [*sic*].[1]

"With such a prospect, as above supposed, of seeing his labours productive of fruit, *he*, I presume, would have no difficulty in finding any quantity of time requisite for the purpose.

"On the other hand, without some such prospect—that is, if in the estimation of the competent official judges, the plan were either positively ineligible, or not of sufficient importance to be worth their attention, I, for my part, know of no point of view in which the publication of my papers, contracted or uncontracted, would present any prospect of being of use.

"In the meantime, as little would it be worth attempting to take up either your time, Sir, or the Doctor's, with the discussion of particular points: and it is on that consideration that I spare both you and him the reading of some pages I had written of that cast.

"It this instant strikes me, that by a '*first publication*' he, perhaps, means not the *open* but the *close* mode of publication above spoken of. If so, it would be necessary that the *pruning-knife* should be set to work for the purpose of such *close* publication, and, therefore, previously to it.

"According to his opinion, there is still a description of persons with reference to whom even the parts that would require, as above, to be cut away, would be of use: viz. 'those who might wish to carry the plan into execution'. But to supply the demand created by this narrowest class, nothing more would be requisite than to throw off a few copies of the sheets as they stand at present, before the press is broken up.

"I am somewhat alarmed by a hint I have just seen in the debates, about an intention of bringing in a bill for the restraining of country paper; for, though some sort of a restriction on *cash paper in general*, is a measure, I myself have been inclined to look upon as necessary, yet I cannot but consider it as very tender ground to tread upon, and I do not well see how a sufficient stock of *data* can be obtained for such a purpose, circumstanced as matters are at present, without preparatory inquiries by a select committee.

"And supposing the plan of government 'interest paper' to obtain

[1]It is highly probable that some words are missing in this sentence, but we have only one text, the printed version in Bowring's *Works*, vol. X p. 372, where a whole line seems to have been omitted by an error of the printer, and cannot fill in the gap.

a sort of provisional[1] approbation, should not some view be taken of its bearings and relations in reference to any such measure for the regulation of *private* paper?

"As to £1 notes, the Doctor's unfavourable opinion of private paper of that size (if meant to apply to that size in contradistinction to larger sizes to an equal aggregate value), the reasons that gave it birth are such as I have not been able to anticipate: by which, however, I do not mean that I expect to find them otherwise than satisfactory, were they to be made known to me. Supposing large paper of all sorts (say £5 and upwards), to have swelled in its amount so as to bear a certain ratio to cash, the existence of small notes to a proportionable amount (say £2 and £1 notes) presents itself to my view as necessary, on pain of a formidable danger, at least universal bankruptcy: viz. by such a demand for *cash*, on the score of *change*, as would indistinguishably be mistaken for, and at length be productive of, a general distrust of paper: though whether the proportions are as yet, or soon likely to be, at that mark, is *among* the problems for the solution of which I have all along been looking in my own mind to Dr Beeke.

"The opening given me in the conclusion of his letter, is by much too valuable to remain unimproved by me; and to this you owe the liberty I take in enclosing the note addressed to him." (*Works* X, 371-373.)

We are not unduly visionary if we imagine that a conclave of our two projectors followed. But if they believed that all would be plain sailing for them now, they were sadly mistaken. Vansittart remained sceptical and decided to call in an expert of his own choice. The man he consulted was Sir Frederick Morton Eden, whose work on *The State of the Poor* had appeared four years before, and whose prestige as an expert economist was then considerable. That prestige was the main reason for calling him in; but there were perhaps other reasons as well. Bentham and Eden were personally acquainted, not to say friends: and they were kindred souls in so far as both were projectors and political inventors. Vansittart may well have felt that a man such as Eden was likely to give him a report on the Annuity Note scheme that would be both expert and just.

Eden's main preoccupation in those days was the foundation of the Globe Insurance Company for which he strenuously tried to obtain a Royal Charter of Incorporation. The Globe was to be a new

[1]Bowring prints "provincial approbation". Cf. ib.

type of insurance company, distinguished from other, older companies by, amongst other things, its acceptance of small deposits, and to that extent similar to a savings bank. When the matter came before the House of Commons, Eden solicited Bentham's support: Bentham's half-brother, Charles Abbot, was an influential man.[1] Bentham's reply to Eden's request was non-committal; but in his heart he was dead against the venture for which, moreover, he claimed the intellectual fathership. He sat down on June 19, 1799, and drafted a letter to George Rose in the following terms: "A Bill, I see, is brought in for the establishment of a company, under the name of the Globe Insurance Company. According to a paper I have received from a gentleman who seems to have been a principal promoter of the scheme, it appears, that whatever there is of originality in it, is in substance and even in name (see Foreign and City Bank) taken from a printed paper of mine herewith enclosed.[2] I am speaking of what is styled, in that paper as well as mine, a Frugality Bank. My endeavour has been to draw a circle round the subject; a circle within the which, amongst other things, whatever concerns *Friendly Societies* should be comprised. I should be sorry to think that anything of mine should have had the effect of giving birth to an institution that might at any time be found to merit the appellation of a bubble: in the note to p.181 may be seen the reasons I have for being apprehensive lest *any pecuniary engagements, depending upon rates of vitality,* stand exposed to this danger, and must remain exposed to it till the *data* therein spoken of shall have been provided." (*Works* X, 334.)

Thus, instead of open support, Bentham's attitude was rather one of sly opposition. He did not, however, send this letter off at once. He had second thoughts on it and decided to try it first on an outsider on whose judgment and decency he could rely. So he forwarded his draft to William Wilberforce and left the decision of the question, to send or not to send, to him. "The enclosed," he writes on June 20, "was on the point of being sent as addressed; but the suggested vindictiveness, and the experienced irascibility and abusiveness of the person addressed, has stayed my hand. If you think it *safe,* do me the favour to forward it; if unsafe, to return it." (*Works* X, 335).

We do not know exactly what Wilberforce did, but it is fairly certain that Bentham's manœuvre did not find his approval, and that

[1]Cf. the letter to Abbot in *Works* X, 333 seq.

[2]*Pauper Management Improved.* The reference is to the paper numbered IV.

he stayed his hand. Thus it happened that, when Vansittart asked Eden for his opinion on the Annuity Note proposal, he was not consulting a man whom Bentham had positively estranged. Bentham, for his part, cannot have been particularly happy to see Eden brought in. He was bound to have a feeling of guilt towards him; and he later assumed that the unfavourable tenor of Eden's report was largely due to the fact that the Globe Insurance scheme and the Annuity Note plan were rivals, in so far as both tried to cater for the petty saver. Whether Eden was influenced by such considerations is more than we can say; he certainly had great difficulties to face and may have been impatient of anything that threatened further complications. On the other hand, there were plenty of reasons for taking an unfavourable view of Bentham's proposal, and personal interest may have been the last motive that determined his attitude.

The calling in of a new expert would have struck a cool and objective observer as a bad omen, but Bentham was neither cool nor objective. He remained in a buoyant mood. On July 20, he sent to Hiley Addington the essay *On the Form of the Supply to the Sinking Funds* which he had laid before Pitt and Rose the year before. He obviously hoped to establish a further official contact. At the same time he had reason to expect that one of his dearest wishes—a personal meeting with Nicholas Vansittart—would presently be fulfilled. Simultaneously with the letter to Hiley Addington, he posted an epistle to Vansittart which shows how near he was to the goal of his dreams, but also how misfortune—sheer bad luck—dogged his steps. "Your obliging appointment for tomorrow," he writes to the Secretary of the Treasury, "will not fail of due obedience. You understand, I hope, that on the former occasion I was at the Treasury at the time appointed (I crossed you in the passage); and that your seeing me so late was owing to some misconception—of which I know not the cause—on the part of the messengers, I believe." (*Works* X, 374.)

While Bentham was thus living in the pleasant expectation of a tête-à-tête with the influential Secretary of the Treasury, a second letter was dispatched by a different correspondent to the same addressee which was destined to bring all his hopes crashing down into the dust. It was also on the fateful 20th July that Sir Frederick Eden sent to Vansittart his considered opinion of the Annuity Note plan. It was anything but favourable. Vansittart forwarded it at once to Queen's Square Place, and Bentham reacted to it in the following terms: "I release you from your obliging appointment for this day.[1] You have cut me out work for several days. I return you the paper—having preserved a copy of it. It answers my purpose to admiration: proving, as it does, that where everything was sought for that seemed capable of being made to wear the semblance of an objection—sought for, and with such ability—nothing was to be found. The force of it—at least the force with which it acted upon me—consisted exclusively in the force of the word 'severity', dropped by yourself in speaking of it. Severity there was indeed in that word, and severely will you yourself be punished for it—punished by the load of paper you will have drawn down upon yourself, and which, but for that word, you would have escaped. Since an answer then is necessary, black and white cannot be answered — not effectually at least — and to any lasting purpose—by anything but black and white: impressions thus made can seldom be wiped away by sounds.

"The judicial was the function I had chosen for the learned baronet: that of advocate-counsel for a rival project, is the character he has taken upon himself in preference. What a Mr Stonestreet[2] is to him, he has made himself to me. His adversary is[3] his model; beginning—middle—end—he emulates Mr Stonestreet. The word, 'portentous', prefixed to the word 'globe' in the title-page of the one, is matched[4] by the 'ewes and lambs' that garnish the first line of the other. As the one concludes with the grave of property, so does the other with the joke about dying of the Doctor. In what degree that style of discussion is calculated for the conveyance of useful information, may perhaps be seen, when the attention bestowed by it comes to be repaid. The misfortune is—all this makes words: and words take time even to write them: not to speak of thinking, even if, like my commentator, a man wrote from imagination, and without stopping to see what was in the text." (*Works* X, 375.)

If we read between the lines here, we see that Bentham's mood was

[1]This letter, according to Bowring, was sent on July 24 (X, 375). As we have seen, Bentham was due to meet Vansittart on the 21st. Did he see him then? Or was the conference again put off to the 24th? Are Bowring's dates reliable? If Eden sent his letter to Vansittart on the 20th, could it possibly have been in Bentham's hands, and copied, on the 21st? All these are puzzles to which we have no clue. Unfortunately such uncertainties make it impossible for us to know whether Bentham ever had a *viva voce* discussion with Vansittart.

[2]Cf. G. G. Stonestreet, *Portentous Globe.* An Enquiry into the Powers solicited from the Crown under an act of 39. Geo III., 1800. (Bowring prints "Storestreet".)

[3]Bowring's text reads "in his model".

[4]Bowring's text reads "watched".

no longer what it had been a few days before. The letter has a definite bitter-sweet flavour. But the main sentiment aroused in Bentham's breast was pugnacity. He sat down at once and plucked "the learned baronet's" arguments to pieces, with the energy of a man who knows that everything is at stake. It was indeed a "load of paper" that Vansittart drew down upon himself. On August 10, Bentham sent him his "Observations by Sir Frederick Morton Eden (in form of a Letter) on the Annuity Note Plan, as contained in the three first printed Sheets with the two Tables: with Counter Observations by the Author of the Plan", covering the manuscript with the following half-serious, half-playful letter: "Dear Sir,—*Before* you had Sir Frederick's *'severity'*, *now* you have it back again with *mine*. You are our *master; we* a couple of school-boys making the declamations you were pleased to set us. As to real spite and enmity—whatever you might otherwise be apt to suppose as you read on (supposing you have the patience to read on), I assure you most sincerely, I have no more against him, than the school-boy who spouts Ajax has against his chum who spouts Ulysses; or than you yourself may have felt when arguing a settlement case against the learned gentleman on the other side. As to Sir Frederick, he is a good-natured man (to judge from everything I have seen or heard of him), and would forgive me, if you gave him the opportunity; but that is a matter for you to judge of. As to this his *jeu d'esprit,* if I have failed of being *severe* upon it, it certainly is not for want of trial—the necessity of defending at all points, what seemed an object on *public* ground worth defending, forbade me to give quarter: but, personally, if he were to have heard all I have said of him, not only before this affair, but since, I think he would not have been dissatisfied with it — excepting always one remark I made t'other day, viz. that for the sake of the public, as well as his own, it would give me more satisfaction to see him at the head of the General[1] Annuity-Note Office, joining hands with his noble uncle at the Post-office, than at the head of the Globe; which last, I am inclined to think would, notwithstanding, experience at least as favourable treatment from me, if it depended upon me, as I should expect to see it meet with from the Crown lawyers.

"Tedious as this operation has been, from the labour of making references, together with the toil of revising an incorrect copy, taken from a most exemplarily rough hand (such as this is, especially when

[1]Bowring, p. 376, prints "Government".

it writes against time to arrest fugitive ideas), I flatter myself it may not be, altogether, labour lost; since, besides the main object, I should expect to find that other *observations,* such as might be looked for from Mr Alcock and others, had been found anticipated by it.

"At any rate, any other objections, fresh or stale, that might present themselves from the same, or any other quarter, I should neither think of answering in a similar tone, nor (probably) look upon it as necessary to answer at equal length—simple references being all I should think it necessary to give by way of answer to objections already foreseen and answered; and if you would have the goodness to distinguish by some mark, any such observations as, in your view of the matter, called for an answer beyond what has been already given, [1]with an intimation of the point at which the *shoe pinched,*[1] it would be an act of charity; unless any objection presented itself to you as a fatal one — in which case, you would give judgment accordingly, and I should have my *quietus.*" (*Works* X, 375-376.)

Although Bentham was not, in general, patient of criticism, the tone of his reply to Eden is on the whole friendly and quiet, and we find it seasoned by a not unpleasant dose of good-natured humour. Bentham had too much respect for his opponent to be really angry with him; nor did he forget that he was writing for a third party. Nevertheless, the first pages speak of "sinister bias", "hostile passions" and "poisoned weapons"—meaning by poisoned weapons the use of words which imply and appeal to prejudices. "Innovation" is a word of this kind: Bentham does not allow that his Annuity Notes are "an innovation": as they are essentially "paper representing capital as well as interest", they are no more than a new incarnation of an old principle exemplified and proved sound by such well-established securities as Exchequer Bills and India Bonds. If Eden insinuates, by speaking of a "large circulating mass of paper", that that mass is going to be *too* large, he is wrong: the Annuity Notes will replace other engagements of the government, and their total circulation will always be in keeping with the needs of the market because they will only be issued when, and as long as, there is a demand for them on the part of the public (par. 1).

Eden asserts that nobody who has £12 16s. at his disposal would be inclined to "sink" that sum in the purchase of a paltry annuity of 7s. 7d. per annum. The money is not "sunk", Bentham replies, because the Note can, at any time, be handed on, like so much cash, in normal

[1] [1]Missing in Bowring.

circulation: and if no private person were willing to take an Annuity Note, the Exchequer and its local offices always would. Nor must the sum of 7s. 7d. be despised as an annuity. The rich can secure as oftentimes 7s. 7d. as they see fit; for the poor it will be a boon, being adjusted to their narrow means, and Eden, the patron of the indigent, should never have forgotten it! (2 and 3.) Indeed, if he asserts that perpetual annuities are suitable only for the use of capitalists, but not of the lower classes, he misunderstands the needs and the possibilities of the lower classes, for there are some purposes for which even the poor can best make provision by the purchase of annuities of some kind (par. 4).

Eden's next criticism touches upon a point in which the technical inventor in Bentham was particularly interested. His contention is that Annuity Notes, whose transfer would require no sort of formality, would be apt to be stolen or lost—irrevocably lost like a threepenny-bit that falls out of one's pocket. Bentham answers by pointing to the divisibility of the Note which he has suggested and recommended as a most desirable feature of all paper money. This divisibility would enable the rightful owner to keep the two parts, for the sake of security, in two different places, and for that reason the proposed currency would give him more safety than cash and coin (par. 5). A similar defence can be brought forward against Eden's next-following objection, namely that a man's children living with him would just appropriate the Annuity Notes they found on him at his death, and thus defraud the Inland Revenue of its Legacy Tax, as well as swindle other children who would not know of this investment out of part of their inheritance. Are not other government securities and ready money as much exposed to this danger, or even more? (par. 6.)

At the next following step Eden brings his Globe Insurance project into the discussion. Granted that it is highly desirable to give petty savers a possibility of making some interest on their money, would not that project be a more promising and less problematic experiment than Bentham's Annuity Notes? With this argument Eden undoubtedly touches a sore spot. Bentham's reply becomes somewhat more peevish, and he does his best to show that his own plan is decidedly superior, especially from the fiscal point of view (par. 7).

A different problem is taken up next: what might, with the ugly but expressive word we have used before, be called the circulability of the proposed annuity currency. Interest-bearing bankers' notes,

Eden urges, do not seem to circulate to any considerable extent. No matter if they don't, Bentham answers; my paper is in so many respects better contrived than country bankers' interest-bearing notes that the question whether these notes are a success, is irrelevant (par. 8). Exchequer Bills, Eden goes on to say, so similar, in the higher reaches at least, to the proposed Annuity Notes, have never performed the functions of money, nor can they very well do so. That is not true, comes Bentham's reply; and if it were true, it would prove nothing against the possibility of circulating annuities. It is not true because Exchequer Bills enter into bankers' cash reserves and thus act as a "succedaneum to money"; and it would not prove anything if it were true, because there are at least ten "features of difference" which show that what applies to Exchequer Bills, need not necessarily apply to Annuity Notes as well (par. 9).

We have now reached the point at which Eden brings forward his heaviest artillery. Money, he says (and who could deny that he is right?), to fulfil its function, must be invariable in its nominal value; it must not be one thing at one time, and another thing at another. Bentham tries to make out that this is a purely verbal argument; but as it is, in fact, a material and not a formal point, his plea is thoroughly unconvincing (par. 10). The variations in value which an Annuity Note would undergo, so Eden continues to press his criticism, would necessitate computations that would make its circulation practically impossible. Bentham, of course, strikes back by referring to the suggested "Table" to be printed on the back of the Notes giving their day-for-day value by "simple inspection". Only an illiterate, he claims, could ever be in difficulties. But it is not alone the variation, by interest, of the *individual* Note Eden has in mind; there are obviously other complications. Say that a man wishes to change an £100 Bank Note into circulating annuities—would this not be an impossibly difficult transaction? Some Annuity Notes at hand would bear interest at nearly 3%, others at 2⅜%; some would be standard Notes, others half or quarter Notes; some would have a number of years' interest due on them, some only a few days': it would be quite an effort to get exactly £100 together. Bentham's answer to this telling argument is rather weak; in fact, it is partly a pure logomachy (pars. 11 and 12).

The following two points raised by Eden are in the nature of an anti-climax. It cannot be economical, he urges, to make a paper-substitute for copper coin; the value of copper coin (and even silver coin) is just not high enough to justify the expense involved. Bentham, in reply, points to the Yorkshire paper-sixpences mentioned by Adam Smith and similar currency expedients which would not have been employed if the cost had really been prohibitive (par. 13). But paper, according to Eden, is uneconomical for yet another reason: it would be quickly ruined by wear and tear, and the print on it still more quickly obliterated. Bentham denies that this is likely to happen—at any rate to such an extent as to interfere with the usability of the Notes (par. 14).

After considering these technicalities, Eden raises the question what proportion of the conceivable £400,000,000 of Annuity Notes would be needed for circulation, and what proportion would be simply a security for annuities. He implies that here lies a difficulty and a danger. But Bentham admits neither the one nor the other. He does not undertake to estimate the numerical relation of circulation and hoarding; he simply insists on the "amphibious nature" of his Notes. "In whichever of its two shapes each Note is most wanted, at each point of time—in that shape will it be employed at that time." The division of the two masses, he argues, is altogether artificial. It cannot be the subject of a rational question. The most interesting passage in this par. 15 is the long footnote: it sums up the conclusions Bentham had arrived at, and the convictions he had formed, concerning the optimum of circulation and the danger of inflation connected with the issue of paper money; and it gives in a nutshell the fundamental idea of all he ever wrote on "paper mischief".

The next three stages of the discussion "contra Eden" are rather fruitless because assertion is set against assertion, opinion against opinion. If the scheme succeeded, Eden asks, would not the Bank of England be damaged? and would not the country bankers be entitled to compensation? Bentham's answer is as conclusive as it is concise: "I neither know nor care!" (par. 16). Again, Eden asks, would not a 3% Consol be more attractive than a 3% Annuity Note, till stock is near to par? Bentham's answer is simply: no! (par. 17.) Would the extension of the plan from buying in stock to paying off the stock-owners be at all practicable, Eden wants to know? Bentham's reply is a simple counter-question: Why on earth not? (par. 18.)

Eden's final attacks are directed against the "moral advantages" Bentham claims for his currency: he deals with settlements and trusts. To cash in the interest due on a Note, he says, the beneficiary of the trust, or a single trustee, would have to *have* the Note, and, as it is payable to the bearer, he could then simply spend the money without further ado, principal as well as interest: hence the security of the investment would be low, not high. Bentham retorts that, according to English law, the trustee of a creditor can receive his debts anyway, so that the introduction of Annuity Notes would make no difference. The divisibility of the Notes into two parts would, however, afford a safeguard, if it were rightly used: if it became customary always to appoint two trustees, each could be made to hand in his half separately and receive it back after the Annuity Note Office had paid the interest, so that neither of them need have the whole Note in his power at any time (pars. 19 and 20). Eden also doubts whether the introduction of some large-type printing into the Note, which Bentham is suggesting, would really help to prevent forgery and thus to reduce crime: but Bentham refuses to discuss this argument because, as he says with some justice, the use of a special kind of letter-press is not the only expedient he recommends.

In his last lines, Eden returns once more to the central problem of circulability. Bentham in his pamphlet admits the possibility of an occasional premium or discount on his Notes. Can anybody, Eden seems to ask, imagine a *stable currency*, whose constituent parts are subject to such *fluctuations in value*? Are we not here confronted with a crying contradiction in terms? Bentham, in reply, declares that a discount is altogether improbable: it could only develop in a state of acute crisis when the nation's confidence in law and order, or at any rate in the stability of established institutions, is rudely shaken, for instance during a foreign invasion or a civil war. A premium is indeed a different matter: it is well-nigh unavoidable at certain junctures: but, then, an increase in price beyond the nominal value is unavoidable for *any* government security when there is more money seeking investment in this form than can be accommodated. Bentham conveniently forgets that this does not matter where the securities concerned are only occasionally bought and sold at the Stock Exchange like Consols, but that the case is very different where they are meant to serve as money, in the everyday transactions of market and shop.

Such are Eden's strictures and Bentham's counter-arguments. Unfortunately, the defence did not impress Vansittart as much as the attack—assuming that he ever cared to wade through Bentham's verbose and voluminous "observations". Eden's report was virtually the end of the whole interlude. The letter-press was broken up, and the pamphlet never published. Bentham, however, remained hopeful for a while even after Eden's devastating critique should have told him that his remaining chances of success were slight and slender in the extreme. On August 11, 1801, he still writes to Dumont in the fond delusion that his proposed fancy currency stands a good chance of being adopted by the government. "Whether it will be adopted, is more than I can as yet pretend to say; but they pay serious attention to it, and appearances are not unpromising" (*Works* X, 376). By this time the whole project had perhaps already slipped from Nicholas Vansittart's mind.

It is a pleasant trait which should not remain unrecorded that the tussle between Bentham and Eden, fatal though it was to Bentham's plans, did not lead to a permanent enmity between the two. Going over old papers, Bentham came, on November 14, 1820, upon the correspondence which we have just been reviewing, and noted on it the following lines: "This letter is from the late Sir Fred. Eden to Nicholas Vansittart. The cause of it was—the project's interfering with a branch of Eden's *Globe Insurance* project. I do not believe this answer of mine was ever communicated to Eden. Notwithstanding this letter, which must have been communicated to me by Vansittart, Eden and I continued till his death upon the most friendly terms. I remember giving him at his request a copy, and I believe the only one I had, of an Annuity Note in its most perfected state. He desired it for the purpose of this rival and successful project of his." (University College collection, IIIb, 359.) This memorandum is certainly not a good summary of the affair, but it speaks the truth when it says that no shadow, not even a temporary cloud, passed over the friendship of the two men. We find them engaged in a friendly correspondence about a year after their clash on the Annuity Note scheme (cf. *Works* X, 395 et seq.)—a fact which seems to prove that Bentham did not take his defeat too much to heart. The reason is, probably, as we have hinted before, that he himself had come to doubt the validity of his ideas and the value of his suggestions.

"PAPER MISCHIEF [EXPOSED]"

In the letter to Dumont of Aug. 11, 1801, which we have just quoted, Bentham told his friend: "Any documents about the state of the country banks in Ireland would be highly valuable to me. Whether my currency be adopted or no, country bankers' paper *must* be stopped from further *encrease*, on pain of certain bankruptcy:

though I cannot tell you exactly on what day, and at what o'clock" (*Works* X, 376 seq.). These words, though they sound a little like a joke, were meant in earnest: they express, in a nutshell, the practical result of a good deal of Bentham's economic thinking since the autumn of the year before. He was now a sworn enemy of the issuing banker. A simple chain of reasoning had led him to this new position and preoccupation. It can be summed up in a short syllogism: every addition to the paper currency of the country leads to an increase of prices and lowers the living standard of those who draw fixed incomes; country bankers continually add to the volume of that circulation; *ergo,* country bankers are a nuisance and should be brought under control. Starting from this conviction, Bentham soon discovered other weaknesses in the existing banking system, especially the one more particularly mentioned in the letter to Dumont: namely, that country bankers promise to exchange every one of their notes against cash; that they issue more notes than they can ever hope to exchange into gold; and that consequently there is a constant danger of bankruptcy which is bound to materialize one day sooner or later, unless energetic steps are taken to improve matters and to put banking on a sounder basis.

Such conclusions unfavourable to the country bankers, and, indeed, to the whole banking trade, must have been preparing in Bentham's mind for quite some time. His friend Patrick Colquhoun had been pushing him in this direction as early as 1799; on November 15 of that year he had expressed himself in a letter as follows: "I have been turning my thoughts a little (and but very little) to the effects of your *circulating medium plan,* and I see in it a vast resource for government. Why should the Charter of the Bank of England be renewed? or why should bankers exist at all? Neither the one nor the other contribute to augment the property of the country; while by dealing in money, and assisting monopolizers, who are always hurtful to every state, they acquire immense fortunes by availing themselves of a resource which properly belongs to the state, and which, under a proper system of management, would not only ease the country of the pressure of war taxes, but would even enable government to pay off the national debt. I daresay you are already convinced of this, from the consideration you have given the subject. But this is not all the good it would produce: those commercial distresses, which beget distrust and produce ruin to many respectable individuals, while they disturb the beneficial intercourse of commerce, *could rarely happen.*" (*Works* X, 338-339.)

However, in 1799 Bentham's mind was not yet made up. It seems that he sought factual information from Patrick Colquhoun, and not theoretical instruction; the next letter from the same correspondent, dated Nov. 29, is of a different cast and tenor. "1. I should conceive the circulation of country bankers' paper to be equal at least to the paper of the Bank of England. No human being can form any accurate judgment of what may be afloat and current at the same time. It must hang upon conjecture, and the best opinion on this subject will be obtained from men of commercial knowledge and good judgment: I should conceive Sir Francis Baring's ideas on this subject of importance. As far as my judgment goes, I should suppose the country circulation of Great Britain about eleven or twelve millions.

"2. I had conceived the circulation of the paper of the Bank of England to exceed ten millions; but Mr Allardice[1] is no doubt right. Since the payment of specie has been suspended, I should conceive the Bank may have extended its circulation one-fourth. This, however, is judging only from appearances: the fact cannot be ascertained. The merchants complain of the directors being less liberal in discounts than the present pressure requires, although they have certainly stretched considerably, and it is probable that their circulation is greater than it ever was. The addition of one, and two, and five pound notes, within the last eight years, must have increased the circulation in a certain degree; but it does not go very far beyond the metropolis.

"3. The country bankers keep very little specie. It varies according to the credit and opulence of the bankers. In proportion as bankers possess confidence in the country, the less specie is required. They have nothing to fear, but from a run upon them, arising from want of confidence, whether proceeding from the credit of the house being shaken, or from public calamity. It is usual for bankers in the country to exchange each other's notes once or twice a week, and the balance is always paid by a bill on London. An extensive credit here is what they trust to more than specie, for supporting them in any exigency; and the want of the means of obtaining this credit, restrains circulation, and prescribes a limit, in proportion to the capital of the bankers. It does not happen once in seven years, that a country banker is called upon to pay specie to any extent; and it seldom happens at a distance

[1]Cf. Alexander Allardyce, *An Address to the Proprietors of the Bank of England*, 3rd ed., 1798, Appendix No 21/22, pp. 76/77.

from the metropolis, that gold coin is to be met with. The risk of light guineas has reconciled the people to *notes,* and nothing else is in circulation. A considerable amount in silver (comparatively speaking) must be kept at the country bankers' houses for change—at least this was the case before the five-pound notes were issued. I should not conceive the gold equal to one-eighth, if so much, of the amount of the notes in circulation; but this is mere opinion. It is the interest of the banker to have as little as possible, and he will act on this principle. If he sees no danger, he will have little or none; if otherwise, he will get temporary supplies from the metropolis.

"If we could suppose a case, where a sudden demand to the amount of one-fourth of the circulation of the different country banks was to be made for specie, I think all of them must stop, because they could not, in that case, assist one another. In this view, specie is not the foundation upon which notes are issued; but the *credit of the issuers,* and their known property and responsibility. It is this that quiets the public mind, since a general impression prevails that the specie is, at all times, very inconsiderable *in* the coffers of the bankers." (*Works* X, 339-340.)

To get to the bottom of the matter, Bentham applied to Sir Francis Baring, as advised. He sent him a letter on Dec. 23, 1799 (Christmas notwithstanding) and asked for guidance on the following four points: "1. Whereabouts may be the amount of bankers' paper (payable on demand) habitually in circulation? 2. If no particular sum can be mentioned, is it supposed to be more or less than that of the Bank of England? 3. Has any and what addition been made to the quantity of Bank of England paper in consequence of the issue of £2 and £1 Notes? 4. What is the rate of interest allowed to customers by such of the bankers as allow interest? as per Sir F[rancis] B[aring]'s Observations [on the Publication of Walter Boyd, Esq., M.P.], 2d edit. p.18."

The banker's answer on all these points was careful but enlightening. He writes: "1. The bankers in London have no circulating paper payable on demand. The country banks always have; but a distinction should be made between paper payable on demand *originally,* and what becomes so, *in consequence of the lapse of the time* for which it is issued—this is partly explained in what I have said about the Exeter and Newcastle banks; for instance:

"Exeter issued *originally* notes on demand, which formed a small part (about one-tenth of their circulation), the remainder being at twenty or twenty-one days after sight with interest.

"Newcastle issued all their paper to commence interest six months after date, and thus payable on demand, conceiving it the best means to keep their paper out; for whoever took out fresh notes must wait six months before interest commenced.

"It is impossible to form an estimate, or even a guess at the amount, which must vary with the more or less internal trade of the country. The proportion of notes issued *originally* payable on demand must be small; but it requires a return of the practice of the great banks to know the degree to which that amount is augmented by the means I have described.

"2. The preceding will explain why no answer can be given to this; but the total quantity or amount of the paper of the country banks must very much exceed that of the Bank of England *in my opinion;* but doctors always differ.

"3. An addition has been made, no doubt; and the sum would have been very much larger, if the Notes had been for guineas instead of pounds. The number which are in circulation may be large, but I cannot think the value or amount to be considerable. I am clearly of opinion that it forms no important part in the circulation of the country. It was *convenient* at the time: it may be so now, and hereafter; but that is the extent of its importance.

"4. The rate of interest from country banks will vary: some are so low as 2½ per Cent, but the most are from 3 per Cent, and upwards. It is probable that war and partial distress may have varied the rate paid by the same banks.

"You should read the report of the House of Lords on examining the Bank; but you must not positively rely, that what are stated as facts, are so in truth. I forget the instances, except some in the evidence of Henry Thornton, which he gives as receiving information from others, but in which he has been misinformed.

"The subject of circulations generally is very tender and difficult at present, for we must have many shocks and convulsions before it can settle in a sound basis; in the meanwhile, it moves quietly and with facility for those who proportion their enterprises or operations to their means; as the distress and failures of 99 out of 100 which have happened in the last six months, has been owing to imprudence, &c, of the parties." (*Works* X, 340-341.)

For the moment, Bentham did not go any further into the matter:

the Annuity Note proposal drove all other problems, however closely akin, out of his mind. But as he began to discover the probable inflationary effects of his circulating annuities, as he came to see that they would do more harm than good because they would affect the price system and the income structure of the country, his thought returned to the general problems of the paper currency and he gave renewed attention to the position and policy of the country bankers. By the fall of 1800, he had done a good deal of thinking on the subject of "paper mischief": but his ideas were not yet quite clear and settled. They were contained in his mind as salt is in sea-water: some extraneous agency was needed to make them crystallize. That extraneous agency was provided by a contemporary pamphlet which Bentham discovered by sheer accident[1]: W. Anderson's *Iniquity of Banking,* a publication with the highly suggestive sub-title: "Bank Notes proved to be injurious to the Public, and the Real Cause of the present exorbitant Price of Provisions".

Apart from Smith's *Wealth of Nations* no book on economics had so deep and lasting influence on Bentham's later thought as this little pamphlet. Bentham accepted Anderson's point of view: he had no quarrel at all with his diagnosis. But he was alarmed at Anderson's practical propositions: the remedy suggested seemed to him a dangerous expedient likely to lead to the death of the patient it was intended to cure. Clearly, Bentham's moral duty was to take Anderson's theories and, entering into them, to bring out of them a policy which would allay the evil exposed, without endangering the economic structure of society.

Anderson's pamphlet contains a clear and straightforward argument. His main thesis is "that Bank Notes are the principal cause of the evils at present most complained of"—the general dearth of commodities, and the especial dearth of victuals; and his main preoccupation flowing from this assertion is "to prove the justice and expediency of putting an end to the paper system". "Having first proved, that increasing the circulation by means of paper is the principal, if not the only cause, of the great increase of the prices of commodities, . . . which is so injurious to every part of the society, but more especially to the poor," Anderson writes, "I shall shew, that the issuing of bank notes is productive of the same consequences as robbery, as by that means the produce of labour is obtained without

[1] Cf. below, p. 429.

labour, and every man in society deprived of a part of his property, or of the fruits of his labour" (pp. III, 10).

To demonstrate the correctness of his assertion and the necessity of his expedient, Anderson appeals to the quantity theory of money, "the truth of which is . . . . generally acknowledged . . . . but . . . seems to have been but very little attended to". He ably recapitulates it and comes, of course, to the conclusion "that increasing the circulation must necessarily increase the price of commodities". If that is so, however, he urges, "it becomes evident, that bank notes, by which the money circulation of this country has been so prodigiously increased, are the real cause of the present exorbitant price of provisions; and such being the case, it must likewise be no less evident, that the banker as certainly robs every other man in the society, by circulating his notes, as by levying a tax, or by putting his hands into their pockets and taking out a part of their money". The supply of a society is limited; hence if some people appear on the market with more money than they had before, they will only be able to increase their share by reducing that of others. "Suppose all the purchasers in a fair . . . . to have each an equal quantity of money, each ought to have an equal share of the commodities: but if one half of them were bankers, and chose to double their money by issuing notes, they would be able to purchase two thirds of the commodities; consequently, those who were not bankers would have one third less than they would have had if there had been no bank notes. Had the bankers, instead of increasing their money by issuing bank notes, increased it by stealing one third of the money belonging to the others, the effect would have been exactly the same . . . . It must be evident, therefore, that the bankers rob the other part of the society." (10-18.)

Certain laws for the protection of property, Anderson goes on to say, are *de facto* abolished or made nugatory, by the freedom to issue bank notes. First, the laws against forgery. "Why do the laws require that both [gold and silver] should be of a certain fineness?" The answer is: to ensure honesty. "Gold and silver were supposed to have cost a certain quantity of labour, in order to be attained, and were therefore made representatives in exchange for an equal quantity of other labour; and the counterfeiting or debasing of these metals was made death, in order to prevent any man from enjoying the fruits of others' labour without labouring himself. But what is the use of such laws, while particular men are permitted to increase their money by means of bank notes? Does it require any more labour to fabricate *a note* than to counterfeit *a guinea*?" Now, this law is not the only one that is virtually set aside by the permission to issue paper. "The laws made for regulating the profits on money are rendered equally ineffectual by the banker; for as he circulates three or four hundred pounds of paper for every hundred pounds of cash that he has, he actually receives *fifteen* or *twenty* per cent for his money, instead of *five,* which is the lawful interest." Thirdly, and lastly, on consideration—if not, indeed, before consideration—"it must be evident that bank notes render the laws against monopoly equally ineffectual with those against counterfeiting and usury": it is the paper system which increases the evil to such an extent that it becomes unmanageable; after all, "it is only by having the command of large sums of money that men are enabled to monopolize", and it is the bankers who, by actually producing money, provide the sums which make forestalling and regrating possible, and thereby sweep away the economic supports on which the effectiveness of a law such as this has to be based if it is to be more than a string of empty words (18-21).

Perhaps it will be argued "that the robberies committed by bank notes differ from all others, inasmuch as that they tend to enrich the nation". This is an erroneous notion, Anderson replies: the nation as a whole is not enriched nor can it be, "since it is as impossible for one part of the society to grow rich and the other not to grow poor, as for one arm of the balance to be raised without the other being depressed". "But enriching one part of the society does not merely impoverish the other; it tends likewise to lessen the number of the inhabitants." More wealth means more country seats, more parks, more carriages. "But by this means, a great deal of land, that now maintains men, would then be set aside for pleasure-grounds, for parks to fatten deer, and for raising corn and hay to feed horses; and as a horse requires as much land to maintain him as is requisite to support a poor family, so great an increase in the number of horses would of itself cause a great decrease in the number of families." Paper money, like a foreign conqueror, lays the country waste, and to the victims it makes no difference "whether they are driven out by the sword or by the obnoxious power of riches". In England, impoverishment has spread abroad; the poor Scots are even forced to emigrate. "Such has been the necessary consequences [*sic*] of suffering men to multiply their money by bank notes, and other similar means: they have been thereby enabled to engross so large a portion of the productions of society, as have either reduced them to beggary, or forced others to emigrate, who have had no means of increasing *their* incomes" (22-25).

After rebutting the suggestion that the general increase in prices is due to enhanced taxation, and not to inflated circulation—a discussion which is, from our point of view, an irrelevant excursion (25-30)—Anderson proceeds to investigate the influence of the paper system on the different classes of society. He deals first with the contention "that the *landed* and *monied* interests are inseparable, and that promoting the one must necessarily promote the other". "Nothing," he insists, "can be further from the truth." His argument is the same as before. Like production, the quantity of "power, consequence, or riches" in society is limited: what the one group gains, the other must lose. "Suppose, for example, that all the lands in England were let for a term of twenty-one years, for a rent of twenty millions, at a time when the revenues arising from money amounted to the same sum, would not the landed and monied men have an equal share in the productions of the society, and in the influence or power arising from wealth? But if the monied men were, during that period, to double their incomes, by increasing the quantity of their money, at the end of twenty-one years their respective power and wealth would be but as one to two; that is to say, the landholders would have one third less of the productions of, and the influence in, the society and the monied men one third more than they had at the beginning of the above period: thence it is obvious, that the bankers, by increasing their own incomes through the means of their notes, do absolutely rob the landholders of a part of their power, and of a part of their property." Rents, it is true, can be periodically readjusted; but they are relatively fixed all the same, and their purchasing power falls constantly while the leases are running, so that the land-holder "must always be a loser in the intermediate time". If he is not even worse off than he actually is, this is due to the corn-laws, "the most iniquitous system that ever was adopted".

A second class to be considered are "those who have fixed revenues, such as stock-holders and annuitants of all kinds, servants in the different departments of government, officers in the army and navy &c &c," and these "must have sustained a much greater injury than the land-holders". Indeed, as their incomes are absolutely fixed, "they are exposed a helpless prey to the depredations of bankers". "The land-holder, by raising his rent, partly indemnifies himself on the rest of the society, and, in a small degree, retaliates on the banker; but the officers and annuitants are pillaged without the least danger of retaliation." The position of money-lenders who are not issuing bankers, is no better than that of the simple annuitants.

Lastly, "people in trade, whether merchants, or manufacturers who trade on real property, are affected nearly in the same manner as the money-lenders; for as the share a man has in the trade of a country, and consequently in the profits arising from trade, must always be in proportion to the share he has of the capital employed in trade, so in proportion as the capital is increased, his share of trade and profit must be diminished: therefore," Anderson concludes with his usual refrain, "the banker, by circulating bank notes, deprives the man of real property in trade of a part of his profits, at the same time that he reduces the value of the whole" (30-35).

This consideration of the traders' case leads Anderson on to a discussion of crises. Paper money, it is said, increases the volume of trade. But the trouble is that, to keep pace with the general rate of economic growth, many a man is forced to go beyond his capital, "and thus a system of credit and speculation has been introduced which has rendered all property in trade insecure: for when men have once recourse to paper, which they must have when they go beyond their capitals, no bounds can be set to speculation. If there be an advantage in issuing one hundred pounds, there is still a greater in issuing two hundred pounds". This leads to an unnatural position on the commodity markets and causes such convulsions as were experienced in 1793 and again in 1796, convulsions which would have been even worse than they actually were if the government had not interfered, to the great benefit of the traders, but at the dire expense of the general public. "Various causes have been assigned for what is called the distress in the commercial world, but certainly without foundation, for the whole proceeds from paper; for as a certain quantity of cash is requisite to make it circulate, when the quantity of paper has been greatly increased there must be an apparent scarcity of cash. That this is the real cause must be obvious, for in 1793, no exportation of money was alleged to have taken place, yet the distresses and embarrassments were as great then as they were in 1796; and there is no doubt but that, while this nefarious system is continued, as no bounds can be set to speculation, distresses and embarrassments will be felt at irregular periods. This must render all property in trade very precarious; and hence it becomes evident that paper must be injurious to the man of real capital in every respect" (35-39). Anderson's argument on these pages is anything but close. But it made a considerable impression on Bentham who grasped the general drift and upshot of it, namely, that the free issue of paper money implies an ever-present danger of general bankruptcy.

Anderson's indictment now draws to a close. He plays one more trump card by referring to the situation of the poor and of the working classes under the paper system. The poor rates have risen "which is a necessary consequence of the great rise in the price of provisions; for all those who had but just sufficient to maintain them before the rise took place, must have starved if the difference of price had not been made up to them by additional rates". There are more poor now than before: and those working men who are not exactly poor, are yet extremely hard hit, because their income is spent mainly on necessaries, and necessaries have risen most. "The injustice done by the circulating of bank notes to this class, is, if possible, more palpable, than that done to any of the others. For although the injustice of depriving any man of that share in the productions to which he is entitled by his property must be sufficiently obvious, yet the injustice of depriving the productive labourer, the man by whose labour the whole society is supported, of any part of the small share he has at any time been allowed to retain of the productions of his labour, must be particularly striking. What words, for example, could we find sufficient to express our indignation at the conduct of a set of men who should combine to deprive the labourer of a part of his wages? Yet this the bankers have positively done; for there can be no difference, whether they take a part or reduce the value of the whole; whether they take four-pence out of a shilling or reduce the value of that shilling to eight-pence. The wages of the labourer will not now purchase two thirds of the quantity of provisions that the wages he had five and twenty years ago could have purchased; therefore the bankers, by issuing their notes, have as effectually robbed him of one third of his wages, as if they had put their hands into his pocket and stolen it" (39-42).

With this rhetorical flourish, the argument has reached its climax. Anderson is satisfied that he has proved the bankers to be highwaymen: he closes his pamphlet by indicting them of cold-blooded mass murder. They are, he says, the main war-mongers in the country. "It has been shewn," we read, "that an increase of the quantity of money to be lent, without a similar increase of the quantity wanted to be borrowed, must necessarily reduce the interest; therefore if the demand for money were not from time to time increased, the constant increase of the quantity to be lent, by means of bank notes, would in time reduce the interest to almost nothing. War is the only effectual means for increasing the demand, and raising the interest on money. War therefore becomes the interest of all money-lenders. The bankers, from their having a great deal of money belonging to other people, which they cannot well employ but in such a manner as to be able to call it in on any emergency, will always be investing large sums in the funds; and as the interest which they receive will be high in proportion as the prices of stocks are low, war, which reduces the prices, must to them be particularly desirable."

The Bank of England, it is true, is not quite in the same position as the country bankers. Unfortunately it also stands to gain by war, if in a different way. "For as all the money raised by taxes is lodged there, the revenue becomes a fund for circulating the notes of the bank. And as the profits of the proprietors depend upon the quantity of their paper in circulation; and as that must depend upon the largeness of their funds; war, which by increasing the national debt and taxes, increases their funds, must greatly contribute to their advantage." Hence, in addition to all the other evils for which it is responsible, the paper system must bear the blame for the frequency of war (42-44). Surely, Anderson concludes, "it must .... be the wish of every honest man to see it abolished" (ib.).

This is the gist of Anderson's publication; it seems that it created quite a stir. It went through no less than four editions in a comparatively short time. As happened so often in the case of successful pamphlets, the author felt tempted, and could not resist the temptation, to issue a second part to it: and—again as happened regularly in such cases—the sequel was not up to the standard of the original tract. We are not interested here in "a further illustration" the author gives "of the injustice of the paper system" (5-19)[1], nor in the enquiry his part II contains "into the nature and probable consequences of

[1]These pages are no more than a somewhat vulgarised repetition of the arguments of part I, esp. of the pp. 35-39 therein. The only new feature is a historical discussion, centring around the thesis that "bankers at first only lent money, but now they *coin* it" (7) which, according to Anderson, goes to show that the evil and iniquity of banking was introduced slowly and surreptitiously, under the cover of political deception.

the Bank Indemnity Bill" (19-33)[1]; but we must have a brief glance at his "plan for removing (or at least alleviating) the evils produced by the circulation of bank notes"—the practical part of the treatise which was sure to attract Bentham's attention above all others.

Anderson introduces his proposal by pointing out that gold and silver have no intrinsic merits as means of circulation but function only on the strength of a deeply rooted convention. "Paper will" in consequence "answer all the purposes of gold and silver"; there is no serious objection to the stuff as such, to the physical matter of which it is made. There is no reason why it should be driven out; nor could it be excluded from circulation without great inconvenience. But it must no longer remain in the hands of irresponsible agents. It must be publicly controlled. There are, Anderson says, "two methods by which the evils now produced . . . . can be either prevented or palliated:—these are, either to oblige every man [who issues notes] to hold a quantity of stock equal to the quantity of his notes in circulation, upon which the interest from the nation shall be withheld while his notes continue to circulate [so that he cannot draw two incomes from one and the same capital]—or to suppress by law all the paper now in circulation, and to supply its place with an equal quantity of national paper". Needless to say, Anderson goes all out for the latter, the more radical alternative. It is in his view "far preferable to the former, and would . . . . be productive of very great national advantages" (33-42).

There is no reason to fear that "national paper when made a general legal tender" would fail to be accepted (42-43); or that it would be more easily forged than the old bank notes (44); or, again, that it would tend to lose its value, "if there be not a greater quantity issued than what is necessary to replace that which is now in circulation" (43-48). The latter point—the question "who will assure us that the government will not issue a greater quantity"—is, of course, of crucial importance, and Anderson admits that a safeguard is necessary. He sets it forth after a momentary relapse into his old argument that the Bank of England has robbed the public and is a willing

[1]Anderson sums up this bill as "a law to make the paper of a particular corporation equal to gold", and says: "By the Bank Indemnity Bill, the whole property in the kingdom is virtually put into the power of the Bank. For as all transfers of property are made by the intervention of Bank Notes, there is nothing to prevent the Bank from purchasing whatever is brought to market; whether it be land, stock or property of any other kind. The Bank has only to fabricate an additional quantity of notes" (21).

supporter of a war-mongering cabinet (49-59). "In order to prevent an increase of the paper beyond what was really requisite for the circulation, the Bank should be obliged to receive from individuals, at a certain interest, any quantity of national paper not below a certain amount; and the government should be obliged to receive from the Bank all the paper that was not necessary for carrying on its business. This regulation would not only prevent, to a certainty, an unnecessary increase of the national paper, but would give it a great superiority over cash; for as people would soon perceive that the former could be used much more conveniently than the latter in all the operations of commerce; and that, when not wanted for other purposes, it could be lent upon the most undoubted security, which would not be the case with specie, there can be no question, but that paper would always be preferred to cash where there was a choice." (61-62.)

It is impossible to imagine that Bentham had any serious objection to the principle and spirit of Anderson's proposal: it promised two reforms, both of which he himself had very much at heart. On the one hand it was out to stop the depreciation of money through the unlimited issue of bank notes; on the other, it tended to make the Bank of England a "frugality bank"—a bank where smaller people excluded from the stock-market could leave their petty sums for a while against the payment of interest—especially as Anderson also suggested that county banks should be erected "on the principle of that in London", provincial branch offices as it were, which would bring the opportunity to deposit "superabundant paper" to everybody's doorstep. The idea of a national currency of this complexion must have been acceptable, both to the Bentham of the *Circulating Annuities*, and to the Bentham of *Paper Mischief*.

But if Anderson's plan was, in its essence, sure to be sympathetically received byBentham, one particular feature of it repelled and alarmed him: the reckless proposal to do away with the banking trade, and that by crude and even desperate methods. This was what Anderson suggested: "Let a law be made to suppress, within a certain period, all the bank or promissory notes now in circulation. This law would make it necessary for bankers to convert their capitals into money in order to redeem their paper. All the property of bankers, therefore, would be brought to market." The private banks would thus, in the true sense of the term, be "liquidated". That part of their property which consists of stock should simply be exchanged for national paper

—a trick by which the public would be greatly benefited as "by this operation all that part of the national debt now in the possession of the bank or bankers would be payed off". Lands and houses would be acquired by people now holding stock who would willingly exchange their stock for the new government currency, and that in turn for lands and houses. "By this means another part of the debt would be redeemed." Lastly, mercantile bills now held by the country bankers would be dealt with by the Bank of England whom the government would grant for this purpose "a sum of national paper sufficient to liquidate all the remaining private paper in circulation" (59-61).

By these tactics the business of the bankers would have been dissolved very much as the estate of bankrupts is usually dealt with. Anderson realized this, but the prospect did not dismay him. On the contrary, he thought it right and proper to treat the bankers as bankrupts since, under the paper system, their assets could never be equal to their liabilities. And he brushed aside the apprehension that the public would suffer under the discomfiture and disappearance of the "coiners" and "counterfeiters". "The fears entertained of some great evil being the consequence of a general bankruptcy among the merchants and bankers, are groundless," he says recklessly. "Suppose that all, or the greater part of the merchants and bankers in London were literally, as they are virtually bankrupts; what might probably be the consequence? should we lose any part of the commodities now in the country? or should we lose the power of producing an equal quantity next year? most certainly not. What would be then this apprehended terrible national calamity? probably a few hundred pounds worth of paper that now passes for millions of guineas, would be committed to the flames; and not a few gentlemen, who without any property of their own, are at present enabled, by means of paper credit to ride in their coaches or chariots, would be obliged to descend to the pavement. As for the rest, every thing would in a few days go on as usual. Credit is not as it has been represented a delicate but a very hardy plant. The man who is a bankrupt to day finds little difficulty in getting credit to morrow. The same would be the case in a general bankruptcy." (II, 15 seq.)

So certain was Anderson that a general bankruptcy in the banking world would not harm but rather benefit the nation, that he proposed to work towards it with all energy, and without delay. He knew very well that "there is not cash enough in the kingdom to discharge one tenth, or probably not one twentieth part of the paper in circulation," and that if "such an alarm were given to the public, as to create a general run, all the banks in the kingdom must instantly stop payment". But yet he says at the end of his first pamphlet: "We must not content ourselves with wishes, we must exert all the means in our power in order to remove so great an evil [as the issuing trade]. The interposition of government is the only effectual means of removing it, and that we must endeavour to obtain: but although government should refuse to interpose, yet a great deal might be done by individuals. If, for example, gentlemen would keep their money in their own possession, instead of leaving it in the hands of bankers, a great fund would be removed which is now employed in circulating paper; and if they were at all times to refuse bank notes, especially in the payment of their rents, a wonderful check would be given to their circulation." If that were done, "it might be expected that the danger people [at large] incur of losing their property, would prevent them from leaving their money in the hands of bankers, or from taking their notes", and that again would have decisive results, as "there cannot be a doubt, but that any serious shock given to public credit would infallibly ruin them all" (I, 44-45). Such talk seemed to Bentham the height of folly and frivolity. A sane and sound theory made the basis of an unsound and insane proposal—wisdom degraded to be the handmaid of error! To take Anderson's analysis of the situation and show that different conclusions could and must be drawn from it, was in Bentham's opinion very nearly a patriotic duty. At any rate, here was a grand opportunity of being "useful". That is the reason why he took up the pen.

As far as we can tell, Bentham attempted two different pamphlets on the paper money question. *Paper Mischief* [*Exposed*] directed against Anderson; and, later, *The True Alarm* directed against a man called Boyd. Neither of them was completed. Of the latter, much will have to be said in vol. III; the fragments of the former will still find room in the present volume. Bentham started on it in the last days of October 1800 and worked at it up to the end of January 1801. Then he must have come across Boyd's *Letter . . . on the Influence of the Stoppage of Issues in Specie . . . on the Prices of Provisions*[1] and decided to make him his quarry, and to let Anderson go. The reason for this change of plans is not difficult to guess: he liked most of what Anderson said, but he liked little of what Boyd was saying,[2]

[1]Cf. *Works X*, 361.
[2]Cf. ib. 364.

and he assumed quite rightly that an attack on an adversary would make a more interesting pamphlet than a discussion with one who was half a friend. There are, then, two reasons for the fragmentary state of the papers labelled for short *Paper Mischief*: one, that this projected publication was dropped altogether; the other, that part of the materials prepared for it was transferred to the bundle entitled *The True Alarm*. Nevertheless, we possess the skeleton of a booklet which, as far as it goes, makes not uninteresting reading.

Paper Mischief [*Exposed*] begins with a genuine and somewhat disarming "*pater peccavi*" on the part of Bentham. Until quite recently, he admits, he had believed that there was a positive connection between additions to circulation on the one hand, and the growth of wealth on the other; as to the rise of prices that manifestly follows on any new influx of money into the economic system, he had simply regarded it as a sacrifice well justified by the greater good with which it is bound up. He had been so firm in these opinions that he had actually occupied himself "with contrivances for adding to the existing mass of the circulating medium". But now, he frankly explains, he has found the assumed connection between the volume of circulation and the volume of wealth "purely imaginary", while he has come to see the evil of inflation, of rising prices, to be an evil of the "most enormous magnitude", and Anderson has confirmed him in this conviction which has been growing spontaneously in his mind for quite some time.

These personal preliminaries over, the "Introduction" bluntly states that the rise of prices which is at the moment distressing the country, is caused by paper money; and that, behind the paper money, there hide the country bankers who issue it, and who are thus, in the last analysis, the real mischief-makers. They unlawfully levy a tax on everybody, but especially on the indigent, whose mite they are constantly reducing in value; and, equally unlawfully, they are all the time usurping the privilege of coining which belongs to the Crown, so that they are, in effect, confirmed counterfeiters of money; yet they are none the less personally blameless—indeed "without the smallest particle of guilt"—because neither they nor anybody else seems to comprehend what is happening.

The plain fact of the matter is that prices have doubled, and the purchasing power of money has been halved, since 1760; and it seems unavoidable that prices should double again, and the purchasing power of money be reduced by half again, in another forty years, unless radical steps are taken to arrest this development. To demonstrate the depreciation, Bentham makes use of figures supplied by Sir George Shuckburgh Evelyn in a learned paper on weights and measures; these figures please him very much because the rise of prices they indicate more or less "quadrates" with the increase of circulation by paper money in the same period, so that we seem to be confronted with a clear picture of cause and effect. (The text, unfortunately, is not complete, but it is easy to fill in the gap, which has been done below in a short paragraph in square brackets. The point Bentham wishes to make is perfectly plain.)

The mischief, then, is mathematically demonstrable, even measurable, and its cause clear. Wherein exactly does it consist? Bentham sees three "heads of mischief"; paper money, he says, is attended by trouble on its creation, on its application, and even on its annihilation. When it is created, it inflates prices and thereby leads to a *de facto* reduction of certain incomes; it has the effect of an income tax, although the Exchequer does not get the benefit of it. When it is applied, it tends to drive prices up in a second way, and again reduces the level of incomes. Through the credit facilities at their disposal, which arise on the issue of promissory notes, the country bankers are in a position to enable manufacturers to withhold their goods from the market and thus to increase their profits at the expense of the consuming public; also to enable dealers to engross goods and form corners, and again by this means to exploit the common man; and they will be tempted as well as enabled to engage in such machinations themselves. Finally, when paper money is "annihilated", i.e. when an issuing bank breaks down and there is a run, a rude shock is given to commercial security. Such shocks are not due to extraneous causes; they are inherent in the nature of paper money itself. The habitual proportion between cash reserve and volume of circulation depends on a purely empirical judgment of what is safe, and consequently it is never really safe because all empirical judgments are risky.

After these considerations which form the core of the pamphlet (or rather which would have formed the core of it, if it had been properly worked out), Bentham introduces a chapter on the "money-hoarding system" which he believes will be instructive because "things are illustrated by their contraries". In it, he tries to follow out the effects of thesaurization, i.e. the economic consequences of a systematic *reduction* of the volume of circulation. At a time when some countries still kept well-filled war-chests, this case was by no means purely imaginary.

Even though this pamphlet is only a fragment, the fundamental idea of it stands well out. An evil and a good go hand in hand: the evil of rising prices, and the good of increasing wealth. But though the two tendencies run parallel, they are by no means inseparably connected: it is possible to check the evil without hampering the good. *How* can this be done? The bulk of the chapter in which the remedies are set forth was transferred to *The True Alarm* and we shall find it in vol. III. Yet even *Paper Mischief* [*Exposed*] enunciates a double desideratum: that the increase of paper money be restrained; and that the increase of cash, too, be kept under control, or at any rate not positively encouraged. These two demands constitute the pivot and principle of the monetary policy which Bentham had now made his own, and which he was determined further to expound and to propagate.

A PLAN FOR
AUGMENTATION OF THE REVENUE

A PLAN FOR AUGMENTATION OF THE REVENUE

BY THE ESTABLISHMENT OF
A TRAFFIC ON GOVERNMENT ACCOUNT
IN LIFE ANNUITIES
AND EVERY OTHER BRANCH OF MONEY DEALING
WHERE ADEQUATE SECURITY CAN BE OBTAINED
UPON A PLAN
ADAPTED TO EVERY MODIFICATION OF DEMAND

1794-95

[Table of Contents]

Introduction

The burthensomeness of the national debt is a truth but too generally felt: but as neither good nor evil is ever pure, even this burthen, grievous as it is upon the whole, is not altogether destitute of compensation. A circumstance that has often been noticed as such, and with great justice, is the convenience it affords to individuals of purchasing an income to any amount, free from all trouble as well as from all risk: properties, in respect of which it is impossible that any individual fund can approach to a public one. If to individuals in general the advantage is considerable, to the helpless classes, the orphan and the widow, to the tender sex in general, and to the antient of both sexes it is unspeakable. In short, where there is property, there is no such thing as orphanage in this age and country: government is the guardian—and there can not be a more faithful [one]—of every infant who has money: from what we see of orphanage now and here, we can have no idea of what it is, in its natural state, in many countries still, and every where in all former times. It is from the sense of this convenience that it has been often doubted whether, were it even in the power of government, a danger in no great likelyhood of being realized, to pay off the whole of the public debt, there might not be a part of the burthen, and that no inconsiderable one, in respect of which it were better that the exercise of such a power were forborn.

The debt having, in point of fact, been productive of this convenience, is tacitly regarded as essential to its existence: erroneously indeed, in as far as taxes for the discharge of the interest of the debt are concerned: but the error, if it be one, is too innocent an one to be worth correcting.

Be this as it may, the bargain, make the best of it, is but too incontestably a bad one: but the worse it is, the more cogent the motive for making in every respect the best of it.

Much is done for individual convenience in the way just mentioned as it is: but every thing is not done that might be done. For the principal demand for secure and punctually receivable income a provision is made, and that a most ample one: but there are other modifications of demand in this line, nor those in small variety or of small account, to which the existing provision in point of supply does not extend. In a word, the branches of that species of dealing which may be distinguished by the general name of money-traffic, I speak not only of what might exist, but of what actually do exist, are in great variety, and this, of selling perpetual redeemable annuities for ready money, though a great one, and the greatest, is but one out of a number. Of these by-branches of money traffic, some, as we shall find, either actually are or have been, as well as the main one, carried on in this country by government itself: others being relinquished to individuals, are carried on by individuals, though under considerable disadvantage: others which, had circumstances been sufficiently favourable, or invention sufficiently productive, might perhaps have been carried on by individuals, have either not been carried on at all, or not to near the extent to which they are capable of being carried, more especially with the aid, or by the hand, of government.

The object of the present paper, then, is to propose that the dealings of government should be extended to every modification of money-traffick: such branches alone excepted, which either from its very nature government is incapable of carrying on, or which, for some particular reason or reasons, it would not be eligible that government should carry on.

By money-traffic in general I mean the exchange of [1]money in one shape, for money in another: to wit, in respect of presence or futurity, certainty or uncertainty, simultaneity of receipt, or diffusion of receipt through an extent of time: the nature of the substance meant by money, being throughout supposed the same.[a]

Not only this proposal is new, but the view of the object itself which the proposal takes for its subject, I mean the view of it in this its whole extent, is equally so. The different branches have, most of them, been the subject of consideration, and some of frequent practice. But they are now for the first time brought together, confronted and formed into a whole. It will be seen whether the result of the comparison is a matter of indifference to the purposes of finance, or to the convenience and security of individuals.

[1] [a][Later filled in in pencil.]

I. Borrowing

Antiently there was a good deal of borrowing by government, and but little paying. Forced loans were frequent: and forced loans were but another name for plunder.

For some generations past, government has in a manner ceased to borrow, at least of the nation at large. What was originally *borrowing* has been changed, and that in a manner insensibly, into the *sale* of perpetual redeemable annuities. Among those that deal with government, the contest now is, not who shall be paid off, but who shall not be paid off, that is, have his annuity redeemed. In new loans at a higher rate of interest than the original rate, the stipulation is that the lender, that is the purchaser of the annuity, shall not be paid off, at least not before certain others are paid off.

What government really borrows, it borrows in comparatively small sums chiefly of the Bank of England.

Paying in promises to pay is a particular mode of borrowing. In the ordinary mode, what a man borrows of one man, is to pay to another: what he borrows at one time, is to pay at another. In this particular mode, he borrows of one man in order to pay the same man: he borrows and pays in one and the same operation, at one and the same time. The issuing of a Navy Bill is a transaction of this sort. The issuing of an Exchequer Bill is another.

Future money not being of equal value with present, borrowing is seldom performed, especially by government, without paying interest to make up the difference. The object of course is to pay as little interest as one can. Government, to the extent of a certain portion of its demand, has some peculiar facilities for giving itself this advantage, such as do not fall to the share of individuals: this advantage it is high time it should improve, and make the most of. A proposal for this purpose will be given in a separate paper, under the title of a *Proposal for the circulation of a [new] species of paper currency, under the name of Government Bonds [or Exchequer Notes]*.

II. Lending

Lending will appear to be a branch of money-traffic not much to be expected on the part of government in this nation and in these times. To lend money, one must have money to lend: and the great grievance of government is the having none.

Those, however, who have property to sell, or credit to borrow upon, may have money to lend to one man by borrowing it of another. And if the rate they lend at is higher than that they borrow at, the transaction will in proportion be a source of gain.

In the most common ways of borrowing and lending, government in this country could have no chance for any such advantage. But there is a particular mode of lending in which it certainly would be in the power of government, poor as it is, to make an advantage, and that no very inconsiderable one: through an advantage which, as we shall see, appears to be more than compensated by the inconvenience to individuals. What I speak of is *pawnbroking*: the lending upon what in one sense may be termed real security, the security of specific property, but that property consisting, not, as in the common case, of what is called real security, in immoveables, but in moveables.

In this country a great pawnbroking shop was set up, not on account of government, but however by authority of government. It was kept by a great joint-stock company, called the *Charitable Corporation*. It had a bad end, the funds being embezzled. But the miscarriage proves nothing against the productiveness of such a business, even if in the hands of government. The accident happened only for want of some regulations which, were the business to do a second time, would not fail to be established.

There seems no reason for thinking that without the aid of a monopoly, this branch of money-traffic could be conducted on government account with any degree of profit whatsoever. It is at present carried on, and that upon the freest footing, by individuals, whose interest it is to carry it on as cheap as possible. Competition is at its height: no apprenticeship is necessary. If it were capable of being carried on a single per Cent cheaper than it is, it would be: a man who could carry it on a single per Cent cheaper than his rivals, would engross the trade for a great distance. The trade has indeed been made the subject of parliamentary regulation; and rates are fixed, above which a man shall not be permitted to take: but as to the doing the business at a less profit, and as much less as a man pleases, every man is free. It is then equally in the interest and within the power of the individual dealer in whose hands the business is at present, to carry it on at as cheap a rate as possible. It could not be made the interest of the agents of government to conduct it upon such low [terms]. Give them a share in the profits, the rate of profit to government would be diminished, in comparison of the present rate of profit, by the amount of that share. At the same time the inducement to diligence and economy on the part of the conductors of the business would be but a fraction of what it is at present. It would be precisely as the share supposed to be given is to the whole. The funds, too, would now and then be embezzled: for it would be necessary they should be trusted with individuals, whose characters and solvency would not in every instance be justly represented to the powers above, nor, if sufficient at the time, would they in every instance continue upon the same footing of stability as they possessed at first. Even by agents of such note and in such small number as the receivers of the Land-Tax, the losses to government are not altogether inconsiderable.

By the help of a monopoly, a profit might indeed be extracted by government from this branch of trade as well as from most others. But such profit would, in every part of it, be a tax, and one of the cruellest of taxes. It has been shewn that there could be no reduction in the expenditure; but must, on the contrary, be a considerable encrease. This encrease would come altogether, in every particle of it, out of the pockets of the most distressed of mankind. It would be worse, if possible, than a tax upon justice: much worse, except in as far as those taxes have the effect of prohibitions. For the persons affected by the tax on justice are all so far distressed indeed, in as much as they are suffering under expences and vexations from which their neighbours are free, but they are not all in a state of pecuniary distress. They are mostly poor indeed, because the classes who are under a physical impossibility of buying justice at the price fixed upon it by the law, are out of comparison the most numerous in the community; but they are not exclusively poor, because they consist of poor and rich taken together, indiscriminately as they come. But the contributors to this tax upon borrowing are uniformly and without any exception in a state of pecuniary distress.

But this is not yet all. They would not only have more to pay for money, but they would have farther to go for it, longer to wait for it, and, in a thousand nameless respects, be worse treated. For the first thing that government would do, when it had got the trade into its own hands, would be to reduce the number of the shops: to reduce it to a half, or a quarter, or perhaps an eighth part of what it is at present. For here would be an appearance of economy, and the only way in which any attempt of economy could be made. The journey which a man would have to undertake, the time which he would have to consume when he should be occupied in supplying in a better way the deficiency in his subsistence, would thence be multiplied in the same proportion. At present, the sensibility of the distressed is screened from the galling eye of curiosity by obscure and multiplied places of entrance: and though the heart of the dealer must soon be steeled by habit against real tenderness, yet his trade depends upon his not letting any such deficiency be perceptible in his deportment. Under the present regimen, that is under the present liberty, we may be assured they are not only as cheap, but as numerous and as civil as they can be. Under the auspices of government, the approaches to the few stations of this kind that would be left, would be crowded by a throng of miserables exposed to all weathers, whose distresses would be aggravated by public shame: on the outside would be a perpetual scene of scrambling and disorder: within, another conflict for preference betwixt those who came for relief, and those whose duty it was, without being their interest, to administer it: while, in the room of civility, brutality in a state of perpetual irritation would rage without a bridle and without a mask. Extortion, too, in such a scene would find a most favourable field: the prices to be carried to the account of government would be fixed: but civility money to its agents would not be comprehended in the rate. Thus much as to those, who could bear the struggle for relief: but a considerable number, and those the most deeply afflicted, would forego it altogether, rather than purchase a chance of it at such a rate.

Compared with the current interest of money borrowed at large, the interest allowed the pawnbroker appears enormous: and the charge of warehouse-room to the account of which so large a proportion of it is placed, wears to an incurious eye the semblance of a pretext. But by far the greatest part of the price which the pawnbroker pays for his receipts is not seen. It is for the time he must employ in examining article by article, goods in many instances so open to deceit: for the skill he must possess in the capacity of an appraiser of such goods: for the risk he runs in the appraisement of goods, the loss on which, in case of latent damage, must be his own. He is paid, too, as the butcher is paid, for hard heartedness: for the distress he must have undergone, ere habit has blunted the edge of whatever sensibility he brought with him to the business. He is paid, as the low publican is paid, for the low company he keeps. All this while, he must be a man of property, or he would not have a capital for his trade. He must have a fortune sufficient to place him upon a line with men of education, and of a rank very considerably elevated above the lowest: while the lowest, and those in their most forbidding garb, are those with whom he has to spend the greatest part of his time.

Speaking of this branch of money-traffic as a resource open to government at large, Dr. Adam Smith quotes the republic of Hamburgh as an instance of its being employed,[1] and the profit, according to the authorities from whence he took it, exceeds indeed what in so small a district one should easily have conceived. But this profit, if the account be true, if indeed it is to be credited, we see at what a price it must be obtained. An establishment of this sort will hardly, I think, now be proposed as an object of imitation. Yet Adam Smith seems to have something of a velleity towards the adoption of it: for though he puts his negative upon it, yet this negative is grounded, not upon any reasons such as are above exhibited, but upon a supposed difference which, to the purpose of the argument, must be an insuperable one, between German and republican management on the one hand, and that in a small state, and British management in the vast mixed monarchy of Great Britain. Were this all the objection, I should by no means despair of its being overcome. But the true objection will, I think, have been seen to be deeper-rooted, and that in causes which one would hope never to see removed: for the great ground of it seems to be the excellent, and perhaps unimprovable footing upon which the business is already carried on by individuals.

III. Banking

1. *Of banking in the way of a bank of deposit: or banking on condition of returning the money on demand, without ever parting with it.*

By banking I mean the sort of business that is carried on by the corporations called banks, and by the individuals called bankers: the taking charge of money for the owner, on condition of returning it upon demand.

This branch of trade divides itself into two others according as the party who takes charge of it is allowed, or not allowed, the liberty of making use of it, that is lending it out to his own advantage.

In the first case it is keeping a mere warehouse, a mere lodging house, for money: no sort of profit can be made but in proportion as a man is paid for the keep of it: and this profit will, on account

[1] [Wealth of Nations, bk. V, ch. II, pt. I.]

of the neat expence of keeping, be far from what at first sight it may appear to be.

What a man gets is, that is, the risks and other inconveniences he frees himself from, are,

1. the risk of its being stolen;

2. the anxiety and expence of guarding it against being stolen;

3. the risk which respects the taking bad or light money. This indeed is what he will not save himself from in respect of the money he receives: but if he finds other persons employing bankers for this purpose as well as he, they may agree amongst them to take draughts upon their respective bankers instead of money, and if they agree to employ the same banker, the transaction will be the more simple, and the confidence the more entire. The same parcel of money may thus pass from hand to hand a thousand times and for any number of years without changing its place: and one operation of examining and counting will have served for the whole. A bank kept for this purpose and upon this footing is what has been called a bank of deposit: and this is the sort of bank of which the bank called the Bank of Amsterdam affords an example.

This is one of those branches of money-traffic which, where there happens to be a demand for it, government may carry on, not only to equal advantage with an individual, but with much more advantage. Under a good government, the security which the government can afford the proprietor is much more substantial than can be afforded by any individual. Government itself can not run away with it: and if run away with by any of the agents of government, government can replace it. It would be worth while, therefore, for the proprietor to give more to government for keeping his money, than it would be worth his while to give to any individual. Government could therefore get more for keeping it than any individual could: as to the difference between interested and [un]interested management, where the business is so perfectly simple and requires no endowment whatsoever but fidelity, it is in such a case as nothing: the expence need be no more to government than to the most frugal of individuals.

But government has in this case other advantages which do not apply to the case of the individual: the advantage of having a pledge for the good behaviour and loyalty of the proprietor: the advantage of saving it in times of danger for the benefit of the proprietor and of the community of which he is a member, by conveying it to a place of security: in a word, the advantage of making use of it on an occasion of extreme necessity for the common good of the whole. These are advantages which, if ever they are felt, must be felt at the time at which this paper is writing—Oct. 26, 1794—by the Bank of Amsterdam.

These advantages, it may occurr, are inconsistent with the nature of the business, as a business which consists of keeping merely, of keeping not as against the owner, but as against all the world besides. True: but in two of the instances the likelyhood is, that the owner should be still more desirous that the money should be disposed of, than the government can be to dispose of it: and were it otherwise, this is one of those cases of extreme necessity where it may be of more advantage that an engagement should be departed from for the moment, than that it should be adhered to: and as the promise of subjection, on the part of the subject, to the sovereign, may receive its dispensation from the extremity of tyranny: so may the promise of fidelity and protection for this portion of property on the part of the sovereign towards the subject find a dispensation from the extreme of disloyalty on the part of the subject, in the extreme of distress on the part of the whole state. Happiness, it must not be forgotten, is the only ultimate end as of individual action, so of political establishment: fidelity to engagements, justice in a word in all its branches, is but as a means to that end, how important an article soever in the catalogue of means. But, in short, whatever ought, in point of expediency, to be the hold of government upon money in such a case, such in point of fact is its hold: and such a hold is not of a nature to be altogether overlooked in the catalogue of inducements.

[2.] *Of banking on the ordinary terms: that is on condition of returning on demand, but with liberty to lend.*

Where confidence has got only to a certain length, and has concentrated itself as it were into a point, a bank of deposit may be the chief or only trust. Indeed, where a bank of this sort happens to have been established, and to have taken possession of the public confidence, it is natural enough that it should have the preference over the other mode. Where a man's whole fortune may be concerned, it may be worth his while to pay a moderate consideration for full security, in comparison of any inferior degree. By the price which he pays for the thus keeping of his money, he insures himself against the failure of private bankers, as by paying a certain premium he may insure himself against fire.

Where confidence has attained a fuller growth, and has spread itself over the face of society in general, a man may committ his fortune to private bankers and upon terms, which in England are the ordinary terms, without being sensible of a risk. And, in short, where, as in England, there happens to be no such thing as a bank of deposit, these are the terms upon which he must entrust his money to be kept, or upon none. In England, however, it seems to be more owing to the growth of confidence than to the want of a bank of mere deposit that the prevalence of the custom of trusting money to private bankers with liberty to lend it, is to be imputed [*sic*]. For the credit of the Bank of England can hardly be looked upon as inferior to that of the Bank of Amsterdam, even in its best days, and surely would be superior, if there were any difference, to that of any private banking company. Yet so it is that, vast as are the receipts of the Bank of England in its quality of cash-keeper, still by far the greatest quantity of money that is trusted in deposit in England, nay even in London in the very contiguity of the Bank of England, is trusted to private bankers, and that without the smallest difference in the terms.

It is certain that in a community where this degree of confidence prevails, a considerable addition to the common stock of property may thus be made. If three people can be made to believe, and kept believing for a constancy, each of them, that he may enjoy a thing at any time which, in fact, only one could enjoy at a given time, if the two others chose to enjoy it at the same time, the stock of enjoyment in the country, so far as depends upon that article, will be trebled. If the same picture could, by any optical illusion, be made to appear in the entracts [?] of three virtuosi at a time, no one of them knowing the felicity of the other, it would be exactly as if there were three pictures instead of one. To the twin brothers who took it by turns to live, as horsemen sometimes *ride* [*and*][1] *tie,* the one in the day, the other in the night, one wife might have been as good as two. *Crede quod habes et habes,* ought to be the motto of the Bank of England. One third of the quantity of money deposited with him is, according to the common calculation, what is a sufficient stock for a banker to keep by him: the rest has two proprietors who, neither of them, ever see it: the true owner and the banker, besides the borrower who pays

[1][The MS reads "in".]

interest for it, and who has it [in] his possession, or passes it on to somebody who has [the means of enabling him to put the capital to use, and thus to reap the profit out of which that interest is paid].

Be this as it may, a stock of real wealth is added to the community, by this addition to the stock of confidence. In the hands of the proprietor, neither he nor anybody would have made either interest or profit by it. For whether it is that there is too little of it to find a borrower for it, or that he knows not where to find a borrower, or has not time to look for one, or knows of none that he would trust, or can not spare it to any one for any determinate time, so it is that he can make no use of it himself, consistently with his own notions of his own convenience: for if he could, he would not part with the whole profit to another. The community, then, receives a clear addition of wealth, in the person of the banker by the interest which the banker gets, and in the person of the borrower by the profit which he, the borrower, makes, over and above that interest: and this although in any instance any specific borrower may have used it in the way of dissipation instead of thrift: for by taking this parcel for the purpose of dissipation, he spares another to equal amount which, had it not been for this, he would have taken and dissipated, thus leaving it to be employed in the way of thrift.

No government, not even that of Great Britain, has ever yet attempted to exercise this branch of money-traffic: but it follows not from hence that no government, not even that of Great Britain for example, ever can. There can not well be a more simple branch, nor [one] more within the competence of government to exercise. Compare it with the pawnbroking branch which is exercised with profit on the account of other governments, which might, as we have shewn, be exercised with considerable profit to government, though with proportionable mischief to the community, even in Great Britain—how great the difference! the extreme of simplicity in one case, almost the extreme of [complexity][1] in the other. In fact, all the difficulty, if there were any difficulty attendant on this branch, would be found already overcome in the daily practice of government, to wit in the receipt of the Exchequer: for in point of difficulty, where is the difference between receiving money on the account of another, and receiving the same money on one's own?

[1][The MS reads "simplicity" even here.]

Government, if it could get custom on one side, [i.e.] if it could get individuals to trust it with their current cash, as they trust the Bank of England and other banking houses at present, need not want for custom on the other: it need not want for borrowers. It need not, perhaps it ought not, to look for borrowers as bankers do in the discounting part of their business among individuals. It would find custom enough in this way by lending to itself, and perhaps on occasion to such a body as the East India Company, of which the responsibility might be ascertained without such a scrutiny as would be too minute for uninterested eyes. But receiving current [cash] from individuals and lending it to itself, or redeeming the annuities with which it is charged, is, in other words, the borrowing so much *pro tanto* without interest: and such accordingly would be the effect of a portion of the banking business, if taken into the hands of government. This could not be done all at once: it ought not, perhaps, if it could, that it might not occasion too sudden a reduction in the profits of the Bank of England and its private competitors. But by degrees the practice might be introduced, and the experiment made with perfect safety, as well as without injustice or undue hardship to individuals.

[IV.] Life Insurance

Another species of money dealing that might be carried on on the account of government, is that which goes commonly by the name of insurance of lives: selling for a small sum paid down in the first instance, a large sum payable in the event of a nominee's dying within a certain period, generally a year.

I mention this as a species of dealing that might be carried on on government account: but it may be a matter of doubt whether for government it would be an eligible one. The sum risqued is great: the sum received is small: the amount of the clear gain this mode of traffic can yield, consequently still smaller: the enquiries that would be requisite for the purpose of ascertaining the goodness of the life would require to be the same, and as troublesome and open to fraud, as in the case where an annuity for the whole of life were the object of enquiry. These considerations, when put together, seem to render it that sort of business which it would be more eligible to government to relinquish to the superior sollicitude and activity of private dealers.

[V.] Annuity Dealing

[A. *Sale of Life-Annuities.*]

[*Sale of life-annuities for the lives of the purchasers.*]

For life-annuities payable for the life of the purchaser there would be no want of demand: the great want is that of supply. Individuals abound, whom it would suit to purchase annuities of this description: but there are few individuals whom it can suit to sell them.

Personal security in such a case neither could be given, nor, if given, would be readily accepted. A man who lives by his industry may pay while he lives and flourishes, but how shall he pay when he is no more? The great object of the customers [i.e.] for those who would purchase annuities for life, is security, the certainty of a provision for declining years. The chief customers for annuities of this description are persons in declining years, or at least in middle age. They are no object for youth. They are not the young man's money, nor the young woman's neither. He looks for provision by industry, she by marriage, and to both prospects capital is much better suited than income for life. When provision by industry is hopeless, or the fruit of it got in without prospect of farther encrease—when marriage or the fruits of it are become hopeless: then is the time for closing the scene by an annuity for life.

Real security is what it would suit every man to accept, but what it would suit very few men indeed to give. Estates tied up by settlement can not be thus pledged beyond the life of the present owner, nor consequently for the life of another. Estates that are free a man will not [be] willing to tie up for so uncertain a term. He can do nothing with it: he can't sell it, he can't settle it, he can't charge it, he can do nothing with it to any advantage. A bare equivalent, the mere price indicated as such by the calculations, it can scarcely be worth his while to take: it can scarcely be worth his while to take a price even considerably greater than such an equivalent. Certainty, a comfortable certainty, is on the side of the purchaser: an unfathomable uncertainty on the side of the vendor. The bargain cuts into his income while it lasts: for that the annuity should ever fail of exceeding [the] interest of the money at the highest rate, is impossible: the purchaser, instead of encreasing income by the sacrifice of principal, would lessen it. It can scarcely, for instance, be worth a man's while to take 18 years' purchase: since on those terms, over and above the greatest interest he can make of the money, he must sacrifice a considerable portion of his income perhaps for his whole life, and those he leaves behind him may, instead of being gainers by the bargain, be losers after all.

At the same time, on the other hand, it can scarcely be worth the purchaser's while to give so much: since if he would content himself with an income but a small matter less, he might spare himself and those that are dear to him the mortification of sacrificing the principal.

Security in the funds may either be considered to this purpose as comprized under the appellation of real security, or places the proprietor in the same case without any difference worth insisting upon.

The public is under no such disability. Wherever there is anything to be got by selling, it can sell. Its immortality enables it to wait for the death of individuals, how long soever it may be before that event arrives. It is not tenant for life: it wants neither to sell nor to settle nor to charge: it is tenant to eternity, to the end of time. The engagements it enters into may be moulded into all imaginable forms: it can with equal facility adapt them to all the modifications of individual convenience.

Assurance, too, of punctual payment is out of all comparison: a main ingredient in the value of such bargains, especially in the case of those forlorn and helpless individuals to whose circumstances such bargains are more particularly adapted.

Sale of life-annuities to persons in classes, with benefit of survivorship: Tontines.

This species of traffic has, in many if not all the instances in which it has been practised, been found, I believe, or at least charged with being disadvantageous. But it is not, in its own nature, necessarily disadvantageous to the grantor more than any other mode. On the contrary, it has in its own nature a peculiar aptitude to be rendered advantageous. It has more of adventure in it than any other mode: and it is the nature of man to pay for adventure more than it is worth.*

*Every instance of gaming is a proof of this: those not excepted where the play is upon what, in common speech and to appearance, are equal terms. The fact is [that] it is impossible for two men to play upon equal terms: terms numerically equal are in fact disadvantageous to both. For the ratio of what a man loses,

Tontine life-annuities and simple life-annuities have this in common, that in both cases the liberation takes place of itself at the long run. In the case of Tontines, the liberation is indeed retarded: retarded in proportion as the plan of the Tontine is in respect of the survivorship advantageous to the annuitant, in comparison with ordinary annuities. But for this retardation, the seller may make himself amends by the lowness of the interest: the rate of retardation is susceptible of an infinity of modifications; and some of them may be convenient to purchasers, without being proportionably disadvantageous to the seller.

A Tontine will be clearly advantageous to the seller if, for the pleasure of embarking in this adventure, the purchaser can be prevailed on to accept of an interest not beyond the current rate of perpetual annuities. Suppose 3 per Cents as low as 60: and we have seen them under 54, and may perhaps again. If, in this state of things, a set of men could be persuaded to take 5 per Cent in this way, it is evident that the difference betwixt[1] perpetuity and the duration of the longest life is so much clear gain to government. True it is, that for all that period these 5 per Cents will be incapable of being paid off: but at such a period the probability is that money will not be to be borrowed at 5 per Cent but upon such terms as will preclude its being paid off to more advantage than the bulk of the existing stock. Either men will insist upon a non-redemption clause, or the money borrowed at 5 per Cent will be funded at 3, the lender being credited for £100 stock at 3 per Cent, paying for it only £60 in ready money.

Another supposition in which a Tontine would be advantageous to the seller, is that of the purchaser's accepting a *rate of accumulation* less than would take place, if the whole amount of the annuities left vacant by death were to be divided among the survivors. If, for example, Case 1.—on the death of an annuitant, the seller were to have the benefit of a certain share of the encrease: ½, ⅓, ¼, or a still less share.

Case 2. The accumulation stops when an augmentation has taken

if he loses, to the remainder of his fortune, is greater than that of what he gains, if he gains, is to the whole. Suppose the stake ⅓ of each man's fortune: if he loses, he loses a third, if he gains, he gains but a fourth. Suppose the stake a $\frac{1}{30,000}$ th part instead of ⅓d: though the disproportion is no longer an object, it is not less real in this case than in the other.

[1][May also read "between".]

place to a certain *amount*: suppose twice, thrice, or any other number of times the original annuity.

Case 3. The accumulation stops when the co-annuitants have arrived at a certain *age*. With my constitution, habits, and turn of mind, my powers of enjoyment, I reckon, last me, I conceive, to 65, 70, 75 years of age: to that age I may be capable of enjoying any accession of fortune: that period arrived, my projects will be at an end, novelty will no longer have any charms, change of habits will be irksome, and any farther accession of fortune will be a matter of indifference to me [since it] will find me incapable of enjoying it. This is a sort of presentiment which most men, I am apt to think, will find themselves disposed to entertain in general, how soever they may vary with regard to the age thus regarded as the *ne plus ultra* of enjoyment.

[Sale of life-annuities][1] *for a man['s] own life, to commence at the end of a certain period, if he be then alive.*

[This] case[2] includes that of the Friendly Societies. To accommodate this species of sale to the convenience of the purchaser, or rather to his physical capacity of purchasing, it is essentially necessary in the instance of that description of persons to whose case this species of traffic is more particularly adapted, that a purchase to a very small amount should be accepted; the smaller the amount, the greater the convenience to the individual.

To give this species of contract the form best adapted to the convenience of the purchaser, that is of all descriptions of purchasers, the following are among the conditions that appear to be requisite.

1. It ought to be carried on on the account of government. This for the benefit of the individual in point of security and punctuality: setting aside whatever profit may be thought fit to be taken by government.

2. A *minimum* ought to be fixed in respect to the quantum of the purchase-money. But this *minimum* ought to be fixed as low as possible: in order to accommodate it the better to the circumstances of the poorest classes, that is to those to whom the establishment would be most useful, and who are beyond comparison the most numerous.

---

[1][The MS, in fact, reads "Purchase of a Life-Annuity". But from the government's point of view, which Bentham usually occupies, the annuity is in this case one that is sold, and the purchaser is the individual customer.]

[2][The MS reads "Case 4th includes . . .".]

3. The minimum thus fixed (say for example 20s*), ought to be accepted.

4. This minimum, or any number of such minimums, ought to be multipliable any number of times.

[1]In virtue of this latitude, the plan will suit itself to the cases and situations, not only of handicraft, of the superior classes, but likewise of artists, and other professional men whose income depends upon faculties, the perfect exercise of which they are more or less liable to survive.

5. It ought likewise to be accepted at any *time*: always understood that by this acceptance of the purchase-money the course of payment appointed for the annuity need not be disturbed. This clause is adapted to the situation of those who are liable to be deficient in respect of the gift of retention, whether the deficiency be the result of moral weakness or that degree of poverty which involves the want of a place where property can be kept.

6. The requisite facilities must consequently be given for transmitting money in such small parcels to the office, whatever it be, in which the purchase is to be made, and for the transacting of the business.

[2]7. Facilities might [or] ought farther to be given for enabling the purchaser to deposit and secure his pittances, as he can save them, till such minimum as abovementioned is collected.[3]

8. Facilities should lastly be afforded for the payment of the annuity, when it becomes due, at the abod[e] of each annuitant, or at least at a place to which he can repair without consuming more time than a man in the most inferior situation can afford. A plan for the payment of annuities of this description through the medium of the Post-Office establishment has been given in the draught of the Panopticon Bill.

[9][4]. If among the objects of this branch of the proposed institution be the securing to the persons in question a sufficient provision for old age, a quantum of annuity ought to be fixed up to which, whatsoever annuities came to have been bought, should remain unalienable: the surplus above that quantum to remain free. This quantum should not be less than what is sufficient to maintain a person at

*Twenty shillings is the sum supposed in all the calculations.

[1][Later brackets.]

[2] [3][A question mark is written over this passage.]

[4][The MS reads "8".]

large upon a footing at least equal to that on which paupers are maintained in Houses of Industry.

[10][1]. The annuitant should be eased of all expence relative to the transaction of the business, at least to the extent of the above-mentioned quantum destined to secure the annuitant from becoming chargeable to the parish.

An Act was passed in the Session before last for facilitating the purchase of annuities of this description where the funds for such purchase have been formed by periodical contributions, made by individuals collected into societies by the name of *Friendly Societies* for that purpose. The Act, as far as it goes, is worthy of every commendation: but the plan of it is narrow, and the benefit of that plan short of what it might be, in comparison of the extent that might be given it in the manner above mentioned. So far as, by forming themselves into such societies, men can find the means of partaking of this benefit, it is well: but how much more extensive the benefit would be made, if, without waiting for a contingency, which in so many instances can not be realized, individuals were enabled to enjoy it each for himself and by himself. Differences of opinion, quarrels, loss of time, ill-digested and inconvenient regulations, convivial expences cutting deeply into the funds, such are among the inconveniences where the concurrence of a multitude of minds, especially of minds so uninformed and unpolished, are necessary to the performance of each man's business. Each little commonwealth is empowered, under the controul of the magistrates of the county, to make its own regulations. Extremely good: but how much better still, if all this complication could be avoided, and each man were enabled to do his own little business for himself, unencumbered by associates and without being called upon to trouble himself about any regulations. Not to insist on the peculiar danger of the present time, the danger of degenerating these Friendly Societies into societies of politicians unfriendly to the peace of the community, discussing the rights of man instead of transacting the humbler business of securing a provision for old age. Things are good or bad by comparison: good itself is bad in comparison of better.*

---

[1][The MS reads "9".]

*The hands are such in which scarce any political power can, consistently with their own good, be trusted. Science, forecast, temper, all are requisite in a high degree to the good conduct of such a business. It is a business particularly exposed to delusion, and to delusion of which the greater part of the societies already instituted with similar views were known to have become victims. Under the

[*B. Purchase of Life-Annuities.*]

[*Purchase of life-annuities for the lives of the sellers.*]

The difference between having to buy and having to sell, is perhaps in no instance so sensibly felt as in this of annuities. Buy an annuity for your own life, you will not get it, for example, for less than 16 years' purchase: sell an annuity the same day for your own life, you will not get for it so much as 8 years' purchase. Buying annuities would therefore, if it were equally secure, be at least twice as lucrative a branch of trade for government to carry on as that of selling them.

The great and only difficulty respects the security. When you sell, the security is perfect, and you have it in your own hands: it consists in the purchase-money you receive. The bargain may turn out a gaining or a losing one, according to the length of the life: but whatever you expected to have, you have: you can incurr no loss that you did not foresee.

The dangers attendant on the opposite branch of business, respect three objects: 1. the goodness of the title to the property pledged: 2. the value of the property pledged: 3. where life is in question, the goodness of the life.

That which respects the goodness of the title, is the slightest of the three dangers: it is slight to an individual, it would be still slighter to government considering the superiority of legal assistance which government would have at command, and, if government thought proper, it might be absolutely done away.

Opinions might be taken, not only of counsel, which would be presumptive, but of judges, which might be made conclusive. This might be done without injustice, if parties interested to contest the title in the event of its insufficiency, had due notice to contest it.

Neither is the danger respecting the value of the subject incapable

---

controul only of county magistrates, power is given them to frame each its own code of regulations. So many societies, so many codes: of which all may be bad, and, if any, but one so good as it might have been. The contents of these codes can not be objects of indifference. In some instances, diversity is excellence: here it is, in proportion as it prevails, departure from excellence. Since one will be better than the rest, all others ought, for that reason, to be like unto it. Even if all were upon a par in respect of individual excellence, they would be all bad in comparison of what they might be, were it only for being various. In laws, uniformity of provision, where uniformity of reason admitts of it, is one of the first of excellencies. The body of the laws as it stands at present, is not too accessible to the apprehension or the memory: it wants no addition of irregular parts to render it less accessible.

of being obviated. The subject might be valued at its saleable value by sworn appraisers, either appointed on each occasion, or, what would be more secure, appointed in the way of office: the pledge of their probity would be their continuance in office. A rule may be laid down, that the money given for the annuity shall fall short, by a certain proportion, of the saleable value of the subject pledged: and, to prevent deperition of the value through poverty or negligence, power to a person appointed on the part of government to enter and repair, after due notice, the subject, [the seller of the annuity] being thereupon to be charged with a farther annuity proportioned to the capital so expended.

Neither in that part of the danger which respects the goodness of the life, is there any thing very formidable. There is nothing but what has in practice been risqued and provided for with success. In the proceedings of the society for the insurance of lives called the Amicable Society, the goodness of the life has regularly formed the most important subject of examination: and the prosperous state of that society is sufficient proof that the want of effectual precautions against fraud in this behalf is not reasonably to be feared.

The composition of the board, the mode of proceeding, especially as to what regards the examinations, are considerations not to be neglected: but being matters of subordinate and subsequent consideration, it would be to no purpose to enter into them, unless the principle of the measure were previously approved.

[*Purchase of life-annuities for a man's own life, against the payment of a principal sum on his death.*][1]

The occasion of the demand is in this case the desire of making a provision for a third person in the shape of a principal sum once paid, instead of that of an annuity as in the first case. The first species of dealing is particularly adapted to the case of persons ill qualified for turning money to account, such as widows and antient females in general. The present species is particularly adapted to the case of persons well qualified for turning money to account, such as men in

[1][The MS, in fact, heads this page with the following title: "Purchase of a principal sum (to an amount certain or uncertain) payable on the death of the purchaser, by payment of an annuity during his life". To preserve uniformity, it was necessary to change the title so as to characterize the type of contract here under discussion from the point of view of government—the point of view usually assumed by the author.]

general, or to whom a principal sum might be particularly serviceable as a help to marriage, such as marriageable and unmarried females.

The terms of this species of dealing might be diversified by a system of modifications, corresponding to the nature of the different sorts of funds which a man might happen to have at command for the purpose of making the purchase. They are, as it will be seen, precisely the same as those that have already been detailed under the head of that species of dealing which, on the part of the individual, consists in the grant of an annuity in return for a principal sum paid to him before hand.

This difference in regard to the period at which the principal sum comes to be paid, makes a great difference with regard to the security, and much to the advantage of the other party, viz. government, who in this case has the staff of security in its hands. Security, none requisite: past payments are sufficient security for succeeding ones: goodness of title and sufficiency of value consequently out of the question. Goodness of life the only source of danger: but the danger is less in this case than in the other: for the consideration money being to the last as yet unpaid, may be made to serve as a[1] pledge and additional security against fraud. If a man dies early, and dies in consequence of a cause of mortality wilfully concealed (which, if due provision for examination has been made, can not have happened without perjury), the stipulated principal sum may be declared forfeited for the fraud: a necessary provision, if in this instance the maxim *no man shall take advantage of his own wrong,* is to have the effect it has so good a claim to.

The business of the Amicable Society [2]above-mentioned[3] is an instance, but a limited and narrow one, of this species of dealing. The terms upon which the society deals are restricted in a variety of ways, partly by the Act of Government, partly by its own caution, partly by the extent and nature of its funds. The annuities subscribed (the grants of which are stiled *policies*), must be to the amount of a precise sum, £5: a man is not permitted to have more than three of these on his own life: his age at entrance must not be above a certain age, 40: the sum paid his representatives upon his death is never a sum certain, but a sum dependent on the number of other deaths that shall happen in the year in which he dies: the number of dealers in

[1][The MS reads "an"—the words "pledge and" being additions made when the MS was read over.]

[2] [3][Later brackets.]

this way (the dealings being between the individual members on the one part, and the whole society on the other) stands limited by the charter of incorporation: originally to 2000: since, by a subsequent charter, to twice the number.

Government might carry on this species of trade free from all those restrictions, considerably to its own emolument, and to the great accommodation of individuals. It might take payment, that is the annuity given in payment, on a variety of future and even contingent or determinable terms, according to the varieties of which a man's funds for payment are susceptible. It need not restrict the quantum of the annuity to any sum: it might vary from 1s to £100 or £1000: it might admitt dealers at any age: it might make the principal sum in question a variable or a fixt one, according to the choice and convenience of the customer.

[*Purchase of interests already existing.*]

Another species of traffic that might be carried on on the account of government, is that of purchasing interests, viz. terms or contingencies already in existence. This species of dealing is in effect comprized under that abovementioned under the general name of purchase of annuities. The only difference is, that in the one case the operation of shaping the object of purchase is concomitant with the purchase, in [the] other case comes after it.

This species of money-traffic, besides affording a profit to government on the same footing with the rest, might in such hands be made to operate in a considerable degree to the benefit of individuals. The price of such contingencies, when sold by auction or otherwise to individuals, is liable to great uncertainty: sometimes it will be adequate or nearly so: more frequently perhaps it is inordinately low, to the great prejudice of the seller. This casual and inordinate depretiation would, if government were to admitt itself into the number of the purchasers, be effectually prevented. The price allowed to be given for government would of course be a somewhat inferior price, else there would be no profit: but it would be superior in many instances to that which would otherwise have been given by individuals, and less than the utmost price allowed to be given for government would in no instance be given: since the rules laid down for the trustees of government on this behalf being known, parties interested would be sure to keep the price up to that mark by employing bidders for the purpose.

[*C. Conjunction of Sale with Purchase.*]

It is by bringing these two opposite branches of trade into conjunction that the advantage they might be made to afford, may be placed in the most conspicuous point of view. Suppose to the amount of £50,000 a year of life annuities to be annually bought, no very extravagant supposition, and to the same amount sold at the same time. Those bought will have been bought, say, at 7 years' purchase, that is upon an average for £350,000: those sold will have been sold, say, at 12 years' purchase, that is for £600,000: the difference is £250,000: £250,000 then, on the above supposition, will be the gross produce of this branch of the resource.

The probability is, that the demand for annuities for the lives of purchasers will exceed, and that very considerably, the demand for ready money in exchange for annuities granted for the lives of sellers. The demand for annuities will always be the demand of thrift undisturbed by penury: the demand for money in exchange for the grant of an annuity for the life of the grantor will, in some instances, be the demand of thrift, but perhaps in more instances the demand of thoughtlessness and extravagance. But thrift is, as Adam Smith has manfully observed in the teeth of old-womanly prejudices, by far the more common case:[1] the case of thoughtlessness and extravagance, though still too common, is yet comparatively as rare as it is deplorable.

The annual amount of annuities demanded will therefore probably exceed, and probably in a very considerable ratio, the annual amount of annuities offered for money. The profit of this surplus will not stand upon so conspicuous a footing as the profit upon the quantity balanced as above: but still there will be a profit, for, upon terms that would not afford an assurance of profit, no such engagement need or ought to be made. There will therefore even here be a profit: and from so pure a source, no portion of profit ought to be despised.

Annuity Dealing: Concluding Observations.

A caution must here be given: and that not merely to serve as a caution, but because were it omitted, an objection might be apt to

[1][Wealth of Nations, bk. II, ch. III.]

take its place. This is that the tables hitherto current, if implicitly deferred to, would lead to losing bargains: they are grounded either on single observations of the rate of mortality, or [derived] from averages. But single observations are insufficient, and averages are delusive. Averages comprehend in the account unhealthy occupations (not to speak of situations) along with healthy ones: some of so pestiferous a nature as to multiply the chance of death eight, ten, or twelve fold. But the purchasers of annuities will be with very few exceptions of the most long-lived classes. Tables calculated for the meridian of the Metropolis, the great seat of hazardous and unhealthy modes of life, would be ruinous to the seller. Tables grounded on the calculated rate of mortality in this or that parish, even among country parishes, would [likewise] be an unsafe dependence. The surest basis as yet existing would be formed by the registers of the private societies for this purpose already in existence: and the superiority in point of longevity displayed in those societies, even in comparison of such country parishes as have hitherto been employed as standards, is equally surprizing and instructive.

But the evidence relative to this matter is, take it altogether, so widely different, and the difference between the rates of dealing that would be suggested by different articles of the evidence so important, and the rate of dealing grounded on the rate of mortality in one place, if the rate of mortality in another place and not that were the proper standard, would be so inordinately disadvantageous, that a compleat collection of this species of evidence by parliamentary authority seems absolutely indispensable in the character of a previous measure. And this then adds one to the many reasons for extending to England, and that with all expedition, the statistical process that has with so much success been carried on in Scotland.

The application of this caution, however, confines itself, we may observe, to any quantity of annuities that government might be inclined to sell over and above the amount (setting purchase money against purchase money) of the annuities which it should have thought fit to buy. For so long as the two amou[n]ts are equal, the rate of mortality taken for the basis of the two calculations being the same, the correctness or uncorrectness of it would be altogether immaterial.

The several modifications of money-traffic that as yet have been adopted or proposed on the account of government or of individuals, are but so many fragments of the universal plan, the outlines of which are here attempted to be given. Complicated the plan undoubtedly is, it must be confessed: complicated in proportion to the extent, variety, and therefore the utility of it. Happily, however, the complication is of that peculiar sort with which government have nothing to do, and which consequently will not, to the members of government, be productive of any expence of time or encrease of trouble. The whole of the mass is what not only may, but must be turned over in the lump to mathematicians: a class of men whose property it is neither to err nor tire: a set of labourers, whose labour, like virtue, is its own reward: who would rather work to no purpose than not work: whose labours are always at the command, not only of government, but of any individual to whom they have the remotest prospect of being of any service: to whom perplexity is pastime, utility but a corollary: and who are but too happy if, in the application of their sublime art, they can descry an occasion for the practice of beneficence.

Mathematicians, though themselves unerring, may lead men into error, and will do so, whenever the stock of *data* they have to work upon is imperfect or erroneous: but to furnish them with proper *data* is not their own province but, in a government concern like this, the province of government. But even this branch of the business will not be, all of it, to do. A great part, perhaps the greatest, will be found to be already done and accessible to the public in different publications.

The making provision for these indispensable grounds of calculation will perhaps appear not only a measure of prudence with reference to the future dealings of government, but a measure of justice with regard to the future dealings of individuals in a species of traffic to which they have been invited by a solemn invitation already given by the Legislature. I speak of the Friendly-Society Act [1]above referred to[2]; the professed object—and surely a very humane and wise one—was to induce as many individuals as possible to engage in this particular branch of the traffick in annuities. The merits of it—the design—I subscribe to most cordially: but in this particular it will perhaps appear to have been in some measure defective in solliciting men to stake their fortunes in an adventure, the conditions of which had not been rendered so well assured as they might have been, to stake their fortunes upon scanty, in truth extremely scanty evidence, where the Legislature had it in its power to afford such

[1] [2][Later brackets.]

ample evidence, in short a compleat body of evidence. If a standard had been fixed by the Act, as the Bill [below][1] referred [to] very wisely did, and had the standard given by that Bill for example been adopted, the adventurers would in so far have been secured. But no standard at all is given, not even that standard, and yet so is even that standard constructed, that the great probability is that calculations grounded [on it][2] may be productive of the severest disappointment, not to say [the] ruin of the adventurers. In those tables the supposition is, that, in country parishes, life is of so little length that, in the compass of a year, one dies in every 26½: whereas if Mr. Howlett's reports[3] be conformable to the truth, the chance is five to one that life, instead of being so short in such situations, is so long that, in the same space of time, not more than one will die in upwards of 54. But the propensity of man in general in these adventures is to be over-sanguine. The history of all the societies of this nature which I have read over in this view, is one continued proof of it: and the lower and less cultivated the class of men, the stronger this propensity. The probability is therefore that the tables the persons concerned will govern themselves by under this Act, will be more flattering than those tables rather than less flattering, more productive of disappointment and distress rather than less so. The wisdom of the Legislature has in more instances than one exerted itself in guarding men against the species of adventures familiarly termed Bubbles: in the present instance the danger is, if my apprehensions do not deceive me, that, with the purest intentions in the world, and with great wisdom displayed in the general design, it may have been leading men into Bubbles. I state the danger, if there be any, with the less reserve and in the stronger terms, inasmuch as if there be any, it is so perfectly in the power of those who [compose] the Legislature which gave birth to it, to remove it.

The Friendly Society Act, as is well known, is the same in principle, however different in detail, with the Bill which, about 20 years ago, passed the House of Commons, but was rejected by the Lords, at the instance of a noble and learned Lord of whom the country has lately been deprived.[4] The reason mentioned by the author of the Bill as

[1] [The MS in fact reads "above".]
[2] [The MS reads once more "even on that standard".]
[3] [Cf. John Howlett, An Examination of Dr. Price's Essay on the Population of England and Wales, 1781.]
[4] [Earl Camden, died April 18, 1794.]

the ground of the rejection, and the only ground I have been able to learn after asking some friends and *quondam* colleagues of the noble and learned Lord who were witnesses to the debate, was an apprehension that the funds might be dissipated in the hands in which, according to the Bill, they were to be lodged. Without staying to enquire whether this consideration, doubtless a very material and pertinent one, might not have been presented with more propriety in the character of a caution than in that of an objection, it may be not immaterial to observe that this danger, which under the present Act exists in equal, if not greater force, would upon the plan here proposed be effectually done away. Government would be the dealer, government [1]would be[2] the banker, government [1]would be[2] the security.

To save a Session, if the saving of a Session should be deemed an object, I would humbly propose that in the tenor of the Act, the settling of the specific conditions upon which the several branches of this species of traffic shall be carried on, shall be referred to the Treasury Board. But if such an authority, if pure and simple, should be thought, as I should rather suppose it would be thought, to confer too great a command over the public purse, it might be provided that the conditions shall not, in any instance, be more favourable to the individual than those contained in the tables framed by Mr Baron Mazeres,[3] and which, for this purpose, might be incorporated into the Act. I mention these tables, on account of their having already entered into the composition of [the aforementioned][4] Bill (Mr. Dowdeswell's Bill) which in the year 177[1] passed the House of Commons. It would be deemed unparliamentary, I should suppose, to refer to it in that character, [i.e.] in the character of a Bill which had passed one branch of the Legislature indeed, but had been rejected by the other, and it is under that idea I propose its being inserted in the proposed Act. But the circumstance of its having passed the Commons, though not sufficient to warrant its being referred to in that quality by the Legislature, is not an immaterial nor an useless circumstance. Though the Upper House can not be called upon to give implicit credit to the Acts of the Lower House, yet the Lower House may be disposed to give credit to its own Acts,

[1] [2][Later brackets.]

[3][Cf. Francis Maseres, Considerations on the Bill now depending in the Commons for enabling Parishes to grant Life Annuities, 1773.]

[4][The MS reads "a Bill".]

though in a former Parliament, especially where the terms may in consequence be made less burthensome to the public purse, and can not be made more so, which will save discussion and expedite the business in the committees. The object is indeed greater, but the nature of the power is the same as that granted in the Post-Horse-tax-Farming-Act, and now t'other day in the last Penitentiary Act.

[Limitations of Government Traffic]

It is of use to know, not only what can be done, but likewise what can not be done. If the former intelligence answers the call of the moment, the latter is necessary to compleat the repose and self-satisfaction of the mind. The species of resource here in question is an unburthensome one: it ought therefore to be pushed as far as it will go. *You propose to carry it thus far,* says the reader, *why carry it no farther?* An answer to this question may very reasonably be required.

Government in general is unfit for the exercise of a lucrative occupation in comparison of individuals. In particular cases it is either fitter than individuals, or even fit to the exclusion of individuals. Why unfit in general?—in what cases, and for what reasons, peculiarly or exclusively fit? If exclusively or peculiarly fit in any cases, in what cases and for what reasons?

With regard to the general unfitness of government, the reason is obvious enough, and it is tolerably conclusive: it is the comparative want of personal interest, that indispensable whetstone to ingenuity and spur to vigilance. The individual acts for himself: the agent of government acts for others. Even in the concerns of individuals, the management of an agent can not, in general, be expected to be upon a par in point of goodness with the management of the principal: but the management of the agent for government wants very much of being upon a par with that of the agent of an individual. The agent of the individual has a variety of motives for probity, diligence and zeal, none of which apply in equal degree, if in any degree at all, to the case of the agent for government. The principal of the private agent is a person whom he knows, a person whom he sees, a person who is watching over him, or ready at any time so to do: a person to whom he is obliged, a person for whom he naturally entertains an affection, who commonly has entertained an affection for, and certainly has had a good opinion of him. The principal of the government agent is an ideal being, whom nobody knows, and for whom nobody cares: who is at nobody's elbow, and [from][1] whom nobody, unless by great chance, can have any thing to fear. Government has[2] indeed its upper agents: but these agents have a variety of occupations, most of which are of a more agreeable and gracious nature than that of prying into the possible defaults and failings of their subordinates, who are of course their obsequious servants, and in many instances their creatures.

Government agency lies under still another disadvantage in point of good management, in comparison of private agency. Partly for the sake of encreasing patronage, partly for the sake of satisfying competitors, partly for the sake of affording to probity that assistance which in such a case it stands so much in need of, it has become a practice in almost every department of government, to committ agency to boards. It has been observed among insects that the more legs they have, the slower is their pace. A board is one of those insects. Every commissioner beyond the first is either a cypher, or a nuisance. But be he ever so much a cypher, he can never be so perfectly so as not to be in a great degree a nuisance. The most obsequious may be occasionally ill or habitually indolent: and the more obsequious, the more likely to be indolent. A man who is not the first, can neither originate nor help forward any thing: but he can and does stop every thing. Boards, too, have their days and their hours when they meet, or at least when they ought to meet: but to have particular days and hours when they ought to do business is, in other words, to have a multitude of days and hours when they are sure not to do business, although they might without any thing to hinder them but the rules of the board, that is, their own regard for their own pleasure. The most assiduous of boards can scarce find half the time for doing business that is found by a negligent private agent, not to speak of principals. Attend an agent for government and think whether any thing in private life can equal the indifference with which he treats your business, although, or rather because, it is the public business, even when he is best disposed towards it. Nothing can be more striking, nor any thing more natural, than the affection with which he clings to the place, even where he gets nothing by it, and the indifference with which he applies himself to the discharge of the

[1][The MS reads "for".]

[2][The word looks almost like "loves".]

duties of it. But if so it is with the single agent, how must it be with boards?

It seems contrary to the nature of things, then, that in respect of any lucrative occupation where individuals are competent to it, government management should in general be upon a par with them. What are the lucrative occupations, to the exercise of which individuals are not competent?

[In a general point of view, the] cases where government is more than upon a par with individuals [in this respect, fall under one or other of the following two categories]:

1. [Superiority on the part of government by dint of] *superior security*: where it can give a better equivalent (for instance a securer) than individuals can give.

2. [Superiority on the part of government by dint of] *superior longevity*: where it is better worth while to government to give an equivalent of a certain *kind* to a certain *amount* than it is, in general, of an individual. [The proposals above outlined find, all of them, their theoretical justification in the one, or the other, or both these circumstances.]

[Conclusion]

It is evident that of all these modes of dealing there is not one, nor, if there were ever so many of them, would be one, that was in its own nature necessarily disadvantageous to the proposed dealer, viz. government. All may be made advantageous, all, if government should be so advised, equally advantageous, to government. But as to individuals, some would be more advantageous to one individual, some to another: and the greater the variety of them, the greater the chance of hitting the *maximum* of advantage to the greatest number of individuals. The proper course, then, for government to take seems to be this: 1. to settle the number of options that shall thus be given: 2. then to frame a set of tables expressive of the *par* in point of advantage with reference to these several options: 3. then to settle what rate of advantage shall be required by government, or rather the limits within which that rate, according to the prudence of administration for the time being, shall be allowed to fluctuate: 4. then to frame a set of tables adapted to the several distinguishable points or stations within the range of fluctuation. Options being provided upon these terms, it will be a matter of indifference to government which option is embraced by the greatest number of individuals.

This sort of equality, however, need not be observed with so much rigour, but that government may exact terms more advantageous to itself in the instance of these plans where it is perceived that individuals, in sufficient numbers to render it worth while, will be content to accept of terms in fact less advantageous to them and, at the same time, more advantageous to government, than the terms of certain other plans: a supposition which, for example, we have seen realized in every case, as it should seem, of *adventure*.

But since some species of adventure are well understood to have an unfavourable influence on the morals of the people [i.e.] of those concerned in them, a caution equally obvious and important is to abstain from all species of adventure of that description as much as may be, giving the preference to innocent ones, at least as far as ever they can be made to go.

PROPOSAL FOR THE CIRCULATION OF A [NEW] SPECIES OF PAPER CURRENCY

PROPOSAL FOR THE CIRCULATION OF A [NEW] SPECIES OF PAPER CURRENCY

UNDER THE NAME OF GOVERNMENT BONDS OR EXCHEQUER NOTES

1795-96

[Table of Contents]

[I.] Government ought to have the Monopoly of Paper-Money as well as of Metal-Money

Bank notes, though bearing no interest, circulate at par. Even private notes, the notes of country bankers, do the same. Government paper not without interest, and that, even when carrying interest at upwards of 4½ per Cent, scarce bearing a premium.

To what causes are we to attribute a contrast thus striking, and so much to the disadvantage of government? Is the disadvantage remediable, or irremediable? If remediable, are there any reasons, and those sufficient ones, against its being remedied? Is not the remedying it, [in the] event of its meeting with a remedy, an event to be wished for upon the whole? Instead of bearing a share comparatively so minute as that which government bears in the business of issuing paper currency, and that upon terms comparatively so disadvantageous, ought it not rather to possess the whole? How stand these questions with reference to general constitutional principles? How stand they upon the footing of particular expediency with reference to the circumstances of the case, independently of the general expediency of adhering to constitutional principles? If obtainable and desirable, by what means can such an extension of the government currency be attempted with the greatest prospect of success? Of what nature are the advantages to be derived from it, and to what length are they capable of being carried?

[1]The advantage is the first object. It is this alone that gives importance to the rest. Call the total present amount of the paper circulating without interest	20 millions
Whereof Bank paper	15 millions
Paper of the country bankers	5 millions
Annual amount of the interest at 5 per Cent, if it bore interest at 5 per Cent, the present rate ...	[£]1,000,000
Five per Cent in round numbers may, for the present purpose, be reckoned the interest government pays at present for the money it borrows	

[1] [2][Crossed out, probably by Bowring.]

upon, or rather purchases upon, the ordinary terms, viz. that of granting perpetual but redeemable annuities: for [£]20,000,000 of ready money, it pays interest in that way to the amount of ...	£1,000,000
Four per Cent is the interest it pays at present upon such of its own paper currency as it emitts and circulates under the name of Exchequer Bills: which, upon the [£]20,000,000 above supposed, would be	£800,000
Gain, upon the supposition of its circulating upon the footing of Exchequer Bills as much as is at present circulated without interest	[£]200,000
Gain upon the supposition of its circulating the same quantity at 3 per Cent	[£]400,000
Gain at 2 per Cent	[£]600,000
Gain at 1 per Cent	[£]800,000
Gain on the supposition of circulating without paying interest, being the footing on which Bank Notes circulate	[£]1,000,000[a]

If [such] advantage, on the whole or any part of it, could be gained, would there be any harm in gaining it? Let us open, in the first place, the great book of the Constitution. Constitutional laws, to be the same in point of principle at all times, should vary as the times, and adapt themselves to the times.

One of the most unquestioned and most innocent prerogatives of the Crown, acting in this as in all other instances under the controul of Parliament, is the monopoly of the coinage.* When there was no currency but metal, the Crown had the sole issuing of that currency: the Crown, therefore, to preserve the prerogative *in statu*

*This branch of the prerogative had its origin in force, with little or no regard to public utility. But so it is with almost every other branch: the King took it, not from any view of the general advantage the nation would reap from his taking it, but because he found his particular account in taking it. But the utility of the institution is not the less real, less really among the effects of it, from the not having been the *final* cause.

The monopoly of the metal coinage, it is to be observed, is confined to the fabrication of such coin as shall be legal tender, i.e. as a creditor shall be obliged to receive in satisfaction of his debt; for as to the fabrication of medals of the same intrinsic value, or purporting to be of the same intrinsic value, there is nothing against it in law, so long as the impression upon them is not an imitation of the medals made on government account. The monopoly then consists in the taking the coin fabricated on the King's account for the sole subject of that part of the law of contracts which prescribes what acts shall amount to the payment of a debt.

quo, ought to have the sole issuing of that currency: at any rate so long as the extension of the monopoly to this modern branch is not attended with greater inconveniences than what accompany its application to the old one.

Nor let it be thought that the expediency of this extension rests upon the mere general ground of adherence to principles sanctioned by general acquiescence—of keeping matters in respect of government as they are; in a word, of keeping up the *vis inertiæ* of government. If the prerogative had utility for its support in its original shape, it is recommended by equal utility in the proposed supplemental one. The use of the prerogative in respect of metal money was, by suppressing counterfeits, to guard the people against loss. In the instance of paper currency, the use and need of it is the same.

The loss to which the subject was exposed by metal money coined by individual hands, was that of the difference between genuine metal and of full weight, and the coin of light weight or base alloy that might be apprehended from individuals. The loss to which the subject is exposed from bad paper currency is of the same kind, but much heavier in degree. Loss by bad metal currency distributes itself in small parcels, and, by the minuteness of the portions to which it adheres, falls with a gentle and almost imperceptible stroke. Loss by bad paper falls in much larger masses. Loss by bad copper is as nothing: loss by bad silver is no great matter: even loss by bad gold is light in comparison of the average rate of loss upon a bad bill.

The justification of the monopoly in the new case is stronger than in the old one, in every point of view. The loss that government endeavours to save the subject from by the monopoly of the metal coinage, it succeeds but very imperfectly in saving him from. Coiners are punished as traitors, and yet the country swarms with coiners. The copper is, three-fourths of it, bad: the pretended silver, a great deal of it, worth nothing, and there is scarce any that is not counterfeit and light. Saving the subject from bad paper is most perfectly in [the government's][1] power. Let it but supply the market with its own paper, and a simple prohibition will keep all other paper out of the market most effectually. Against the fabrication of bad coin, capital punishment is expended in vain: against the fabrication of paper, which, under the danger of its turning out so much

[1] [The MS reads "its".]

worse than bad coin, it seems expedient to prohibit, a mere pecuniary penalty will be perfectly sufficient.

[1]Will the prerogative, when extended to paper, be abused? No more than it is now that it confines itself to coin. [3]Good faith as towards subjects is a jewel too deeply set ever to drop out of the British Crown: it can as little be expected to shake in any one part as to drop out altogether[4].

[5]At the time this branch of the prerogative took its rise, currency had but one form and one species of subject, that of the pretious metals. For a long time it has had a partial substitute, to wit paper, and that to a value, or at any rate to an amount, little, if at all, inferior to that of the article of intrinsic use[2]. Hence it is that this branch of the prerogative, though nominally the same now as heretofore, has in reality been stript of half its power: originally it embraced the whole of the currency: and now it includes scarce half[6].

If, in the whole scheme of government, there be any where an instance where the idea started by Machiavel [7](and in the mind of Machiavel who broached it, as well as of so many others who have repeated it, seemingly but a loose one)[8] is susceptible of a determinate signification and an useful application, the idea of the expediency of bringing back institutions to the standard of first principles, the present will, I believe, be found among the number. Compare the advantage resulting to the community from the monopoly in the respective instances of the two species of currencies, we shall find it in every point of view greatly superior in the instance of the paper currency, [the currency] of factitious[9] value, to what it is in the instance of the currency of natural value, the metal currency.

[II.] Paper Money—why not circulated by Government without Interest, as well as by Individuals

The contrast between the terms on which Bank paper is received, and those on which government paper is received, has been already brought to view. The inferiority of the latter can never be owing to any inferiority in point of credit. The credit of the Bank of England can never be greater than that of the Government of Great Britain.

[1] [2][A question mark is written over this passage.]

[3] [4][Put into brackets at a later time.]

[5] [6][Crossed out, probably by Bowring.]

[7] [8][The brackets are of a later date.]

[9][Bowring's text, *Works* III, p. 149, reads "fictitious" instead of "factitious", although the MS leaves no doubt as to the correct version.]

One reason that may save the looking out for others is this, that the capital of the Bank having been, the greatest part of it, laid out in the purchase of government annuities, the Directors of that Company can never distribute these annuities in the shape of dividends amongst the stockholders any further than as they have received them from government. A man who would trust government with his whole fortune, to the amount perhaps of £100,000, will not give more than a few shillings above par for an Exchequer Bill for which he will receive interest at the rate of 4½ per Cent, at the same time that he will give £100 for a Bank Note to that amount, for which he can receive no interest. The same man, too, will not only take a promissory note from that great Company, of whose opulence the opinion is so universal and so high, but perhaps even the note of some country banker, of whom, except from such his note, he has no knowledge. The cause of the disadvantage government paper lies under in this respect, in comparison of Bank paper, can never, therefore, consist in any inferiority in point of credit. It must be looked for, therefore, in some other circumstance.

There are several circumstances which cooperate towards giving to the Bank paper the perfect aptitude it possesses with respect to circulation. The want of any of these properties, or the possession of it in an inferior degree, will account *pro tanto* for the inferiority of the terms upon which the government paper possesses the degree of circulation it has obtained.

These properties seem to be: 1. the being payable [1]to the bearer[2] on demand; 2. the being transferable, like coin, from hand to hand, without indorsement or any other formality; 3. the being issued for such small sums as £20, £10, and now lately even as low as £5; 4. the being impressed on paper which, in point of size, is neither so large as to take up much room, nor so small as to be liable by its minuteness to escape observation, and be lost, and in point of thickness is thin enough to bear folding without cracking, at the same time that it takes up little room in the pocket or the pocket-book: nor is it yet so thin but that it will bear to be written upon, by which means any proprietor may put his mark upon the note as a means of identification, to enable him to vindicate his property in it, in case of loss; 5. its having been so long in possession of the national confidence, and that to such a degree as to be the only paper which individuals all over

[1] [2][Put into brackets at a later date.]

the Kingdom are universally in the habit of accepting upon the same terms as the current coin*.

An Exchequer Bill (I speak of those issued in virtue of the Statute of last year) bears interest to the amount of upwards of 4½ per Cent: the interest upon a Bill of £100 being 3d a day: which, by the year, makes £4 11s 3d: and it is made payable to bearer. Upon hearing thus much of it, what one should suppose is, that it should bear a premium to the amount of the interest: since a Bank Note for that sum payable to bearer and carrying no interest bears no discount, but is received at par. Upon being informed that, though an Exchequer Bill does indeed bear a premium, that premium is very far short of being equal to the interest, a natural inference would be, that the difference was owing to the difference between the credit of government, and the credit of that opulent, but, in comparison with government, private body.

[1]That no such difference in point of credit is the cause of such difference of market price, is, however, evident beyond doubt, and that from this one circumstance. While the depretiation of Exchequer Bills, in comparison of Bank Notes, is to such an amount, and such an amount only, that, by purchasing them, a man makes almost, but not quite, 4 per Cent, the depretiation upon Navy Bills upon the new establishment (called in the Alley *New Navy*) is such that, by buying them, a man makes at the rate of from 5¼ to 5½ per Cent by the year: difference from 1¼ to 1½ per Cent. But, in these two cases, the security is one and the same: it is government security in both. Difference therefore in point of security and credit is not the cause of the difference in point of current price between government paper and Bank.[2]

The depretiation seems to be owing to the combined influence of several causes, viz. 1. the want of Bills for small sums of a size adapted to the general run of the demand; 2. the not being made payable to the bearer at any time, but only after the interval of about half a year after issuing; 3. the want of that simplicity in respect of the terms and mode of payment, which is observable in the paper of the Bank of England; 4. to which may perhaps be added something (of which presently) in the sensible properties of the instrument itself by which the engagement is expressed.

---

*A Bank Note has other properties calculated to guard it against forgery: these will be spoken of a little lower down, but do not belong to the present place.

[1] [2][Crossed out, probably by Bowring.]

That the want of sufficient division has a very considerable share in the production of the effect, can scarcely be a matter of doubt. Exchequer Bills are all to an amount, viz. £100: they are never issued for any less sum. Bank Notes are issued for £100, for £50, for £20, for £15, for £10, and now, within this twelvemonth, or thereabouts, for £5. In the instance of Exchequer Bills, the magnitude of the sum is of itself sufficient to render this species of paper unfit for general circulation: it is of itself sufficient to throw it out of the ordinary current of private dealings. It is a commodity so few are qualified to bid for that those few can not but enjoy by that means a considerable advantage. It is so few men's money, that that circumstance is of itself sufficient to prevent this species of paper from being generally known. Accordingly the circulation of it is confined in great measure, for aught I know, to the Metropolis: it is confined to the neighbourhood of the Alley: to bankers, stock-brokers, and the other classes of money-dealers. A man may have enjoyed a large income, a man may have had very extensive dealings in the way of trade, and yet go out of the world without having ever set eyes on an Exchequer Bill.

The Bank, it may be said, issues Notes for sums as large as £100: indeed for sums to a prodigious degree larger: and yet there is no more discount upon these large Notes of the Bank, than upon the very smallest ones. True: but then, along with these larger Notes, the Bank issues the smaller Notes abovementioned, and that in such plenty, as to be in readiness for change of the larger Notes, whenever and by whomsoever such change is wanted: nor are such larger Notes ever issued to any one who chooses rather to have the smaller Notes.

The small Notes of the Bank, it may be observed in reply, afford no facility to the circulation of the large Notes of the same Company that the Exchequer Bills of government do not equally possess: for, admitting that the value of an Exchequer Bill of £100 would not be quite so great, setting aside the article of interest, as that of a Bank Note to the same nominal amount, still the Exchequer Bill has a known value, and a value in the market, as experience shows, not much less than that of the Bank Note. It ought therefore to be as easy, were this all, to find change for a £100 Exchequer Bill in Bank Notes, as for a £100 Bank Note.

To this it may be rejoined that the facility in the two cases is not in truth alike. Every body being equally acquainted with Bank

Notes, any body who has £100 to keep for a little while, before he will have to change it, will as readily take it in a single £100 Bank Note, as in ten £10 Notes: for though he may never have seen such a thing as [a] £100 Bank Note before in his life, yet the perfect resemblance it bears in every respect but the quantity of paper, engraving, and writing, to the ten £10 Notes, makes it, so long as he does not want to change it, exactly the same thing to him: the security is the same, the conditions and time of payment is the same, and, what is no small matter, the appearance of the instrument is exactly the same, the variation in respect of the sum excepted—a sort of variation which he is already accustomed to by the smaller Notes. A man who has a £100 Bank Note need not fear, therefore, the getting smaller Bank Notes to the same amount from any one who has them, and is in no immediate want of such lesser sums in the way of change: whereas a man who has only a £100 Exchequer Bill, may see very good grounds for doubting whether he shall be able with equal facility to get such change for such Exchequer Bill: since among twenty people to whom he may offer it, every one may perhaps be altogether unacquainted with it, and, if not absolutely decided in regarding it as a species of paper of less value, may still be unwilling to give himself the trouble of satisfying himself whether it be of equal value or not.

The want of sufficient assurance of putting off this species of paper with as much facility as a Bank Note to the same amount, gives this species of paper a disadvantage, or at least is among the causes which contribute to give this species of paper a disadvantage in point of prompt circulation, in comparison of a Bank Note. But since, accordingly, the Exchequer Bill is not, like the Bank Note, every man's money, the consequence is, that, in order to find out a person whose money it is, it must be sent to the great market for money in different shapes, the Alley: it must go into the hands of a broker: and the expence, but much more the time (for the expence is but $\frac{1}{2000}$ per Cent) places it thus on a ground of considerable disadvantage in comparison of the Bank Note.

So far as this disadvantage goes, instead of operating as current cash, it has the effect only of so much capital in the funds, operating in the shape of principal money, as carrying interest, and serving as a source of income. In this quality, the price it bears will approach to that of stock—to that of a government annuity given in exchange for so much money, rather than to the price of so much money receivable at any time. It will, however, in point of price, have the advantage of such an annuity, and that on several accounts: it is transferable with so much less trouble and expence, and the value of it rises by keeping, according to a visible and certain law, in a visible and certain proportion, and that day by day: whereas the price of so much stock, though it may rise in much the same degree upon the whole as the period of payment approaches, yet, as it can rise by no less intervals than ⅛ per Cent, amounting in 5 per Cents to $\frac{1}{40}$ of the whole, it can rise by no shorter steps than one step of at least nine days, and even then the rise is so liable to be disturbed by fluctuation as to be, in the character of a rise proportioned to [the] lapse of time, and the consequent accrual of interest, in a manner imperceptible.

It might be thought, that though the £100 Exchequer Bill is, for the reasons above pointed out, not every body's money—not the money of so many people as the £100 Bank Note, still it might be worth so many people's money as to bear the same price, or nearly the same yet still not to the same degree as the Bank Note: it is their money dealers in general. It certainly is the money of bankers to a degree: yet still not in the same degree as the Bank Note: it is their money upon a footing more nearly approaching to that on which so much stock is their money, than that on which the Bank Note is their money. A banker may lay out [his][1] money in this way for the purpose of making it produce an interest: and thence he may lay out in this way such part of his receipts as he allows [himself] to lay out for his own benefit. But [he] can not lay out in this way, as he may in Bank Notes, any part, or at least any considerable part, of the money which he deems it necessary to keep by him in readiness to answer drafts: because, as has already been observed, he can not be equally sure of the Exchequer Note's being accepted of by a person who comes with a draft, as he can of the Bank Note's being so accepted of.

He can keep it therefore upon no other footing than that of a title deed to a principal sum bearing interest: in a word, than as a source of interest. But in the capacity of a source of interest, it must bear the interest it purports to give, or at least a very considerable part of it: if it did not, it would not answer the purpose: it there-

[1][The MS reads "their" and, in the following cases, "'themselves" and again "they".]

fore can not bear, in this quality, a premium eating out that interest, or any considerable part of it. It may indeed be worth his while to take somewhat less interest upon such a security than he could make of the same money in the funds, because it will cost him rather less time, and at any rate less money, to convert it into cash at any time, than to convert into cash so much money in the funds: and this accordingly is the case: a man makes almost 1 per Cent less in this way, than by buying into the funds.

At the same time, the circumstance of the Exchequer Bill's not existing to any amount less than £100 can not, it may be thought, be the sole cause of its depretiation in comparison with the Bank Note: for a Navy Bill may be issued for any sum, however small: and yet the depretiation upon Navy Bills, even the new Navy Bills, is still greater than upon the Exchequer Bills. It must be allowed, however, that though Navy Bills may be demanded and issued for sums much smaller than the amount of an Exchequer Bill, for sums for example of an amount not greater than that of the smallest Bank Note, yet in fact there are not many issued for such smaller sums.

As to the circumstance of the Exchequer Bill's not being payable on demand, [or rather of its] not being payable in fact till half a year after the time of its being issued, neither is this circumstance sufficient of itself to account for the depretiation. Taken by itself, it seems in fact to have but little or no influence. If this were the sole cause of the depretiation, this cause being removed, the effect would cease: before the time when principal and interest became payable, or at least at the time of issuing, an Exchequer Bill would indeed bear no premium: but no sooner were that period arrived than it would bear a premium, and that equal to the interest. This, however, is so far from being true, that, as far as I can learn, the arrival of this period makes in this respect no perceptible change. At the time of issuing, the Exchequer [Bill] bears a small premium equal to about ½ per Cent, reducing the [rate of] interest that can be made of it from about 4½ to about 4: at the arrival of the time of payment, it continues to bear that premium, but does not bear any more. The truth is, that the inconvenience of not being payable for half a year is foreseen, and as far as it is reckoned for any thing, allowed for from the first: it has already taken its station among the commodities of the Alley, as a paper fitter to constitute a source of income than for general circulation, and this station the change in its nature, operated by the arrival of the time for payment, is not able to remove it from.

The comparative want of simplicity, in respect of the terms and mode of payment in comparison of a Bank Note, can not but have some share in the comparative depretiation of an Exchequer Bill. To be adapted to general circulation, an engagement of this sort ought to be such, if possible, as every body of a condition high enough to have property to such an amount pass through his hands, will be able without effort to apprehend. The engagement taken by the Bank, a promise on the part of an individual to pay the sum in question on demand, and that to the bearer by whom the instrument of engagement shall be produced, possesses this property in the highest degree of perfection that can be conceived. In the instance of the Exchequer Bill, several circumstances concurr in keeping down the terms of the engagement considerably below that mark of perfection. It is to be paid indeed to the bearer, that is, if it be paid at all. But will it be paid at all? This appears to depend upon a variety of contingencies, viz. if aids happen to be granted for the service of the next year, then out of the first of such aids. But will any such aids be granted? This is expressly stated to be a matter of uncertainty: it is stated that perhaps no such aids may be granted before the 5th of July in the next year: provision is accordingly made for that contingency, and, if no such aids [be granted], then the money is to be paid out of a fund called the Consolidated Fund. But if paid out of this Consolidated Fund, when is it to be paid? and where? and by whom? These are questions it leaves in utter darkness. Is it, too, in other respects a good Bill? Grounds of suspicion, and those of the strongest kind, present themselves upon the face of it. A period is expressly avowed, during which it will not be accepted of as such by the very government that issues it. It is not to be current, or pass in any of the public revenues, aids, taxes, or supplies whatsoever, or at the receipt of the Exchequer, before the 6th day of April in the next year, that is, for half a year and upwards. Before that period, then, it will not be treated as a good Bill; this it expressly says: will it afterwards? and when?—of this nothing is said: it is left open to conjecture.

Nor is this all: [here is] another ground of uncertainty and suspicion. How soon it is to be paid, it does not state, but what it does state is that it is not to be paid till another sum, amounting perhaps to several millions, has been paid. "Registered and payable after

1,754,400," says a Bill, No. 17545, I have before me. When is it, that this £1,754,400 will be paid? This again is all in darkness.

To a person acquainted with the mechanism of government, all these points are in a state of perfect clearness: he knows that with all these apparent difficulties and uncertainties, the Bill that presents them is at least as good as a Bank Note. But among persons who are not unaccustomed to the simple language of a Bank Note, not one out of a hundred, or perhaps a thousand, has any such acquaintance with the mechanism of government.

Even the introductory words, inserted with the view of indicating the authority on which the Bill is issued, are of a nature more likely to excite doubt and difficulty in an unlearned mind, that is, in the mind of the bulk of readers, than to command confidence. "By an Act of Parliament, Tricesimo quarto Geo. III. Regis. For raising a certain sum of money by Loans or Exchequer Bills for the service of the year 1794." In this formidable mixture of English and Latin, interlarded with terms of art and the language of finance, a man is sent to an Act of Parliament, to know whether the Bill will be paid or no, and if so, when and how and by whom it will be paid, the rather as in the Bill itself no answer to any of these questions is to be found: and upon his putting a right construction upon a Revenue Act of Parliament, he who perhaps never read an Act of Parliament in his life, and almost certainly (if not a lawyer) is not in the habit of trusting himself to find out the sense of an Act of Parliament, depends his knowing whether the Bill will, or will not, be paid, and so forth. It is a case for him to consult his lawyer upon, as he would think it necessary to do upon other Acts of Parliament, and where property to much less amount than £100 (the amount of an Exchequer Bill) was at stake. But the occasion does not allow time for consulting a lawyer: and if it did, the expence of consulting him would eat a good way into the profit to be made by the interest of which the Bill holds out the prospect, in addition to the principal that would be promised by a Bank Note to the same amount.

[1]The instance of a Navy Bill may perhaps be thought to afford another ground for attributing a considerable share in the comparative depretiation of the value of an Exchequer Bill to the want of simplicity in the statement of the conditions and mode of payment[2]: the depretiation in the instance of the Navy Bill going so far, that from 5¼ to 5½ per Cent may be made by taking Navy Bills in

[1] [2][Crossed out, probably by Bowring.]

payment, at the same time that scarce 4 per Cent can be made by taking Exchequer Bills. But perhaps in the instance of the Navy Bill the case may be, that a still greater share in the depretiation is borne by a cause that remains now to be touched upon in the last place.

The fourth and last of the causes that have been mentioned as appearing to concurr in the production of the depretiation in question, is the quality of the instrument in respect of its sensible properties: the bulk and thickness of the paper. A Bank Note is perhaps in respect of both these properties as convenient for circulation as can be imagined. In point of size and thickness neither so large as to take up an inconvenient quantity of room in the pocket or pocket-book, not even when a considerable number are taken together, nor yet, on the other hand, so small as to be liable to escape notice and be lost: while, by reason of its extraordinary thinness (besides being so much the better guarded against fraudulent alteration, which is the principal object) it is the better adapted to bear folding to reduce it to a compass fit for the pocket and pocket-book, without cracking at the edges, and so coming to pieces.

In these particulars, the difference between the Bank Note and the Exchequer Bill is not great: though, as far as it goes, rather to the disadvantage of the Exchequer Bill. In point of size, the Exchequer Bill is much upon a par with the Bank Note: not quite so long, a little broader—these differences [are] not at all material; but the paper is a great deal thicker, rather of a thick and brittle sort than otherwise, so much so as to be to appearance more exposed to crack than any of the papers commonly used as writing papers.

In the Bank Note, too, there is something in the neatness of the engraving, and the conspicuous and emphatic display of the sum, that can not but be particularly attractive and fascinating to an ordinary eye. In the Exchequer Bill, there is no such display of the sum, and the impression of the long-winded explanation of the conditions of payment has nothing particular to recommend it.

A Navy Bill is in all these points in a most remarkable degree inferior even to the Exchequer Bill. It is, the whole of it, in ordinary writing, without any of those engraved embellishments which decorate in a small degree an Exchequer Bill, but in a much higher degree a Bank Note. It has, in short, exactly the appearance of an ordinary tradesman's bill. It occupies, too, a whole sheet of folio paper; and, what is more, this sheet is not transferable from hand to hand without an assignment in form, occupying another sheet. Either of these sheets forms a mass so much too large for the pocket or the pocket-book, as to unfit the instrument in a very considerable degree for general circulation: both of them together consequently still more. The assignment, too, instead of being expressed in the concise significance of the mercantile stile [*sic*], is loaded and perplexed with the superfluities which characterize lawyer's language. But wherever the hand of the lawyer is visible, diffidence follows of course.

There is another point very material to the purpose of circulation, in respect of which the Navy Bill is in a very remarkable degree inferior to an Exchequer Bill. An Exchequer Bill is always for an even sum—£100—a circumstance which, of itself, affords a great facility in respect to the calculation of the interest, in comparison of a Bill for an odd sum, such as Navy Bills are; they being issued for any sum as it may happen, according to the value of the goods that happen to have been furnished upon the occasion by the person to whom the Bill is issued. To this facility is added another still greater, and which seems to have been the result of design and calculated for the purpose of this very advantage: I mean the reckoning the interest by the day, and putting it at an even sum, viz. 3d: making *per annum* £4 11s [3]d[1], instead of reckoning the interest by the year, which would have rendered the interest *per diem* an uncalculable fraction. In the Navy Bill on the other hand, the principal itself is commonly a fraction, consisting of an odd number of pounds, shillings, and pence: the interest *per diem* consequently a most intractable fraction, not to be computed with any tolerable facility but by persons particularly conversant in arithmetical operations.

Till very lately, the price of a Navy Bill was so much lower than that of an Exchequer Bill that, by buying a Bill of the former kind, a man might sometimes make as far as 9 per Cent. At that time it carried no interest till half a year after it was issued, at which time it began to carry 4 per Cent, and the time of paying off the principal was altogether uncertain: at that time the depretiation on it was more than twice as great as that upon an Exchequer Bill. At present, according to the new plan, it is put exactly upon the same footing, as well in point of immediate commencement of interest as in point of certainty of the time of payment in respect of the principal, as an Exchequer Bill: and yet, as we have seen, the depretiation is from 1¼ to 1½ per Cent greater, from 5¼ to 5½ per Cent being to be made

[1][The MS in fact reads "6d." Cf. above, p. 160.]

by Navy Bills, while scarcely 4 per Cent is to be made by Exchequer Bills. The two species of currency being in point of security precisely the same, both being issued by government, and the good faith of government being in both cases equally pledged for full and punctual payment, the cause of so great a difference in point of depretiation is to be looked for solely in circumstances of an inessential and apparently trifling nature, such as those that have just been pointed out.

[III.] Remedies proposed to the Depretiation [of] Navy Bills [and other types of Government Currency]

Upon the whole, comparing what the state of the paper currency is, with what, upon this view of it, there seems some ground for supposing that it might be, we see a very great loss, or, to speak in the most moderate way, a very great failure of advantage, annually incurred by government. The avoiding of this loss, the attaining of this advantage, so far as it may prove attainable, would surely be an object not altogether unworthy the trouble of consideration, or even the hazard of experiment.

I shall here proceed to state a variety of measures which may, any or all of them, be taken with this view, leaving the determination in respect of eligibility to those to whom it appertains.

One is, to cease issuing Navy Bills altogether, paying Navy debts with Exchequer Bills. Upon this measure alone, if it can be effected, the saving would amount to from 1¼ to 1½ per Cent upon all the paper that would otherwise be issued in the shape of Navy Bills.

This, it may occurr at first sight, will make a proportional glut of Exchequer Bills: a glut which, it may be apprehended, may produce a depretiation as great as, or still greater than, that at present existing in the instance of Navy Bills. But of the money which would otherwise have been employed upon Navy Bills, not a penny can now be laid out in that species of security any longer. It must therefore betake itself to some other employment: and a part at least, if not the whole, it can not but be supposed, will apply itself to the additional mass of Exchequer Bills. It may be said the *whole,* and *that* notwithstanding the superior price of Exchequer Bills: since Exchequer Bills yielding only 4 per Cent, are notwithstanding worth as much, as appears by the course of the market, as Navy Bills yielding 1¼ per Cent more. The argument, however, will probably be found not to be universally conclusive: for the market of funds and private security are equally open, and many of those who at present prefer Navy Bills to these two species of security as well as to Exchequer Bills, will betake themselves to one or other of these other species of security rather than to Exchequer Bills, if Exchequer Bills retain the same inferior price as at present. Their object is to make as good interest for their money as they can: at present they accept of Navy Bills, because they can make ¼ per Cent more by them than by discounting the paper of individuals, for example: but when they can not make their 5¼ per Cent upon Navy Bills, they will rather make their 5 per Cent upon private paper than put up with 4 per Cent from Exchequer Bills. It may occurr, on the other hand, that this conflux of new money upon private paper will throw an equal part of the old money which would otherwise have been employed on private paper, upon Exchequer Bills: but this will hardly be found to be the case. Unless the influx of money upon private bills were to lower the discount upon such bills, no such influx could tend to throw any money out of that market into any other. But it does not seem likely that any such influx should produce any such depression. For while stocks are so low as to pay almost 5 per Cent, and Navy Bills ¼ per Cent more, the probability is that a quantity, and that a very considerable one, of undoubted private bills are unable to meet with discounters: so many, that all the money that can be thrown out of the market for Navy Bills, will not be sufficient to answer the demand.

On the other hand it must be allowed that private bills are not the money of every man whose money Navy Bills and Exchequer Bills are. For when a man has once parted with his money by discounting of a private bill, say that has six weeks to run, he has no way of getting it back during the six weeks: whereas when he has laid it out in the purchase of Navy Bills or Exchequer Bills one day, he may get it back the next, if any sudden occasion for calling in his money should present itself. Upon the whole, then, the probability seems to be that, in the event of the conversion of the present stock of Navy Bills into Exchequer Bills, the latter would not preserve the whole of their advantage, nor lose the whole, but preserve a part, insomuch that not the whole of the 1¼ per Cent or 1½ per Cent would be gained by government by the operation, but only a certain part of it: what precise part of it is, I believe, more than any one will undertake to say with confidence.

Were this course to be pursued, the simplest mode of pursuing it would, it should seem, be this: an Act to be passed, in virtue of which the Navy Board, instead of giving a Navy Bill, [were] to give a draught upon the Auditor of the Exchequer: the Auditor, in payment of such draught, to make out an Exchequer Bill. Exchequer Bills, it may be said, are not now made out but to a certain amount, predetermined by Parliament. But, Parliament consenting, it would be just as easy to make out bills to an amount uncertain in the shape of Exchequer Bills as in the shape of Navy Bills.

Of this measure, were it successful to the utmost possible extent, the profit would be small in comparison of the profit of doing away the depretiation to the amount of 4 per Cent, suffered by Exchequer Bills in comparison of Bank Notes: in other words, of obtaining for government paper a general circulation upon a footing with that possessed at present by the Bank of England without stint, and by country bankers in a limited degree. An attempt of this sort is equally susceptible of a variety of shapes.

One is to pass an Act for issuing, and to issue accordingly, government notes to a limited amount, and that at first a small one, say one million, payable to bearer at a certain office, exactly upon the plan of Bank Notes. They should be made at the same time universally and *immediately* receivable as cash in all offices and by all agents of government. On the other hand they will in this case be tendered of course by all such offices and agents, in as far as they have money to pay on account of government. The obligation of accepting a certain number for circulation might be tacked to a loan, to the sale of lottery tickets, or to any other such negotiation, should any advantage be expected from any such forced mode of circulation.

The experiment, it may occurr, will be an expensive one, since, as nothing can be foreknown with regard to the degree of its success, cash must be provided beforehand and kept in store, sufficient to answer all demands that can be made, as well as to cover all deficiencies that can take place on this account in the receipts of government. But to be thus in readiness, it must have been borrowed, which it can not be at a less rate than 5 per Cent, to which, if, in order to induce people to take them in the infancy of the experiment, it should be necessary to allow a discount on them, there must be added the amount of that discount.

It should seem, however, neither proper nor necessary to allow any such discount. Not proper, because if the Notes thus issued were to be received at any time by the government offices as cash, or changed at the new office appointed for that purpose, the allowance of the discount would be a present made to the bearer without any advantage. Whoever took a bill with such discount, though it were but an ⅛ per Cent, would immediately take it to the office where he could get the full amount of it: allowing the discount would be paying so much porterage for carrying the bill from one office to another. As any discount, even the smallest, would therefore be too much, and the allowance of it improper, it should seem accordingly not to be necessary: inasmuch as it can not well be imagined that a man would refuse at one office a bill, of which he could get the full amount at another.

As to their coming to bear a discount in the hands of individuals after having been taken by individuals at full value, the loss, were such a thing to happen, could be but very small, and even that would not fall upon government. In remote parts of the country even Bank Notes have been known, and that within this year or two, to bear a discount. In the same manner, and from similar causes, whatever were the causes, might such Exchequer Notes come to bear a discount in similar situations. But, in or near the Metropolis, no such discount was ever borne by Bank Notes. Why? because the office of the Bank was at hand; and as at [that] office a man might always have the full amount for his Note on presenting it, of course no man would take, or expect another to take less. The facility of changing being by the supposition the same for these Exchequer Notes, the impossibility of their bearing a discount would in the same situation, the Metropolis and its neighbourhood, be the same.

It is scarce conceivable, however, that there should be any difficulty in the circulation of such Notes. Private bankers in the country have got their notes circulated without difficulty, and that among people they were unknown to: can it be supposed that the credit of government would, at this period, be inferior to that of an obscure and unknown individual? I suppose these government notes to be endowed with all those engaging sensible qualities which concurr in recommending those of the Bank: qualities which, though the Bank, it will be thought, can not, yet individuals may without scruple, be debarred by law from giving to their notes: but of this afterwards.

The expence of the experiment might however, it should seem, be without difficulty reduced to nothing, by the simple expedient of empowering the Treasury to issue to the same amount in Exchequer

Bills. In as far as the Exchequer Notes are taken and not returned, the power of issuing the Exchequer Bills remains unexercised: so far as the Notes are either refused or returned, the power is exercised. A Note is tendered in payment to a creditor of the Navy Board, instead of a Navy Bill. If accepted of, government, instead of losing, is a gainer to the amount of from 1¼ to 1½ per Cent, although the Note should immediately be offered for payment and thereby government obliged, *pro tanto,* to make use of its power of borrowing upon Exchequer Bills. The interest paid upon the Exchequer Bill is, it is true, ½ per Cent more than [the interest] born[e] by the Navy Bill. But upon the Exchequer Bill there is a premium of about ¾ per Cent; while upon the Navy Bill there is a discount of about 1¾ per Cent, which, though not paid directly by government, is [borne by it] in effect, since whatever the discount is, a man who deals with government is obliged to add so much to the price at which he offers his goods to government. That this is the case, government is well persuaded, or it would not, for the sake of diminishing such discount, have made the new arrangement for the fixing and accelerating the payment of these Bills, which it has so lately made.

The smaller [the][1] sum of a Note is, the less scrupulous a man will be about taking it, and the less disposed he will be to look out for interest as a consideration for taking it: the more numerous too the hands capable of giving value for it, the better the chance it will have for meeting with an easy circulation. The smaller these Exchequer Notes were made, the better therefore their chance for circulation, especially in the remote parts of the country, from whence, when once got thither, they would not be so apt to return to the Metropolis for payment. The lowest Bank Notes were till lately for £10: now, within this year or two, they have been issued for so little as £5. The Bank, I make no doubt, find their account most amply in the innovation. Were the Exchequer Notes to be, some of them, so low as for £2 10s and £1 5s, they would by their smallness be capable of circulation in many a case and in many a hand to which even Bank Notes can not at present find their way.

About twenty years ago, the country was deluged with private notes to bearer for very small sums. An Act of Parliament* was made to prevent this, [i.e.] to limit the amount below which no such note should be issued, viz. 20s;—why? because of the extreme facility with

[1] [The MS reads "a".]

*15 Geo. [3]. ch. 51; 17 Geo. 3. c. 30: continuing; 27 Geo. [3]. ch. 16: perpetuating.

which such notes obtained currency whoever were the issuers, and thence the facility given to men of no property to obtain credit, and to dupe those who trusted them. A stronger prognostic of success than this fact affords of the success which government notes would meet with, were the experiment to be made, can scarcely be conceived. Government refused to trust individuals any longer with the power in question: and it did wisely. But it trusts the Bank of England in this respect without reserve: and it were strange indeed, if it could not venture to trust *itself*.

Government could not without the imputation of hardship give itself, as against the Bank, the monopoly of any of those species of currency which the Bank [is][1] in possession of issuing: it could not without exposing itself to that imputation forbid the Bank [the][2] issuing Notes in the form in which it is accustomed to issue them, to the amount of £5 and upwards: but it might, and that without any imputation whatever, preclude the Bank from issuing Notes of any sort which it never has issued, Notes for instance to a less amount than £5: giving itself thereby, as against the Bank, a monopoly with respect to the issuing of Notes to such inferior amounts.

Another advantage besides the encreased chance of circulation attending the issuing of such small Notes on the part of government, would be the security which their smallness would afford against the danger of a *run*. Such small Notes would be much more widely dispersed than larger ones: they would get into remote parts of the country, into which the present large ones scarce ever penetrate. The hands among whom they would be distributed would be more numerous, and many of them more remote from all intercourse with the Metropolis. On account of that remoteness it would be the more difficult for many of the holders to present their Notes for payment, and on account of the smallness of the Notes it would be the less worth each man's while. At the same time, in case of a run it would on several accounts take up more time to pay a given sum in such small Notes than in the present large Notes. It would, for example, take up at least four times the time to give change for four Notes of £2 10s each, that it would to give change for one of £10, even supposing them all brought by the same person: and, if brought by four different persons, the time would, it is obvious enough, be more or less protracted by that circumstance. Government would therefore con-

[1] [The MS reads "are".]
[2] [The MS reads "from".]

stantly and *ex necessitate rei,* and therefore without the smallest imputation upon its credit, be gaining that time which the Bank of England [has][1] occasionally and very rarely been driven to give itself for the preservation of its solvency, to the great disparagement of its credit.

No reason can be given (except the universal objection of its not having been done before) against government's issuing notes of this description, which does not apply, and with still greater force, against the issuing of the present Exchequer Bills. If government ought not to trust itself with the faculty of borrowing money without interest, still less ought it to trust itself with that of borrowing money with interest.

Money has always been borrowed by Administration at interest without the sanction of Parliament, viz. by Navy Bills and Ordnance Debentures, and, till lately, at very exorbitant interest. In this way, and without interest, not a penny would be borrowed by Administration without the sanction of Parliament. Why then should Parliament be distrustful in the present instance? Of whom would it be distrustful, but of itself. And why be distrustful of itself in the present instance more than in any other? It has for this century past, from the very birth of the Company, trusted the Bank of England, and never once seen reason to repent its confidence. Shall it thus give unlimited confidence to a trading company, and refuse all confidence to itself? Yet to restrain the Bank from imprudence in this way, there is nothing but the casual prudence of a fluctuating body of men, acting too in perfect secrecy, without the smallest check from the public eye: whereas Parliament could not give itself this faculty to the amount of a penny without the fullest discussion, carried on in the face of the whole world.

Were it ever so disposed to imprudence, it is difficult to say how in this way it could contrive to run into imprudence. Were it at any future period to issue, or rather try to issue, too much of this paper, the difficulty it would find of getting people to take it would, at the same time that it afforded proof of the imprudence, prevent its having any bad effect.

Suppose a run upon government. We have seen the defence that government would, upon this plan, have against a run, which the Bank of England has not. The Bank of England has never yet been hurt by runs; how then should government be hurt by any such

[1] [The MS reads "have".]

accident? The stock of cash which the Bank has to defend itself against such accidents, though large, is limited: it might be exhausted, and would necessarily be exhausted, if a number much less, I will not pretend to say how much less, than half the amount of its paper were to be brought for payment at once: it might, and in short must, unavoidably be exhausted, and then the Company would be altogether without resource. Government, besides the temporary expedient of postponing such of its payments as are postponable, has the whole property and credit of the nation to back it, and annuities to sell without end.

Another mode might be, to make provision for issuing, and to issue accordingly, a number of notes for a limited sum, (say the same sum, a million,) in point of sensible properties and succinctness of expression similar to Bank Notes, as likewise in respect of the division into small sums as £20, £10, and £5, not without interest as according to the former plan, but bearing an interest, though inferior to that given upon the present Exchequer Bills: say 2 per Cent, or rather as much less than 2 per Cent as will make the interest *per diem* come to what may be called to this purpose an even sum, an aliquot part of a pound: payable, too, not on demand, but at a fixed future period, principal and interest, in the manner of Exchequer Bills. This, in other words, would be an attempt to reduce the interest upon Exchequer Bills, by rendering them fitter for general circulation than they are in the form they wear at present.

Another plan would be, to make the Bills in other respects of the nature of those last described, and in particular in respect to the carrying interest, but to make them payable, interest and principal, on demand.

Another mode might be, to make them payable as to the principal on demand, but as to interest not before the end of a certain period, half yearly for example, that being the period at which government annuities are payable, or yearly.

These several ways of allowing interest I give rather for the purpose of illustration, and to compleat the view of the subject, than as expecting that any one of them will be deemed preferable to the most simple and most advantageous expedient of a paper without interest.

It has, I hope, been made pretty apparent, that there can be no reason for supposing that interest should be necessary. But if not necessary, besides being so much thrown away, it may be doubted whether, instead of promoting the circulation, it might not tend rather to impede it. Allow interest, and you put the paper *pro tanto* upon the footing of the present Exchequer Bills—you bring it into comparison with Exchequer Bills, and the comparison is in point of interest seen immediately to be to its disadvantage. By Exchequer Bills, we may make from 4 to 4½ per Cent interest: by this new paper not so much as 2 per Cent. This disadvantage strikes at first sight, and is within the reach of every observer: the expected advantage, expected to arise in point of superior facility of circulation from the smallness of the sum, or from the faculty of obtaining payment of principal, or interest, or both, upon demand, is matter of inference and reasoning, and comes not within the grasp of every eye.

Should the interest, on the other hand, operate according to its value, and, by being superadded to the advantage resulting from the faculty of obtaining payment on demand, enable the new paper to bear a premium, such a premium, though a proof of the success of the experiment in one point of view, will be a proof of its miscarriage in another. The premium will be so much gain to the first takers of the paper, but it will be no gain to government; on the contrary, it will be so much loss: it will shew that government has given just so much more than it need have given.

[But if, in a theoretical and long-term point of view, the payment of interest appears both unnecessary and undesirable, it may well be desirable and necessary as a practical means to introduce the new species of government paper into circulation. This is why the plan set forth in the following pages makes the grant of 2 per Cent *per annum* an essential feature of the proposed currency in the first stages of its existence.]

[IV. Plan for the Establishment of the new Government Currency]

A. [*Framing and Introduction of the proposed Exchequer Notes.*]

The introduction to the business will be the borrowing at low interest. The mode and the prospect of success are taken partly from the practice of the Bank in the instance of Bank Notes, partly from the practice of the East India Company in the instance of its Bonds.

The promissory notes of the Bank of England bear no interest: yet being made payable to the bearer, they are received as cash, and mostly in preference to cash. It is no wonder that they are so. The credit of the Bank remaining unimpeached—that is, the Bank being looked upon as prepared to give money for them to any one who demands it—they have a variety of advantages over money.

1. They are portable without the smallest expence or trouble.

2. The genuineness of this substitute for money takes infinitely less trouble to ascertain and is upon the whole much more secure than that of real money.

3. The facility of screening it from depredation or from fire is much greater, on account of the lightness of its weight, and the smallness of its compass. A Bank Note or two, proof being preserved of the contents, might be swallowed without inconvenience in case of danger, and by the liberality of the Bank, the loss would be replaced.

4. By an improvement of not many years' standing, it may be transmitted by the post to any distance, without the smallest danger from depredation or any other mischance.

The bulk and texture of the materials, as well as the form of the impression, are accordingly all of them admirably well calculated for improving those advantages to the utmost.

To replace *pro tanto* to a certain degree what are now called Bank Notes, [i.e.] the promissory notes of the Bank of England, what I propose is the issuing of what I will call Exchequer[1] Notes. The object then will be, to give these new creatures of finance the preference over those which are their competitors in the market, and which are at present in exclusive possession of the market, as abovementioned.

The main pillar of this preference must be the making them bear an interest: in this point they will have a clear advantage and ground of preference to the amount of the interest: as to other points, it will be a considerable thing done if they can be brought upon a par with those exquisite productions of art, Bank Notes. These other points are, the giving every facility to the circulation, and the giving them every possible security against forgery. In the former article it seems impossible fully to equal the Bank Note, consistently with the indispensable addition of the interest: in the latter it seems not impossible to exceed them.

For the obtaining the preference, let them bear interest, at least at the outset of the experiment, at the rate of 2 per Cent: by this means, reckoning the peace rate of interest at 4, and the war rate at 5, there will be a saving of from 2 to 3 per Cent *per annum* on so much of

[1][The word "Exchequer" was later crossed out, and replaced by the word "Annuity".]

this substitute for money as government can find means to circulate, [i.e.] as individuals choose to take, and government think fit to give.

To facilitate the circulation, let the principal be such as that the interest shall amount to an aliquot part of a pound, shilling, or penny, per day. Suppose it a farthing: the principal of this interest, at 2 per Cent, is £18 19s 2d: but this being an uneven sum, and not of a piece with the sums men are accustomed to in Bank Notes, let the note bearing this interest be a £20 note: the interest will be so much under 2 per Cent, and the gain to government so much the greater.

Upon this plan, the interest *per diem* and *per annum* upon a series of notes in aliquot parts of a pound at the rate of 2 per Cent, bating the reduction that results from the discarding of the small fractions, would run as follows: giving no interest for the five odd days of the 365, nor for the intercalary day of a leap year:

Interest *per diem* at nearly 2 per Cent	[Interest *per annum* at exactly 2 per Cent]	Principal Sum at exactly 2 per Cent	Principal Sum proposed at nearly [2] Per Cent	Full Interest *per annum* at 2 per Cent	Proposed Interest *per annum* at nearly 2 per Cent
d	£	£	£	[£]	£
1	1 10 5	75 16 8	80 0 0	1 12 0	1 10 0
½	0 15 2½	37 18 4	40 0 0	0 16 0	0 15 0
¼	0 7 7¼	18 19 2	20 0 0	0 8 0	0 7 6
½ of ¼	0 3 9½+⅛	9 9 7	10 0 0	0 4 0	0 3 9
¼ of ¼	0 1 10¾+ 1/16	4 9 0½	5 0 0	0 2 0	0 1 10½

To preserve simplicity in respect of the calculation of the interest as much as possible, the component articles of the series of notes should, all of them, have one common multiplier, viz. 2, as here: the other sums in use at present, such as £100 and £50, would easily be made up by adding notes of different amount together.

To give a farther facility to the calculation and thence to the circulation, a table should be added to the impression, exhibiting the encreases of interest accrued at a certain number of equal periods in the year: say 15 periods of 24 days each: throwing out, as before mentioned, the odd days.

[The] table for a twenty pound Note may be as follows.

Table shewing the interest that will have accrued upon this Note at different periods in the year, each consisting of 24 days: and thence the encrease of value that it will have received thereby: and so for five successive years: and the price which will accordingly be to be given for it, if received at par.

To find the value of this Note on any day not mentioned in this table, add a farthing a day to the sum opposite that one of the days mentioned in it, which immediately precedes the day in question.

	1796			1797			1798			1799			1800		
	£	s	d	£	s	d	£	s	d	£	s	d	£	s	d
Jan. 24	0	0	6	0	8	0	0	15	6	1	3	0	1	10	6
Feb. 17	0	1	0	0	8	6	0	16	0	1	3	6	1	11	0
Mar. 13	0	1	6	0	9	0	0	16	6	1	4	0	1	11	6
April 6	0	2	0	0	9	6	0	17	0	1	4	6	1	12	0
April 30	0	2	6	0	10	0	0	17	6	1	5	0	1	12	6
May 24	0	3	0	0	10	6	0	18	0	1	5	6	1	13	0
June 17	0	3	6	0	11	0	0	18	6	1	6	0	1	13	6
July 11	0	4	0	0	11	6	0	19	0	1	6	6	1	14	0
Aug. 4	0	4	6	0	12	0	0	19	6	1	7	0	1	14	6
Aug. 28	0	5	0	0	12	6	1	0	0	1	7	6	1	15	0
Sept. 21	0	5	6	0	13	0	1	0	6	1	8	0	1	15	6
Oct. 15	0	6	0	0	13	6	1	1	0	1	8	6	1	16	0
Nov. 8	0	6	6	0	14	0	1	1	6	1	9	0	1	16	6
Dec. 2	0	7	0	0	14	6	1	2	0	1	9	6	1	17	0
Dec. 26	0	7	6	0	15	0	1	2	6	1	10	0	1	17	6

Interest has been paid upon this Note for the years . . . .

With these advantages, there seems no occasion for making them payable, either in respect of principal or interest, more than once a year.

With respect to the interest, a time may be fixed within which the Notes must be presented for payment: Notes not presented within the time not to be paid till the paying season recurrs in the next year. On such terms, the number of days allotted for payment in each year can not, consistently with good faith, fall much short of what would be sufficient for paying the interest upon the whole number of Notes if presented, should they happen to be presented, which, however, is supremely improbable: though at the outset the presumption upon which the arrangements are grounded should, all of them, be as unfavourable as possible.

The first emission may be, for instance, on, or a little before, the first day of some year: the first day then for the payment of interest will be the first day of the year ensuing. As the Notes circulate from hand to hand, the interest that has accrued at the time of each transfer will naturally be added to the principal: and it is to facilitate this operation, that the table above given is proposed to be given on the face of each Note. This addition, I say, will naturally be made, because it actually is made in the instance of India Bonds. Without such a table, the trouble of calculation would be too great, the interest, especially on the small Notes, would, rather than submitt to the trouble, be given up, and thence the great inducement to take these Notes in preference to Bank Notes would be lost. As to the intervening days between the several periodical days set down in the table, they are so few and quadrate so exactly with a division that is in universal use, the division of small money, that no difficulty capable of embarrassing the most ignorant individual can arise.

To shew up to what time interest has been paid, and thence how much, if any, remains due, a stamp may at the time of payment be put to each Note, expressive of the year up to which such payment has been made.

For the payment of the principal, the same period may suffice: though the hope is, that few indeed will be presented.

That no breach of engagement might ensue in case of a run, government might reserve to itself the option of giving by way of payment instead of cash an engagement under the name, for example, of an Exchequer Annuity Bond, granting a perpetual redeemable annuity. To ensure acceptance of this equivalent, the rate of interest might be made somewhat higher than the rate at which government borrows at the time. Were this rate to be even higher than necessary, no lasting prejudice, if any, could result to government from the excess: since by borrowing [cash] at the current rate of the time, it could always free itself from the charge. Nor could the demand for payment be unexpected, since there would always be a full year to look out for it and prepare for it.

From this option, no prejudice to the circulation seems likely to ensue. True it is that, among those who, in case of an assurance of obtaining cash in payment, would be likely to accept of these Notes, there may be comparatively but a very few who would be disposed, or could afford, to accept an annuity instead though at ever so high a rate of interest. But there will always be others in abundance, equally able and willing to accept of such annuity in lieu, and who accordingly will be willing to pay the full price for the notes or bonds entitling them to such an annuity. The proposed Annuity Bonds would therefore find their full value in the market according to the rate of interest they bear, just as so much stock of any of the existing species does at present.

There seems no ground, then, to apprehend any prejudice to the circulation from this condition any more than ensues to the circulation of Bank Notes from the circumstance of their not being exchangeable for cash at the pleasure of the holder any where else in England but at the office of the Company which issues them. What the holder of the Note depends upon, in respect of the assurance of getting cash for them, is the finding individuals ready to take them from him as he took them from others: and the expectation of this facility seems not less reasonable in the case in question than in this. The annuity payable in exchange for a small Note, such as £20 or £10, though at the encreased rate, say 5 per Cent, would, it is true, be a poor pittance of an annuity, scarce worth the trouble of receiving: but neither would this consideration be any prejudice to the circulation: for those who wanted annuities of a considerable amount might always obtain them to any amount, only by buying a sufficient quantity of such Annuity Bonds: if they could not find them in sufficient numbers, it would be because they were scarce in the market, which could only happen from their being valued at a high rate.

There are [in fact] grounds for expecting [the proposed Exchequer Notes][1] to bear a very considerable premium: while Bank Notes bear none. To assist the conception in forming an estimate of the probable amount of this premium, I will begin with three suppositions at the outset: returning afterwards to correct the error that may be the result of what they want of quadrating with the truth.

The first supposition is, that the credit of the government is as good as that of the Bank: that is, [that] the ability to discharge engagements of every kind is equal in the former case to what it is in the latter.

The second supposition is, that government were not obliged[2] to pay the interest half yearly upon the footing of the existing annuities, but [obliged] to pay the principal upon demand at any time, at the same time that [it][3] should be in the holder's option whether he would ever have it paid off, at least so long as any of the existing annuities remained unpaid off.

The third supposition is that of government's not having the option of paying off the Exchequer Note transferable from hand to hand, by an Exchequer Annuity Bond transferable no otherwise than in the way of other government annuities, by means of the government

[1][The MS reads "them".]

[2][In the MS, the word "not"—a later addition—stands *after* the word "obliged". It seems, however, certain, that it should stand where it is placed in the text. The whole passage is not very clearly worded. Bentham assumes that the interest on the proposed Exchequer Note would be paid out once a year only, not twice, as in the case of the then current types of government annuities.]

[3][The MS reads "in".]

books of which the Bank, by agreement with government, has the charge.

On these suppositions, what would be the value of a Note of the sort proposed? It would be the value of the principal money added to the value of the interest, that is added to another sum being the capital for which a perpetual annuity to the amount of such interest might be bought at the current price of the day. The former value it would possess in the character of a circulating note: because the Notes of the Bank of England with which these are, by the supposition, upon a footing in point of credit, possess that value. The latter value it would possess in quality of its being a grant of a perpetual annuity: because perpetual annuities to that amount do, by the supposition, bear that value. Now, the value of the note as a circulating note is £20: and the value of an annuity of 2 per Cent upon £20, that is of 8s, money being at 5 per Cent as it nearly is at present, is £4 [*sic*]: £4 then is the premium which, on the above suppositions, an Exchequer Note ought to bear.*

[It might be urged that it is unlikely the proposed Exchequer Notes should ever attain so considerable a premium, since the three assumptions above made represent the case in too favourable a light.] But the circumstance of the Notes' not being payable on demand, and that of the interest['s] being paid annually only, and not half-yearly, do not, either of them, promise to make any sensible diminution in the value. As to the faculty of obtaining payment for it on demand, if a man had it, he would not use it, since by doing so he would lose the whole value of it in the character of a note bearing interest: this he would never think of doing while he could meet with any body who would give him any thing for the interest. As it would clearly never be worth any body's while to make use of any such faculty, the Notes' not conveying any such faculty does not seem likely to detract any thing whatever from the value. [And if the Notes should thus pass current, as there is every likelyhood they will, the precaution taken with regard to the danger of a run, viz. the right of government to give for them by way of payment, instead of cash, Annuity Bonds, will not, in the ordinary state of things, produce any alteration in the value put upon them by the market.]

*[Strictly speaking, the premium would only amount to] £3 10s.: deducting what interest is proposed to be deducted from the rate of 2 per Cent for the sake of even money, as above stated: but, to simplify the business, the consideration of the deduction may as well be omitted.

B. *Term* [*of the Circulation*].

Upon the principle exemplified in Bank Notes, they might be divisible into two portions, each bearing sufficient marks of its belonging exclusively to the other. This contrivance might in the present instance be productive of a farther advantage, of which presently.

It might possibly be found advisable to limit the currency of these Notes to a certain period—say, for example, 5 years—at the expiration of which they must be presented to be exchanged, on pain of losing all farther interest that should have become due: possibly also to assign a farther period, say 5 years more, at the expiration of which, if not presented in the mean time, even the principal should be no longer payable. One use is to enable government at the expiration of that period, in the event of their bearing a premium, to pay off this first set of Notes, for the purpose of replacing them by Notes bearing an inferior rate of interest, and thereby obtaining money on so much the more advantageous terms. There does not seem much danger that these conditions should afford much obstruction to the circulation of these Notes: the time being, at the commencement of the circulation, which is the only trying time, remote, and act appearing to be always and easily in a man's power. One use is, if any forgery should have been committed, the bringing it to light at a time when the traces will be in some degree of freshness, and the discovery of the offence present the better chance of leading to the discovery of the offender. 2. Another is the advantage that may thus accrue to government from accidents and negligences such as individuals, feeling prevention to be in their own power, will take no account of. The establishment of these conditions will be a sort of extension, as it were, though in a much more productive as well as milder shape, of an antient and still existing prerogative. The money that would have been due upon Notes thus grown out of date, will, in the hands of government, be so much *treasure-trove*. 3. There will be a certain number of years, at the end of which the whole of the space left vacant would be covered with the stamps expressive of the years for which interest has been paid. This would itself create a necessity for a call in at some period or other, though if the surface of the Note were to be extensive, this period might proportionably be a long one. 4. There will be a certain period, by the end of which a considerable number will have been more or less defaced by wearing: at this period it will be necessary that some should be exchanged, and this period might serve for the whole number.

C. *Advantages* [*to Individuals*].

These Notes, being equally convenient to individuals of all descriptions, promise to be an object of competition to individuals of all descriptions. By this means, a man may have the satisfaction of keeping in a state of improvement every particle of his fortune, even of his current cash: no part whatever, except the change for a £5 Note, need ever be lying dead. By keeping his own, a man will be lending it to government and getting paid for it. Even a very poor man may thus have a method, and that a sure one, of improving his little pittance. The same article will in this way be answering the double and hitherto irreconcilable purposes of a capital and running cash: a man puts his money out at interest, without parting with it out of his hands. If a man calculates justly with regard to the quantity of currency he may be able to keep for a certain period, it is so much gain: if his calculation proves erroneous, and demand comes upon him sooner than he had expected, still he is under no difficulty nor experiencing any loss. On the contrary, how little soever be the time he has kept the article, he is all the better for it. Like generous wine, it improves by keeping: nor yet, like wine, is it exposed to spoil by keeping, nor has its progress in the career of improvement any limits, as is the case with almost every sort of wine.

It will be a sort of practical lesson and standing encouragement to economy to those classes who are most liable to stand in need of such lessons. A pin a day is a groat a [year][1], says the homely proverb: by this means a man may exemplify the truth of this proverb upon an enlarged scale: he will see what is to be got by the inaction, by the mere forbearing to part with an individual thing, and without any such constant effort as is necessary to add article to article to form a hoard.

Every man in this way may be his own banker, every man making banker's profit upon his own stock. The facilitating this point of frugality was one of the reasons for proposing the extending to these Notes the divisibility given by the Bank of England to their Notes.

If a man's being his own banker will in this way have its profits, it has its perils too: the perils from theft, fire, and accidental loss. From

[1][The MS reads "a day".]

these perils, the proprietor of a Note thus divisible may make himself, humanly speaking, pretty secure, by dividing it and keeping the two halves in different places, one, suppose, in the custody of a friend. This security a man never thinks of giving himself in the instance of Bank Notes, unless it be for the accidental purpose of distant conveyance, because nobody can get any thing by keeping Bank Notes, nor therefore thinks of keeping them for any length of time. But here it would be worth while: keeping one of these Notes would, to a poor man, be like buying a little fortune into the funds, and all without the expence of agency, brokerage, and stamps, which in the funds would cut up the profit upon a capital several times as large.

To bankers, the value of this species of currency will be still more apparent, as presenting itself in so much larger masses. At present, according to the common calculation, a banker is obliged to keep in reserve, to answer contingent demands, to the amount of a third of the exceedings of the sum of his ordinary receipts above the sum of his ordinary payments. By the proposed Notes, if he can get them, the whole arm of this third will become productive. What he lends out, he lends at 5 per Cent: what he thus keeps, he gets but 2[1] per Cent for. His profit, then, in this way will be $\frac{2}{5}$[2] of the [normal rate on the] third he must keep in reserve. If his reserved third is fifty thousand, his profit will be what he would have made by adding [twenty][3] thousand pound to the amount of his loans: it will be nearly a thousand pound a year.

D. [*Possibilities of*] *Agio* [*and Discount*].

The price of this species of currency in the market will shew with precision the quantity of it that can be issued. Suppose the quantity issued at first in the way of experiment to be £2,000,000. If at the end of the experimental period, suppose a twelvemonth, it bears a premium to a certain amount, it will be a sign that another parcel may be issued, and perhaps, if the premium be considerable, at a still lower rate of interest: till at length, should the premium ever rise so as to equal the interest, it will be a sign they may be issued without any interest, upon the footing of Bank Notes.

It seems no unreasonable expectation that, in time, they may [come

[1] [Over the "2" is written a "3". When this passage was brought to paper, Bentham was probably in doubt which rate of interest it would be proper to suggest.]

[2] [The MS in fact reads "$\frac{3}{5}$".]

[3] [The MS speaks of "thirty".]

to] be upon a par with Bank Notes, or even upon a superior footing: they surely ought to be. In the instance [of Bank paper], the quantity issued is unknown to the public: whether it will always be confined within the exact bounds of the sufficiency of the fund for their discharge, depends upon the uncertain prudence of a shifting body of individuals. Runs may take place, too great for the ability even of this vast and opulent Company: for it is of the essence of that Bank as of all others, to receive more than, if called upon, it would be able to pay: it can have no profit but in proportion as its ability is transgressed. Accordingly one hears of periods when, in order to gain time, they have paid in sixpences (A. Smith[1]). But what government undertakes for, being not the return of the principal but the payment of an annuity in lieu of it, no run whatever can expose it to difficulty even for a moment. The only possible case in which it could be exposed to any such difficulty would be that of a difficulty to pay the amount of the annuity: but the proposed annuities being upon the same footing in respect of the security as all the other annuities, nothing could shake the credit of this species of currency which did not act with equal force and effect against every other branch of the funds. Of this government currency, not a penny can be issued but by an Act of Parliament specifying the amount. It is therefore impossible there should be any sudden glut of it; or that there should be any more of it issued than what it shall have appeared, after the fullest and openest discussion, the market will be able to bear. In the case of a glut of Bank currency, what the holders of Bank Notes would have to apprehend would be, not only the loss of a part by a discount, but even the loss of the whole: apprehension would have no certain resting place. In the case of the proposed government currency, a discount, and that a very slight one, is the utmost which any man could have to fear.

There would be a period at which a regular, though very inconsiderable, abatement in the price of such currency would be to be expected: this is the approach of the time for the payment of the interest. The attendance upon the office, or offices, for the purpose of obtaining payment would be a loss of time: a real inconvenience, which imagination would perhaps be more likely to magnify than to diminish. To get rid of this inconvenience, such as wanted to receive their interest would at that time shew a more than ordinary forwardness to exchange their Notes: for the same reason those who had

[1] [*Wealth of Nations*, bk. II, ch. II.]

cash would not be so ready to take these Notes; they would by this means abate at this period something of their ordinary price. Moneyed men who were in habits with the offices would take advantage of this temporary depression to buy what would be to them a bargain: and this readiness on their part would, to a certain degree, counterbalance the operation of the cause of depression, and keep up the price so much higher than it would be otherwise. The greater the number and value a man got of this currency in his hands at the time for the payment of the interest, the less would be his loss of time in respect of each particular Note. This, then, would be a sure way of a man's employing his time and capital to account. It would be a branch of the business of the stock-broker, just as the keeping of stock for the purpose of carving out slices of it adjusted to the exact amount of the demand of each purchaser, is another.

In comparison of the larger Notes, the smaller Notes would be subject [to] a cause of rise on the one hand, and to a cause of depression on the other. The cause of rise would be, that they would be more men's money: the cause of depression would be the superior trouble of receiving the interest, in comparison of the amount of that interest, since the trouble upon a £5 Note, and that upon a £5,000 Note, would be the same. The cause of rise would be permanent: the cause of depression would be temporary: hence the agio would be somewhat greater upon the smaller Notes [than][1] upon the large ones. The agio, however, never could mount so high as to be productive of any thing at all approaching to distress: the utmost amount of the depression would be, not a loss upon the holding the Note, but only a slight diminution of the gain. In the remote parts of the country, the agio may in proportion to the distance and comparative non-abundance of currency of all kinds, be expected to be somewhat greater than in the Metropolis. From Scotland for example, about the time of the payment of the interest, Exchequer Notes may be expected to be on their travels to London by the post: the rate of exchange between the Scotch towns and London will, at that period, be rendered somewhat the more against Scotland. These are little effects, of no consequence in themselves, but of which it may be proper the financier should be pre-apprized, that he may be prepared against all results, and that, by the consciousness of foreknowledge and fore armament, [and] by having a commanding view of the whole subject, his mind and conscience may be at ease. Till the conception

[1][The MS reads "that".]

has learnt to get a view of what will be the precise consequence of things, it is apt to be frightened, and fills up the vacuity with undefined and magnified disasters.

E. *Objections.*

Objections to such a plan, alarms for the consequences, would not be wanting. The alarms might be entertained by any body: the ground for alarm will be confined to the Bank and bankers. Damage there certainly would be to the Bank, and it would all fall upon that great Company: advantage to government and to every individual: injury to nobody. If I chose to be my own banker, my present banker would be a sufferer, and he would naturally do what depended upon him to prevent it. Yet every man may be his own banker, as he may his own brewer: and no reason can be given, why government should not as well as any body else.

But the credit of the Bank, it may be said, would be ruined: and the credit of the Bank is the great prop of the credit of the nation: and so the nation would be ruined: and as to government's attempting to be its own banker and supplant the Bank, it won't do: it can never have credit for it.

The Bank will probably experience a diminution of its profits, [1]possibly to the amount of the interest it makes upon a principal sum equal to two thirds, or thereabouts, of the amount of the principal of the proposed Notes.[2] Its profits may be curtailed, but its credit can not be weakened in the smallest degree. On the contrary, if at all affected, it would be improved rather than impaired. What the actual property of the Bank consists in, what its solvency depends upon, is the cash it keeps in its coffers, the cash due to it from individuals to whom it has lent, that is whose Notes it has discounted, and the annuities it has bought of government: from none of these will any subtraction be made by any diminution in the faculty of issuing its Notes. What its credit is put in jeopardy by, is the quantity of its Notes which it issues, that is the quantity of money it promises to pay without having wherewithal, if payment for the whole or but the half of it were demanded at the same time. Its profits are certainly in proportion to the number of these Notes which it induce[s] people to take instead of cash: but in the exact proportion in which its profits, so long as its credit last[s], are encreased in this way, in the

[1] [2][Later brackets.]

same proportion is its credit strained. There is not a Director that can have any doubt but that, if the number of its Notes were to be doubled, for example, its credit would presently be gone: if there were [a chance of the credit's remaining unshaken], he would not acquiesce in that number's remaining as it is; he would propose, not to double it perhaps, but at least to add to it. There is not a Director that can entertain a doubt, but that if the credit of the Bank wanted strengthening, the reducing the number of its Notes, though it were to half its present amount, would strengthen it. This then and no more, is the effect [which] the issuing of the proposed Exchequer Notes would produce upon the Bank: an obligation to withdraw to the amount of an equal sum out of the amount of the Notes it issues at present, on pain of departing *pro tanto* from the line of its present prudence. From what precise source this obligation might arise, whether solely from unmixed prudence, or from a mixture of prudence and necessity, I will not take upon me absolutely to determine. I should rather expect a mixture of necessity: and that this necessity would save the expence of prudence.

Upon the issuing of this Exchequer currency, or at least upon its beginning to find its value, I should expect a small discount upon Bank Notes. When a man had the option between a paper that brought him no interest, and a paper equally secure that brought him interest, he would naturally prefer the latter: if a debtor proffered him Bank Notes, he would say, *no, I won't take your Bank Notes: if you have Exchequer Notes to give me, well and good: but if you have not, I won't take your Bank Notes (and you know you can't oblige me): I may find a difficulty in getting them off, since other people will be for getting Exchequer Notes, for the same reason that I am: I won't take your Bank Note then, unless you will allow me a discount upon it: if you won't, you must give me cash.*

[1]Bank Notes then, it is probable, will for a short time after the issuing of the Exchequer Notes, bear something of a discount: but by knowing the amount of the interest borne by these Exchequer Notes, we know the utmost possible amount of the discount that can be demanded upon the Bank Notes: at the very[2] [worst, it could not come to much: and any objection to the present proposal grounded on the supposed slight depretiation of the Bank currency, any more than on any other apprehended interference with the business of the Bank, would be proportionably unavailing].

[1] [2][Crossed out in the MS.]

F. *Precautions against Forgery.*

In the endeavours for guarding against forgery, it is not sufficient to save the party charged with payment, the government office in the present instance, from being imposed upon by the forgery; it is a matter of equal importance to save individuals in general from similar imposition, in respect of the danger of their receiving of the counterfeit paper in payment: and this not so much on account of the loss to the individual, as on account of the loss to government, by the depretiation of the paper which may be the consequence. The last point is perhaps of still greater importance than the other. Whatever acts as a security as to the first point, does so in regard to the other: but the latter, which is the easier point to compass, may be provided against, and that perhaps pretty effectually, by means which would have no application to the other.

Forgery may be attempted in the way of fabrication, or in the way of alteration. The precautionary contrivances will take a different turn, according as they are levelled against an attempt of the one or the other nature.

The difficulty of attempting a scheme of forgery with any prospect of success may be enhanced by a variety of circumstances.

The success of any project of forgery will appear the more hopeless, according to the degree of skill necessary to the attempt,* according to the time it would require, the elaborateness of the apparatus, if any, which would be necessary to the same purpose, the space necessary for the action of such apparatus, and thence the difficulty of working it without the betraying of the purpose, and according to the number of persons whose concurrence would be necessary in the character of accomplices.

The idea of introducing the human figure into the substratum of a legal instrument may be seen exemplified in several of the blank instruments that are charged with stamp-duties: those for Patents for example. Ornament was perhaps the only object in these

*The necessity of extraordinary skill on the part of the artist augments the improbability of a successful attempt in a double way: the more skillfull [*sic*] the artist must be, the fewer there are that would be *capable* of the attempt [1]in point of ability[2]; and the more skilfull [*sic*] again the less likely, since the greater a man's skill in this or any such line, the more he may make by it in a safe and honest way, and the less he is on that account exposed to the temptation of seeking profit by such dangerous and dishonest means.

[1] [2][Later brackets.]

instances: but in the instance of the proposed Notes, such decorations will have a more substantial use.

At the time of the publication of a pamphlet, twelve or fifteen years ago, of the present Earl Stanhope's (then L[or]d Mahon), on the coin,[1] I remember being much struck with the ingenuity of this idea as exemplified on that subject. I remember being struck in a similar manner at the hearing of Mr. Bolton's machine intended for the copper coinage, a machine in the instance of which the elaborateness and consequent expensiveness of the work, as well as the great room it would take up (a steam engine forming but a part of it), were circumstances trusted to, as I understood, in the character of safeguards against forbidden imitation. But in spite of all this ingenuity, the difficulty of counterfeiting with success an impression in metal seems much inferior to that of counterfeiting the impression of an engraving of the human countenance, executed by a masterly hand. In the instance of the coin, [i.e. of] metallic impression, the alterations which wear and tear may make on the original operate as a cover to deception in the spurious copy. Sharp prominences become obliterated: sinkings fill up, partly by dirt, partly by rubbing down of the prominencies.

The Notes might contain a head, or a number of heads, or part of a human figure, elaborately engraved, and by the artist whose works shall have been deemed most inimitable. Art does not afford an object so unsusceptible of being imitated in such manner that the copy shall pass for the original, as a good engraving of the human countenance. The imitation of such an engraving, even though attempted in a loose manner, would be a work of considerable time: during almost the whole of which time, as the posture and size of the intended figure would be given perhaps at the first sitting, the offender would continue exposed to detection.

Engraving after drawing and engraving after writing are, moreover, two different branches, just as drawing and writing are themselves. It is rare that the same person who practises the one, practises the other, at least to any perfection, to any degree of perfection approaching that which would here be requisite. The quantity of engraved writing, as above proposed, though in other respects rather of inconvenience, in as much as by its complication it may tend rather to perplex an ignorant individual and disincline him from giving the prefer-

[1][Cf. Considerations on the means of preventing fraudulent practices on the Gold Coin, 1775.]

ence to this species of currency over the simple currency of the Bank; this quantity of engraved writing is therefore, as a safeguard against forgery, a very considerable addition to the security: since it requires either the concurrence of two ingenious criminals instead of one, or at least such an one as, even in the whole assemblage of honest members of the profession, may scarcely be to be found. The greater the quantity of engraving to be forged, the greater the room for those errors and deviations by which forgery is detected.

To the engraved work of the kind abovementioned, in which the figure is exhibited by colouring, may be added engraved work of another kind, in which the figure is exhibited in relief without colour, by the mere raising or depression of the paper, as produced by a stamp, in the manner employed upon paper when made the subject of the species of tax called a stamp-duty. By this means the concurrence of a third branch of the graphical art, [or rather of a third] artist, is rendered necessary to every attempt at forgery.

As to the subject of the figure, the head of the Sovereign is an article that, for decorum-sake, and by analogy to the coinage, can not well be refused a place. There is, however, a reason why that effigy alone is less adapted to the purpose than any other human effigy. The subject chosen for this purpose should be a subject which no man would think of executing, at least in the particular manner in question, otherwise than in pursuance of a design of forgery. But the head of the Sovereign, a subject beyond comparison more popular than any other whatsoever, is a subject which artists of all description will, without any forbidden intention, be perpetually executing in all modes and sizes that can be imagined. Taking the head of the Sovereign, then, for the principal figure, and consequently of the largest size, other heads of smaller dimensions might be added in a groupe or line, the heads of persons bearing an official relation to the subject, of such descriptions as have never yet been represented in the manner and size in question, nor were ever likely to have been so represented for any other purpose: the Lords of the Treasury for example, to whom might be added the Auditor and the Barons of the Exchequer.

The paper might thus be decorated with an engraved border, single or double, on one, two, or three of its edges, or on all four, partly in the way of ordinary engraving, partly in the way of stamping.* The

*Paper has lately been made with stampt borders very neatly executed, in which the King's head, with the King's arms and other devices, are introduced.

effigies of the Sovereign might be crowned, partly for shew, but more particularly because there is perhaps scarce an example existing of its being exhibited in any such *costume,* at least of a size at all approaching to that which would be adapted to the purpose here proposed. The heads of the Barons of the Coif, exhibited of course in their dress of office, should for that reason be executed in the way of engraving: in order that that branch of the art which admitts not of such minute and elaborate execution, viz. the stamping branch, may be reserved for the effigies of those officers whose offices are not marked by any peculiarity of dress.

Security against forgery is not the only advantage that may result from a stile of decoration which, to a first glance, might appear puerile and frivolous enough. It may help the circulation of this new currency among individuals of a certain class, a class in which the bulk of the people may be found included. A man must have made very little use of the gift of observation who is ignorant of the power of sensible images over the human mind. The wealthy yeoman who, in bringing part of his property into the substantial shape of *terra firma,* estimates the goodness of his title by the bulk of the parchments which are given him as evidence of it, will, in weighing in his own mind the comparative value of a Bank Note and an Exchequer Note to the same amount thus adorned, find his judgment warped in no small degree by these fascinating decorations.

Against that branch of the art of forgery which consists in mere alteration, and which requires accordingly a genuine document for its subject, chemistry and mechanicks will be found to afford several antidotes in addition to such as have already been employed.

A fraud of this sort can scarcely be practised to advantage but upon that part of the Note which expresses the sum, and must consist in the substituting by addition, erasure, or alteration, a larger sum for a smaller. In one instance, if the prints of the day were correct in this particular, a Bank Note of fifteen pound was altered into one of fifty, and that by obliterating the two *ees* and the *n,* and filling up the vacancy with a *y*. In what particular mode the obliteration was performed, I can not take upon me to say: I do not recollect that it was stated at the time, nor should I well know in what precise way to produce such an effect, if the task rested upon me. From a paper of such chosen thinness, the obliteration could hardly have been performed by erasure, or in short by any mechanical means: how printer's ink could be discharged from such a ground by any chemical solvent, especially without leaving traces of the operation upon the ground, I am equally at a loss to know: yet this chemical mode appears much less unfeasible than the mechanical one.

Two expedients occurr, by either of which, it should seem, any such chemical mode might be rendered impracticable.

One is the following: by a stamp containing the same characters, and those impressed upon the same places, except that the characters on the stamp may, each of them, stretch a little beyond, or terminate a little within, its corresponding engraved character. In this case the obliteration of the engraved characters would not answer the fraudulent purpose, since the stamped characters would remain.

Another expedient is to impregnate the paper with a powder which, upon the application of any fluid, would take a conspicuous colour, and give warning of the deceit.

Falsification considered as applying itself to writing performed with a pen seems at first sight not to have any application to the present subject, since the characters expressive of the sums are in Bank Notes made, not with writing ink and a pen, but with printing ink by an engraved plate. As an additional security, however, the sum might be repeated somewhere in words or figures with a pen, and then a falsification effected on the characters made by engraving would fail of its purpose, unless a similar falsification could be practised upon the characters written with a pen.

Against an attempt of this kind, there might be more defences than one. One is, the impregnating the paper with a powder of the same property as that above mentioned: the other is, the adding to the common ink an ingredient which would render it incapable of being obliterated by any of those acid menstrua by which ink of the ordinary composition may so easily be made to disappear.

A security which confines itself to the office without extending to individuals is, as hath been already observed, a very incompleat one. This purpose, as far as it goes, is or may be pretty effectually answered by the antient and well known expedient of checks, or counterfoils as they are called in that part of the annual Malt-tax Act which relates to Exchequer Bills.

An additional security to this purpose might be given by leaving breaks, and those large and frequent, and of different lengths, in the series of the numbers used for marking the individuality of the Notes. A Note being brought to the office bearing a number not in the list, the forgery would be apparent at first glance.

The publication of this irregularity might add something to the danger of forgery, and thence to the sum of the restraining[1] forces an enterprize of that sort would have to overcome. The addition would not, however, be very considerable, since, the list of the omitted numbers being a secret every where but at the office, an excluded number would not any where but at the office be discernible from a genuine one.

G. *Limits* [*to the Emission*].

[2]The limits of emission with regard to this species of currency will be a very natural subject of enquiry: in other words, what quantity of it it seems likely that government should now or at any other given period, meaning a period sufficiently distant to admitt of time for the gradual introduction of it, be able to emitt to advantage.

The answer to this question seems not very difficult to give. Just as much as what would have been the amount of the paper currency of the country[4]: just so much as, were it not for this government currency, the Bank of England, together with any other banking houses that would otherwise have been in the practice of issuing promissory notes, would have issued. Now, then, as to the profit. What the amount of the paper currency in England, I mean that payable to bearer, [is,] I do not pretend to know. Call it, for illustration sake, 40 millions: of which 30 issued by the Bank of England, the other 10 by the country banking houses. On this supposition, the profit to government by the monopoly of the paper currency will be the difference between the interest they pay upon these 40 millions, and the amount of the annuities they would have had to grant for the same capital, had it been obtained upon the ordinary terms. If it ends, as there seems reason to expect it should, in the circulation of such Notes even without interest, the profit will then be the borrowing 40 millions without interest, or, to speak more correctly, the obtaining *gratis* 40 million of the money they have employed.[3]

H. [*How to secure a Government*] *Monopoly* [*of emitting Paper Money*].

To secure to itself the possession of this advantage it might be necessary, and it would, it should seem, not be unjustifiable, for

[1][The word looks in the MS like "restrainting".]

[2] [3][A question mark is written over the whole page of the MS.]

[4][The MS seems to read "that country".]

government to pass certain prohibitory laws, calculated to give itself the monopoly of the emission of paper currency.

1. One regulation would be, to prohibit any individual or company [the][1] emitting notes payable to bearer and on demand, together with any interest for the same.

2. Another would be, to prohibit any individual or company [the][1] issuing any notes payable to bearer on demand, with any of the letters or figures thereon marked in the way of engraving, or any otherwise than in the ordinary mode of writing with a pen: to which might be added a limitation in respect of the paper, confining it in respect to bulk as well as thickness to the paper commonly used for writing.

The notes emitted by the country banking houses are calculated to take advantage of the ignorance of the bulk of individuals, and by imitating, as far as the law will permitt, the exterior semblance of Bank Notes, share in the credit which people are in the habit of giving to those Notes. This they certainly do to a considerable degree: and even where, in point of credit, they are estimated at no more than they are worth, still the probability derived from these expedients is a very considerable advantage.

It is not so much that these notes are ever taken for the Notes of the Bank of England: few individuals capable of paying the price of a note to such amount, that would be capable of falling into such a mistake. The mistake consists in imputing to these private banks a degree of solidity which does not belong to them: in attributing to people whose draughts are accompanied with these pompous exhibitions a degree of opulence and solidity superior to those whose notes are drawn in the usual manner, and in a modest stile.

A man who sets up in a county or in a country town, decorates his house too with the name of the county or the town: it is *the* Bank of such a county or such a town: as if the capital of it consisted of the whole wealth of the county or the town, poured into that one house. A title like this, adorned with rich flourishes upon a thin paper, is a fascination too strong to be resisted by the common run of eyes. To look upon the suppression of this licence of paper coinage as a benefit, it is not necessary so much as to entertain a doubt with respect [to] any of the banking houses as yet existing: if they are unsolid, it were time for that reason that they should be suppressed: if they are not unsolid, yet the credit, which is but the due of the existing race, will be usurped and turned to a bad account by unsubstantial houses,

[1] [The MS reads "from".]

to which the confidence justly reposed in these substantial ones will give birth.

The stripping them of their flourishes would go a great way: but it is not absolutely certain that it would compleat the business. Sooner than not issue their notes, they might comply with the law by issuing them in the way of common bills, but escape from it by outbidding government in respect of the interest: it is on this account that the prohibition of notes to bearer bearing interest, is proposed.

It would be an untrue objection to the measure to say that it would be prejudicial to private credit, meaning to private confidence. A man will be left at full liberty to make promises to every body that he knows: all he will be prevented from, is the making promises to any body whatsoever—the obtaining credit for promises made to persons whom he does not know.

I. *Why* [*the Experiment was*] *not* [*made*] *before.*

If the measure you propose be a feasible one, how comes it never to have been attempted before? This is that sort of question which naturally presents itself to every new measure, and which has always a claim to the best answer than can be given to it.

The non-institution of this experiment is the natural result of the habit so prevalent in governments, and a habit which can not but be expected to be prevalent, of taking things as they are found, without setting themselves to enquire how they might be. At the institution of the present paper currency, a paper without interest would not have done: at least there were the strongest appearances of its not doing, and none at all of its doing. Things are by this time settled into such a state, that, as we have seen, there is the highest reason for being assured that the experiment would succeed: but it is gradually and insensibly that [we] have arrived at this state: nor has there been any particular period at which any man could have said, to-day it will do, yesterday it would not have done.

It may well be said, the experiment would not have done. [1]Three things were wanting to its doing[2]: no such experiment had ever been made by any body; had it been made and succeeded in other hands, there was no appearance of its succeeding in the hands of government; and, what is more than all, there were no means of making it.

When government began to borrow money for a permanency, to

---

[1] [2] [Put into brackets at a later date.]

borrow it upon perpetual redeemable annuities, it was of the Bank of England that it borrowed it. It was before the Revolution was well consolidated: the nation was at war: the necessities of government were at the extreme: no such thing as general credit existed, and if there had been any, government would have had no share in it. In this exigency it found a set of people hardy enough to trust it with £1,200,000*—a prodigious sum in those days—upon the terms of receiving eight per Cent for it till paid off, and being aggregated into a corporation: this corporation was, and is, the Bank of England. It was from this corporation that paper currency of a general nature, a promise of paying so much money on demand to any one who should produce such promise, took its rise. Experience shewed the solidity of such promises: and experience shewed at the same time the convenience of a man's having a small slip of paper of extreme thinness to keep or carry about him, instead of a heavy load of metal, good and bad, heavy and light, as it might happen.

When government borrowed money upon a sudden emergency or for a short time, when it borrowed it otherwise than upon perpetual annuities secured upon a new and certain fund, it was always, or almost always, of the Bank that it borrowed it. The Bank always had either money or credit sufficient for the purpose. No individual and scarce any other corporation had any such sufficiency of either. The Bank had always in possession or at command a large quantity of ready money that it could spare: government was frequently in want of that commodity, and it never had any of it to spare. It was in this state of things that the practice of borrowing money upon Exchequer Bills took its rise. Government in those days paid 2d a day, a trifle more than £3 *per annum*, for every £100 to the bearer, besides £3 to the Bank for circulating them and lending them its credit; total a trifle more than £6: it now pays 3d a day, a trifle more than 4½ per Cent to the bearer, without any thing for circulating them. As to the time and conditions of payment in other particulars, they remain precisely upon the same footing now as then.

Governments are seldom the first to spy out their own advantages: that they should be as early as individuals to spy out their's, is out of the course of nature: without time, without personal interest, it is not to be expected: it is a great thing if they will make use of those advantages when pointed out to them by those who have both. The Bank (as already stated) were the creators of general credit: because

*5. W & M c. 20.

it was by that great Company that money was first collected in a quantity capable of pretending to any such advantage. It was not till the present reign that it entered into the conception of any body that it was possible for any body but the Bank to have a share in it. Not long after the commencement of the present reign some bold adventurer made the experiment, and it succeeded: succeeding, it did not want for imitators, and it spread at such a rate, and among hands so ill deserving of the credit they obtained, that government conceived itself called upon to stand up and put a check to it. Putting a check to the exercise of this faculty in other hands was one thing: stepping forth to take a share in the exercise of it, is another and quite a different thing: the transition was not easy. Appearances were even against it. Paper currency government had always had: and that currency, though carrying interest, had never borne any considerable premium, never a premium approaching to the amount of the interest. Bank paper in the mean time had always circulated without interest: so of late the paper of individuals. But in both instances the sum promised was payable on demand: and to pay on demand, one must have ready money in store: and to be expected to pay on demand, one must be at least thought to have money in store—but for government to have money in store! Government the arch spendthrift, the universal borrower, for government to have money in store! when was such a thing ever known? to whose conception could it ever shew itself as possible? The possibility of it has now, I think, been shewn: and that by means as simple as they promise to be efficacious.

ABSTRACT OR COMPRESSED VIEW OF A TRACT INTITULED CIRCULATING ANNUITIES

ABSTRACT OR COMPRESSED VIEW OF A TRACT INTITULED CIRCULATING ANNUITIES

EXHIBITING A PLAN FOR THE CREATION, CIRCULATION, AND PAYMENT OF A PROPOSED NEW SPECIES OF GOVERNMENT PAPER CURRENCY UNDER THE NAME OF ANNUITY NOTES

OF WHICH THE OBJECT IS TO AFFORD FACILITIES WHICH ARE NOT AFFORDED BY STOCK ANNUITIES OR ANY OTHER EXISTING GOVERNMENT SECURITIES FOR THE INVESTMENT OF SMALL, TEMPORARY, OR FLUCTUATING SUMS: WHEREBY MONEY MAY BE OBTAINED BY GOVERNMENT AT A REDUCED RATE OF INTEREST:

THE PRICE OF STOCKS RAISED AND UNIFORMLY SUPPORTED:

THE REDUCTION OF THE RATE OF INTEREST ON THE NATIONAL DEBT ACCELERATED AT THE SAME TIME WITH THE REDEMPTION OF THE PRINCIPAL:

A NEAT ADDITION MADE TO THE MASS OF NATIONAL CAPITAL, THE EVER-ENCREASING SOURCE OF NATIONAL INCOME:

FRUGALITY PROMOTED AMONG INDIVIDUALS OF ALL RANKS AND DENOMINATIONS:

THE MEANS OF PROVIDING FOR FUTURITY UPON THE SECUREST TERMS PLACED FOR THE FIRST TIME WITHIN THE REACH OF THE INFERIOR ORDERS: AND THEIR ATTACHMENT TO THE ESTABLISHED GOVERNMENT (THE BASIS OF NATIONAL SECURITY AND TRANQUILLITY) STRENGTHENED BY NEW TIES

1800

[Table of Contents]

CIRCULATING ANNUITIES, &c.*

Introduction

The *main principle* of the proposed measure consists in the opening the market for government annuities on terms of profit to government—viz. at a *reduced rate of interest*—to a mass of money, which, by existing circumstances, is either excluded from the faculty of yielding interest to the owners altogether, or, in the hands of bankers or otherwise, they are obliged to accept, on inferior security, a rate of interest inferior, all things considered, to that which, with a very considerable degree of profit, might be allowed by government. The annuities, thus created, to be charged upon the existing fund; and the money thus raised to be employed, as it comes in, in the redemption of debt, and thence in exoneration of that fund. The result and benefit of the measure, taking it on the *smallest* scale, will, besides the above profit to government, consist in the affording to the least opulent and most numerous class of individuals (Friendly Societies included)—in a word, to the great bulk of the community—the means of placing out *small hoards,* however minute, with a degree of advantage unattainable by any other means,† and this, too, even at *compound interest*—a mode of accumulation which, familiar as it is in *name,* is not in *effect* capable of being realized by any other means in favour of individuals, though so happily brought to bear in favour of the *public* in the instance of the *Sinking Funds;*—not to speak of the collateral advantage obtained, by creating on the part of the *lower* orders, in respect of the proposed new species of property, a fresh and more palpable interest in the support of that government, on the tranquillity of which the existence of such their property will depend.‡

*When the pen was first set to work upon these pages, there was generally understood to be a deficiency of paper money. At present, there is at least no such deficiency:—a superabundance seems much more probable. At the time of the want, the proposed paper presented itself as a remedy against the want: now, at the time of the superabundance, it presents itself as a safeguard against the sort of mischief—past, present, and impending—which may be traced to the superabundance.

†See Chap. [XVI. As Bowring changed the numeration of the chapters, this edition must deviate from his as far as such references are concerned.]

‡See Chap. [XVII.]

On the *larger* scale upon which it may be expected to expand itself, the measure, after accelerating the *otherwise* rapid ascent of government annuities to the par price,* and clearing away the 4 and 5 per Cents,† would afford the means of bringing the further reduction of the rate of interest on those annuities to its *maximum* in point of effect, *rate* of reduction and *rapidity* taken together;‡ *reduction* of *interest* accelerating, too, in this way, *redemption* of *principal,* instead of taking place of it and retarding it, as on the plan pursued in Mr. *Pelham's* days.§

Other paper currencies have been either (like the French *Assignats* and *Mandats,* &c.) engagements for money in *unlimited quantity,* and without *funds* for performance; or promises of *minute* portions of a species of property (for example *lands* and *houses*) incapable of being reduced into such portions; or, like some of the American currencies, promises of metallic money, payable at a period altogether *indefinite,* dating, for instance, from a fixed day posterior to the conclusion of a war.

By the *proposed* currency, nothing is engaged for but to pay such *moneys* as there are already funds for paying, and at such *times* at which there are funds for paying them; and this in a *quantity* which, by the terms of the engagement, has its *ne plus ultra,* and can in no case add to the existing amount of the engagements it finds charged upon those funds; reimbursing immediately, and with profit, the fund on which it draws, it stands distinguished by this prominent feature from all currencies as yet exemplified.‖

The losses, experienced or apprehended, from rash or penniless issuers of promissory notes, gave birth to the restrictions imposed on issues of sums below a certain magnitude. But this reason has no application to notes expressive of engagements, of the sort proposed, on the part of government. Issuing from such a *source,* the sums of the notes cannot be too minute: incapable of encreasing, certain even of diminishing, the amount of the engagements they find existing, the influx of them cannot be too great. The *smallness* of the *notes* adds to the *multitude* of the *customers;* the *multitude* of the notes *divides* the mass of the engagements, and does not *add* to it. Confined

---

*See Chap. V.
†See Chap. [VI.]
‡See Chap. [VII-IX.]
§See Chap. [XV.]
‖See Chaps. I, III, and IV.

within those bounds, the magnitude of the emission adds not only to the *profit* of the measure, but to the *security* of the fund.

A species of notes was *not long ago* proposed, whereby government annuities were to stand mortgaged, and *yet* (it was supposed) without diminution of their value:—and which were expected to pass, and be paid for, *as if* they had engaged for the payment of so much money, though without binding any assignable individual to the payment of it. But the *now* proposed plan engages for no payment for which adequate funds are not *already* in existence; nor without imposing on a determinate individual the obligation of making the payment out of those funds; not yet *burthens* those funds, without immediately *disburthening* them to a *superior* amount.

By taking from the load of government annuities which is found pressing on the market, the *sale of the Land Tax* for stock has bettered the terms of all succeeding loans. On the measure now proposed hangs a profit the same in kind, superior in degree.*

Reducing the mass of the national debt, the operation on the Land Tax *takes nothing* from the mass of national capital;—the proposed measure *adds* to it. The former borrows from capital, but refunds immediately, with 10 per Cent to boot; the latter adds still more to capital, and that as speedily, without having borrowed anything.†

Every penny of the national debt redeemed, if redeemed with money not borrowed from capital, is so much added (it will be shown) to that part of the national capital which does not consist of money. The addition made by the Sinking Fund to the mass of national capital is little inferior to the defalcation it makes from the mass of national debt. So many years as, by the aid of the proposed measure, may come to be struck off from the period which would otherwise have been occupied in the redemption of the debt, so many years' interest, upon the sum equal to the greatest amount of that debt, will therefore have been added, and that at *compound interest,* to the amount of national capital, by the operation of the proposed measure.

A sort of discovery in political economy has been made of late (for such it seems to be,) that commercial security is not less liable to suffer by *deficiency* than by *excess,* in respect of the customary quantity of paper in circulation. Among the advantages attendant on the proposed paper will be found that of affording a remedy, and that of

*See Chap. [X.]
†See Chap. [XI.]

the preventive kind, against the shocks which commercial security might otherwise have to sustain from such deficiency or excess.*

Shocks of that kind are not, however, the only mischief to which the community stands exposed, not only by the *abuse,* but even by the *use,* of every species of circulating paper as yet known. *Rise of prices* is another mischief, less heeded, but not less real. By gold and silver money to the same amount, the same mischief would (it is true) be produced, and in the same degree; but the magnitude of the mischief is in proportion to the *suddenness* of the addition, not to the *absolute quantum* of it; and, in the shape of cash, the influx is not susceptible of any such suddenness as in the shape of paper. To be capable of opposing an effectual barrier to a torrent of this sort, will be found to be among the properties of the proposed paper. To point out measures adequate to that end, is among the tasks undertaken in the plan of the proposed measure.†

The extent of the proposed emission being given, neither the *efficiency* nor the *utility* of the measure will be found open to dispute: the only room for *uncertainty* regards the *extent.* As to that point, cases are collected, presumptions offered: but nothing short of experience can determine.

CHAPTER I. PLAN FOR THE CREATION, EMISSION, PAYMENT, AND EVENTUAL EXTENSION, OF A PROPOSED NEW SPECIES OF GOVERNMENT PAPER, UNDER THE NAME OF ANNUITY NOTES

1. *Creation, Emission, and Payment.*

ART. 1. That there be issued from his Majesty's *Exchequer,* in whatever *quantity* (1) it shall be applied for by purchasers, on the *conditions* hereinafter mentioned, through the medium of such *local* or *sub-offices* as are hereinafter mentioned, and the *interest* or *dividends* paid in such manner as is also hereinafter mentioned, a competent number of *transferable promissory notes,* to be termed ANNUITY NOTES; importing, each of them, the grant of a *perpetual redeemable* annuity, payable to the purchaser or other *holder* of the Note, in consideration of the *principal* sum, on the repayment of which such annuity is made redeemable, and which accordingly constitutes the denominative *value* or *principal* of such Note; such interest to be paid half-yearly, (2) immediately after the expiration of each half-year.

*See Chap. [XII.]

†See Chapters [XIII and XIV.]

(1) Art. 1. (*In whatever quantity.*) The money thus raised being appropriated to the redemption of stock annuities, when that redemption is completed, the emission will cease, by articles 6 and 20; and, subject to that limitation, the more copious the emission, the more profitable the measure.

As to the mode of limiting, in cases of necessity, the portion producing the effect of money in the circulation, see note to Art. 16, and Ch. [XIV.] *Rise of Prices.*

(2) Art. 1. (*Half-yearly.*) Yearly would be more simple (as may be seen in the form exhibited for that purpose in Table II.) as well as more profitable to government; but being unconformable to the established usage, it would be apt to strike the customer as a great drawback from the value, stand in the way of the profit expected as under mentioned, by forbearance on the part of note-holders to receive the interest (see Ch. V.) and would be in a manner destructive of the advantage obtainable in the way of *compound* interest by persons keeping the paper in hand, as stock is kept in hand, for that purpose.

Art 2. That the interest be in such sums as to be capable of being computed *daily*, as in the case of *Exchequer Bills.* That the daily interest allowed upon the *standard Note* (so termed with reference to any smaller or larger Notes that may come eventually to be added to the circulation upon the same principle) be a *farthing;* (3)—and that the principal or denominative value of such standard Note be £12 16s; and that the interest, in order to afford a profit to government, be inferior to the current rate borne by government annuities at the opening of the issue, say £3 per Cent *nearly* (4)—a small sum being added to the principal sum, corresponding precisely to that rate, for the sake of making the sums the more *even*, especially at the bottom of the scale. (5)

(3) Art. 2. (*A farthing.*) By taking, for the standard Note, a principal sum, having for the amount of its *daily* interest, at the proposed rate of interest, an *even* sum (*i.e.* a sum having an existing piece of coined money or number of pieces of coined money, corresponding to it,) the *multiples* of this *standard* Note will in like manner have *even* sums for the respective amounts of their daily interest, and their *aliquot parts* will have for their amounts of interest, sums capable, when put together, of being made up into even sums.

Here, as in Exchequer Bills, the interest is computed daily, that each Note may receive from each day a *determinate* addition to its value, and may pass accordingly in circulation.

The smallest of all Notes possessing this property is taken for the standard Note, because the smaller a Note, the greater the number of persons that are capable of becoming customers for it.*

The standard Note being scarcely small enough in this view, it were better, perhaps, that not only the *half*, but the *quarter* of it should be issued at the same time.

The larger Notes will serve to protect the smaller ones from the contempt which might otherwise attach upon them, by reason of the smallness of the daily, and even weekly, amount of interest.

(4) Art. 2. (3 *per Cent.*) For the reason why no higher rate of interest could

*Had the *Bank* been sufficiently aware of this, would they have waited, till compelled by necessity, before they issued their £2 and £1 Notes?

be allowed with profit on a series of notes carrying daily interest, nor any lower above 2⅜ per Cent, which in the first instance might be too low, see *Currency Table*, note *m*. [Cf. Table I and pp. 223/224.]

(5) Art 2. (*Bottom of the scale.*) See *Currency Table.*

Art. 3. That each Note contain, on the face or back of it, a *table*, whereby the value of it, as *encreased* by daily interest, may be seen for every day in the year, by inspection, without calculation; also a table, whereby in case of forbearance (6) to receive the interest, the value of a Note of that magnitude, as encreased by daily interest, added to yearly interest so forborne to be received, may be seen, for any number of years, by a single addition; together with an indication, by means of which it may be seen (also by simple inspection) for what number of years, if any, the interest on the particular Note in question continues unreceived.

(6) Art. 3. (*Forbearance.*) See *Currency Table*. On a Note which passes on from hand to hand, any number of years may elapse before the interest on it is received from government; since the interest may be received by each holder with less trouble from the individual to whom he passes it. Hence one source of the profit to government (see Chap. V.). It is only where a man *keeps* a Note in his hands as a source of income, that the interest of it will be applied for at the offices. In fact, it is only in the case where a man means to hoard up at compound interest, that it will be necessary for him to receive the interest upon his paper from government; inasmuch as, without trenching upon the principal, he may spend the income from his Notes, by passing off a *proportion* to that amount, keeping in hand the rest.

Art. 4. That the interest on each Note, whenever issued, commence on the first day of each year of our Lord; and that, on Notes issued on the several days after such first day, the interest to the day of issue be *added* to the purchase money. (7)

(7) Art. 4 (*Interest added.*) Upon all Notes of the same denomination, interest must commence upon the same day (say the first day of the half year,) otherwise 365 Notes of the same denomination might be of so many different values: and if interest is to commence on that day, a purchaser in the way of issue must pay for the Note accordingly; otherwise customers would be apt to delay taking out their Notes till the last moment; keeping their money in their pockets, or employing it in other ways in the meantime; and then they would pour in, all at once, in crowds too great to be served.

Art. 5. That no such annuities be ever issued at a less price, (8) (*i.e.* so as to bear a greater rate of *interest*) than the *first* issue, and accordingly, that as often as any money comes to be raised at a higher rate of interest by *perpetual* annuities, it shall be by the creation of *stock annuities*, &c. as at present; and that a clause to this effect be a *fundamental* article in the contract made with the purchasers on the part of government, and be *inserted* accordingly in the tenor of the Note.

(8) Art. 5. (*At a less price.*) Want of security against depreciation has hitherto

been the bane of government currencies, and is *among* the reasons why banker's paper, yielding a low interest, is taken, notwithstanding the existence of a government currency (Exchequer Bills) yielding a higher interest. Government must, it is true, have the money it wants upon any terms; but so long as it reserves to itself the faculty of selling any *one* species of annuities (*ex. gr.* the existing stock annuities) in a quantity commensurate to the amount of the money it wants, at the *times* price, it may refuse to sell any other (such as the proposed note annuities) under a *fixed* price. As anybody may have as much of these annuities as he will at par, nobody will ever give more; and as no more can ever be sold than is applied for, and the demand for these annuities will encrease as the mass of existing stock annuities comes to be redeemed, by the money raised by the sale of these note annuities, backed by the money from so many other funds, no man need ever part with them at a less price; since, by taking an Annuity Note in the way of circulation, a man will save the trouble of going to the office for it, and taking it out in the way of issue, not to speak of the small fee which it may be necessary to require. (See Art. 17, and Chap. IV.)

Art. 6. That, at that price, the issue be kept open, so long as any of the redeemable stock annuities existing at the commencement of the issue, continue unredeemed, and no longer; and that this be *another* such fundamental article. (See Art. 20.)

Art. 7. That no such *note* annuity be paid off till the whole mass of *stock* annuities existing at the commencement of the issue, or created subsequently, shall have been paid off, (9) and that this be another such article.

(9) Art. 7. (*Paid off.*) By an assurance to this effect, nothing can ever be lost to government; because, so far from profit, while an annuity to the amount of £3 a-year can be paid off by £100, an annuity to no more than £2 19s a-year can never be paid off but to a loss: and it will be no small recommendation, especially when, by the operation (as will be seen) of this measure, the complete redemption of the existing mass of annuities has been brought to view. (See Chap VI.)

Art. 8. That for every £3 a-year annuity thus created, an equal portion of stock annuities be forthwith bought in and extinguished within a time to be limited; and that this be another such article.

Art. 9. That the *profit* resulting from the difference between the price at which each such annuity shall have been sold, and the price at which an equal mass of annuity shall have been bought in, be carried to the Sinking Fund, subject to such other dispositions, if any, as from time to time may be thought fit to be made by Parliament with respect to a predetermined portion or portions of it.

Art. 10. That, at the outset, no other Note be issued than the *standard* Note (£12 16s) with the *half*, or with the half and quarter of it.

Art. 11. That, by degrees, the series of Notes be extended *downwards*, each successive Note being the half of the one immediately preceding it (with or without the *omission* of any term or terms in such descending series) until it has descended to the lowest piece of silver coin in common currency, viz. a sixpence; and that it be then considered whether to give it a further extension downwards, viz. to the level of the copper coinage. (10)

(10) Art. 11. This, if not stopped by the expence (which encreases with the number and not with the value of the Notes,) would be attended with several advantages.

1. The Copper Notes, the receiving of interest upon them being attended with a degree of trouble, in proportion to the number requisite to produce a principal yielding a mass of interest worth regarding, would stay in the circulation, and by lessening *pro tanto* the amount of the supply capable of meeting the demands of those who want their paper to hoard for the purpose of income, it would encrease the scarcity of the paper of the first issue, and render customers the more willing to accept a second issue at a reduced rate of interest.

2. The profit by *forbearance to receive the interest* (see Chap. V.) would take place upon the whole of this branch of the currency.

3. The proposed paper, being so effectually guarded (as will be seen) against forgery (see Explanations to the *Form of an Annuity Note*,) and the copper coinage so much exposed to that crime, notwithstanding all the exertions that have been made to rescue it, the saving to the public, especially to the inferior and more numerous classes, on this score, would be a matter of considerable and almost universal accommodation:—and,

4. The saving to government, by the diminution of the expence of renewing the copper and other coinage, would be proportionably considerable.

How far the expence would be capable of being paid for by the profit, would be learned by experience from the *Silver Notes*.

The minuteness of the small Notes would be protected from contempt by their relation to the large ones; and to go in change for one another, they must, all of them (even *copper* not excepted,) bear an *interest*, and the same *rate of interest*.

A reason for making the extension *gradual*, may be to avoid perplexing the public mind with a multiplicity of Notes of different values, before it has been familiarized with any of them. But, at the worst, the magnitudes would be little, if anything, more numerous than in the case of Bank Notes.

Art. 12. That the Notes having for their respective values sums not exceeding the largest silver coin in use (viz. 5s) be distinguished by the appellation of *Silver Notes*, all above being for the same purpose termed *Gold Notes;* and that to facilitate the discrimination, a corresponding peculiarity of colour be given to the *Gold Notes.*

Art. 13. That, moreover, as convenience may suggest, the series be extended to a correspondent length, or otherwise, *upwards;* (11) in which case the series will, if complete, consist of *nine terms below* the standard Note, and as many *above* it—total, nineteen; having *two* for their common difference: values as by the annexed table.

(11) Art. 13. (*Upwards.*) The time for issuing *large* Notes, *i.e.* Notes of the magnitude of the *smallest Exchequer Bills* and upwards (in a word, all Annuity Notes above the £50 8s Notes,) will not arrive till after stock 3 per Cents are at par; for, till then, Exchequer Bills, yielding more interest, will draw off from the proposed Annuity Notes all customers whose quantum of money capable of being

kept in hand extends to such a purchase; unless possibly in the remote parts of the country, where Exchequer Bills are unknown, or not in use.

Art. 14. That when the credit of this paper has been established, or even from the first, Notes already taken out by individuals be received (as Bank Notes are at present) at the several government offices (12) in the country as well as in the town, and re-issued from thence in the way of circulation, as they would be between individual and individual, charged with the intervening interest, to as many as may think proper to receive them at that value.

(12) Art. 14. (*Received at government offices.*) Were this to be done from the *first*, a great lift would certainly be given to the proposed currency at once: the only objection seems to be, the possibility lest, in case of any sudden turn taken against it by the public mind, the Exchequer should for a time be overloaded with it, *i.e.* labour under a *deficit* of cash (the only money that nobody can refuse) to the amount of it. But in Chapter IV. the improbability of such an event, and at the same time an effectual remedy, is pointed out.

Supposing Bank Notes to be driven out of the circulation,* the same sort of *necessity*, or supposed necessity, which gives employment to *Bank* paper in the transactions of government† and in other transactions upon a large scale, in preference to cash, to save *counting, examining,* and *luggage,* would create an equal demand for the *Annuity Note* paper on that score.

Art. 15. That the offices from whence the proposed paper is issued to the purchasers, be, *in the first instance,* the several *local Post Offices* (13) in town and country, with the eventual addition of any of the other local government offices (such as the Stamp and Excise Offices,) or in case of need, other offices to be established for the purpose, in such situations and numbers as may be found necessary.

(13) Art. 15. (*Post Offices.*) *Dispatch, punctuality, cheapness* in the transaction of the business, *sufficiency of number,* and *equality of distribution* in regard to the *stations,* forming the characteristics of the Post Office establishment, as compared with all other provincially-diffused official establishments. These form the properest *stations* for the transaction of the business, as well as the properest, or rather only

*This (it would seem) would depend upon government; since if government, in the issues of Annuity Notes, refused to take Bank Notes in payment for them, the unwillingness to take barren paper, when interest bearing paper was to be had, would soon become general, if not universal. As to the propriety of this, or any further measures in the same view, see Chapters [XIII] and [XIV].

†"Guineas *cannot* be used in any considerable dealings," says Mr. H. Thornton, in his evidence before the Committee of the House of Lords on the stoppage of the Bank. (Report, p.72; reprinted in Mr. Allardyce's Address on the Affairs of the Bank, Appendix, p.54.) By Mr. Abraham Newland's evidence, in the above Report (p.62,) it appears that the payments of cash into and from the Exchequer, are small in comparison with the payments in Bank Notes; not above £50,000 or £60,000 a-day, upon an average, remaining in the Exchequer in the shape of cash; forming a daily total of money (cash and paper together) averaging about £151,095 (see Chap. V.). And out of £20,000,000 paid on the score of dividends at the Bank, not above £1,300,000 or £1,400,000 is paid otherwise than in Bank Notes.

proper, standard for the *mode* of conducting it. In the London Penny Post Offices, deliveries of letters six in a day; therefore once every day cannot be too often for deliveries of packets of Annuity Notes. Six times a-day go letters, some of them with money in them; therefore *once* in a day cannot be too often for money to go without the letters.

The oftener the receiver's hands are emptied of the principal money, the less the degree of pecuniary responsibility that need be required of him: few of the existing Post Offices, town or country, that may not be trusted with a day's stock (say £200 or £300) at a time (more in some places, according to the opulence and populousness of the spot;) many whom it would not be prudent to trust with a month's stock, say thirty times that amount.

This public money being required to be kept unmixed with any other monies, and in a government package, and the officer declared to be a *"servant"* of government,—in respect of its deficiency, otherwise than from accident, he *might* be treated on the footing of embezzlement;—capital felony in case of absconding; single otherwise.

In the Penny Post Office, one-tenth of a penny is the pay in respect of each letter, for marking each with two stamps; besides the trouble of examining and receiving the money, and occasionally of giving change, in the case of those letters with which money is paid.

The proper quantum of pay is in all cases the least that will be accepted by a person competent to the business; such cases only excepted in which, from the nature of the service, the value of it is capable of being raised to an indefinitely encreasing pitch of excellence by extraordinary exertions.

With this exception, quantity of *trouble, not value* of the subject-matter, any otherwise than with a view to pecuniary responsibility, is the proper standard and efficient cause of demand for pay. *Poundage,* considered as a mode of remuneration, is therefore very apt to be disproportionate and excessive.

On a letter, for which no more than a penny is received—out of which penny the expence of conveyance must be defrayed, as well as a portion of the expence of general superintendence, and a profit made—10 per Cent for the trouble of receiving it, is at the same time almost as little as *can* be given, and yet (though in this case no more than the tenth part of a penny) as much as *requires* to be given. For receiving the price of a set of stamps, some of them as high as several pounds a-piece, the same poundage would be acknowledged to be excessive.

If the trouble attending the issuing of an Annuity Note (the filling up the blanks, and examining and taking care of the purchase money) were no greater than that of receiving a penny-post letter (allowance made for the proportion on which money is received, and the requisite extra trouble taken,) experience shows that the tenth part of a penny would be a sufficient recompence: but the trouble would be in a considerable degree greater—perhaps three, four, or five times as great: —therefore so, it would be necessary, should the pay. A halfpenny might in this way be necessary, and at the same time sufficient, in the case of the standard Note of £12 16s; and upon a Note of this magnitude, not only a halfpenny, but several pence, might perhaps (as will be seen in Art. 17,) without much inconvenience be thus imposed; and thus, as far as Notes of that magnitude were concerned, the expence of management at the local offices might be thrown upon the individuals—the purchasers. But though a purchaser might not grudge a few pence for the profit to be made in the way of interest upon a £12 16s Note, he certainly would not give so much as a halfpenny for the profit to be made upon a sixpenny Note, as it would be three or four years before the interest would have reimbursed the fee thus advanced. In Notes that were to a certain degree below the standard Note (say in the £3 4s or £1 12s Notes,) it would be necessary that the fee upon each, though not remitted altogether, should be reduced below the amount of the lowest coin,—a farthing; which would be the case, if Notes under the £3 4s Note, for instance, were not to be taken out but in *parcels*, and a halfpenny or a farthing were the fee upon each parcel; in which case it would be necessary that government should make up the difference. This it would be well worth its while to do, even upon the Copper Notes; since, in Yorkshire, according to Adam Smith, before the restriction on small notes, sixpenny notes were issued by individuals in abundance. [Cf. book II, ch. II.]

As to the *general* Annuity Note Office,—having no intercourse with individual customers, nor with the local office-keepers but by letter, the nature of the business admits of its being conducted with perfect regularity, and upon a plan extremely simple. (See Chap. VI, *Profit in respect of management.*)

Art. 16. That to save trouble in the issue of the smaller Notes, especially the *Silver Notes,* government reserves to itself the power of fixing the *least* quantity (14) of Annuity Note money, which an individual shall be allowed to take out at once; as also to *prescribe* the *composition* of that quantity, taking care to leave to the customer the choice of the composition, as far as it may be a matter of indifference to government.

(14) Art. 16. (*Least quantity.**) A Note under this amount would consequently not be capable of being taken out singly, but only as one in a parcel, with other Notes of the same or different magnitudes. So also, *perhaps*, in regard to the carrying in Notes to the local office to be sent up to the general office, to be returned from thence with the interest; as likewise in regard to the changing large for small Notes, or *vice versa*, or injured Notes for fresh ones. But instead of a prohibition, as above, the same end might be answered, perhaps more advantageously, in some, at least, of the above instances, by a small fee, acting as a penalty to the amount of it, as by the next article.

By this means, the offices would be kept clear of the most troublesome, as well as numerous, class of customers. *Silver* Notes, for example, would in that case be taken out, not *singly* by *journeymen* manufacturers, but in *parcels* by *masters*, by whom at pay-day they would be distributed among their journeymen.

Interest would by this means be *capable* of being received at the offices upon the smallest Notes (which, as above, is necessary to their passing in change for large ones;) though what is probable is, that on the small it will scarcely ever be demanded. (See on this head, Chap. V. *Profit by interest undemanded.*)

What is the least Note that can be issued with profit, will be determined by the quantity of *time* occupied in the operations necessary to the issue of it. Possibly on this account, in the Silver, or at least in the Copper Notes (if any,) the actual signature of the local office-keeper might be dispensed with, and a stamp of some kind (affixed at the time of issue at *his* office, or previously at the *general* office) be employed in its stead.

In this power is included that of suspending the issue of Notes of any particular magnitude or magnitudes; by which means, in case of an *inordinate* demand for the proposed paper (viz. such an one as shall threaten to swell to a pernicious magnitude the quantity of it producing the effect of money in the circulation,) a stop may be put at any time to the inconvenience. (See Chap. [XIV], *Rise of Prices.*)

---

*Not less, for instance, than the amount of the *quarter* Note (the £3 4s Note) or the *half quarter* (the £1 12s Note).

Art. 17. That powers be given to the King in *Council,* or to the *Treasury,* from time to time to declare, whether any and what *fee,* not exceeding a certain amount, shall be paid by the *purchaser,* on the emission of each Note or parcel of Notes constitutive of such or such a sum; as also on the *exchange* of an old Note for a fresh Note, at the instance of the holder—regard being had in both cases to the magnitude of the sum constituting the value of the Note or mass of Notes; as also to *call in* at any time any such Note or Notes, so it be without expence to the holder, for the purpose of their being *examined* or *exchanged;* and, by suspension of interest, or other penalties, to enforce obedience to such calls; as also to declare whether any and what *fee* shall be paid by the holder on the *receipt* of the *interest* due on each Note or parcel of Notes. (15)

(15) Art. 17. (*Emission, exchange,* or *payment of interest.*) Imposing, after the opening of the Office, the minutest fee on any of these occasions, would be a breach of engagement, and moreover, if otherwise than by authority of Parliament, an invasion of parliamentary rights.

In regard to the fixation of the amount, no harm could result from allowing to the executive government a moderate latitude; such as from a farthing to sixpence on the standard Note of £12 16s; and room would thus be allowed for following the dictates of convenience, as indicated by experience. Without being so great as to check the *issue,* the fee might perhaps be made to favour the *circulation.* In the circulation it might produce a *premium,* the *maximum* of which would be the amount of the fee.

The progress of the issue being known everywhere, it is scarcely possible that, in one and the same *place,* this paper should be meeting with customers in the way of issue, and at the same time meet with refusals in the way of circulation; the *trouble of taking out,* however small, being, with or without the *expence* of the proposed fee, so much saved by taking the Note in the course of circulation. Not even as between different places does it seem very likely that any such contrariety should take place; but were the inconvenience to happen, the proposed fee, if made a little larger than would otherwise be necessary, might afford something of a remedy. Suppose the fee on the £12 16s [Note] to be 4d, and the circulation dull at York, while the issue was brisk at Bristol: a York banker, taking them at par at York, might, by sending them to a correspondent at Bristol, sell the Notes there at 2d or 3d premium, especially if a correspondence of that sort were favoured in regard to postage. So long as this lasted, the issue at York would be stopped; instead of getting them at the government office, the customer would get them at the bankers, whereby he would save 1d or 2d, besides a part of the trouble; and the load upon the market at York would be taken off. An agio to an *unlimited* amount would indeed be destructive of one of the characteristic advantages of the measure; but an agio to an amount thus strictly *limited,* would scarcely (it is supposed) be felt as a disadvantage. Were the Note kept in hand, though it were but for a few days, the interest on it for that small space of time would afford complete reimbursement of the greatest possible amount of loss.

If, in regard to the quantum of the fee, the principle were, that it should amount to just so much as would be sufficient for the remuneration of the local distributor,—this, again, would be a reason for making it variable within certain bounds; for, under any given plan for conducting the business, it would be matter of experiment what is the lowest fee that would be sufficient; and by such improvements on the plan, as reflection fed by experience might indicate, the time and trouble, and thence the quantum of remuneration necessary, might from time to time come to be reduced.

Art. 18. That periodical accounts be *published* of the progress of the issue, (16) as regularly, and circulated as extensively, as the prices of stocks are at present, under heads expressive of the day, the *place*, the number of Notes of each *magnitude*, and the *total amount* issued on each day at each place; together with the *encrease* or *decrease* of the amount, as compared with former periods; and any such other particulars as may be of use.

(16) Art. 18. (*Accounts published.*) The uses of such publication are as follows:—

1. That, from seeing this paper taken out in the way of *issue*, people may be the more ready to take it in the way of circulation.

2. That in case of its proving to be in any degree an impediment to the circulation of Bank and country banker's paper, the parties concerned may, by observing how the paper spreads, have timely warning to withdraw or keep out of the market any superfluity in their own paper.

3. That in case of any local difficulty as to the circulation of the paper in *one* part of the country (for instance, by reason of any sudden and extraordinary demand for cash) the load of the paper in the market may be lightened, by sending it to *another* part of the country, where the issue is observed to be going on briskly.

4. That from the amount of the issue in the course of each given period, indications may be deduced of the degree in which any *temporary* cause of depreciation must have operated, before it can have the effect, not only of stopping the *issue*, but subjecting to a *discount* the quantity already *in circulation*.

5. That *data* may be afforded, from which the several classes of persons interested may be able to foresee the approach of the several results or effects in which they are interested; such as the *rise of stock* 3 per Cents to par, the growing *scarcity* of government annuities, the *reduction* of the *rate of interest* paid by government in respect of them, the encrease in the mass of national *capital* by the paying off the annuitants, the *reduction* of the rate of interest *in general*, &c.

2. *Eventual Extension.*

Art. 19. That if, by this and other means, three per Cent stock annuities should ever have risen to par, the produce of the issue of note annuities be thereupon applied to the *paying off*, instead of *buying in* stock annuities; and so *toties quoties*, buying in whenever they are *under* par, paying off whenever they are *at* or *above* par.

Art. 20. That inasmuch as the paying off stock annuities, the greatest part thereof carrying three per Cent, will lead to a rapid and almost simultaneous *conversion* (17) of the whole amount thereof into note annuities, bearing nearly the same rate of interest;—and inasmuch as, upon the redemption of the last parcel of redeemable stock annuities, the emission of note annuities at this rate of interest must (according to article 6) immediately cease;—and inasmuch as the mass of government annuities will in the meantime *have* already been much reduced, and by the continued operation of the continually encreasing powers of the existing Sinking Funds, the scarcity *will* be growing greater and greater every day (notwithstanding that, being continually exposed to be paid off at par, they will be incapable of bearing any considerable *premium*), the offices be opened thereupon for the emission of a *second* issue, at a *reduced* rate of interest, say £2 7s 5d—*i.e.* 2⅜ per Cent nearly—(viz. by raising the price of the standard Note from £12 16s to £16;)—the produce of such *second* issue to be applied to the paying off the Notes of the *first* issue, and the second issue to *close* as soon as the redemption of the Notes of the first issue shall have been completed.

(17) Art. 20. (*Conversion.*) *Conversion* is a word used for shortness, to indicate the result of two operations:—on the part of government, the redemption of such or such a mass of stock annuities; and on the part of the stockholders so expelled, a purchase made of the fresh mass of note annuities to equal amount—a result which, in the case where a man does not choose to part with the mass of annuity he receives from government, is a necessary consequence.

That the disposition to accede to such conversion should be nearly universal, seems altogether probable. The loss of interest is but a sixtieth; and, in all other points, the change will be greatly to a man's advantage. In a very short period it cannot fail of taking place. When stocks (three per Cents) are no higher than par, the £2 19s note annuities are (it is true) worth, as far as interest only is concerned, no more than £98 6s 8d; —but no sooner are three per Cents up at 102, than the £2 19s per Cent, are worth upwards of £100¼.

Among any such group of annuitants thus forcibly expelled, there will always be a certain proportion (it is true,) who at the time of the expulsion were desirous of disposing of their annuities, and would have done so, had the matter been left to their choice. But, by the supposition, there will be at the same time another group desirous of purchasing a mass of annuities, equal at the least to that which is thus wished to be disposed of; otherwise the price of the article would not be at par, which it is supposed to be:—therefore, setting the one demand against the other, the whole amount of the mass of annuities paid off at or above par, may be set down as so much taken from a set of proprietors, who will not part with such their property, but will accept of it in the proposed new shape.

Proposed mode of effecting the conversion.—Adjoining to the room where a man signs in the stock-book a recognition of the redemption of his mass of stock annuities, are two other rooms—a money-room (as at present the dividend-warrant room) and an Annuity Note room. Question by the clerk: "Is it money you want? yonder is the room for receiving money, and here is the warrant for it. Do you keep your annuities? yonder is the Annuity Note room, and here is your warrant for the amount in Annuity Notes."

On this occasion, *two* provisions, customarily inserted in the Acts, will require observance:—1. That notice (a year in some instances,* half-a-year in others†) be given of the intention to pay off; and that the masses paid off at once be not less than of a certain magnitude—£1,000,000 in some cases, £500,000 in others. Of the *former* the object was, as it should seem, that a man may have time to form his

*25 Geo. II. c. 27 (the first consolidated Act); 39 & 40 Geo. III. c. 32.

†3 Geo. III. c. 10.

plans in regard to the employment of his money; of the *other*, to obviate the suspicion of personal preferences, which, if the masses were small and undetermined, might be manifested in favour of individuals; viz. by paying a man off, or respiting him, whichever were most advantageous at the time.

To comply with these conditions, as far as appears either practicable, or material, or consistent with the practice and intention of the Legislature, suppose the course taken, in regard to the redemption of the *stock* annuities, with a view to their proposed conversion into *note* annuities, to be as follows, viz.—

1. Notice to be given, in the usual form, on the day immediately preceding the *next* day for a half-yearly payment, or on any earlier day subsequent to the then *last* day of half-yearly payment;—such notice to be expressive of a general *intention* on the part of Parliament, from and after the day mentioned in such notice, to pay off the then remaining mass of stock annuities, in masses or lots of not less than the above stipulated magnitude of £500,000, as fast as the sums of money for the making of such payments shall respectively be completed;—the order in which the masses shall be paid off, to be determined by a lottery, unless changed in the way next mentioned.

By the publication of the progress of the issue in the newspapers, it will be known all over the Kingdom, day by day, what sum is in hand applicable to this purpose. The masses being marked in numerical order for this purpose, each stock-holder will see, day by day, whether the mass his portion of stock belongs to is ripe for payment, or if not, how soon it is likely to become so.

That a *general* notice of the *intention*, in contradistinction to a particular notice for the very day, was all that was meant by the Legislature, may be inferred with some degree of assurance from the practice in Mr. Pelham's case. Fifty-seven millions worth, and upwards, was the mass of capital in relation to which notice was given on that occasion—that, in the event mentioned, it should, on a particular day mentioned, be paid off: so that, if the invitation given had remained altogether without compliance (an event which for some time was highly probable*) the whole would on that one day have been to be paid off, and the money put into the hands of as many as on that one day might happen to apply for it. But, that such payment could have taken place, either in respect of the whole of the mass, or so much as the greater part of it, and that, either on the day fixed, or on any assignable subsequent day, within a week's or a month's or even a quarter's distance of it, is a result that does not present itself as probable.

To borrow nearly fifty-eight millions in the lump, and at that early period too—or even nine and twenty millions, and that payable all in one day—presents itself as an affair of no small difficulty, even on the ordinary footing of mutual obligation as between the two contracting parties. How much greater the difficulty, if (as by the supposition contended against) one party (composed of the eventual lenders) was to be bound, while government, the eventual borrower, was to remain loose!

It seems, therefore, that (according to the interpretation put in that instance by Parliament) by a notice that the capital of government annuities will, to such amount, be paid off on such a day, nothing more is to be understood than that (as here proposed) a *part* will be paid off on *that* day to such as apply for it, and the *remainder* at some *subsequent* day or days, according as the money for paying off shall happen to come to hand.

If not—and if it were regarded as an article not to be dispensed with, that no one parcel of the consolidated 3 per Cents should be paid off but on one of the half-yearly days in use for the payment of the dividends on those annuities, and that

*Sinclair, [*The History of the Public Revenue of the British Empire*, ed. 1785] ii, 112.

day posterior, by one day at least above a twelvemonth, to the first day on which the notice to that effect shall have been made public—the consequence will be, that upon the *first* parcel so paid off, the loss of *time* and *interest* will amount to a full twelvemonth; but that upon all *subsequent* parcels, the loss of time will be such as cannot amount to less than a year and a quarter upon the whole. For paying off the *first* parcel—say on the 25th of December 1804—the latest day on which notice can be made public, will be the 24th of December 1803. For paying off the *second* parcel, the earliest day that can be appointed will be the 24th of June 1805. Should a parcel of the magnitude required by the Act (£500,000) have come in or been made sure by the 25th of December 1803, notice may be given on the next day, appointing, as the day of payment in respect of that *second* sum, the 24th of June 1805. But on this *second* transaction, 1½ year, all but a day, would be lost. If, again, by the 23rd of June 1804, a *third* sum happened to have been collected or made sure, and notice given accordingly for the 24th of June 1805, as before—then upon that sum no more than a year and a day would be lost, as above mentioned; and upon the *whole*, supposing the intermediate days—of collection perfected, and notice given accordingly—to run in a regular series between such earliest day and such latest day, it would, by the nature of an arithmetical series come to the same thing as if the quantity of time thus lost amounted to 1¼ year in *each* instance.

2. Meantime, by way of encouragement to stockholders to *expedite* the measure by their concurrence, *books* to be opened, in which each individual may *subscribe* his consent to take Annuity Notes for his stock at the same price. The amounts of stock thus subscribed to be made up into masses of a determinate size, as above,—the lot which is first filled to be the last paid off—and so on in the order of the lots;—and the operation of the lottery to be confined to such parcels of stock as shall have remained unsubscribed.

By subscribing, and subscribing as soon as possible, a man (it has been seen) will have nothing or next to nothing to lose, and he will have much to gain.

As the holders of Annuity Note paper of the first issue will all of them, sooner or later, be paid off, and as, when any such Note of the first issue is paid off, the holder will have no certain means of placing his money out at interest upon the same sort of security, otherwise than by purchasing into the second issue at the reduced rate of that issue, he will naturally be upon the look-out for paper of the first issue. But as this will be the case with regard to all such expelled note-holders as fast as they are expelled, such paper will (it is evident) bear an encrease of price:—which encrease will of course be greater, the more remote the period appears, at which the mass, to which the Note belongs, is about to be paid off.

From every such mass of Annuity [Notes] of the first issue, it is known that sooner or later one quarter of the amount will be struck off, unless a man chooses to receive the principal or purchase-money instead of it; and this quarter, compared with the reduced remainder, may be considered as a sort of temporary annuity, for a term not altogether certain, but longer and longer in proportion as the Note stands higher on the privileged list.

Under these circumstances, the opening of a second issue will immediately (it is evident) give an encreased value to the whole remaining paper of the first issue;—which encrease cannot at any time, nor in the instance of any class, amount to quite so much as 25 per Cent (the difference between the rates of interest on the first and last issues,) payable during the time of respite—and from thence will vary, in a series decreasing down to 0. The Notes of each class will at all times be worth something more than the Notes of the same magnitude, in an inferior class; and as the time for the redemption of the highest or last redeemable class, and thereby for the reduction of the rate of interest upon each class, is seen to approach, the extra value of the Notes of all the classes will sink together.

At the outset, this rise in value will approach the nearer to the 25 per Cent, the less quick the progress of the redemption promises to be. Suppose it to be no more than 12½ per Cent, or even 6¼ per Cent, even at the very outset, and in the case of the very highest class, the prospect of it will still hold out a very ample *premium* or *bonus* to subscribers. The subscription will be a sort of *lottery*, with all prizes and no blanks; since the worst that can happen to a man will be, not to receive more than he ever paid principal and interest; nor yet so entirely a lottery, but that diligence will encrease his chance.

As between Note and Note in the same class, the order of priority in respect of redemption might be determined, either by the number of the Note (as in the case of Exchequer Bills,) or by lot.

The *complication* incident to this state of things may present itself at the moment as an objection to the measure:—Notes of two issues current at a time; those of the closed issue bearing a premium, different in the several classes, however numerous; those of the open issue, bearing no premium; and each Note encreasing, and thereby varying in value every year, half-year, quarter, month, week, or day, as time advances, according to the magnitude of the Note. But as to government, the complication will not be attended with any embarrassment. Whatever variation the price may be subjected to in the way of *circulation*, there will be but one price for government to *pay* on *redemption*, or *receive* on *issue*. To individuals, the variety is productive of neither loss nor trouble. Where the premium is an object to a man, he will accordingly pay it on taking a Note, or make a demand of it on parting with it; where the difference is no object, he will neither pay it nor demand it. It cannot be productive of any dispute; since whatever may be the amount, no man has any *right* to claim it: there will be no authoritative *table* to fix it, and attest the reality of it, as in the case of the augmentation by *lapse of time*—I mean by daily or half-yearly interest unreceived. To those who will take upon them the trouble of attending to the variation, and whose dealings in relation to it will thence be conducted on a large scale, it will afford a source of profit; and in that character may afford to two classes of professional men, the stock-broker and the stock-jobber, a compensation for any loss they might otherwise sustain from the measure.

Even the owners of the 4 and 5 per Cents might find in this arrangement, not only an inducement to come cheerfully into the measure, but such a compensation, or at least mitigation, in respect of their loss, as on the score of humanity (for *strict justice* is out of the question) may perhaps not be disapproved. For such of them as shall have come in by a time to be fixed, the highest classes may be reserved, in preference even to the earliest subscribers of the 3 per Cents;—the 5 per Cents being ranked in this respect above the 4 per Cents.

As the purchasers of these extra-interest annuities have had the less to pay for them, on account of the prospect of their redemption, inasmuch that, at a time when 3 per Cents are at 64, even 5 per Cents are 3 per Cent below par, the redemption might, under the above terms, be, in appearance at least, rather profitable than otherwise; and really and indisputably profitable in the instance of all such as, at the time in question, would have been disposed to employ their money in other ways.

Even in the case of such as were prevented by *distance* from subscribing within the time, an expedient might perhaps be found for preserving the individuals as well as the public from being deprived of the advantage; stockholders, for example, resident in, or on a voyage to or from, the East or West Indies.

At the instance of a spontaneous though unauthorized agent, a person so circumstanced might be admitted to the benefit of the subscription, the portion of stock annuities cancelled, and the amount in Annuity Notes kept in deposit for him at the Office, such agent undertaking to indemnify the proprietor against *any loss* by the subscription, and finding such sufficient security for the fulfilment of the undertaking as shall be appointed for that purpose.

As to the clause restricting government from paying otherwise than in such large masses as the £500,000 and £1,000,000 above mentioned, supposing the object above conjectured (viz. the exclusion of personal preferences) to have been the real one, the expedient proposed (viz. determination by lot—an expedient employed in similar instances under the old French government) will be equally competent to the attainment of it. In all events, the difficulty would not extend beyond the conversion effected by the *first* issue. The *paper*, if accepted, would stand clear of this and other such clogs.

Were it otherwise, a stipulation of this sort might be attended with some inconvenience and expence. As by the nature of the process of reduction, the charge precedes the exoneration (since it is by the charge, and that alone, that the money for the exoneration is to be furnished,) the consequence might be, that, to the extent of a certain amount of paper, a half-year's charge, on the score of interest, might be incurred upon so much paper of the *open* issue, before the sums were collected that would be necessary to effect the exoneration by the redemption of a correspondent quantity of paper of the *closed* issue.

Art. 21. That the amount of all interest saved, as well by the redemption of stock annuities redeemed by the produce of the existing or other future funds (and, therefore, without the preparatory emission of a mass of Annuity Note paper to the corresponding value) as by the progress made in the reduction of the rate of interest in the way just mentioned (viz. by the preparatory emission of a mass of Annuity Note paper, at a lower rate of interest, followed by the redemption of a correspondent mass of stock annuities, or note annuities, at the higher rate,) be carried (immediately) to the Sinking Funds—on the principle of the provision made, in the like behalf, in and by the existing Act (viz. the New Sinking Fund Act, 32 Geo. III. c. 32, § 2).

Art. 22. That, *immediately* upon the redemption of the last parcel of note annuities of the *first* issue, the offices be *again* opened for the emission of a third issue at the next lowest rate of interest suitable to the nature of note annuities on which interest is computed daily, say £1 9s 6d—*i.e.* 1½ per Cent nearly (18);—viz. by raising the price of the standard Note from £16 to £25 4s;—the produce of such *third* issue to be appropriated to the redemption of the note annuities of the *second* issue as above: with like provision as above in favour of the *Sinking Funds*: and so *toties quoties*, in so far as any such farther reduction may be deemed eligible.

(18) Art. 22. (1½ *per Cent nearly.*) See Table I. Note *m*. From 3 to 1½ is no greater reduction than from 6 to 3;—being that which, in the course of 33 years, viz. between 1717 and 1750, took place in regard to divers parcels of stock, though the reduction of the great mass from 4 to 3 per Cent was not completed till 1757. (See Sinclair on the Revenue, II. 112.)

When Adam Smith wrote, the rate of interest in the Dutch funds was already as low as 2 per Cent (B. I. ch. ix.).

Art. 23. That inasmuch as, so long as any portion of the redeemable annuities remain unextinguished, there may remain two parcels of Annuity Note paper, bearing two different rates of interest—the higher *closed,* the other *open*—provision be made, that in case of the creation of any portion of capital in stock annuities, at any time thereafter, by reason of money borrowed for the support of a war or otherwise, powers be given for extending the issue of note annuities to the extent of the capital so created, and at the rate of interest the then last or open issue of note annuities shall receive.

[NOTES TO TABLE I]

a Standard Note, or Unit, to which the other Notes bear reference; those above it in the scale being *multiples* of it and of each other; those below it *submultiples.* Common measure, 2.

b In the series marked thus the fractional parts of a farthing are omitted, as not capable of being paid, nor requiring for any other purpose to be taken into account.

c Rate of interest reduced thereby to £2 19s 4d¾ per Cent, fractional parts of a farthing being neglected.

d Magnitudes, inserted in the series for uniformity, but supposed to be superfluous.

e By putting together the *six* sizes marked thus, the sum of £100 exactly may be made up.

f By putting together the *five* sizes marked thus, the sum of £1,000 exactly may be made up; likewise by ten £100 Notes, if £100 Notes are admitted.

g The Notes marked thus may be termed Silver Notes; all above them being styled Gold Notes. It is proposed that the paper for the Gold Notes shall, for distinction sake, be *yellow.*

h In the Daily Augmentation Table on the back of each Note, the periods will vary in number according to the magnitude of the Note. In the standard Note it is proposed they should be periods of *eight* days; and so in the double, quadruple, octuple, and half of it—amount of encrease by the end of such period in the standard Note, 8 farthings (=2d). On any intermediate day the exact sum will be made up by adding 1, 2, 3, 4, 5, 6, or 7 farthings, half-pence, twopences, or half farthings, according to the distance of the day in question from the last *tabular* day (*i. e.* day mentioned in the Table). In the higher Notes the periods might be more numerous; in the lower Notes they would of course be less numerous, since a period indicating an encrease under a farthing would be of no use. Among the Silver Notes, in the 4*s* Note the year could contain but *four* such periods; in the 2*s* Note but *two*; in the 1*s* Note but *one*; and in the sixpenny Note but a part. To give a whole farthing will *here* require a whole year and part of another. In this there will be no *Daily Augmentation* Table; and in the other Silver Notes the *daily* and *yearly* table will be combined into one. In the four intermediate Notes between the Silver Notes and the half of the standard Note, periods of 32 days will suffice.

i In this series the fractional parts of a farthing are inserted, as being requisite to be taken into account in respect of payment of interest by government, or allowance of interest, as between individual and individual in the way of circulation. For though on the lowest Note (the sixpenny Note) the interest will not amount to so much as a farthing by the end either of the first or second half-year, yet by the end of the third half-year it will amount to a farthing with a fraction over, and consequently, on *three* such Notes taken together, it will amount to a farthing by the end of the first half-year, and on two by the end of the second half-year.

k The reduction being from £2 19s 4d¾ per Cent to £2 7s 6d¼ (fractions of a farthing neglected) viz. a trifle *more* than 2⅜ per Cent.

l By putting together the *three* sizes marked thus, the sum of £100 exactly may be made up.

m The two series or scales here given, with their respective *halves* and *doubles*, &c. will be found to be the *only* convenient series for a currency on which *daily* interest is to be computed. The series which has the £12 16s Note for its standard Note, giving for the rate of *yearly* interest £2 19s 4d¾, being a trifle *less* than £3 per Cent; the series which has the £16 Note for its standard Note, giving for the rate of *yearly* interest £2 7s 6d¼ being a trifle more than 2⅜ per Cent.

By each of these series or scales *even* sums (sums having a certain number of pieces of existing coin exactly corresponding to them) are given for the amount of the several Notes respectively exhibited by them; in any other series that could be interposed *fractional* sums (sums *not* having any number of existing coins exactly corresponding to them) would present themselves in several places.

By altering the principal sum (or purchase money for the *standard* amount of interest, viz. a farthing a day) from £16 to no more than half as much. viz. £8, the rate of interest would be *doubled*; that is, raised from a trifle more than 2⅜ per Cent to a trifle more than 4¾. But, were this to be the rate allowed at the present period (viz. anno 1800), instead of *profit* there would be loss. The rate given by the *last loan* (21st February 1800) being no more than £4 14s 2d¼ per Cent, instead of £4 15s 0d½, which would be the rate allowed, if no more than £8 were taken for the above standard amount of interest.

By altering the *principal* (or *purchase money* of the said standard amount of interest) from £12 16s to as much again, viz. £25 12s, the rate of interest corresponding to that amount would be reduced by one-half; *i. e.* reduced from almost £3 per Cent to £1 9s 8d¼—being a trifle less than 1½ per Cent.

If, instead of being *reduced* by one-half as above, the *purchase money* of the said standard amount of interest were to be *doubled, i. e.* raised from £16 to £32, the rate of *interest* corresponding to that amount would be reduced by one-half—*reduced* from a trifle *more* than 2⅜ per Cent to a trifle *more* than 1 3/16 per Cent.

For all these rates of interest, as well as for any number of *multiples* or *aliquot parts* of them, this same Table (it is evident) may be made to serve; viz. by conceiving the series of *principal sums* to be *shifted* so many degrees higher or lower; the corresponding series of *amounts of interest* remaining *unmoved;* or, *vice versâ*, by conceiving the series of *amounts of interest* to be *shifted* so many degrees higher or lower, the corresponding series of *principal sums* remaining *unmoved*—the number of series or scales which differ in such a manner from one another as to give the amounts of the several sums comprized in them *throughout*, and which in both instances give none but *even* sums, being (as above mentioned) but *two*, viz. that which has £12 16s, and that which has £16 for the price of the *standard Note*.

CHAPTER II. FORM OF AN ANNUITY NOTE

(See Table II)

CHAPTER III. COMPARISON OF THE PROPOSED, WITH THE EXISTING GOVERNMENT SECURITIES, ETC.

I. *Features possessed in common with other Securities.*

1. Rate of interest low, inferior to that afforded by money laid out on the purchase of stock annuities. Exemplified in the notes of country bankers.

2. *Perpetuity* of the mass of interest granted, subject to redemption. Taken from stock annuities. Agrees with Irish Debentures and India Bonds. Differs from Exchequer Bills.

3. *The principal not demandable.* Taken from stock annuities. Agrees with Irish Debentures and India Bonds: also Navy, Victualling, Transport Bills, and Ordnance Debentures. Differs from Bank, bankers', and private notes and bills.

4. Interest *without special fund,* over and above the general Consolidated Fund. Taken from Exchequer Bills. Differs from the common practice on the creation of stock annuities. Agrees with all the other above-mentioned government engagements.

5. The quantity issued, *incapable of exceeding the quantity demanded at the original price.* Agrees with Bank paper, and in practice with bankers' paper. Differs from stock annuities, Irish Debentures, Exchequer Bills, and Navy &c. Bills.

6. The evidence of the engagement consigned to a *portable* instrument, instead of a fixed book. Taken from Exchequer Bills. Differs from stock annuities. Agrees with Irish Debentures, and the now disused Navy, Victualling, Transport, and Ordnance Bills or Debentures: also with India Bonds, Bank Notes, bankers' promissory notes, and private promissory notes, and bills of exchange.

7. The *paper,* by its *size, shape, texture,* and *thinness,* particularly fitted for circulation. Taken from Bank paper. Agrees more or less with bankers' paper and with the French Assignats. Differs from all the other above-mentioned engagements: except from some late issues of Exchequer Bills in respect of *size.*

8. Application of the *profit* of the measure *towards the reduction of the national debt.* Taken from the sale of the Land Tax, i.e. the exchange of so many portions of the annual produce of that tax for portions of stock annuities. Differs from all the other engagements above mentioned.

[II.] *Features altogether new.*

9. Secure provision for the *instant* extinction of the debt created by it.

10. The amount of it incapable of exceeding the amount of the existing debt.

11. Funds no other than those already provided for the existing debt; but the security better, in respect of the appropriation of the *profit* to the exoneration of the fund, by the continual redemption of a greater mass of debt than the mass continually created.

12. Interest receivable, with scarce any trouble or expence, wherever *letters* are receivable.

13. The note or instrument serving as security for the interest, purchasable of government, with *scarce any* trouble or expence, wherever *letters* are receivable.

14. Ditto receivable in the course of circulation and with the interest, *without any* trouble or expence. N.B. Exchequer Bills, India Bonds &c. are not obtainable in the course of circulation, without the expence of brokerage, to which is added, out of London, the expence of postage, and the expence of professional, or obligation of gratuitous, agency.

15. Quantity obtainable, adapted to every purse, from the largest to the smallest. Bankers' notes, limited as they are on the side of diminution by law, and in point of variety of magnitude by the narrowness of the market &c., in the instance of each banking house, share this advantage in an imperfect and inadequate degree.

16. Facilities afforded for ascertaining by inspection without calculation, the amount of interest due, &c.

17. Securities against forgery.—See Ch. 2, Table II. *Form of a Note.* (Notes 14, 22, and 24.)

18. Facility thence afforded for *ascertaining the value in respect of genuineness*:—an advantage it has over gold and silver coin, and which is shared with it in but an imperfect degree by Bank and bankers' papers, &c., for want of the securities against forgery.

19. Means afforded of making *compound interest* without hazard, trouble, or expence. Shared in an imperfect degree (being attended with hazard, trouble, and expence) by stock annuities. Compleatly impracticable by any other means.

20. *Security against depretiation.* The price can never rise because any quantity may be had at the original price, so long as any portion of stock annuities remains unredeemed. In the *ordinary state of things,* no man need take an inferior price in the way of circulation, while men are giving the full price for it in the way of issue. As to the probability of any state of things so extraordinary as to produce a discount, see Ch. IV. *Grounds,* &c. Bank and bankers' paper are incapable of rise, but in several instances the one has experienced a partial, and the other a total loss of value.*

CHAPTER IV. GROUNDS FOR EXPECTATION, IN REGARD TO THE PROPOSED MEASURE

What is expected of the proposed currency is:—

1. That it will be taken out in the way of issue,
2. „ „ at the fixed price put upon it;
3. „ „ be received in circulation,
4. „ „ at the same price;
5. „ „ with the addition of the interest,
6. „ „ and without undergoing any subsequent depretiation;
7. „ „ and will thus continue to circulate among individuals of all classes.

That it will be taken out in the way of issue, and pass in the way of circulation, at 3 per Cent nearly (the rate of interest put upon it) notwithstanding the higher interest yielded by stock annuities, Irish Debentures, Exchequer Bills, and India Bonds, is proved by the example of bankers' paper, the interest on which runs from 2 to a nominal 3 per Cent, but really not so much, by reason of divers conditions which reduce the value of it; besides that in these instances the engagement is not perpetual, nor the security so good.

That the *interest* due will be allowed for in circulation, is put out of doubt by the usage in the case[1] of Exchequer Bills, Navy &c. Bills,

*A government engagement could not, like this, have been rendered *depretiation proof,* but for the pre-existence of stock annuities, and its connection with them, as above. The exigencies of government not being susceptible of limitation, no species of engagement could be offered, of which the price should be fixed, and the quantity limited to what could be disposed of at that price, but for the co-existence of some other species of engagement, unlimited in respect of the quantity offered at market, and thence exposed to an unlimited diminution of price.

[1][Bowring's text reads "course".]

and India Bonds, though none of these papers are provided with the tables which do away the trouble of computation altogether, however small the sum, and however short the time.

The following may serve as a view of the masses of money (cash or Bank paper) *capable* of being employed in the purchase of this paper, whether in the way of issue, or in the course of the circulation:—the time when the paper is capable of being taken in hand being the time when the several masses of money respectively come in hand; and the time for parting with the paper being the time when the money must or would have been parted with.

I. Moneys capable of being employed in the purchase of the proposed paper, for the purpose of *perpetual* or *permanent* income. *without* any view to circulation; and that would thereby afford to the noteholder, so long as the paper were kept in hand, a mass of perpetual annuities on a small scale.

1. Money actually kept up in the form of a *petty hoard,* or hoard upon a small scale, with or without accumulation, to serve as a fund for demands more or less remote and certain, but *determinate;* such as marriage, apprenticing or portioning out children, provision for widowhood or superannuation, purchase of articles of stock in agriculture or manufactures, building or furniture of such a price as to require a persevering course of frugality to raise the amount.

2. Money, the amount of which *would be* kept up in the shape of the proposed interest-bearing paper, if the proposed encouragement were held out.

3. Money actually kept in reserve for contingent and *indeterminate* expences.*

*This (should it ever come into existence) will be the only species of property known, which not only pays for keeping, but pays without either risk or trouble. To the aged and parsimonious, it will be a new discovered treasure. Timidity and indolence are the natural accompaniments of that disposition to parsimony, which is so natural an accompaniment of old age. To place money out at interest in any other way is a work not only of exertion but of hazard: in this way a man escapes from both.

To *hoard* money—to keep in hand any quantity that might be placed out at interest—is to suffer a continually encreasing loss. Yet the habit of sustaining this loss is found a concomitant, nor that an infrequent one, of the habit of parsimony. At the hour of death, ready money in large masses has been found in the hands of the parsimonious of all ranks, from the beggar to the prince. But what prince, or what beggar is there, who will hoard metallic money, when, by simply forbearing to part with this new species of paper money, he may, every day of his life, be not only preserving his property, but adding to it?

4. Money that *would* be kept in reserve for such purposes.

II. Moneys that could not, or would not, have been employed in the purchase of the proposed paper, but *with a view to circulation*: the amount being destined to be otherwise employed or spent within a smaller or larger compass of time, in masses or in driblets, as the money (cash or Bank paper) would have been employed or expended.

5. Money coming in in the shape of *fixed* income, i.e. to an amount certain, and destined for current expenditure.

6. Money coming in in the shape of *casual* income, i.e. to an amount uncertain, and whether in driblets or large masses, and destined (as above) for current expenditure.

7. Money received in the shape of income *in trust* on *private account*: *ex. gr.* by land stewards, Army and Navy agents, guardians, receivers of the estates of corporations, of estates thrown into Chancery, &c. See Ch. 13.

8. Money received in trust on *public* account, in its passage to or from the Exchequer: *ex. gr.* by collectors and receivers of the Land Tax, customs, excise, stamps, assessed taxes, boards and individuals receiving impress money for various services. See Ch. 5.

9. Money already in capital sums (whether received on the score of debt, or by sale of lands, houses, government annuities, shares in a joint stock company, succession, testament, or gradual accumulation) *under engagement* to be laid out, on a day certain or uncertain, in a mode of *permanent investment*: *ex. gr.* purchase of land, houses, or government annuities; shares in a joint stock company, loan on mortgage or bond, stocking of a farm or establishment of a manufactory.

10. Money already in capital sums *not under engagement*, but waiting for opportunities of being laid out, as above.

11. Money already in capital sums not under engagement, but waiting for opportunities of *temporary* employment: such as loan by discount of bills, purchases in the above ways on speculation, purchases in the way of trade, &c.

12. Money as yet in small sums (whether saved from fixed or casual income) kept in hand for accumulation.

13. Money *received* in the shape of *capital* in trust on private account: *ex. gr.* by assignees of bankrupts and insolvents, prize-agents, executors, and administrators turning assets into money, &c.

14. Money destined for the discharge of debts, and kept in hand while accumulating into the sum due, or waiting for the time when due, or for their being demanded.*

The ground of the expectations thus entertained on behalf of the proposed currency will appear the stronger, the more closely the advantages conferred by the possession of it are compared with the advantages afforded by the several other sorts of securities [or] modes

---

*Of the annual amount of money received in the shape of income, and *capable* of being employed in the purchase of the proposed paper, a conception may be formed from the supposed amounts of the several component branches of the national income, as exhibited in the income table framed for the purpose of the Income Tax, and printed in Mr. Secretary Rose's Finance pamphlet of 1799[1]: to which are subjoined the amounts of the same articles according to the estimate of Dr. Beeke.†

	Official Estimate	Dr. Beeke's Estimate
Land rents	£25,000,000	£20,000,000
Farming profits	19,000,000	15,000,000
Tithes	5,000,000	2,500,000
Mines, navigation and timber	3,000,000	4,500,000
Houses	6,000,000	10,000,000
Proportion for Scotland	5,000,000	8,500,000
Income from possessions beyond sea	5,000,000	4,000,000
Interest in Funds, deducting foreign property	15,000,000	15,000,000
Foreign trade	12,000,000	8,000,000
Shipping	———	2,000,000
Home trade	18,000,000	18,000,000
Other trade	10,000,000	———
Labour	———	110,000,000
	[£123,000,000	£217,500,000]

Observations. The more regular the receipt, and the larger the masses received are, in proportion to the total income of the year, the better adapted they are to the purpose of the proposed temporary employment. Stock dividends occupy the highest point of the scale: professional profits, where accumulation is out of the case, the lowest. The weekly pay of a labourer would afford him no inducement to take out Annuity Note paper in the way of issue, unless in case of hoarding: but, in the way of circulation, it would at least be upon a footing with cash.

The amount of the sums which, having been received in the shape of *capital*, are susceptible of the proposed temporary employment, is altogether unsusceptible of calculation. In the course of the year, is it *greater* or *less* than that of the sums received and kept for the purpose of current expenditure?

[1][George Rose, *A Brief Examination into the Increase of the Revenue, Commerce, and Manufactures of Great Britain*, 1799, Appendix 7.]

†*Observations on the* [*Produce of the*] *Income Tax*: second edition, 1800 [pp. 128 *et seq.*].

of placing out money, considered as coming in competition with it: viz. *stock* annuities, *Exchequer Bills,* and the market constituted by the demands of *individual borrowers, country banking houses* included, as well as those afforded by *cash* itself, and by *Bank* of England *Notes.*

I. Compared with the market afforded by *stock* annuities, we shall find it possessed of the following advantages:—

I. in regard to *purchase*—

1. No trouble or expence on the score of journeys to London, or attendance there. 2. No expence on the score of agency, 3. brokerage, 4. stamp duties, 5. fees for powers of attorney, or 6. postage. 7. No danger of loss by buying to a disadvantage.

II. During *custody*—

1. Interest daily:—not so much as a day's interest need ever be lost. 2. Interest receivable without trouble. 3. Compound interest capable of being made with certainty and facility. 4. Settlements of money in trust may be made, by this means, without trouble or expence.

III. In regard to *transfer*—

1. No expence or trouble on the score of journeys or attendances. 2. No expence on the score of agency, 3. brokerage, 4. stamp duties, 5. fees for powers of attorney, or 6. postage. 7. No danger of loss by selling to a disadvantage. 8. The capital of the mass of Notes employable in the shape of circulating capital, in whatever portions may from time to time be requisite, just like so much cash, without trouble or expence.*

*The following *bill of costs,* exhibiting the charges attendant on dealings in stock, though it were for the minutest portion, in cases where, by distance of residence and want of connections at the Metropolis, the party is obliged to have recourse, in the regular way of business, to professional assistance, may serve to shew how ill adapted government annuities are, upon their present footing of stock annuities, to enable a man to employ in that way to advantage, either a *small* sum for any length of time, or even a considerable sum for a *short* time: and this even independently of those contingencies which in the latter case have so frequently the effect of converting expected profit into positive loss. The charges are such as I have reason to look upon as rather under- than over-rated. By doing certain parts of the business himself or getting them done gratis by a friend, a man may save so much of the expence; as his wife might save the expence of a mantua-maker, by making her own gown: but a contingency of this sort does not prevent the professional charge from being, in a *general* point of view, the proper standard of expence.

II. To money circumstanced as in the case last supposed—viz. to be laid out either in small parcels or parcels of any magnitude for a short time—the purchase of Exchequer Bills is in some measure free from the objections to which the purchase of stock annuities is exposed, but it is open to others:—

1. The period for which they are issued is limited in general to a

---

I. *Charges on Purchase.*	*s.*	*d.*	*£.*	*s.*	*d.*
1. Country attorney's attendance on the party to take instructions for the purchase of the stock in the party's name	3	4			
2. Town agent's attendance on a broker for that purpose	3	4			
3. Broker's fee on the smallest purchase	2	6			
4. Attendance on the Bank for blank power of attorney to accept stock and receive dividends, agent's and attorney's fees together	6	8			
5. Price of the power of attorney	11	6	2	5	8
6. Attorney's attending and attesting execution of ditto, with two witnesses	6	8			
7. Attendance at the Bank to get it passed (agent's and attorney's fees together)	6	8			
N.B.—This is commonly charged, but, if contested, not allowed.					
8. Letters and parcels (a usual lumping charge).	5	0			
II. *Charges in respect of Receipt of Dividends.*					
1. Agent's attendance at the Bank to accept stock (both fees as before)	6	8			
2. Fees on receipt of each dividend (both)	6	8	0	18	4
3. Letters and parcels	5	0			
			3	4	0
III. *Charges on Sale.*					
1 Attendance to give commission to a broker for the sale (both)	6	8			
2. Attendance for a blank power of attorney, from the principal to the agent in town, for selling (both)	6	8			
3 Power of attorney	11	6			
4. Attendance on execution (both)	6	8	2	5	8
5. Attendance at the Bank to make the transfer (both)	6	8			
6. Broker's fee	2	6			
7. Letters and parcels	5	0			
			5	9	8
IV. *Contingent Charges.*					
1 Fee on private transfer,—if the books were shut at the time of the purchase, 2*s* 6*d*; the same if they were shut at the time of the sale; charges therefore on both together			0	5	0
			£5	14	8

If the party die before the stock is resold, the whole of the above expence of £2 5s 8d will be to be repeated; and to it there will be to be added the expences attendant upon proving the will, or taking out letters of administration to the deceased.

time of war; besides which, their existence is at all times precarious.

2. The quantity of them is continually liable to encrease, as well as the time of payment to retardation, and thence their marketable value to depretiation to an unknown amount.

3. Exchequer Bills are never issued for sums less than £100; by which circumstance every mass of money less than that considerable amount is excluded from this branch of the market.

III. *Circumstances of comparative disadvantage* attending the private market may be reckoned up as follows: viz.

1. Trouble and expence and loss of time attending the enquiry necessary in many cases to the meeting with a fit opportunity of placing out money at interest. N.B. *In the case of the proposed market, this circumstance of disadvantage is wanting altogether.*

2. Want of coincidence between the *quantum* of the sum wanted to be borrowed and that of the sum ready to be lent.—*Wanting altogether.*

3. Want of coincidence between the time for which money is wanted to be *borrowed,* and the time for which it can conveniently be *lent.* *Wanting altogether.*

4. Difficulty of obtaining sufficient assurance respecting the competency of the security in its several points of view:—the borrower's trustworthiness in every point, moral character and pecuniary sufficiency included: *Wanting altogether.*

5. Trouble, expence, loss of time and interest attendant on the adjustment of the pecuniary part of the security.—*Wanting altogether.*

6. Trouble, sometimes expence, loss of time and interest attendant on the process of demanding and obtaining payment of the interest alone, or of principal and interest together, as the case may be.—*Trouble and loss of time reduced to next to nothing: expence and loss of interest, wanting altogether.*

7. Danger of loss and particular incidental inconvenience by unexpected delays in regard to payment—*Wanting altogether.*

8. Danger and fear of the necessity of litigation. — *Wanting altogether.*

9. Unwillingness to deal with a stranger, in consideration of the uncertainty respecting his trustworthiness as above defined.—*Wanting altogether.*

10. Unwillingness to deal with the individual, if a stranger, in respect of the risk of being eventually obliged either to distress him

by pressing for payment, or to submitt to loss for want of such importunity in many cases. In the instance of a friend, in case of any apprehension on the score of want of solvency, still more if on that of moral trustworthiness, unwillingness still greater. — *Wanting altogether.*

11. Unwillingness to accept of interest from the individual, if a friend, especially if it be on a small sum, or for a short time.—*Wanting altogether.*

12. Unwillingness, through shame, to accept, much more to demand interest for sums and times separately trifling, how considerable soever in their collective amount.—*Wanting altogether.*

13. Embarrassment, disputes, and loss of time in the computation of interest on small or fractional sums, or for short and fractional periods.—*Wanting altogether.*

14. Danger of loss by death, marriage, or other change of condition on the part of the borrower, whereby, as far as mere personal security is concerned, a security originally sufficient may become bad or precarious.—*Wanting altogether.*

Being the holder of an Annuity Note, there is not a person living whom I have any right to call upon to give me value for it: but had it not been for the advantage accruing from the holding of the Note, I should not have become the holder of it: and as the advantage thus accruing to me from the holding of this Note is no greater to me than it will be to thousands of other people—in a word, to every man without exception, to whom it can lie in my way to offer it—in the event of his becoming the holder of it in my stead, the certainty of my obtaining value for it at any time wants nothing of being entire.

No one living is bound to give me silver for the guinea I have in my pocket; yet who is there that ever hesitated to receive a guinea, under the apprehension of not being able to get change for it? Not only the self-regarding advantage of making profit by goods sold for part of the value engages my neighbour, the shopkeeper, to change it for me, on my laying out to the value of a few halfpence with him, but the social consideration of amity and neighbourhood is sufficient to procure for me the same accommodation at his hands without any such personal advantage. In the case of the Annuity Note, the social consideration not only operates with equal force, but has the personal consideration of the advantage to be gained by the holding of the Note to back and strengthen it.

The material question is—will it be received? This being answered, and answered to satisfaction, the other question—why will it be received? how comes it that it will be received?—is matter only of curiosity and speculation.

CHAPTER [V.][1] FINANCIAL ADVANTAGES

The advantages of the financial kind that may be expected from the proposed measure, will require to be distinguished in the first place according to the *periods* or stages[2] above marked out, in regard to the progress of it.

Period I. From the opening of the first issue of Annuity Notes to the arrival of 3 per Cent stock annuities at par.

The branches of profit or advantage that may be looked for in the course, or at the conclusion, of this first period, may be stated as follows:—

1. Profit on sale: profit by the difference between the price for which a 3 per Cent annuity, as secured by an Annuity Note, is sold, and the price at which an annuity to the same amount, as secured by an entry in the books of the stock annuities, is bought in with cash raised by the above sale—in a word, profit by difference between selling price of Note Annuities and buying price of stock.—N.B. This branch of profit ceases altogether on the termination of Period I.*

2. Profit by interest forborne to be received on Annuity Notes.

3. Profit by Notes in hand: profit by interest of Annuity Notes received by government in the course of circulation, while kept in the hands of government.

4. Profit by Notes lost under circumstances which either do not admitt of, or do not call for, compensation.

5. Profit by Exchequer Bills: profit by reduction of the rate of interest paid by government for such moneys as it is in the habit of

[1][The MS in fact reads "Ch. 8".]

[2][The MS reads "three periods or stages".]

*This branch of profit will have for its accompaniment, and that, as we have seen already, an inseparable one, the effect, and that an advantageous one, of taking out of the market a mass of stock equal to the mass of annuity paper issued, although the burthen on government, in respect of the mass of annuity to be paid, remains the same. But though this effect is produced immediately and at all events, the profit resulting from it depends upon two other circumstances:—viz. the having money to raise by the creation of government annuities, and the arrival of the period which will put into the hands of government the power of bringing its annuitants to consent to a reduction in the amount of their several annuities. These constitute two perfectly distinguishable branches of profit, which will be considered in their respective places.

borrowing by annual anticipation, by issue of Exchequer Bills, whether on account of the service in general, in a mass, or on account of particular branches of the service as occasion arises, viz. by Navy Bills, and other bills of that class.

Profits peculiar to Periods II. and III.

6. Profit by saving upon the expence of management.

7. Profit by fractional interest: i.e. by the 7d per £100, difference between the £3 per Cent yielded by stock annuities, and the £2 19s 5d yielded by £100 worth of Note Annuities.

8. Profit by redemption of 4 and 5 per Cents: and thereupon, by extinction of the masses of extra-interest.

Profit peculiar to Period III.

9. Profit by reduction of the rate and quantum of interest upon the mass of national debt.

10. Profit peculiar to a state of war: i.e. to those years, in which money is to be raised by the creation of fresh masses of government annuities. Profit on loans: profit or saving by lessening the loss by those transactions, by raising the price of government annuities as compared with money, and thereby lessening the loss by the difference between money [received] on the creation and sale of government annuities, and money paid on redemption of the same.

11. Profit by yearly interest instead of half-yearly: a profit mentioned as being obvious, and capable of being realized, but not (it is supposed) to advantage.

If to prove the proposed measure to be an advantageous one, and advantageous to a sufficient degree to give it a claim to be carried into practice, it were necessary to prove the quantum of the advantage, or even to give a calculation that had pretension to exactness, its chance for adoption would be weak indeed. Happily for the plan, no such proof can reasonably be required: whether the profit be £10,000,000, or no more than £10,000, still, although that advantage stood alone, yet supposing it to stand clear and not to be attended with any degree of disadvantage capable of counter-balancing it, the conduct indicated would be just the same: it would be worth adopting, though the advantage were worth no more than £10,000: and it could but be adopted, though the advantage were worth 100 millions.

Profit 1. Profit by difference between selling price of a £3 a year Note Annuity, and buying price of a do. stock annuity.

In the calculation of this branch of profit there is one element, the quantum of which may be assumed upon unimpeachable authority. This is, the probable average price of stock 3 per Cents taken out of the market upon the buying-in plan before the commencement of the period during which, these annuities being at or above par, the paying-off plan will have taken place of the buying-in plan. In Mr. Secretary Rose's Finance pamphlet for 1799, this average price is stated at 85.* Selling price constantly £100: buying price, on an average, £85: difference, on the profit side, £15 per Cent.

Such being the rate of profit, the quantum of profit will be as the quantum of Annuity Note paper issued, and consequently as the quantity of stock bought in by the produce of the sale of Annuity Note paper, by the day of the arrival of 3 per Cents at par; from which day, casual and momentary depressions apart, the profit on this score will be altogether at an end.†

---

*6th edit. pp. 26, 37, and Append[ix] No 3.

†This branch of supposed profit (it may be objected) is ideal, or rather so much loss: since the same profit would have been made by the existing Sinking Funds, and at the end of the period in question, the Commissioners of those Funds will have to pay so much the dearer for every million of capital they redeem.

The answer is—No: make the most of the objection, the assumed rate and mass of profit is neat profit, and the existence of it indisputable. If at a time practically speaking the same, you sell for a million the very selfsame article (£30,000 a year perpetual annuity) that you purchase for £850,000 the propriety of setting down to the account of profit the £150,000 difference is altogether beyond dispute. Such is the money gained: were the amount of it afterwards thrown into the sea, the profit in the mean time would not be the less real. It is not thrown into the sea, but employed in buying in a correspondent portion of the national debt: why?—because this, according to a judgment by Parliament, approved by the nation, and confirmed by 14 years' experience, is the most advantageous of all applications that could be made of it. The first moneys applied to this purpose, the first moneys from whatever source obtained, take away all profit from the succeeding ones: but if this were an objection against the making this application in question of the produce of the proposed new Sinking Fund, so would it against the making the like application of the produce of the two existing ones. The ultimate object is the discharge of the debt: for this object it is, that such enormous sacrifices are made: that by means of £5 millions' worth of fresh money applied to this service, the object will be accomplished so much the sooner, is not to be disputed. From what source soever the money comes with which the £360 millions of debt, or thereabouts, as yet unbought in is to be redeemed, such is the nature of the case, that upon the first portion, say from 5 millions to 50 millions[1], a certain profit is to be made, but upon the remainder, nothing: the bargain can never be regarded as a losing one, if for a sum of 5 million which, by this fresh influx, happens to be shut out of this portion of profit to the amount of £750,000, another five million which would

2. The expectation of profit by interest forborne to be received is grounded on the following proposition, viz. that in general a man will not bestow either trouble or expence, much less both, how inconsiderable soever the quantity, in compassing an end, which he has it in his power to compass to equal perfection without any such trouble or expence.

The trouble (not to speak of the expence) attendant on the receipt of the interest on these annuities, has been reduced to the smallest amount possible: because the greater it had been, the greater the danger lest, by the contemplation of it, individuals should at the outset have been repelled from the purchase of these annuities; but be the reduction ever so great, still the remainder will be something: and this remainder, it may reasonably be expected, should, in the ordinary state of things, be sufficient to turn the scale. On the other hand, suppose the circulation of this paper to be once established upon the terms on which government paper is in the habit of being received—(I speak of Exchequer Bills, Navy, Victualling and Transport [Bills], and Ordnance Debentures, not to speak of India Bonds)—viz. the allowing for it, in addition to the amount of the principal, the amount of the interest that has become due upon it, a man, by simply paying away an Annuity Note upon that footing, will receive, from the individual who takes it of him, the amount of such interest, without the trouble of applying for it elsewhere.

The smaller the amount of interest or other money to be received, the greater the *ratio* which the trouble of receiving, whatever it be, will bear to it: accordingly, if there be any difference, it is in the instance of the smaller Notes, and the more certainly the smaller the Note, that the dependance on this forbearance will be more assured.

But the disposition to forbearance will be the more steady, the more perfect and unbroken the facility of receiving the money in the event of its being thought fit to receive [it], appears to be. It is on the strength of the persuasion entertained by a man that the amount of a banker's note which he has taken in payment would, if demanded,

---

otherwise have been to be raised by taxes and taken out of the old Sinking Funds, is saved.

Another consideration that may help to shew the reality of the branch of profit here assumed, is—that the sooner stock annuities are raised to par, the sooner will that period have been made to arrive, at which the possessors of redeemable government annuities may, to save themselves from being paid off, consent to accept of a reduced rate of interest, as in Mr. Pelham's time: for which see Period III.

[1][The MS reads almost "80 millions".]

be paid at any time, that his forbearance to demand it is grounded.

It is on this account that, whether or no the payment of the interest upon a fresh Note be deferred till after the end of the year, or be divided into two payments, the first of them to take place at the end of the first half-year, at the end of the year it seems most advantageous upon the whole, that the *even* amount of the year's interest should be made demandable at any time.

In regard to the proportion of interest that would be likely to be forborne, thus much may be observed:

1. In regard to whatever portion continued to be employed as currency, the forbearance would probably be general and continual.

2. In regard to whatever part was hoarded for the purpose of furnishing *compound* interest, it could not take place. To obtain an interest upon a year's interest due on any Note, it would be necessary for a man to receive that interest, and with the money take out a fresh Note or assemblage of Notes: a second year's interest is a year's interest and no more, in addition to its own amount: it does not give him the interest he might have made on the amount of this same second year's interest, by receiving it in the shape of money, and employing that money in the purchase of a fresh Note carrying its interest, or (what would come to the same thing) by receiving it at once from the Office, if upon his application the Office were to furnish him with it in that shape.

3. In the case of a mass of Annuity Note paper kept in hand for the purpose of income, but without any determinate plan of accumulation in the way of compound interest, it seems difficult to say whether receipt or forbearance would be most apt to take place. The purpose of receipt might be equally answered by forbearance, viz. by paying away at each period a mass of paper of an amount equal to what the whole mass had gained in value on the score of interest by that time. But this would require provision to be made accordingly in the composition of the sum constituted by the Notes: and which of the two masses of trouble would be the greater, that of making the provision in question, or that of receiving the interest at an office, would depend upon circumstances.

Mean time this consideration operates as a reason for rendering the composition of the series of Notes as favourable as possible to the purpose of affording interest in the way of simple circulation as above described, without the necessity of coming upon government for the payment of it: that is, to render the gradation of the series more regular, and the *terms,* or degrees in it, more numerous, than might otherwise be necessary or advisable. The more compleat the series of Notes, the greater the chance it has of meeting the demand of each individual with reference to this purpose.

As to the quantum of this branch of profit, the principal part—that which may be regarded as certain—will depend upon the quantity of the paper thus employed, and upon the time during which each parcel of that quantity remains in circulation. It will depend consequently on the duration of this first period.

Should this period prove a short one, the probable length of it (according to a supposition that will be stated a little further on) not exceeding two or three years, this branch of profit will be proportionably inconsiderable: but whenever it vanishes, it vanishes[1] (as will be seen) only to make way for a branch of much superior importance. So long as stock annuities are to be purchased under par, none of those whose circumstances it suits to become customers for stock annuities will, in respect of that portion of their money, become customers for note annuities, which will not be to be had but at par price. But no sooner are stock annuities arrived at par price, than these note annuities will be at least as well suited to the circumstances of the customers for stock annuities: and inasmuch as the mass of stock annuities will be lessened every day by the operation of the Sinking Fund, while the mass of note annuities can not be encreased [without] diminishing by at least an equal amount the mass of stock annuities, the owners of the continually encreasing mass of money seeking to be employed in the purchase [of][2] government annuities, to serve as a source of permanent income, will have no other resource than to lie in wait for Annuity Notes as they pass from hand to hand, and so impound them and take them out of the circulation.

3. The third head of advantage consists in the saving or profit that may be made to accrue on the score of interest upon Annuity Notes, which, after being received by government from individuals on the score of taxes or otherwise in the way of circulation, remain at the command of government till wanted to be re-issued.

This head of profit will again require to be distinguished into three branches:—

1. Profit by Annuity Note paper lying in the Exchequer.

[1][The MS places the brackets by mistake after the word "as".]
[2][The MS reads "for".]

2. Profit by do. lying in the hands of receivers of all classes on its way to the Exchequer.

3. Profit by do. lying in the way of imprest in the several offices of expenditure, waiting till re-issued.

1. As to the first of these three branches of profit, what the probable annual amount of it may be, is compleatly out of the knowledge of the writer of these papers, but as compleatly within the knowledge of those to whom they are addressed: I mean in so far as the past is in this respect capable of serving as a guide to the future. Add together the 365 sums respectively existing in the Exchequer on the 365 days of the year, and divide the sum by 365: the quotient will be the principal, the interest of which will thus in the course of the year be gained or saved to government, supposing the whole of the money to be in the shape of Annuity Notes. From this gross amount of principal will require to be deducted the amount of that proportion of money which is, upon an average, in the shape of cash: but this proportion is capable of being calculated with tolerable precision, even by the public at large, from the information that has been given on this head in the evidence laid before the two Houses of Parliament in or about the month of March 1797, on the enquiry into the affairs of the Bank. The ratio of paper to cash will, in the supposed period, be at any rate at least as great as in any past period: and in past periods upon an average it appears to be very great indeed. In the supposed period it will naturally, and on the supposition of due vigilance in this respect on the part of government, be considerably greater: inasmuch as a profit to the amount of 3 per Cent *per annum* will thus accrue in respect of every penny of money thus received and kept in the shape of Annuity Note paper, and no profit at all in respect of whatever quantity may come to be received and kept in the shape of cash.

2. As to the second of the above three branches of profit, it will rest with government whether to take it into its own hands, or to leave it in the hands of the receiver in this or that proportion, and for this or that length of time, according to circumstances.

[1]Whatever sum it may be deemed necessary to leave in the hands of the receiver for any length of time, whether as a fund for the answering of contingent demands or otherwise, that sum the receiver, if the profit on the score of interest is to be his, will be sure, so much

[1][This half page and the two following pages are crossed out in the MS, but it is very likely that they were crossed out by Bowring.]

of it as is not already in the shape of Annuity Note paper, to carry day by day to the local Annuity Note Office of the place, that it may come back to him in the shape of Annuity Notes. In other ways more interest would be to be made of it, were the ground altogether sure, in regard to *security* as well as *time*: but in this way alone can it be perfectly sure, in regard to either of those points.

As this would be the course taken by each such individual receiver, on the supposition of a due attention on his part to his own interest, there is one consideration that presents itself in the character of a reason why government should not leave the matter to the individual, but take it into its own hands. Guided solely each by his own interest, the quantity of Annuity Note paper taken out by money drawn from this source might come to be so great within a given space of time, as in conjunction with the quantity taken out by individuals within that time, might come to produce a glut of this paper and sink the price. So long as it depended upon the individual, and supposing, as must be the case, that the Annuity Note paper so purchased would be received at the Exchequer or other principal government office at par, no degree of depretiation thus produced would be sufficient to prevent, or so much as check, the practice: since whatever were the amount of the depretiation in the money market at large, every £100 worth of this paper being received from him by government at £100, with the interest up to the day when so received, his profit would not be in the least diminished by it.

Government would in the other case take care that no such depretiation should ever take place, at least in any degree worth regarding: in the very first stage of such depretiation, though it were to be but a farthing upon the standard Note of £12 16s, government would give the requisite orders of stopping the exchange.

It may here occurr, that if the government money were in this way to come up to the Metropolis to the principal Annuity Note Office to be exchanged for Annuity Notes, as well might it come up to the Exchequer, the Custom House, the Excise Office, or other such principal office of receipt at once, and there stay, without being remanded to the local officer in the country, by whom it would afterwards be to be remitted to the Metropolis, viz. to that one of the above-mentioned offices to which he is subordinate. The answer is, that the observation is just with regard to all sums but such as the nature of the service requires to be kept in the hands of the local receiver, as a fund for the answering of contingent demands: accordingly the sums thus excepted are the only sums, in regard to which the exchange in question is proposed to be allowed.

If shared between government and the office, in what mode shall the profit in question be shared? by allowing him the whole profit for such a length of time, accounting for it after that time to government, or by allowing him a part, and but a part of it, from the first? These are questions which, in the present stage of the proposal, it is sufficient to start: the time would be early enough for the discussion of them at a much maturer stage.

Either plan supposes an exact account kept of the sums received by the officer on each day, distinguishing what part in cash, and what part already in Notes, the charge against him on the score of interest to commence on the earliest day on which a return could be made to him in paper in exchange for the cash, bating such allowance in point of time as shall be thought fit to be made on the score of accidents.[1]

3. In regard to the last of the above three branches, little need be said. The money being already in the shape of Annuity Note paper yielding an interest to government, so long as it is in the hands of government, all the difficulties in regard to the conversion of it into that shape are out of the question here.

Under the existing plan, much anxiety has every now and then been entertained to prevent this or that subordinate officer of expenditure from getting inordinate sums by way of imprest into his hands: under the proposed plan, the money being in the shape of paper, that paper yielding its interest to government, so long as it is in the hands of any office or officers keeping it on the account of government, whether the power of disbursing it, when disbursed on account of government, rests with this or that officer, will make in this respect no difference: though the quantity issued from the Exchequer to this or that office, upon this or that occasion, should happen to be more than sufficient—in other words, to be excessive—it would be no matter: since not only the temptation to produce the excess, but even the mischief of the excess if produced, would, in the proposed state of things, be done away.

4. Profit by Notes lost under circumstances which either do not admitt of, or do not call for, compensation.

As this source of profit will go on encreasing as the quantity of Annuity Note paper encreases, and will consequently be inconsider-

[1] [Here ends the passage which appears to have been crossed out by Bowring.]

able in this first period, even at the close of it, in comparison of what it will be at the close of the second period, at which time the conversion of the whole mass of stock annuities into annuities secured by Annuity Note paper will have been compleated, it is to the second period that what there may be to say, in regard to this source of profit, may with most propriety be referred.

5. Profit by reduction of the rate of interest, paid on other government paper, viz. Exchequer Bills, and bills of the nature of Navy Bills.

With the fall in the rate of interest yielded by money lent and borrowed on stock annuities, the fall in the rate of interest paid by government on Exchequer Bills will at least keep pace. At present, the interest paid on money thus borrowed is by the day 3d½; by the year £5 6d for every £100: rate of interest, 5⅓ per Cent nearly. This at a time that 3 per Cent stock is between £62 and £64.

In the year 1724[1], the interest on the same species of paper was no more than by the day 2d, by the year £3 0s 10d: rate of interest, a trifle (not worth reckoning) above 3 per Cent. Yet at this time, 3 per Cent stock was very considerably below par, i.e. below the price to which, by the end of the first period, it will by the supposition have been raised.

The rate of profit, therefore, by the last day of the period, will have risen to about 2⅓ per Cent upon whatever may be the last amount of the last portion of debt of this kind incurred on the occasion nearest to such last day: average rate for the whole of the period, 1⅙th per Cent.

As to the absolute quantum of profit on this head, that will of course depend on the amount of Exchequer Bill paper issued within the time: a quantity, in regard to which any calculations or conjectures that could be given, would be of little use.*

---

[1][Filled in at a later date.]

*In regard to Navy Bills, and the other government papers of that class, nothing particular need be said: paper of this class being since the recent improvement placed on a footing so little different in this respect from Exchequer Bills, the rate of profit may be taken for the same.

Peace and war will, however, make this difference. When war ceases, and the war accounts are wound up, the issue of Navy Bills will cease: while that of Exchequer Bills, if the old established practice under this head should be persevered in, will continue in regard to a certain sum, which however will be growing less and less every day, as the amount of the Land Tax taken out of the hands of government by sale, encreases.

This being the case, upon the supposition[2] that this first period consists of an

6. Profit (if taken) by difference between yearly and half-yearly interest. I have already stated that my leaning is not to assume this head of profit, and for what reasons. [To][1] form the better judgment on this question, the best way will be to defer the consideration of this source of profit till it has attained its *maximum*, which will not be till the close of the second period.

CHAPTER VI. [FINANCIAL ADVANTAGES CONTINUED]

Period II. From the arrival of stock annuities at par, to the redemption of the last portion of stock annuities; whereupon follows immediately the opening of the second issue of Annuity Notes at the reduced rate of 2⅜ per Cent.

1. Profit (in the shape of principal money) *by sale of Notes* ceases; but, in the event of the creation of a fresh parcel of stock annuities revives and continues till the redemption of such stock annuities.

2. Profit *by interest undemanded* will continue, and with encrease. The profit above mentioned as produced by the Notes in *circulating hands* will encrease, as the quantity of paper taken out with a view to circulation encreases: this branch of profit may be termed the *standing* or *regular* branch. To this will now be added the profit produced by the Notes in *hoarding hands,* viz. the expelled stockholders who take this paper with a view to permanent income, as they held their stock. This branch may be termed the *casual* branch: it will arise out of such casual forbearances only, as take place at present in the case of dividends on stock. The probable rate of it might be estimated from the course of the payments on this score made at present at the Bank.

The quantity of government annuities, stock and note annuities taken together, will, it is true, be growing less and less every day: while the quantity of money, capable of being employed in the purchase of them, will be growing greater and greater: so that the scarcity will be growing at both ends. But inasmuch as, the issue being open all the while, every body will be at liberty to supply himself with whatever quantity of this paper he chooses, whether

equal portion of years of war and years of peace, the assumed rate of profit upon the whole period taken together will be to be reduced to half that which is assumed in the case of Exchequer Bills, because being the same as on Exchequer Bills, it continues to be reaped for no more than half the time.

[2][The MS reads "The above made supposition".]

[1][The MS reads "The".]

for the purpose of hoarding, or with a view to circulation, the diminution will fall exclusively upon the stock annuities, the quantity in circulation will not be absorbed in any degree by the demand for the purpose of hoarding, and the only effect of the encreasing scarcity, even when the issue is at the point of closing, will be to make the demand and consequent emission the more rapid to the last.

3. Profit by *Notes in hand.* This inconsiderable source of profit seems likely to continue from the first period, without any variation worth enquiring into. It admitts of no encrease from the encreased amount of Annuity Note paper produced by the *conversion,* that part only which is [in] circulation being capable of finding its way into government hands.

4. Profit by *Notes lost.* During the whole of this second period, this source of profit will be on the encrease, a quantity of Annuity Note paper equal to the whole amount of stock annuities being in the course of it added to the mass.

It is neither to be expected, however, nor to be wished, that the rate of profit to government ([or] loss to individuals) upon the large masses hoarded for the purpose of income should approach to that upon the small Notes continually passing from hand to hand.

5. Profit by reduction of interest on *Exchequer Bills.* This source of profit will probably have begun to manifest itself in the course of the former period, but it is not till now that the amount can be easily submitted to calculation. During the whole of this second period, the rate of interest will be that reduced rate towards which it will have been moving on during the first period.

The rate of interest on these temporary loans, has been for some years past 3d½ a day, making by the year £5 6s 5d½ per Cent, bearing at present a premium from 1s to 6s, at a time when 3 per Cent perpetual annuities are about 64 or 65.

During the whole of this second period, i.e. while stock 3 per Cents [are][1] at 100, and £2 19s per Cent note annuities at the same price, the rate of interest on Exchequer Bills may be expected to be no higher than 2d a day, making £3 0s 10d a year, or, at the highest, 2d¼ a day, making £3 7s 7d¼ a year. For in 1730 (by Stat. 3. G. 2. c. 16), the interest on them was not to exceed "3 per Cent": and 3 per Cent perpetual annuities could scarcely have been much above par at that time (so as to yield a less interest), if they were not rather

[1] [The MS reads "being".]

below it: for in 1731, the lowest price was 95, and the highest, 97.* Under these circumstances, the difference between the superior rate of interest made on Exchequer Bills, and the inferior rate afforded by stock annuities (which difference constitutes all the profit to be made by Exchequer Bills in preference) must have been very inconsiderable: and it appears that the reduction of the rate of interest on stock annuities was followed by a reduction of the rate of interest on Exchequer Bills to a level very little, if any thing, above that of stock†.

Two pence a day, making £3 0s 10d a year, is the rate that, to this purpose, may be regarded as being in the case of Exchequer Bills on a level with the £2 19s per Cent afforded by Annuity Note paper of the first issue. 1s 10d is the difference between the two masses of yearly interest (£3 0s 10d and £2 19s), and is the result of the small addition made to the price of Annuity Note paper for the sake of even money upon the smaller Notes. The next step above is 2d¼, making, by the year, £3 7s 7d¼.

Annual interest paid on Exchequer Bills, at the present price of stock 3 per Cent perpetual annuities: Exchequer Bills at 3d½ per day (making £5 6s 5d½ a year) bearing a small premium	1. On the ordinary amount £6,500,000	2. On the *extra-ordinary* amount occasioned by the Income Tax as per last account‡ £20,360,700
	£345,989	£1,083,745
Do. at the said expected rate of £3 7s 7d¼ ...	£219,755	£688,210
Annual profit	£126,234	£395,535

*Sinclair [*History of the Public Revenue of the British Empire*, 2nd ed., 1790], II, Appendix, Table of prices of Stocks.

†The subject of Exchequer Bills, with reference to that distant period, is attended with several little obscurities, the clearing up of which would not pay for time or space, with reference to the present purpose. What is evident enough and at the same time sufficient, is—that a reduction of the rate of interest on permanent annuities must be attended with a correspondent reduction in the rate of interest on those temporary loans: and that the difference, on which ever side it be, can never be very considerable.

‡22 April 1800: Commons Finance Accounts No. VII.

This head of profit will be an enduring one: no degree of plenitude on the part of the Exchequer will supersede it. It is not with Exchequer Bills as it was with Navy Bills. It would (as already observed, Ch. IV) be bad economy to make and keep on foot a *perpetual* loan to a certain amount, in order to save *occasional* loans to the same amount, and at the same, or nearly the same, rate of interest: and to keep in hand a sum in cash to the same amount would come to the same thing, since, by the application of that sum, a proportionable part of the perpetual debt already existing might be redeemed. The maximum of advantage under this head is therefore what results from keeping the rate of interest on such temporary loans from rising more than one step [above] the level of the rate paid on perpetual loans.

The *principle,* therefore, to which Exchequer Bills owe their rise, or at least their continuance—viz. that it is necessary to allow a somewhat higher rate of interest on a temporary than on a permanent loan—is of a nature to continue. Whether, under the order of things introduced by the proposed Annuity Note paper, the plan of the present Exchequer Bills would be the most advantageous plan of all for the borrowing money on such temporary loans, is a distinct question, the examination of which would be requisite in case of the adoption of the proposed measure, but would at present be premature.

6. Profit by saving in the expence of *management*:—*transfer* and *allowance of interest,* as between *individual* and *individual,* being performed *without* expence: and the expence attached to the issue and to the payment of interest on *government* account, being defrayed, in part or in the whole, by *fees.* See Ch. I. Plan, Art. 17.

Present annual expence of management, per million ...	£450
Total of present annual expence of management, adding Emperor's perpetual loan and loan of 1800 (capital 32,000,000) but not risk, and deducting annuities not perpetual, and redeemed annuities	£209,249*
Expence of the proposed General Annuity Note Office, suppose	£9,249
Remains annual profit	£200,000

*House of Commons Finance Accounts, No VI, 24 Mar[ch] 1800.

Annual expence of the Post Office in salaries and emoluments (General and Penny Post included) A° 1797* £45,851. On looking over the list of offices included in that expence, it will be seen, that by far the greater part have no application to, nor equivalent in, the present instance.†

This profit, being a rateable profit on the amount of debt, will of course diminish in *amount*, as the amount of the debt diminishes.

7. Profit by *reduction of interest* from £3 to £2 19s.

This profit results from the conversion of stock annuities into note annuities at the par price of both, which will be the price throughout this second period. It amounts to exactly 1-60th part of the interest at 3 per Cent. It comes in a manner without design, the difference being the unavoidable result of the defalcation of a few fractions which it was necessary to get rid of, in order to leave even and commensurable sums‡. The amount of annual profit on this score on each million of capital in stock annuities *converted*—i.e. on each £30,000 of interest on the said capital—is £500.§

Present amount of the capital of the redeemable part of the national debt: including loan of 1800, £32,180,000, and Emperor's loans, £7,502,000: but not *Irish* loans, nor capital redeemed; £436,507,237: say— ... ... £436,000,000[1]

*7th Finance Report, A° 1797, Append[ix] C, p. 83.

†See Ch. I *Plan*. Art. 15, Note.

‡Table, shewing the principal sums of the several Notes entering into the composition of £100 worth of Annuity Note paper, with their respective amounts of interest, taken from [the] Table of Annuity Note Currency.

Principal of the Notes.			Amounts of Interest.		
£51	4	0	£1	10	4
25	12	0	0	15	2
12	16	0	0	7	7
6	8	0	0	3	9½
3	4	0	0	1	10¾
0	16	0	0	0	2¾
£100	0	0	£2	19	0

§To so much of the mass of stock annuities, as will have been either redeemed or converted into note annuities in the course of the *first* period, the £500 per million will of course have been to be added in the account of *that* period: but the amount of that portion being uncertain, it seemed most commodious to defer the rendering an account of it to this *second* period, at the end of which it will have attained its *maximum*: thenceforward the amount of it will, of course, annually decrease, as the amount of the debt is diminished by the operation of the Sinking Fund.

[1][The six noughts were filled in in pencil, probably at a later date.]

Annual amount of profit by reduction from £3 per Cent to £2 19s upon the above capital (exclusive of profit by reduction from 4 and 5 per Cent, as per separate account following), at £500 per million	£218,000
Deduct profit on the portion of the debt redeemed during Period I—say, at random, 36 million ...	£18,000
Remains amount of annual profit by reduction of interest from £3 to £2 19s per Cent, at the commencement of Period II, but diminishing, as the amount of the debt diminishes	£200,000*

[8.][1] Profit by reduction of 4 and 5 per Cents to 3 per Cents.

This will be seen from the following table: in which the assumed order of redemption is that which is most advantageous, [2]viz. to[3] the public, if any, that would be consistent with the terms of the respective loans.

Species of Stock	Amount of each species	Amount of interest on each species	*Rate* of profit by reduction	*Amount* of profit by reduction
4 per Cent† ...	25,000,000	1,000,000	1 per Ct.	250,000
5 per Cent‡ ...	28,125,582	843,765[5]	2 per Ct.	562,510 [*sic*]
4 per Cent remainding[4] ...	19,759,859	790,392[5]	1 per Ct.	197,598
5 per Cent Loyalty,§ 23 Dec. 1796	20,250,000	1,012,500[5]	1 per Ct.	202,500
	[£]93,135,441	[£]3,646,657		£1,212,608 [*sic*]

*According to Art. 21 of the plan (Ch. I), in order to preserve the powers of the Sinking Fund undiminished, as soon as any portion of stock annuities, the interest of which has been subjected to any *reduction*, comes to be redeemed, so long as the interest is not extinguished, but kept alive in their hands, to be employed in continuing the redemption, the amount of the reduction, upon that portion of stock, will be immediately to be *replaced*.

[1] [The MS reads "13".]

[2] [3] [The two words appear in the MS in the opposite order.]

†These would, of course, be reduced, along with the 3 per Cents, to the 2 19s per Cents: but, as credit has already been taken for the reduction of the 1s per Cent upon the whole amount of stock annuities of all sorts, it would be repetition to add [it] to the account here.

‡By the terms of the loan, none of these 5 per Cents are to be redeemable till the redemption of 25 millions of either 3 or 4 per Cents has been accomplished:

CHAPTER VII. [FINANCIAL ADVANTAGES CONTINUED]

Period III. From the opening of the second issue at 2⅜ [per Cent] nearly (viz. £2 7s 5d per Cent) to the redemption of the last portion of the paper of that second issue; whereupon follows immediately the opening of the third issue at £1 9s 6d, being a trifle less than 1½ per Cent.

Rate of interest on the *closed* issue during this period ...	£2 19 0
Rate of the *open* issue	£2 7 5
Difference constituting the rate of profit by the operation	£0 11 7

Profit 1. Profit by *reduction* [1]*of the rate of interest*[2] from £2 19s per Cent, to £2 7s 5d per Cent.

This result constitutes the characteristic profit of this third period: the proportionable amount of it is nearly the fifth part of the interest on the mass of annuities remaining at the commencement of this third period.

The annual rate of this branch of profit is upon each million of capital of Annuity Notes remaining in the hands of individuals, and thereby upon each £30,000 a year of interest on 3 per Cents	£5,791 13 4
1. Profit by reduction of 11s 7d per £100 of capital or £3 of interest, of the redeemable part of the	

but, since the option is left to government as between the 3 and the 4 per Cents, of course when the time comes for *paying off*, i.e. redeeming at par, 4 per Cents will be paid off before 3 per Cents: but, so long as neither 4 per Cents nor 3 per Cents are as yet at par, which of them will be paid off on each occasion, will depend, of course, on the comparative price.

§These Loyalty Loan 5 per Cents would be liable to be paid off at par, and thereby reduced to 3 per Cents, by the conversion attached to the proposed measure, with a profit consequently of 2 per Cent, instead of the 1 per Cent assumed, were it not for the stipulation by which the stockholder has it in his option, at any time within three years after the signature of the definitive treaty of peace, to call upon government to convert each £100 of the 5 per Cents, into £133 6s 8d of 3 per Cents, giving him thus instead of his 5 per Cent, 4 per Cent upon the original £100 of stock: an offer which in the case supposed, can not but be universally embraced.

By this option, an addition to the amount of £5,062,500 will be made to the capital of the debt.

[4][Bentham here appends the following fragmentary footnote: "This remainder would be greater (the whole amount of 4 per Cents created being £ . . .), were it not for £ . . . which on the . . . had been bought in by the Commissioners." There seems little point in trying to fill in these gaps.]

[5][Filled in in pencil.]

[1] [2][Crossed out in the MS.]

national debt, supposing the whole to have continued unredeemed from the present time to the end of this third period—£5791 13s 4d × 436	£2,525,166 13 4
2. Deduct profit on the part redeemed during the first period (say, as before, £36,000,000), £5791 13s 4d × 36	£208,500 0 0
	£2,316,666 13 4
3. Deduct profit by reduction of £3 per Cents to £2 19s per Cents during the second period ...	£200,000 0 0
	£2,116,666 [13 4]

4. Deduct restitution to the Sinking Fund of profits by reduction of 3 per Cents to £2 19s per Cents, and by do. of 4 and 5 per Cents to 3 per Cents (—a quantity not susceptible of previous calculation).

5. Remains clear annual profit, during this period, by the reduction peculiar to this period, supposing the whole reduction to be effected on the first day of the period.

6. Half of this gives the amount of the reduction, and thence of the profit, for each year of the period.

2. Profit on sale, i.e. by difference between selling price of Annuity Note paper and buying price of stock annuities, remains, as in Period II, extinct by the extinction of stock annuities; subject to revival in the event of a fresh creation, as before.

[3. & 4.] Profits by *interest undemanded* [and] by *Notes in hand;* continue as in Period II, with little change.*

[5. & 6.] Profits by *Notes lost,* and by saving in respect of the expence of *management,* being rateable profits, their amount per million's worth of paper continues unchanged, but their total amount diminishes of course in some degree, as the amount of Annuity Notes (which, from the commencement of this third period, are the only redeemable government annuities remaining) is diminished by the operation of the Sinking Funds.

For some time at least, the paper of this second issue carrying but

*Profit *by interest undemanded* ceases (it is to be remembered) at every reduction, in proportion as the conversion from paper bearing the higher rate into paper bearing the inferior rate goes on: because, whenever a Note is paid off, the whole amount of interest remaining due upon that Note must be discharged as well as the principal. It follows that, in regard to the paper of each issue, the *time of forbearance* can not date from any *earlier* period than the *opening* of that issue.

£2 7s 5d a year interest, the demand for it, with a view to *circulation,* will be more certain than the demand for the purpose of *permanent* income on the footing of stock annuities: because to the former set of customers, the whole amount of interest, reduced as it is, will be as so much *gain,* being a profit which, but for this species of paper, they would not have made—perhaps at all—certainly not in this commodious way, and by government annuities: whereas the reduction will sit heavy on the customers for *permanent* income, who, if they continue their money upon government security, must submitt to see their incomes reduced to this amount; and whose capital, to a considerable amount, will accordingly, for the purpose of escaping such reduction, be withdrawn from this employment, and either laid out upon other *securities,* or be embarked, along with the owners, in some branch of *trade.*

The progress of the operation may notwithstanding not be diminished upon the whole: for, to the amount of the demand with a view to circulation, no assignable limits can be found.

7. Profit in respect of *Exchequer Bills.* During this third period. in comparison with the second, the rate of profit will receive an encrease. For the money wanted for occasional purposes during the second period, it will (as has been seen) have been necessary to give a rate of interest one step higher than that which, by the continual emission of Annuity Notes at that rate to all customers, it was in the power of every body to make. But the first issue being *now* closed, it is no longer in the power of every body, or any body, to obtain government annuities at that rate; since though the paper of the first issue will still be to be had of individuals, it will not be to be had but at an advanced price. The profit, by the saving of this advanced price, will be sufficient to engage customers to take Exchequer Bills at the par price of the *closed* issue, to an amount adequate to any money that can be wanted on the footing of a temporary loan.

CHAPTER VIII. [FINANCIAL ADVANTAGES CONTINUED]

Period IV. From the opening of the third issue at 1½ per Cent nearly (viz. £1 9s 6d per Cent) to the redemption of the last portion of paper of that issue: whereupon follows immediately the opening of the fourth issue at £1 3s 8d½ per Cent, being a trifle more than 1⅙ per Cent.

Rate of the *closed* issue during this period	£2	7	5
Rate of the *open* issue	1	9	6
Difference constituting the profit of the operation ...	£0	17	11

The annual amount of this head of profit for this fourth period, at 17s 11d per £100 of capital, is, for each million of capital remaining in the hands of individuals, i.e. for each £30,000 of interest at the original rate of 3 per Cent, £8958 6s 8d.

Profit, by *reductions of interest* up to this period inclusive is, per million of principal of 3 per Cents, and per £30,000 a year of interest, as follows:—

Period II. Profit by reduction of £3 per Cents to £2 19s per Cents	[£]500	0	0
Period III. Do. by do. of £2 19s per Cents to £2 7s 5d per Cents	[£]5,791	13	4
Period IV. Do. by do. of £2 7s 5d per Cents to £1 9s 6d per Cents	[£]8,958	6	8
	£15,250	0	0[1]

Profits by *Notes lost,* and *by expence of management saved,* will continue, as before, with little change in regard to the rate, but, in respect of the total amount, reduced [of][2] course, as the quantity of the annuities in question is reduced.

So in regard to profit *by interest undemanded,* and profit *by Notes in hand.*

Profit in respect of *Exchequer Bills* will, at this period, if not before, be so far fixed, as that the rate of interest upon these temporary loans will never be higher, and more likely lower, than that of the closed issue. For although the reduced rate of the open issue should not be accepted of by the expelled annuitants of the closed issue, nor even by any more of the customers for Note paper with a view to circulation, yet, for the reasons given with reference to Period III, the premium given for the paper of the closed issue will, notwithstanding, be considerable: the more so as the drop from the rate given by the closed issue (the second issue) to the rate given by the third issue (being the issue that remains open till the very close of this fourth period) is so great. Second issue, £2 7s 5d; third issue

[1][Bowring, p. 128, misread Bentham's handwriting, and gives the figure as "15,259".]

[2][The MS reads "in".]

£1 9s 6d; difference, 17s 11d: more by 6s 4d than the drop from the first issue to the second. Between the two amounts in question, a profit sufficient to draw purchasers for Exchequer Bills can not but find room to place itself; and the interest on Exchequer Bills during this period may be expected to be considerably less than £2 7s 5d.

CHAPTER IX. [FINANCIAL ADVANTAGES CONTINUED]

Concluding Period. The precise number of reductions which the rate of interest upon this paper might be destined to experience, is what it would be too much to attempt to fix. But a picture of the last moments of the expiring debt, at whatever stage the reduction of interest may then be, may be not without its use.

It will present the profit *by interest undemanded* in an enlarged and interesting point of view: strike off in effect the last 10 or 20 or 30 millions of the debt: and strike off perhaps the value of a year or two or more from the duration of that load.

After the exoneration thus effected in the course of the fourth period by the reduction of the rate of interest to the £1 9s 6d which is the rate given by the paper of the third issue—is it or is it not likely that the reduction of interest should have descended any lower before the redemption of the last portion of the principal of the debt?

The reduction of the rate of interest on the money that had been thus lent to government, will stop short of this mark, or stop at it, or go beyond it, according to the influence which the rate thus allowed by government turns out to exercise over the rate of interest in general. That the influence which the government rate of interest has in its rising state maintained over the general rate of interest, has been considerable, is matter of known experience: though the operation of the restrictive laws, which stop the rise at the point of five per Cent, even on the slenderest security, has rendered the amount of this influence scarce capable of being measured. The influence of the rate of interest paid on the debt can not but encrease with the magnitude of the debt, to which the magnitude of the mass of capital poured into the market (as will be seen) by the redemption of that debt, will be proportioned. The effect of 436 millions thus poured in can not but be double (it should seem) to that of 218 millions, at least if poured in within the same compass of time.

The influence of the capital poured in by the redemption of the national debt, at the time the reduction of the interest on that debt is going on, will (it is true) not depend solely on the quantum of the capital thus poured in, but also on the magnitude of the general mass of national capital into which it flows. But the general mass of national capital is also of itself in a rapid state of encrease; and to such a degree on the encrease, as to be of itself in a way to effect a reduction in the rate of interest in general, without any aid from this or any other factitious source. Accordingly the factitious cause of reduction — the factitiously accumulated capital which is thus poured in by government, so far from finding any obstruction in the magnitude and *vis inertiæ* of the mass into which it flows, finds a powerful assistance in the operation of that mass, acting as it is already in a direction tending to the same end.

If, then, while the two forces, the *natural* and the *factitious,* are thus acting in the same direction, the influence of the factitious should be strong enough to bring the other to the same pace, things will continue on in the same state as already depicted in the account of the fourth period: paper of a *closed* issue, in a quantity which can not be encreased—paper of an *open* issue, in a quantity which will be continually and rapidly on the encrease, till, by the produce of it, the paper of the closed issue has been paid off; when a *fresh* issue will be opened, at a still lower rate, and the *now open* issue *closed*: and so on—always paper of two issues, at two rates of interest, till the last applied portion of redemption money comes, and sweeps them both out of the market at once.

If, then, the reduction of the rate of interest goes on to the *last* year of the debt without stopping, the state of the paper, during that last year, in respect of its being divided into paper of two issues (viz. a closed issue, and an open one) will be the same, at that supposed last period of the existence of this paper, and of the redeemable part of the national debt, as is exhibited in speaking of the advantages belonging to the fourth period of its existence: the paper swept off by the last mass of redemption money will be paper of two different issues.

On the other hand, if the emission and consequent reduction have stopped any where, there will, at that last stage, be but one rate of interest paid by government on the redeemable part of the debt: the Annuity Note paper remaining at the time will be, all of it, of the same issue, viz. the then *closed* issue: there being at that time another issue *opened,* but no paper of that *proffered* issue in existence because nobody will purchase any at that price.

For illustration sake, let the last issue which meets with customers be the above-mentioned third issue: the issue at £1 9s 6d, with the opening of which the fourth period commences. Let 30 millions at this time be the amount of the whole remainder of the debt: of which let 10 millions be the amount of the paper of the second issue now closed, bearing interest at £2 7s 5d per Cent, and let the other 20 millions be paper of the third or open issue, bearing interest at £1 9s 6d per Cent: and let the 10 millions at £2 7s 5d per Cent be, all of it, in the hands of persons who keep it in hand as a source of permanent income; while the 20 millions at £1 9s 6d is, all of it, in a state of circulation more or less rapid, being all of it in hands that *took it out,* or received it in that view.

The Sinking Funds, taken all altogether—the Sinking Funds present and future—being now in a condition (suppose) to pay off 10 millions in the course of a year, let such payment be made accordingly. This extinction, falling of course upon those 10 millions, strikes off the whole of the hoarded paper, and leaves only that part which, being in circulation, constitutes so much of the circulating capital of the country. Upon the redemption of the last parcel of these 10 millions, the opening of the fourth issue follows of course, by Article 22. If any purchasers presented themselves at the rate of this fourth issue (£1 3s 8½d per Cent) the reduction of the rate of interest would go on. But, by the supposition, no such purchaser *does* present himself. The persons who had been keeping their capitals in the shape of Annuity Note paper of the second issue at £2 7s 5d, are, by the redemption of the remaining paper of that issue, put to their option —either to cease letting their capital lie on that sort of security, or to accept of £1 3s 8½d per Cent. By the supposition they all reject the paper bearing this new and lowest rate: they will not meddle with it, not even for a time, and with a view of putting it into circulation by employing it in the ways in which they determine to employ the capital thus thrown upon their hands. It is still taken, and that to the amount of 20 millions, by the customers for temporary income in the course of, and with a view to, circulation: but by this 20 millions, the demand, on the part of that class of customers (it may be supposed), is satisfied.

When the *two* masses of paper, that had till now been in the market, are thus reduced to *one,* that one will, all of it, be in the hands of noteholders who take it with a view to circulation. For whatever rate of interest is accepted on the footing of permanent income.

there will be always persons in abundance to whom it will be worth while to accept of the next lowest rate, with a view to circulation. If, by the growth of national opulence, a rate so low as £2 7s 5d appears now, is raised to such a pitch of relative value, as to be worth acceptance in the character of a source of permanent income, the *next* lowest rate, though so low as £1 9s 6d, will be raised along with it in the scale of importance, and will become not less worth acceptance in the character of a source of such temporary profit as could not, with equal security and convenience, be made by any other means. And if the £1 9s 6d comes itself to be thought worth acceptance in the character of a permanent provision and sole dependance, the next lowest rate, though now reduced to £1 3s 8d½, will no more be regarded with contempt in the character of a source of temporary profit, than the £1 9s 6d was before. If, then, the demand for Annuity Note paper should stop altogether at any period prior to that of the compleat extinction of the debt, it is with the customers for *permanent* income that it will stop, and not with the customers for *temporary* income with a view to circulation.

Compared with cash, the interest afforded by the Annuity Note paper to those who take it, or keep it, with a view to circulation, will, be it ever so small, be so much *profit*. Compared with the preceding higher rate of interest, the reduced rate afforded by the Annuity Note paper to those who, if they take it, will, to the extent of their respective capitals so invested, have nothing else to depend upon for their respective incomes, [1]present itself as so much loss by the amount of the difference.[2]

Under these circumstances, though, for illustration sake, the supposition has been that the fresh issue would at some period remain open without customers, it seems not easy to abide by it. At the time the Sinking Fund came with its ten millions, and swept off all the paper of the second issue—all the paper that was in the hands of customers for permanent income—the demand on the part of the customers for temporary income with a view to circulation had got no farther than the remaining 20 millions. But, under the accumulation of wealth inseparable from the state of things thus supposed, it is scarce possible that the demand, from that class of customers, should, for any length of time, be altogether at a stand. If, in a

[1] [2][The MS in fact reads "by the amount of the difference, present itself as so much loss". The transposition of the text was necessary to give clarity to the sentence.]

twelvemonth, but a single £100 worth were wanted by any person for a few weeks or months, more than could be met with without giving such a premium as would make it dearer than the paper of the open issue, he would betake himself to the open issue.

Even in the case of the last group of now-expelled noteholders, by whom this paper had been held as a source of permanent income, the supposition of their rejecting the paper of the fresh issue *altogether*, appears scarcely tenable. They would still, to a certain degree, be customers for Annuity Note paper, though with different views: *before* their expulsion, for the purpose of *permanent* income: *after* their expulsion, for the purpose of *temporary* income, till a better income or better prospects could be obtained from some other source.

True it is, that by the paper taken out of their hands they made £2 9s 6d a year: while, by the paper of the fresh issue, they would make not half the money—£1 3s 8d½. But £1 3s 8d½, which they might begin making from the very instant of their expulsion, would be £1 3s 8d½ better than nothing—which is what the interest of a considerable part of their 10 millions of capital would be reduced to, for a time more or less considerable, if it rejected this accommodation. And, though no more than a single £100 of the expelled 10 millions were to betake itself to this employment, though it were but for a day, from thence would be to be dated the birth of the paper of the fourth issue.

If, however, at the period in question, there remains no paper but of one issue, it is, all of it (as we have seen), in the hands of the customers for temporary income with a view to circulation, who would, generally speaking, betake themselves to the *circulation* for the interest of it, upon which the *demand* for interest at *the Offices* would nearly cease. But the same cessation *might* take place, although there were to be paper of *two* issues: and *would* take place, if the paper of both issues were to be in the hands of the customers for temporary income with a view to circulation. Nor is this any more than what might well enough take place, since the paper of the closed issue would bear a premium, corresponding to the superior rate of interest it afforded;* and it would be seen by government to be the

*The premium is a necessary condition to the co-existence of two papers of the same denominative value bearing different masses of interest: a man would never give £100 or the value [of £100] for a mass of paper called £100, and yielding £1 3s 8d½ a year interest, if for the same price he could get a mass of paper which, though called but £100, yielded £1 9s 6d a year interest.

case, if the interest upon the paper of the closed issue were seen to remain undemanded.

In this state of things, many millions of government paper still in circulation, and little or no interest demanded on it, there seems nothing to be gained and something to be lost by carrying the redemption any further. As to so much interest as continues to be undemanded, the debt *ceases* to be a burthen; the taxes, from which the redemption money would be to come, *are* a burthen; and the paper taken out of the circulation by the redemption would be so much taken from the mass of circulating capital: as much so as if gold to that amount, after having been received by government on the score of taxes, were to be thrown into the sea. A defalcation made to any such amount as the supposed 20 million in the course of two years, might, by its suddenness, be productive of inconveniences such as it would not be easy to estimate:* similar, in a word, to those which have been attributed to the diminution in the quantity of Bank of England paper in circulation.

Were the redemption thus to cease, it might be of use to declare, at the time that such cessation were declared, that from thenceforward, as often as a Note were sent in for payment of interest, interest and principal should be paid together,† as is the practice at present in the case of Exchequer Bills: and at the same time to declare a respite of the redemption for a certain time.

The advantages would be—

1. The continuance of the source of profit in question (profit by interest undemanded) would be more steady and assured. For, in proportion to the length of [the] respite declared, the paper thus respited would come to bear a premium in circulation: the amount of which premium, though *limited* by the rate of interest yielded by the open issue (resorted or not resorted to) would not be prevented by it from taking place. This premium a man would lose, by sending in his paper to be paid off at par: *in general,* then, paper will not be sent in for that purpose, nor consequently any interest be paid by government.

2. No payment would thenceforward be made upon the proposed paper but that a payment to a far greater amount would go in

*See further, Chapter [X. *Advantage by Addition to*] *National Capital.*

†By this restriction, the amount of the premium might perhaps be made less than it would have been otherwise: but that would comparatively be of little moment.

redemption of principal: whereas, without such regulation, no part of the money paid would take that profitable course.

The undemanded interest (it might be thought) might in this way come to accumulate to such a mass as might be productive of inconvenience, if, by a sudden turn of affairs, it were to become a matter of advantage to the whole body of annuitants to claim payment of it at once. But, on a second glance, the inconvenience would be seen to vanish altogether. Supposing, as before, the amount of the paper 20 millions; rate of interest £1 9s 6d; the whole amount of a year's interest would thus be short of £300,000. Being *simple* interest, not *compound*, the whole amount of it in twenty years would be short of 6 millions, supposing the whole of it to remain undemanded, and the principal undiminished all that time. No issue (it has been seen) can carry more than its own interest: because, as the open issue fills, the paper of the close[d] issue is paid off, interest and principal together. *Respite* is indeed proposed: but the term of respite need not be so *long* as to preclude government from providing such a course of redemption as should ward off any inconvenience that might ensue from a too sudden diminution of this part of the currency, and at the same time prevent the interest from swelling to any such amount as to become formidable. At the worst, at such a period, interest so low, money so abundant, £6,000,000 would be but a trifle to raise by an immediate and temporary loan, as now by Exchequer Bills.

CHAPTER X. WAR LOANS

By so many per Cent as the market price of old annuities is raised by any cause, by so many per Cent (it is well known) is the price of new annuities raised to those who give money for them to government (i.e. the terms of the loan bettered) by that same cause: since, as between old and new the value is just the same, it would be in vain for any man or set of men to insist upon any considerably greater price in annuities for their money (allowance made for depretiation by encrease of quantity and for dealer's profit) than people in general are disposed to take for theirs.

Whatever takes stock out of the market without taking out or keeping back the equivalent in *money*, adds in proportion to the price of stocks. The proposed measure takes stock out of the market without either taking out or keeping back money: it therefore adds in proportion to the price of stocks.

True it is that even previously to the absorption of stock annuities which it takes out of the market, it has created other annuities to a considerable part of the amount: for it is only with the money received for those *new* annuities, that the *old* are taken out. But of the money thus received for the new annuities, there is not any part that would have gone to market for old annuities: because, while stocks are under par, no money that can be employed with advantage in the purchase of stock, can be employed otherwise than to a manifest disadvantage in the purchase of the inferior rate of interest afforded by the proposed note annuities.

Any melioration thus produced in the price of stocks, and thence in the terms of the loan for any given year, will operate (it should be remembered) not only on the loan of that year, but on all succeeding loans during the existence of the existing debt: since, whatever additions the debt may come to experience in the course of any number of succeeding years, it will always be the less by the amount of all the defalcations that have been ever made from it.*

Were it not for the operation of the *Sinking Fund*, the profit on this account would be so much clear:[1] but, inasmuch as, to the extent of the stock purchased in the year by that Fund, government loses exactly as much as it gains on the stock sold in that same year in and by the loan, the amount of the *loss* by the *purchase* will be always to be deducted from that of the *profit* by the *sale*.†

*This, though so evidently true as to appear little better than nugatory, will be apt enough to be overlooked, or even appear disputable: for, such will naturally enough be the case, if, after rising the first year of the application of the given cause of elevation, stocks should, in consequence of fresh causes of depression, experience a fall the next or any other succeeding year.

[1][Bowring's text, p. 131, reads "clearer".]

†Money raised by loan of 1800‡, contracted for 22 Feb. 1800§ ...	£20,500,000
Deduct income of the Sinking Funds on the 24th March 1800 exclusive of the dividends on the stock put in the hands of the Commissioners by the sale of the Land Tax‖	£4,649,870
Remains amount of money on which the profit by melioration of the terms of the loan takes place	[£]15,850,130
Deduct year's dividend on the stock purchased by sale of Land Tax as above	[£]437,659¶
	£15,412,471

To this account, some corrections might be made, by observations relative to *dates;* but the benefit would not be worth the trouble.

‡39 & 40 G.3. c. 22 dated 10th March 1800.

§*Times* 22 Feb. 1800.

‖Commons' Finance Accounts 1800 No. VI, dated 24 March 1800.

¶Mr. Rose's Brief Examination, p. 77. 6th edit. 1800.

To calculate the probable amount of profit on this score, for one, two, or more years, would require two sets of *data*: viz. 1. amounts of the several other *causes* of *elevation*, together with those of *depression*, in each year; 2. amount of *Annuity Note paper sold* in each year. The former would scarce yield to calculation: the latter bids defiance to it altogether.

CHAPTER XI. ADVANTAGE BY ADDITION TO NATIONAL CAPITAL

Among the advantages promised by the proposed measure, may be reckoned the addition it promises to make to the mass of national productive capital, and thence to the mass of national wealth, viz. by the acceleration it will give to the operation of the existing Funds, in respect of the redemption of the national debt.

That an addition to the mass of national capital—an addition to the value of £100 once paid—is the result of every £100 paid in discharge of the national debt, is a proposition which, though hitherto it seems to have engaged but little, if any, attention, will be assented to almost as soon as mentioned. That the putting of money into men's hands on this occasion, in lieu of the income they are obliged to part with, has no tendency to encrease the ratio of the amount of money expended in the way of *prodigality*, to that of the money expended and employed in the way of *thrift*, is evident enough. But if, in employing the money put into his hands in lieu of a source of income of which he is deprived, a man employs it otherwise than in the view of making it productive of a mass of income to equal amount, he employs it in the way of prodigality: and, if he employs it in the view of making it productive of income, it must be, either by expending it *himself* in the production or improvement of such articles as constitute a mass of *capital*, to the amount of such expenditure, or by lending it, directly or ultimately, to somebody else, by whom it will be applied to that same purpose.

If the money thus put into the hands of the expelled annuitant in lieu of his annuity were taken from the mass employed in the shape of *capital*, there would be neither loss nor gain by the operation, on the score of addition to the mass of national wealth.*

*This supposition is actually realized in the case of money employed in the redemption or purchase of portions of the Land Tax, and laid out in the purchase of masses of stock annuities on government account, to be added to the Sinking Funds. The money for a purchase of that sort can not be supposed (unless here

But the money thus employed by the existing Sinking Funds is *not* taken from any such mass. It is the produce of *taxes* — of taxes levied on income, either directly or through the medium of expenditure—and is taken out of that fund, the whole of which (after a small deduction on account of savings) would otherwise have been expended within the year, in the way of *current expenditure*: that is, in the purchase, partly of unproductive labour, such as that of servants, coach and saddle horses, players, musicians, and the like, partly in the purchase of articles consumed mostly within the year, or some other such short period of time, without having produced any equivalent encrease.

Of the money thus put, in the shape of capital, into the hands of the public creditors, on the redemption of their respective portions of the public debt, that part which is received by *British subjects*, will, *in general*, be employed in adding to the mass of capital contained within the limits of the British Empire: on the other hand, that part which is received by *foreigners*, will as naturally be employed in adding to the mass of capital contained within the dominions of the states to which they respectively belong—in adding to the quantity of *foreign*, not of *British* capital.

Deducting, then, from the whole amount of the money payable on the redemption of the redeemable, but unredeemed portion of the funded debt (£463,723,534)* that part of it which is in the hands

and there by accident) to be saved out of the income of the year, and defalcated from what would otherwise have been the unproductive expenditure of the year, unless in the case where, without any such call, a sum to the same amount would have been saved up, and employed or lent out, in the shape of *capital*. It is therefore so much *taken from* the mass of national capital. On the other hand, when handed on to the stockholders of whom the stock is bought, and in payment for their stock, it is *then* so much *added to* the mass of national capital, being so much which would not have taken that course, had it not been for the measure. It therefore leaves the amount of national capital where it found it.

*Remaining unextinguished of the redeemable debt, due from Great Britain to the holders of stock in the British Funds (after deduction of £12,133,375 *extinguished* before 5 Jan. 1800, by the sale of the Land Tax) as per House of Commons Accounts No. VI. p. 8, 24 Mar[ch] 1800 ... ... £451,699,919

Deduct redeemed and transferred to the commissioners, as per do. Account, to 1st Feb. 1800 ... ... £44,733,294

£406,966,625

Add capital created by the loan of 1800, as per Stat. 10 March 1800, 39 & 40 G. 3. c. 22 (Money raised £20,500,000) £32,185,000

£439,151,625

of foreigners (say, upon an allowance supposed to be excessive, the odd 63,723,534), the remainder (£400,000,000) is the sum that, in the year in which the last portion of the debt comes to be redeemed, will have been added to the mass of national capital from this source, independently of any effect produced by the proposed measure.

Whatever amount of profit the proposed measure may be attended with, this profit being also applied, in aid of the other Sinking Funds, to the redemption of the debt, will act in acceleration of that effect. It will therefore, in proportion to the acceleration, be productive of a distinguishable addition to the mass of national capital, in proportion to the acceleration thus produced by it. In a rough way, the amount of this addition may be stated as equal to the interest, at compound interest, at the rate at which the national capital is accumulating, upon the above £400,000,000, for the term of years struck off by the acceleration.*

Taking 5 per Cent *compound interest* for the rate at which the national capital accumulates, and no more than 5 years for the amount of the acceleration, the amount of the addition to the mass of national capital on this score, would be £110,512,624.†

Add capital that will come to be added to the 3 per Cents, upon the reduction of the £20,250,000 Loyalty Loan 5 per Cents to 3 per Cents, as per Ch. VI	£5,062,500
	£444,214,125
Add borrowed for, and due from, Ireland, but payable, as above, to British stockholders, as per do. Accounts	£12,175,000
	£456,389,125
Add borrowed for, and due from, the Emperor of Germany, but payable, as above, to British stockholders. Capitals created 7,502,633.	
Deduct redeemed and transferred to the commissioners, up to 1st Feb. 1800, as per do. Accounts, 168,224.	
Remains unredeemed	£7,334,409
Total of the money requisite to be paid in London for the redemption of stock annuities	£463,723,534

*This calculation would require great corrections: but these requiring more room than would be thought worth bestowing, are omitted with the less scruple, inasmuch as the result of them would be altogether in favour of the measure: it would operate in addition to the rate of profit here assumed.

†The rate of accumulation, indicated by the amount of the exports from Great Britain, for the 14 years ending in 1798, agrees, to a wonderful degree of exactness, with the assumed 5 per Cent. At that rate, in 14 years, £1,000,000 nearly doubles itself: it becomes £1,979,931‡. According to the Table of British Exports

From this, in any accurate course of computation, would come to be substracted that proportion of the national income, which, had it not been taken by taxes, and thence in the shape of redemption money added to capital, as it were by force, would have been saved up, and, without changing hands, have thus [been][1] added to capital of its own accord: at random, say, for instance, an eighth. Hence would be required two deductions—

From the amount of the *restitution** to capital, by redemption of the debt, independently of the proposed measure, viz. the	£400,000,000
deduct one eighth, viz.	£50,000,000
Remains	
	£350,000,000
From the amount of profit from the proposed measure on the score of addition to national capital by acceleration of the redemption, as before, viz. ...	£110,512,624
deduct one-eighth	£13,814,078
Remains neat profit	£96,698,546

given by Mr. Secretary Rose§, (old valuation) amount in 1785, £16,086,000: amount in 1798, £33,800,000: a little more than double.

The rate of accumulation on a branch of productive industry, favoured as this may be supposed [to be] by the war, may accordingly be supposed greater than on other branches. This, however, seems open to dispute: but what will scarcely be deemed open to dispute is—that in time of peace, when an annual defalcation by war-loans to the amount of upwards of 22 millions, upon an average (over and above what has been restored to capital by the operation of the Sinkings Funds), is at an end, the accumulation can not but go on with much greater rapidity than in a period of the same number of years divided in equal proportion between war and peace.

‡Smart's Tables, p. 53.

§Brief Examination [&c], Appendix No. 1.

[1][The MS reads "gone".]

*I say *restitution*: for, as the amount is *added to* productive capital upon the redemption of the debt, so was it *taken from* productive capital on the creation of the debt.

The capital created (it may here occurr), is always more than the money borrowed: and therefore, deducting from the capital created the amount of the money borrowed, the difference will be—not *restitution*, but neat *addition*: so that, supposing £100 million borrowed in 3 per Cents at 50, and paid off at par, i.e. by payment of £200 million, the restitution would be effected by one of the hundred millions, and the other would be so much neat addition, made to the mass of national capital by the war.

If this statement were correct and full, it would follow that in point of productive capital, and thence in point of wealth, as far as mere disbursement and receipt were concerned, the nation would be a gainer to this vast amount, instead of

To the account of the addition thus promised to the mass of national capital, in respect of fixed[1] capital, and such other parts of the mass as are of an *intrinsically productive* nature, it may naturally enough [be] expected that I should add the augmentation promised

being a loser, by the war: and if the account were taken of profit and loss on other scores, viz. loss by destruction and *captures suffered* on the one hand—profit by insurance-money and *captures made* on the other, the result would (I have reason to think) be still more favourable.

But, besides that, upon the redemption plan now pursued, a considerable part of the debt will be redeemed, not at par, but for a considerably inferior price—the money, added to productive capital by redemption, is added at periods of time much *later* than those at which the money was defalcated by war expenditure: so that, upon the whole, account being taken of money raised, average proportionable amount of capital created, average price paid for capital redeemed, periods of redemption, and quantity redeemed at each period, in the case of the present war, it would be all *restitution* without any clear addition, nor would the restitution be compleat. This, however, depends altogether upon the proportions as between the above several quantities: insomuch that a case *might* be put (and that, how far soever from being a *desirable*, by no means an *impossible*, even very *improbable* one) in which, in point of *ultimate wealth* (were that alone considered) a nation might, under the *Sinking Fund* plan, and even with some ill success and no good success, be a gainer by war.

I need scarce observe—and yet (rather than appear subject, for a moment, or to any eye, to the imputation of broaching paradoxes, and those of the most pernicious kind) I *will* observe—that money to A is no compensation for loss of money, life, or limbs, to B—that the acquisition, if made, is made by no other means than that of the most cruel pinching, for a period greater than the average of human life—and that if the money wrung from *pleasurable* expenditure had been added, the whole of it, in the first instance to productive capital, instead of being consumed in *misery-making* expenditure, the addition to productive capital and wealth would have been so much the more abundant.

Be this as it may, the calculation would be a very curious and instructive one: and, at any rate, at the *conclusion* of the war, so many of the above *elements* will have been[1] *given*, that it might easily be ascertained by what degree of acceleration, practicable or impracticable, the profit to national wealth, by *redemption* of debt and *restitution* to capital, would be exactly equal to loss by *borrowing* and war-expenditure.

A practical advantage derivable from such a calculation, and the views which suggested it, as above, is—the helping to reconcile the public in general, and in some degree the parties affected, to the loss that must inevitably ensue to many descriptions of persons, by the influx, or rather reflux, of capital, which will be seen to pour in from the redemption of the debt: I mean principally the fall in the rate of the interest of money, and thence the defalcation from all incomes flowing from that source. Such (it is true) will be their suffering, from the redemption, from the Sinking Fund, from the war with its debt: but such *would have been* their suffering, and still greater, had there been neither borrowing nor redeeming, and had the country been reposing all the while in a state of uninterrupted peace.

[1][The MS reads "ben".]

[1][Bowring's text, p. 133, reads "freed capital".]

in the shape of *circulating* capital, viz. to that branch of it which consists of money.

That in certain circumstances an augmentation of this sort would be among the natural consequences, and even, unless prevented by special care, among the necessary consequences, of the measure, is a proposition, the truth of which will, I imagine, appear with sufficient evidence: but, so far from taking credit for any such result, in the account of *advantages*, probity requires that I should give warning of it as a source of *danger*. To point out the means of obviating this danger, will be the business of an ensuing chapter.[1]

CHAPTER XII. ADVANTAGE BY ADDITION TO COMMERCIAL SECURITY

Another advantage expected from the proposed paper, is—the addition it promises to make to commercial security—the support it holds out to commercial solvency. It presents itself, not only as being itself exempt from those shocks to which the ordinary species of paper money are essentially exposed, but as affording to the community a remedy, and that of the preventive kind, against the disorders to which it stands at present exposed, by the constitutional weaknesses of those other papers.

For a property thus valuable it is indebted to two features belonging to it and altogether peculiar to it. One is—the making no addition by its quantity to the quantity of cash engaged for. It is by this, that it is itself preserved from that brittleness which is of the essence of those other papers. The other is—the faculty of being employed in either of two capacities at pleasure: 1. as a permanent source of income—like so much stock—so long as it is kept in the same hand; 2. as a circulating medium—a species of money, as often as it is passed on from one hand to another. It is by this latter feature that it is enabled to fill up whatever gaps may come to be made in the quantity of money in circulation by a deficiency in the quantity of those other papers.

That, in point of *security*, commercial wealth is liable to suffer from an excess in the comparative quantity of paper money, is a truth but too often felt and sufficiently understood. That, in point of *quantity*, it is liable to suffer a kind of negative loss from a deficiency

[1]Ch. XIV.[2] [Rise of Prices &c.]

[2][The MS reads "XVI".]

in the quantity of paper money, is a truth rather understood than felt, but equally out of doubt; because, inasmuch as every fresh £100 worth of paper money is so much added to the mass of circulating capital, to the amount of the value at which it passes,* the national capital is of course so much the less for every accession of this kind which it *might have* received, consistently with commercial security, and fails to receive. That, by a deficiency in the quantity of paper money, commercial wealth is liable to suffer—not in point of *quantity* only, but even in point of *security*, is a sort of *discovery* in political economy, seemingly of very recent date.† Till the pressure upon the Bank of England in 1797, it seems to have been generally understood, that, in the article of paper money, *deficiency* was the *safe* side: but on that occasion it became apparent that in regard to paper money of the kind in use,[1] there is *no safe side.*

While there is stock to sell, and in such abundance, how (it may be asked) *can commercial wealth be liable to suffer in point of security by a defalcation* (*which can never be a very large one*) *from the quantity of paper money?—when, by selling stock, a man who has either stock enough, or credit to borrow stock enough, may at any time raise as much money as he pleases: he will be a loser* (*it is true*) *by the interest of the stock sold out, from the time when sold to the time when replaced, and so far wealth suffers in point of quantity: but there ends the damage: security remains entire.* Raise money? Yes, doubtless;—so a man may:—but on what terms? On the terms of taking the precise amount from some one else: the deficiency is *shifted* only, not *lessened.*

Stock may be sold for money: and in that *figurative* sense it may be *converted* into money: but in the literal sense, it can not be converted into money: and it is in the *literal* sense that an article must be capable of being converted into money to answer the purpose in question here. *Stock* convertible into money? Yes, in the same figurative sense in which *land* and *houses* and *goods* are convertible

*See Ch. XI.

†The source to which I am indebted for it, is the evidence of Mr. Henry Thornton, as printed in the several unpublished Reports of the Committees of Lords and Commons on the Affairs of the Bank in March and April 1797, and reprinted in Mr. Allardyce's published *Address to the Bank Proprietors* in the same year. In the form of a note, the substance of that evidence would form a valuable addition to the future editions of Adam Smith.

[1][Bowring's text, p. 134, reads "in view".]

into money—and no other. Annuity Note paper *is* convertible into money (paper-money) in the *literal* sense.

Stock is one thing: paper money (the sort at present in use) is another; Annuity Note money, and that alone, is both in one. It has two natures: and is, at all times, either the one thing or the other, whichever is most wanted.*

The defalcation made from commercial security by the defalcation of a given mass of *money* (*cash* or *paper* makes to this purpose no difference) would upon examination be found greater than might have been supposed. The amount of the annual receipts of the country, on the score of income and capital taken together, may (without any error capable of affecting the argument) be stated as not much over or under three times the amount of the money of the

*It is a fact no less curious than true, that by a mere *collateral* circumstance, such as the *mode* of transfer appointed, and the nature of the *evidence* required in *proof of title*, the nature of a species of property, *in itself* the same in both cases, should undergo so material a change. Without a degree of expence destructive of a part or the whole, or even more than the whole, of the value, *stock*, as we have seen, can not be broken down into masses corresponding to those small and diversified portions into [which] money is and must be divided:—nor can it, at any expence, be either bought, or sold, on any occasion without loss of time, and the obligation of personal attendance at one certain place, the same for the whole island, wheresoever the residence of the parties happens to be in each instance. It can not be carried by a man in his pocket and so, like so much cash, distributed among any number of hands, at the very instant the occasion for each disbursement comes. Annuity Note paper, like cash and Bank of England paper, but still more divisible, is already broken down into a multitude of portions still more various, and commensurate to all purposes: and, like cash, is to be had at all times and in all places.

I have a weekly bill of £1 12s to pay to my baker. The £1 of it which should have come to me in Bank paper has, in consequence of the million of supposed deficiency of that paper, failed me. Can I say to him, "*Come to the Bank, and I will transfer to you £1 12s worth of stock*"? His answer would be—"*True, £1 12s is the worth of the stock you will give me to-day, but what will it be to-morrow? I have my batch of bread to mind, my journeymen to overlook, my customers to wait upon: Can I find time (do you think) to go with you to the Bank to-day to receive your stock, another day to receive the interest, and another day to sell the principal?: and what will the principal amount to when brokerage is paid out of it? No: it would be cheaper to me to give up the debt, than to obtain payment for it on such terms.*"

How different would be the case, if instead of stock, I had my £1 12s worth of government annuities in the shape of an Annuity Note! "*Here* (I should say) *is your money. £1 12s is what I have just been giving for it: pass it to-day, any body will take it of you at the same sum. Keep it till to-morrow sennight, any body will allow you an additional farthing for it, and so on, a farthing for every eight days, for as many time eight days as you may think fit to keep it.*"

country, cash and paper taken together.* Call, then, the quantity of Bank of England paper *habitually* issued and kept in circulation, £10 millions: and of that habitual £10 millions suppose, at a *particular* time, one million cancelled or kept back: for instance by a defalcation to that amount from the usual discounts. Here, then, is produced, already by the defalcation of this single million from the quantity of money in circulation, a defalcation to the amount of 3 millions from the mass of money that should have been received in the course of the year: and this without any allowance made for the proportion of the money of both sorts (cash and paper) that will always be hoarded and kept out of the circulation in the shape of *capital waiting for employment*, or the *cash* that must always be kept up in the same way as a *fund of reserve* for answering the engagements contracted by that part of the currency which is in *paper*.

*Total of national income, according to Dr. Beeke (the official estimate not including income from labour, and therefore not being applicable to *this* purpose)	£217,000,000
Quantity of national metallic money, gold, silver, and copper together (gold alone being, according to Mr. Secretary Rose, near £44 millions), say	£45,000,000
Bank paper, before the pressure of 1797, and the consequent extension by £2 and £1 Notes, as per accounts published, on an average about	£10,000,000
Country bankers' circulating paper, by loose estimate (see below)	£12,000,000
Common bills of exchange, by random conjecture for the purpose	£3,000,000
	£70,000,000
Addition by £2 and £1 Notes, say	£3,000,000

Quere as to the addition made to the amount of Bank and banker's paper by allowance of smaller Notes, considering the effect, if any, of the late tax imposed on that species of paper?

Are Exchequer Bills to be considered as entering into the composition of the mass of paper money? They perform that function, at any rate in the neighbourhood of the *Change*, with not much more difficulty than Bank Notes of the same magnitude: the intervention of broker's assistance and broker's fee being, though convenient in some instances, not necessary in all. In this point of view, the recent addition to the quantity of this species of paper, in consequence of the additional sums raised within the year, by the trebling of the assessed taxes, and since by the Income Tax, may *help* to account for the great plenitude that has so rapidly succeeded to the preceding scarcity.

The particulars afforded by the printed documents are—*numbers* of banking houses at four different periods, 400 the highest; *comparative quantities* of paper issued by a certain portion (16) of that number at different periods; and *absolute quantities* of paper issued at those periods by a lesser number of houses (6), all of them in a particular town (Bristol); the quantities of paper issued in a particular county (Devonshire); and the quantities of paper issued by a single bank in another county, viz. one of the Newcastle banks, at the two first of the above periods, viz. at the first £120,000; at the second, upon the extinction of a rival bank, [£]200,000.

As to the main point—that which, to the present purpose, is the main object of

Call the amount of money kept up on both these accounts in the shape of capital one fourth of the whole, then will a defalcation, as above, from the mass of money by a defalcation to that amount from the quantity of Bank paper issued and kept out, produce, instead of the above supposed defalcation of *three* millions, a defalcation of *four* millions from the mass of money receipts.

Suppose again that, by reason of the alarm excited by this defalcation from Bank paper, and whatever was the cause of such defalcation, another million (cash and paper together) is hoarded up and kept out of circulation, out of the portion which otherwise would have continued in the circulation: on this supposition, the defalcation from the mass of the year's money receipts swells from the *four* millions above spoken of, to *eight* millions.

But it is on the quantity of money ready to be transferred to those to whom it is *due,* or by whom it is otherwise *expected,* whether out of the portion which is kept in general circulation in *small* masses, and which serves as a vehicle for *income,* or out of the portion kept up in *large* masses, in the shape of *capital,* that the body of commercial men, in their capacity of *debtors,* depend for their ability to fulfil the aggregate mass of their engagements. If, then, the influx of money in the course of the year into commercial hands be thus diminished by the amount of eight millions on the score of income and capital taken together, eight millions, or some such large sum,

---

enquiry—viz. the total absolute quantity of paper in issue at the several periods from all these houses taken together, the light afforded is faint to an extreme. In looking for the quantity per house, £60,000 a year—the quantity afforded by a place standing so high in the [scale of] commercial eminence and population as Bristol—a place second in both these respects only to the Metropolis—seems too high for the whole of England taken together, including so many comparatively petty towns and even villages, even for the period of greatest abundance: and yet at a period of inferior abundance, we find £200,000 the quantity issued by a single house in a town of inferior rank—Newcastle! How small may be the quantity in issue in the instance in which it is smallest, it seems impossible to say—no more than a few thousands, or even hundreds: in that case, a few such instances as Newcastle, and many there can hardly be, would go but a small way towards making up the deficiency of the houses of the smaller and more numerous classes to such a degree as to give any such average as the Bristol complement of £60,000, upon the whole.

Meantime, in this account no other paper (it is to be observed) is comprized, than what is called cash paper, paper payable on demand: of the paper bearing other conditions—for instance, payable so many days after sight (of which, according to private information, examples are not wanting)—the amount remains in total darkness. Quere concerning paper carrying interest, but the interest not commencing till a certain number of months (six months in the instance of certain Newcastle banks) after date? Is this comprized, or not, under the denomination of cash paper?

will be the amount of engagements *broken* in the course of that year, by reason of the defalcation of a single million's worth of Bank paper (unless in as far as the deficiency may have been made up from other sources): and to this amount will the commercial wealth of the country have suffered, not only in point of *quantity*, but in point of *security*.

I speak of *security*, in contradistinction to *quantity*, *i.e.* to actual wealth to a *liquidated* amount: for if, to the above liquidated loss, be added the loss by failure following upon failure in consequence of the shock given to *security*, the ultimate loss may rise above the supposed eight millions, to an indefinite amount.

The want of a circulating medium as such, that deficiency of which so much was said in 1797, is not felt now, but it may recurr at any time. By the united wisdom of all parties interested, it received a cure at the time from a number of concurrent measures, all of them perfectly well adapted to the production of the effect. From true wisdom it received for the time a perfect cure:* but by any other means than the sort of remedy here proposed, to prevent the evil from recurring again and again at any time, is not within the reach of the most

*1. On the part of the *Bank*, the extension given to the quantity of their paper—not in Notes of the then usual magnitudes, but in Notes of the reduced magnitudes—the £1 and £2 Notes: whereby the market was enlarged to such an extent as, if given to it at an earlier period, would, it seems probable, have prevented the exigency.

2. On the part of *government*, the suspending to a certain degree the action of the restrictive laws by which individuals had been prevented from issuing notes below a certain magnitude.

3. On the part of the *commercial body*, by their agreement to accept of Bank of England paper without demanding cash for it.

4. To the force of these *factitious* remedies was added that of the *natural* remedy, the return of the hoarded money of both kinds into the circulation, upon the cessation of the alarm.

As no man can keep any unnecessary quantity of money by him for any length of time but to a loss, would not this natural remedy, together with the preceding one, have been sufficient?

That the exigency of the case would have admitted of the waiting for the operation of these two last-mentioned remedies, is more than I will undertake to say. But that if it would, the application of the first two might have been omitted with great advantage on another score, is an opinion that will, I imagine, be acceded to by whoever recognizes the mischief pointed out as flowing from every addition to the quantity of money, metallic or paper, in Chap. XIV. on the *Rise of Prices*.

perfect wisdom:* and prevention is still better than the most perfect cure. To be liable at any time to become the instrument of mischief, and that in either of two opposite ways, by being in too great quantity, or in too little, is of the essence of all such promissory paper: for its not being in *too small* a quantity, it depends upon the wisdom and even humour of a few individuals: for its not being in *too great* quantity, it depends not only upon the wisdom and humour of individuals, but upon contingencies of the day, and the humours and prejudices of the uninformed, and ill-informed, and hasty and impetuous multitude: upon the former, as to their not exceeding in their issues the amount warranted by the rules of prudence: upon the latter, as to the not frustrating and setting at default all the rules of prudence, by crowding in to demand for their paper, without need, such a quantity of cash as is not in existence.

The sort of promise given by Bank and banker's paper, is that sort of promise, the fulfilment of which, taken in the aggregate, is physically and constantly impossible: the promise given by the proposed Annuity Note paper, is that sort of promise, the fulfilment of which, whether taken in the aggregate or in parcels, has never yet been found to fail:—which possesses all the certainty that is to be found any where in human affairs:—and which becomes less and less liable to fail, the greater the quantity of money of which it conveys the promise.

Were the proposed paper the *only* paper money, national wealth would not be liable to suffer either in point of *quantity* or in point of *security*, either from *excess* or from *deficiency* in the quantity of paper money, in any degree: since, even without the exercise of human reason on the part of any body (except on the part of each noteholder, in so far as his own particular interest, and that the interest of the moment, were concerned) it would adjust itself, as it were of itself, as to what concerns the demand for circulating money, to the exact quantum of the demand: it would be *stock* one moment and *cash* the next, whichever were most wanted.

* [1]To a theoretical glance it might be apt to appear that the lesser quantity of money might serve to convey the same quantity of annual receipts as the greater, if, in proportion to the deficiency in the *quantity of matter*, the *velocity* of the circulation were to be encreased. But upon examination, I do not imagine it would be found by what means the velocity would be capable of receiving any adequate encrease. The natural effect of those pressures, to which such encrease would be a relief, is—not to *accelerate* the circulation, but to *retard* it.[2]

[1] [2][A question mark is written over this note.]

In the other case, were it but one ingredient, amongst others, in the composition of the currency of the country, it would, as far as it went, and to the extent of the quantity kept in hand, principally with a view to income,* act as an occasional supplement to other paper money, and as a remedy of the preventive kind to whatever inconveniences might otherwise have arisen from a *deficiency* of that article.

Against an *excess* in the quantity of other paper money, its operation would not be quite so efficient or so manifest. But by presenting to every eye a species of paper money unsusceptible either of excess or depretiation, it would at once, and at all times, take the pretence of necessity from the rashness that might otherwise be disposed to hazard an excessive issue: and it would render the public in general the less disposed to accept, in an excessive quantity, a paper essentially hazardous, seeing that a paper essentially exempt from hazard was at their command, to any amount, at any time.

CHAPTER XIII. PARTICULAR INTERESTS CONCERNED

Of the four distinguishable effects looked for by the proposed measure, that which will probably be regarded as the principal, is the degree of acceleration and assurance promised by it to the redemption of the national debt. To the accomplishment of so desirable an object, in a way consistent with existing engagements, no damage accruing to particular interests has ever been considered as opposing any bar that ought to be regarded as insurmountable. That a reduction, say from 4 to 3 per Cent, is a tax, and that a perpetual[1] one, to the amount of 25 per Cent upon the income of a particular class of men, is a proposition too obvious to be overlooked. Yet the design of effecting a reduction of the same sort, and that to an undefined amount, is a design rooted in the mind of the Legislature, evidenced by the practice of preceding Parliaments,† and by the express declarations of the last.‡

The nation at large and the stockholder are *borrower* and *lender*,

*It therefore would not begin to act in this capacity till after Period I.: but from thenceforward the quantity would be more than adequate to the purpose here in question, in a prodigious degree.

[1][Bowring's text, p. 136, reads "proportional".]

†In the compass of thirty-three years, viz. from 1717 to 1750, interest on divers parcels of the national debt was reduced from 6 to 3 per Cent. (Sinclair, II. 214.)

‡32 G. III. c. 55.

debtor and *creditor*. When the money is to be raised, it is the lender's harvest, and he takes advantage of the borrower and his necessities to the utmost of his power. When debt comes to be paid off, it is the debtor's turn, and it is neither unnatural nor unjust, nor illaudable, nor ought it to be unexpected, that he, by his agents, should take the like advantage.

The stockholder of the *paying-off* season is not (it is true) in every instance the same individual as the stockholder of the *borrowing* season. He is, however, either the very same, or one who, with his eyes open, and for valuable consideration, has put himself in the other's place: succeeding to all his rights, it would be in vain to repine at the thoughts of having succeeded to any of his obligations. From a *creditor,* in some cases, and on the score of humanity, *mercy* may, with more or less reason, be expected: but from a *debtor,* what *mercy* was ever looked for? The words *"merciless"* and *"debtor"* are words scarcely to be coupled with a grave face.

Expressions, however, and the momentary effect they may have on the *imagination,* are not the proper standards of right and wrong in this case any more than in any other. *Human feelings,* and the effect of measures upon those feelings, *do* constitute that standard, in so far as they can be *ascertained.* A stockholder is as much a member of the community—as great a part of the community—as any other man. Such as his *expectations* have been, such will his feelings be, when the event takes place. But what *have* been his expectations? It is from his *situation,* and that only—from the terms of the contract by which his situation in that respect is constituted—that any judgment can be formed.

Thus stands it with regard to the public creditor—the stockholder—who, on the comparative return or encrease of general prosperity and opulence, has in former instances seen that part of his income reduced by one half, and who, within a period already in prospect, may be doomed by the like cause to a reduction to the like amount.

But in comparison with the interests of *this* vast branch of the community, what can be the amount of all the *other* particular interests put together! and in comparison of the degree of sufferance in *this* case, how trifling will be the degree of sufferance in any of those *other* cases!

The destiny of the stockholders is not hypothetical: it originates not in the proposed measure. It has been fixed and made known by the Legislature, and built upon for years and years, by determinations several times repeated and brought to view, without a doubt from that or any other quarter on the head of perseverance. It is for want of means, and not of determination, that the redemption with all its consequences has not long ago been accomplished.

In comparison of *such* interests, whatever lighter interests may be found to stand in the way, might therefore appear as scarcely worth a glance. But though all *particular* interests put together will not prevail for the rejection of a measure beneficial, *in a superior degree,* to the *whole,* yet a view of the particular *ways* and *degrees* in which they may respectively come to be affected by it, will not be without its use, were it only by way of warning of the probable *sources* and *grounds* of *opposition,* and of the nature of the obstacles which may be to be combated in the course of the exertions necessary to bring the measure into effect.

During Period I, while no part of the mass of government annuities is taken but on terms on which the holder is *desirous* to part with it, benefit to particular interests will run along with, and probably preponderate over, the damage. From the commencement of the period when the species of property in question is taken out of unwilling hands, the damage, as far as particular interests are concerned, will be apt to outweigh the benefit.

The only interests that belong in strictness to the present enquiry, are those which are affected by the particular mode of operation employed by the proposed measure. The consideration of any such interests as would equally be affected, whatever other mode were employed, is foreign to the present case.

The particular interests on which it bears are of course the several interests concerned in the species of paper money already in circulation. The *parties* in question are therefore—1. the Bank of England; 2. the country banking houses; to which will be to be added (although not concerned in the emission of paper money, but on another account); 3. the banking houses of the Metropolis.

1. If the paper of the Bank of England should be accepted by government, in payment for Annuity Note paper issued, at the local Annuity Note Offices, on the footing of cash, as it is at present at the other existing government offices, the circulation of Bank Notes would not (it should seem) experience any diminution from the proposed measure. It might even receive assistance: since, in virtue of

the same properties by which Bank paper is rendered preferable to cash for all other purposes,* it will be no less so for this purpose.

Should the public in general testify for Annuity Note paper the expected preference as compared with cash, the Bank, by keeping that paper as the stock in reserve to answer calls for change for their own Notes, might keep so much the less cash, and derive £2 19s interest from a portion of their stock which at present yields them none. But the profit from the present state of things is simple and certain: the result of the proposed measure upon the affairs of the Company would appear wrapped in clouds. The Bank, according to their intelligent censor, Mr. Allardyce,† have not been forward to step out of the beaten track where the step has been ever so obvious, and encreased emolument ever so certain a fruit of it: the probability, therefore, seems to be, that the plan of the proposed rival paper would not be viewed from that superb edifice but with a rival's eye.

Should damage eventually accrue to the corporation, and should the case be regarded as calling for compensation, the profit would afford an ample fund, and the situation of the party damnified is such as would render it easy to reserve compensation in a variety of shapes. But to put the public to any expence in rendering any such compensation would be a departure from former practice. When by threats of forced redemption government has compelled the Bank to accept of a reduced rate of interest, [and] made a defalcation to the amount of 25 per Cent upon the greatest part of its income,‡ compensation has neither been granted by one party, nor demanded by the other.

To government, whose own manufactory of paper money§ is of no less standing than that of the Bank, it will be difficult to say why it should be forbidden to follow the example of the Bank, and cut down its paper into as many smaller sizes as it found convenient. To government, which, for the benefit of the community at large, has made no scruple of restricting the dealings of other manufacturers of paper money, it would be strange, if in the same view it were not allowable to take its own course in the manufacture of its own paper —in the management of its own affairs.

---

*See Ch. IV.

†Address to the Proprietors of the Bank, 1798.

‡By the reduction of interest on government annuities from 4 to 3 per Cent in Mr. Pelham's time, A° 1749, 1750; 23 G. II. c. 1 & 22.

§Exchequer Bills.

But the *resource* [afforded by loans from the Bank] (it may be asked)—*Shall government deprive itself of such a resource?* The answer is short and simple. The resource can not be taken away by the measure till profits have been produced to a greater amount than the fee simple of it. Bank paper need not—would not begin to be withdrawn out of the circulation till the paper of the country banks had been driven out of it altogether. Call both together £25 millions: the sum to which the pressure ascribed was not £12 millions: a sum equal to that seems not very likely to be again granted by one party, or asked for by the other. But the profit by 25 millions of Annuity Note paper sold, adding no more than the profit by the two first reductions—viz. that from £3 per Cents and that from [£]4 and 5 per Cents to £2 19s (not to mention the ulterior or minor profits) would be several times that amount.

It is only in time of war that the resource is of any value. The quantity of money in the country will not be lessened at any rate by the proposed measure: the great and only danger is, lest it be encreased too much. Upon any emergency, the same quantity of money would therefore be to be had, and always to be had, only through a *channel* perhaps different, and at a rate of interest, possibly, though not certainly, a little higher. At the worst, to set against the gain of the twenty, thirty, or forty millions, two or three times in the course of ten or twenty years, an extra expence to the amount of £50,000 or £100,000 might be incurred. Upon these occasions, a quantity of money might come to be raised upon bills in the nature of Exchequer Bills, under powers previously and regularly obtained from Parliament, instead of being raised by Treasury Bills without powers from Parliament.

The resource, such as it is, might or might not be reduced, but at the worst would be but reduced. Even now, profit by paper issued is but a part of the profits of the Bank.

2. As to the country bankers, the effect of the measure upon their interests appears by no means clear. On the one hand, if the quantity of cash in the country is not lessened by the proposed government paper, the demand for banker's service in keeping that cash will not be lessened. Should the proposed government paper come to be universally received in preference to cash, the supply of cash kept by these banks for answering draughts may be made to assume that form, yielding £2 19s per Cent while kept at home, while an equal amount in cash is sent abroad, in the way of discount in exchange

for bills. On the other hand, the money which is now attracted to a country bank by the *nominal 3 per Cent,* or whatever interest it is that is paid for it at present, will no longer find its way thither, being turned aside by the *full £2 19s* a year, with so many other advantages that attend the proposed paper in comparison with the paper of country bankers.

[1]The loss, if there be any, to which this species of trader would be thus exposed, is at any rate among the slightest and least to be regretted of any to which man is exposed by the vicissitudes of trade. It is a mere cessation of gain, or rather of gain in this particular shape. A banker's capital is all in money: it is not with a banker as with a manufacturer: no loss by removal of stock, or by forced sale in the lump, and thereby to a disadvantage, to avoid the other greater loss. A banker steps into his trade without trouble, and goes out of it without loss.[2]

In Nov. 1792 (according to Mr. Chalmers)* the number of country banks was upwards of 400: before the month of March 1793 (according to the evidence given on the 1st April 1797 to the Committee of [the House of] Lords† they had decreased to about 280: on that same 1st of April 1797, according to the same evidence, they did not exceed 230. If, in consequence of the proposed measure, the numbers of these banks should experience a further reduction, or were to be swept away altogether, the change is of a sort that threatens not to be either preceded or followed by *distress. Failure* can not be among the consequences. The banks will have had ample warning, time for getting in their debts, and contracting their issues. Of the issue of the proposed paper the progress from the very opening of it, will be known day by day, the whole island over, to a penny.‡ *Months* at any rate, not to speak of *years,* will have intervened between the first authentic mention of the measure, and the establishment of it.

From withdrawing without failure—from withdrawing, should it take place in consequence of the advancement of the proposed Annuity Note paper — little damage would ensue to the few individuals particularly concerned, and none to any body else. From failure, as often as it happens, ruin ensues to the individuals con-

[1] [2][In a Secretary's hand.]

*Estimate [of the Comparative Strength of Great Britain] &c. Edition 1794. Dedication, p. LXI.

†By Mr. Ellison, Agent to the Association of Country Banks. Lord's Report, p. 87.

‡By Art. 18, Ch. I.

cerned, and much mischief to the community at large. An entire substitution of the proposed government paper to the paper of country bankers, would prevent the recurrence of this mischief and that ruin. It is no light matter. Out of the 400 and odd country banks above spoken of (according to an account taken by Mr. Chalmers), "a full fourth", upwards of 100, failed.* Of more recent failures I say nothing, having nobody to quote.

By expulsion from this branch of trade the whole body of the trade would thus be secured from failure. By the failure of a part, though it were but a tenth part, more distress would at any time be produced, reckoning that of the trade alone, than by the expulsion of the whole.

3. For the banking houses of the Metropolis, there seems less cause of apprehension than for the *country banks.* They have no paper for the government paper to annihilate. True it is, that on the one hand many persons who now keep their money at a banker's, because, by keeping it themselves they could make no interest, would not keep their *Annuity Note paper* at the banker's, if by keeping it there they could make no interest of it, while by keeping it at home they could make £2 19s per Cent of it. But the inducement to keep money at the banker's does not consist solely in the consideration of *safe custody,* but in that and other advantages put together: in the saving in point of time and trouble in regard to the counting of money, and doubts and disputes about the goodness of money offered, together with the convenience of a man's having the account of his expenditure kept by other hands. For these remaining conveniences, some might be willing to waive their claims to the small and unusual gain of 2d per £100 per day upon expenditure: others, though unwilling to give up the whole, may be willing to give up some part of it; and in this way a man might keep his Annuity Note paper at his banker's, as he does his cash, but *upon terms,* and the profit by interest on the paper might thus come to be shared between the *owner* of the paper and the *keeper* of it. Capital sums, however, which now are, in so many instances, suffered, through indolence, and while waiting for a distant and undetermined employment, to lie dead to the owner at a banker's, would not be quite so apt to lie there, when, in the shape of Annuity Notes, they might be productive of interest to the owner, without prejudice to such their destination, and without any encrease of trouble.

**Ib.* LXII.

Here, then, we see two new sources of profit opened by the measure to the banking houses of the Metropolis:—1. Profit by interest of Annuity Note paper kept in reserve, instead of cash, to answer drafts; and 2. Profit by Annuity Note paper kept for customers *upon terms*. Suppose the quantity of cash in the Metropolis to be undiminished by the measure, the amount of the above profits will even be *neat*. *Will* it remain undiminished? The affirmative seems highly probable. (See Ch. XIV.)

Among the effects of the measure is one, that to a certain degree can not fail to encrease that quantity. The cash which now remains, and would otherwise have remained in the hands of the frugal poor, in unproductive hoards,[1] being now poured into the hands of the Commissioners [for the][2] redemption [of the national debt] through the medium of the Annuity Note Offices, in return for Annuity Note paper, will be restored to the circulation, and add to the quantity put into the hands of bankers.

CHAPTER XIV. RISE OF PRICES—HOW TO OBVIATE

I have already stated an extra-rise of prices as among the *conceivable* results of the proposed measure. Taken by itself, it is evidently an *undesirable* one: it is a tax on income to the amount: a tax which comes out of every body's pocket, and goes into nobody's. Being, with reference to the proposed measure, an *unfavourable* result, I may be received with the less difficulty, when stating it as a *probable* one.

Supposing the *influx* of the proposed paper not to be followed, or rather kept pace with, by an *efflux* of other money to an equal amount, and supposing it too *sudden* to be productive of an influx of vendible commodities, to an amount worth regarding in this view, within the assumed space of time, the result presents itself as a *demonstrable* one. For the price of the whole mass of vendible articles taken together sold within the year, is, in other words, the same thing as the quantity of money given, or undertaken for, in exchange for them within that time; so that the quantity of those articles remaining the same, the greater the quantity of the money is that has been given for them, the higher has been the price.

It has already been observed, that it seems impossible to say with

[1][Bowring's text, p. 139, reads "hands".]
[2][The MS reads "of".]

any precision to how small or how great a length the emission of the proposed paper may eventually be found to extend, previously to the arrival of stock 3 per Cents at par: that, at some part or other of that interval, a small quantity at least can, however, scarcely fail to find acceptance; and that a small quantity, a very few millions for example, issued previous to the conclusion of it, would be sufficient to operate the conversion indicated, and thereby give the form of the proposed paper to the whole of the remaining mass of annuities composing the national debt—that, although the quantity of that species of property will be continually and rapidly on the decrease, while the demand for it will be as continually and rapidly on the encrease, it will nevertheless be difficult, if not impossible, to prescribe any determinate limit to that portion of it, which, in this way, may come to have introduced itself into the circulation, on the footing of current *money*. For the open issue will remain equally open to the customers for *temporary* income (who, when they have kept it as long as they can afford, will throw it into the circulation) as to the customers for *permanent* income: and it seems impossible to say in what proportions, at any given time, the quantity of Annuity Note paper, remaining at that time, will find itself distributed between the two classes.

On these considerations, it will be matter of prudence to be prepared for the several possible cases and degrees, in which it may happen to constitute a clear addition to the mass of money in circulation, to any such amount as to be in a sensible degree productive of the apprehended inconvenience.

Of such preparation, the practical result will be, to take such measures as shall be effectual for the prevention—not of the rise of prices, which is impossible—but of any addition to that degree of rise, or rate of encrease, which would have taken place, in the natural course of things, independently of the proposed measure.

If, after having expelled, of itself, the whole amount of paper money of other sorts, it were to keep on encreasing without expelling metallic money to an amount equal to its own, it would thenceforward, if not restrained, make a proportionable addition to the quantity of money of all sorts in circulation, and thence to the prices of vendible commodities. In this case it would be necessary to apply the check to the proposed paper itself, by limiting the quantity that should be suffered to enter into the composition of the mass of money in circulation: for example by stopping the issue of all Annuity Notes below a certain magnitude; say, for instance, the £102 8s Notes. By an expedient thus simple (the requisite powers being given to the executive government *ab initio*) the end might be accomplished, in the possible event supposed, without any fresh interference on the part of the Legislature. That the means thus proposed would be adequate to the end, will appear clear enough (it is supposed) from what has been said on this subject in a former Chapter.*

That in proportion as the proposed paper advanced in the circulation, country banker's paper and Bank of England paper would quietly withdraw themselves, is a result that appears more probable than the contrary, according to what has already been observed.†

Should it fail of taking place in the requisite degree of itself, it would require to be produced by means directed expressly to that end.

The first of the two species of paper attacked, would naturally be the paper of the *country banks*. Collectively modern, individually changeable, they have no such claims on government as plead in favour of the incorporated Bank.‡ Express *prohibition* would not be necessary: by *taxation* the same effect precisely might be produced: by a simple extension of a tax *already* imposed for other purposes. By this means, if necessary, about half the utmost possible amount of the supposed redundant mass of paper (25 millions) would be cleared[1] away.§

Secondly, and lastly, would come the paper of the *Bank of England*. In this case, as in the other, the same means would be sufficient to the same end. Perhaps, however, in this case, they would not be necessary.

*Ch. IV. *Grounds*, &c.

†Ch. XIII. *Particular Interests*, &c.

‡The case of the incorporated banks of Scotland does not appear to differ materially in this respect from that of the unincorporated country banks.

[1][Bowring's text, p. 140, reads "chased away". The error is a natural one, since the critical word in the MS looks almost like "chased", but on closer inspection it is seen to read correctly "cleared" as above.]

§By the tax recently imposed on country banker's paper, government has already taken to itself a share in the profit on that paper. In so far as banker's paper came to be extruded by the proposed government paper, this comparatively minute profit would fall, of course, to be deducted from the sum total of profits promised by the proposed measure.

The present amount, as indicated by the return for the first quarter (£9,821), appeared to be about £40,000 a year.‖

‖Commons Finance Accounts AO 1800 No. II p. 21, dated 29 Jan. and 5 March. The date of the Act (39 G.3.c.3) is 12 July 1799.

A simple refusal on the part of government, to receive at its own offices any other than its own paper, might be adequate to the effect.*

It may be asked—to what end throw the whole burthen of the measure upon the two particular classes in question, instead of letting it spread over the community at large in the shape of a rise of prices?

My answer is—to reduce the amount and pressure of it to its *minimum*. At an estimate greater than any possible one, the former loss would not be to the latter in so high a proportion as that of interest to principal. To the banking class it is not clear (as hath already been shewn) that the loss would in fact amount to any thing. But put an extreme case, and take it, in the instance of each individual, at the utmost possible amount it could rise to in the instance of any one. Call the total amount of Bank and banker's paper, as before, 25 millions, and upon the whole of this paper suppose a neat[1] profit of 5 per Cent, annually made. Upon a supposition in a variety of points thus excessive, the total loss is but £1,250,000 a year. Call, on the other hand, the total quantity of money of all kinds taken together 73[2] millions: and suppose (according to the position brought to view at the commencement of this chapter) that the addition made to the prices of vendible commodities taken together is in the exact proportion of the supposed addition to the mass of money: viz. as 25 to 75 = as 1 to 3.

On this supposition, the rise of prices being supposed equable and therefore universal, every income which did not receive a rateable encrease from the supposed sudden influx of 25 million would in effect be diminished by a fourth: the whole income of a man so circumstanced producing him no more than three-fourths of the quantity of vendible commodities it produced to him before. Call, with Dr. Beeke, the annual income of the country (including income from day labour without stock) £217,000,000, or for round numbers £210,000,000. Then will the annual burthen on the country by rise of prices, on the non-expulsion of the paper money in question, be £70,000,000: *per contra*, the utmost possible annual loss to the bankers and Bank proprietors by the expulsion, not so much as £1,250,000; the probable loss, scarce so much as the odd £250,000.

The amount of the loss would, it is true, be made good in money, in a certain degree, to every person whose circumstances enabled

*In this case, nothing would be receivable at the Annuity Note Offices but cash.

[1][Bowring's text, p. 140, reads "real".]

[2][Bowring's text, p. 140, reads "75".]

him to make in money an addition to his income equal to the degradation thus sustained by it; for although the real value of the total mass of money—its value in respect of the quantity of vendible commodities it purchases and conveys—is not greater after the supposed addition to the mass of money, yet, on the other hand, neither is it less. The misfortune is, that although the pressure from the defalcation would be felt in all its force, and felt by all parties, indemnified as well as unindemnified, the indemnity would in comparison be scarce perceived. The loss by rise of prices would be felt as so much loss: the gain by the share in that extra influx of money by which the loss had been produced—this gain, not being coupled and set down *per contra* in the mind of the party and confronted with the loss, would present itself in the shape of an independent gain, unconnected with any such effect: and by an indisputable law of the sensible faculties of man, sums and circumstances equal, the enjoyment produced by gain is never equal to the suffering produced by loss: if it were, the main reason for affording protection to property would cease.

That an encrease in the quantity of real wealth, i.e. of vendible commodities, has been produced by an encrease in the quantity of nominal wealth, viz. current money, cash and paper together, seems by no means clear of doubt. But what seems not exposed to doubt is, that the quantum of such addition, if real, accruing in the compass of a year, can not amount to more than the produce of the fresh quantity of unemployed capacity for labour brought into employment by the application of a proportionable quantity of the supposed fresh influx of money, over and above that which would have been brought into employment: so that, if at the commencement of the year all hands capable of employment were full of employment, and so would have continued during the whole course of it, no addition could in the course of that time be made to the quantity of real wealth or vendible commodities by the influx of money in question, howsoever copious. But whatever quantity of money, being introduced into the circulation, has not the effect of producing a correspondent quantity of vendible commodities, can not but have the effect of producing a correspondent degradation in the value of the existing mass of money into which it flows, thereby producing what is in truth no more than the same effect expressed in other words, a correspondent *rise of prices*.

Let £6,000,000 be the quantity of extra influx money introduced into the circulation in the compass of the year: let the quantity of extra labour produced by this extra influx be equal to full employment for 100,000 fresh hands. The allowance would be perhaps sufficient as applied to the whole amount of fresh labour produced within the year by all causes, the existing quantity of money and the supposed extra quantity taken together: applied, therefore, to the latter alone, it will be excessive. It is not a matter of necessity that any addition at all to the mass of vendible commodities shall have been produced by the extra influx of money: since a particular application of the existing quantity of money in the country, without any accession to it whatsoever, is altogether adequate [to] the producing the utmost possible degree of accumulation. But for illustration sake, the supposed state of things may serve as well as if it were more correct. Call the average value of the produce of their labour 12s a week for each: this, in round numbers, will be £3,000,000 a year. £3,000,000, then, is the quantity of extra influx money remaining, the efficiency of which is spent altogether in degrading the value of the mass into which it flows, and producing the correspondent rise in the price of vendible commodities.

CHAPTER XV. REDUCTION OF INTEREST—PROPOSED MODE COMPARED WITH MR. PELHAM'S

Reduction of Interest is a declared object with Parliament:* the only question is as to the *mode.*

To exhibit the comparative eligibility as between the two plans—(the one here proposed for the future, and the one pursued in time past by *Mr. Pelham*)—I will consider them together under the several heads of *expence—celerity of operation—previous assurance of success*—and *gentleness of operation*: not forgetting, on the occasion of Mr. Pelham's, its [possible] application to present times, with their almost eightfold mass of debt.

I. As to *expence*—viz. as compared with profit.

In Mr. Pelham's time, the profit consisted in reducing to 3 per Cents the whole amount of the then existing quantity of 4 per Cents: that is, reducing the quantum of interest paid on the nominal capital of about £57,703,475, from about £2,308,136 to about £1,731,102.

When the operation was first mentioned by him in Parliament, it is [*sic*] a sign that *then* at least the state of the money market was ripe

*New Sinking Fund Act 32 G. 3 ch. 55.

for it: otherwise he could not have obtained the requisite assurance of the money for paying off in case of refractoriness: how much longer it might already have been ripe, it would be in vain to attempt to calculate. This being assumed, whatever respite he allowed—whether as to the whole, or as to a part of the interest proposed to be struck off—is to be considered as a price, or *bonus* which, under the plan pursued, it was looked upon as advisable in point of prudence to allow to the stockholders, in order to purchase their acquiescence, and insure the plan against the hazard of failure. [1]I say to prudence: for[2] as to sympathy for the sufferings of the individuals damnified, the professedly vindictive measures pursued afterwards against the *repugnants* are a sufficient proof that no such motive was consulted in the arrangement of the terms.

1. A year's interest was allowed in the first place[3] without reduction: i.e. the amount of the one per Cent that was to be afterwards struck off by the reduction. £577,034 was allowed for the first year.*

2. Half of the one per Cent ultimately struck off was allowed for seven years more. This, for one year, was £288,517: for the seven years, £[2,019,619][4]. Adding the one per Cent for the first year, makes the total price paid for consent, £[2,596,653]. Deducting discount for the several years to come £426,980, leaves the amount of the price paid for the £577,034 a year thus saved, £[2,169,673].

This £2,169,673 [5]thus paid for consent to the reduction[6] amounts to a little more than 1-27th of the amount of the capital of £57,703,475, upon which the reduction of the 4 per Cent per annum to 3 per Cent was thus effected: a little less than [7]£2,308,136, which would be the exact amount of[8] four years purchase of the perpetual annuity

[1] [2][In a Secretary's hand.]

[3][May also read "plan".]

*This (it may be thought) should not be considered as constituting part of the *bonus*, inasmuch as in some of the Acts, and probably in all [1]the Acts[2] prior to that date, it will be found that a year's notice previous to redemption was among the stipulated terms. On the other hand, if, instead of waiting for meditations and negotiations, and observations to be taken of the times, a plan had been adopted in the first instance, such as (like the proposed plan) would have given the public the benefit of the reduction from the instant that the rise, in the rate of interest in general, and of the money in the Funds in particular, had rendered the commencement of it practicable, the probability seems to be, that the extra interest, not only of the year in question, but of one or more preceding years, might have been saved.

[4][Bentham's MS in fact reads "£2,016,119". Bowring corrected the mistake. Instead of the two following figures appearing in the text in square brackets, Bentham's MS speaks of "£2,593,158" and "£2,166,178".]

[5] [6][Put into brackets at a later date.]

[7] [8][In a Secretary's hand.]

thus struck off. Such then, is the price that, on Mr. Pelham's plan, would be to be given for a consent which, upon the proposed plan, would be obtained *gratis*.

On the proposed plan, the quantum of interest that would be struck off by the first reduction ([1]meaning[2] the reduction effected in the course of the two first periods, by conversion of 4 and 5 and 3 per Cents into capitals bearing £2 19s per Cent) by means of the paper of the first issue, would be £1,212,608.*

That, upon any proposed reduction, to be effected at *this* time of day, the same terms precisely should be offered, as were offered at *that* time of day, would, under the vast difference of circumstances, be a supposition altogether untenable: but, as it would be a fruitless attempt to determine what *would be* the terms now offered, the only terms on which any argument can be grounded are the above.

On that supposition, the price to be paid for a consent to the striking off a mass of perpetual annuities to the above amount of £[1,212,608] a year, would be a little less than four times *that* sum: it would be £[4,559,458]: exactly four times would be £[4,850,432].†

3. A *sacrifice* which may be added to the expence attending the reduction of *interest*, as above, is that of the faculty of going on with the redemption of the principal of the debt. By Mr. Pelham's plan, this latter mode of liberation was given up: [1]even in[2] point of right, for eight years, and, in intention, perhaps for ever. Since the establishment of the existing Sinking Funds, it could not *now* be given up upon *any* terms: and, supposing it possible, and deemed eligible, to adopt the principle of [1]Mr. Pelham's reduction[2] plan to a certain extent, it could not be adopted without such modifications as would be necessary to render it compatible with the institution of those [1]Redemption[2] Funds.

On the proposed plan, reduction of interest, and redemption of principal, afford assistance to each other: reduction to redemption, by the supplies it pours into the Fund; redemption to reduction, by the sums which, by expelling them out of the old annuities, it drives into the new.

[4.][3] Another sacrifice that [1]would be to be made upon Mr. Pelham's plan is[2] [that] of the eventual advantage of *ulterior* reductions: the

*See Ch. VI. Period II.

†As £577,034 is to £2,169,673, so is £1,212,608 to £4,559,458. [Bentham's own figures are, in consequence of his faulty multiplication, necessarily different. His text runs in fact: "As £577,034 is to £2,166,178, so is £1,440,259 to £5,406,713".]

[1] [2][In a Secretary's hand.]

[3][The MS reads "3".]

very *right* given up for eight years as before: and, for any subsequent period, no foundation laid, nor prospect opened, for any thing that appears.

On the proposed plan, issue follows issue, reduction reduction, as wave follows wave, execution treading, without respite, upon the heels of possibility. What space of time each reduction would occupy is scarce open to conjecture: thus much is certain, that there is not a moment's interval between the completion of one reduction, and the commencement of the next.

II. *Celerity of operation* constitutes a head of comparison different in name, but in effect carried to account already under the head of *expence.* A given sum is worth the less, as the time for receiving it is more distant. *Acceleration* is *profit; retardation, loss.*

III. *Previous assurance of success.*

That Mr. Pelham's plan was practicable, was proved by the event. But for a long time it "*was likely to have failed*": * and had it failed, it would have failed *in toto*: since, if the reduction had not been submitted to in respect of nearly the *whole* mass, it could not have taken place as to any *part.* Had not the quantity of *uninscribed* stock (about 3¼ millions) been small enough to admitt of its being paid off, the submission, testified in respect of the *subscribed* stock, could hardly have been accepted: nor could the plan have taken place in any degree, without a joint and simultaneous operation on the part of one or other of two numerous sets of parties; viz. the *stockholders,* who were called upon to submitt to the reduction, or the moneyed men, from whom, as far as the expected submission failed of taking place, the money was to come, for paying off the *repugnants.*

But though practicable *then,* in respect of the 57 or 58 million in question then, it does not follow that it would be practicable *now,* in regard to the £444 million in question now: not even although by the time of the arrival of stock at par [1]some such sum as[2] the odd £44,000,000 were to have been redeemed and struck off. The reduction of the 73 millions or thereabouts of 4 and 5 per Cents is (I should suppose) the *last,* as well as the *first* object, to which the view of government could well be directed, but for some such assistance as that [1]which is held out by[2] the proposed measure. Redemption of principal being left to operate on the remaining mass of 3 per Cents, redemption and reduction would be thus conciliated.

*Sinclair II. 112.

[1] [2][In a Secretary's hand.]

In regard to reduction, on the proposed plan, success, as we have seen, is independent of all contingencies. In each *year—month—day*, the process has gone on to the utmost extent consistent with the state of the money-market at that time. By the proposed[1] *subscription* plan—by the consequent competition for respite from further deductions—the first reduction might be rendered in a manner instantaneous: and a very short space of time would be sufficient for the accomplishment of it, even without any such aid:—the 5 or 6 [millions] (which would, by that time, be the amount of a year's produce of the Sinking Funds) this (call it) 5 million, thus vibrating without ceasing between the stock market and the Annuity Note market, would be sufficient to dispatch the reduction, and with prodigious rapidity, although the subscription plan were untried, or tried without effect. In the machinery thus put in motion, no part is liable to stop of itself for want of the assistance of any other: and, as it is at the beginning, so is it to the end.

During the first issue, every Note *then* issued pays off by the money it produces, and thus *converts* into note annuities, a corresponding portion of stock annuities; and contributes so far to the extinction of the 25 millions of 3 or 4 per Cents, which must be paid off before the 5 per Cents can be begun upon. During the *second* issue, every Note *then* issued converts in the same way into paper bearing the reduced rate of interest of *that* second issue, a correspondent portion of the paper of the first issue: and a single Note, thus taken out in the way of issue, would bring about the reduction upon that *portion* of capital, and, in a determinable time, even upon the *whole* capital, although not another Note were ever to be issued on the same terms.

Once put in motion, the machine keeps going of itself, without any fresh winding up, so long as there remains a particle of the debt for it to act upon and cut down: nothing [is] left to depend on the circumstances of the moment: nothing on the humours of individuals. No interval between reduction and reduction; no pausing, deliberating, negotiating, debating, fumbling. Nor yet is the process exposed to the charge of precipitation or excess: government having it in its power to stop or retard the operation at any time, by stopping or retarding the influx of the *primum mobile* from the Sinking Fund.*

[1][In a Secretary's hand.]

*The being so perfectly opposition-proof is a feature by which the proposed mode of reduction stands distinguished in a very striking point of view from every other. Though this consequence of the proposed conversion were ever so clearly foreseen by

IV. Lastly, as to *gentleness of operation*. Of Mr. Pelham's plan, it is upon record that it experienced much opposition and created much dissatisfaction. It was in the nature of it so to do. It brought forward the Minister in an obnoxious attitude, calling upon men to submitt to a loss to the amount of a perpetual tax of 25 per Cent upon income, subject only to an abatement to the amount of about four years' purchase, on condition of their lending their hands to a sacrifice of which they were the sole victims.

Accordingly, though on the ground of justice, nothing could be more unimpeachable, ill humour on one side appears to have begot ill humour on the other: on the part of the authors of the suffering, as well as on the part of the sufferers themselves. On those who stood out at first, harder terms were afterwards imposed: and, to judge from the debates, the professed motive was not merely economy, but vengeance.*

By the proposed plan, no such invidious task is put into the hands of any one. Before any thing of hardship shews itself (at least to the great class of individuals here in question—the stock-holders) the measure has been known—known for years as a measure of universal accommodation. Every man's money has been breeding money in his pocket: every man who has sold out, has sold to an advantage. When hardship comes at last, it is at the end of a long chain of causes and effects, the first link of which has been removed by time, almost out of the reach of observation. The immediate cause,† being every body's act, is nobody's. No new act—none at least that carries any thing of compulsion on the face of it—is required at *this* (or indeed at *any* time) on the part of government.

---

those who, either from factious motives, or on the honest ground of personal interest,[1] were disposed to thwart it, though it were even expressly announced by government (as indeed virtually it could not but be) it would not be in the power even of conspiracy, so much as to impede it. By refusing the paper, each conspirator would make a compleat and certain sacrifice of his own personal advantage, without the smallest chance of affording any sensible help to the common object of the conspiracy. Limitation only, not prevention—limitation, to a degree altogether without effect—would be the utmost possible result of the most unanimous and most persevering opposition on this ground.

[1][Bowring's text, p. 143, reads "motives" even here.]

---

*In the case of the *second* set of subscribers, two years were struck off from the half per Cent for seven years that had been allowed to the *first* set. First act, 23 G. II. c. 1. Second act, 23 G. II. c. 22.

†The quantity of paper taken out.

On Mr. Pelham's plan, every thing turning upon subscription, a man knew not but that he was subscribing to his own *loss*. On the proposed plan, the loss takes place at any rate, and the effect of a man's subscription is all *gain* to him. The quantity of this gain depends upon his own exertions: and the bustle of competition serves to call off the mind from the suffering which is to come.

CHAPTER XVI. MORAL ADVANTAGES

To the head of *moral* advantages may be referred two very distinct results: *prevention of improbity,* and *promotion of frugality*: prevention of improbity, by furnishing (as we shall see) a new *means* or *instrument of prevention;* promotion of frugality, by the offer of a new species of property, which, by annexing an unprecedented *remuneration* to the exercise of that virtue, operates at once as an *incentive* and as a *means.*

I. As to *prevention of improbity*. The class of persons in whose instance it may operate to this effect, consists of *trustees* of every description, to whom it belongs to *receive money* on account of their principals: *executors* and *administrators, guardians, stewards* and *receivers, assignees* of *bankrupts, prize agents, factors* and the like.

To cause *trust-moneys,* as often as a suitable case presents itself, to be laid out in the purchase of government annuities, for the benefit of the principals, is, in the Court of Chancery, matter of long-established practice: a practice which by an Act of very recent date has received express support from Parliament. The credit of the proposed new government annuities having been previously established by sufficient experience, let a similar investment of all trust-moneys, as they come in, be rendered a matter of general obligation by an Act of the Legislature. A trust *receipt book* to be kept with a trust *till*. In the *book,* an entry to be made of each sum received with the day on which it was received: the statement of the day to be indispensable. The money, if not received in the shape of Annuity Notes, to be sent to the Office on that day or the next, to be changed into Annuity Notes: the Notes received to be entered by their numbers: if the day be not entered, the first day of the year to be presumed, for the purpose of charging the trustee with the interest. The trust-paper, as received, to be deposited in the trust *till,* to save it from being confounded with money of his own. This not to prevent the disposal of the amount to superior advantage (i.e. at a higher rate of interest than what is afforded by Annuity Notes) in as far as the nature of the trust admitts of it.*

What is thus proposed to be rendered *obligatory*, for the benefit of the principal, is no more than what a *careful* trustee would do *spontaneously*, either for the benefit of the principal or for his own, according to the texture of his conscience. Should a precaution thus simple and unexceptionable be neglected, the institution of Annuity Notes will be but too apt to operate as a premium for *vice* as well as *virtue*; a premium for *improbity* in the one situation, as well as for *frugality* in the other.

II. Lastly, as to *promotion of frugality*. We have seen the peculiar advantages which the proposed new species of property holds out to the acquirer. Within a trifling and unavoidable fraction, 2d a day: £3 for every £100 by the year: not for *risk* of lending, but for mere *self-denial* in not spending. Income, receivable without *expence*, and without *stirring* from his home. No *attendance*, no *agency fees*, no *brokerage fees*, no *stamp* duty, either on *purchase* or on *sale*. No loss, on either occasion, by fluctuation of price. Not a day without its profit —profit by keeping, for the *minutest* as well as for the *largest* portions of time: conveyance obtainable for it by *post*, in the *minutest portions* as well as to the most *distant parts* of the island. Security afforded by division against misadventures of all sorts — against accidents and against crimes—in the *house* or on the *road*—by fire, water, or forgetfulness—from theft, robbery, burglary, or breach of trust. *Compound interest* brought within the reach of *individuals* for the first time.

In proportion to the degree in which it presents these several accommodations, in that same proportion does it act as an incentive to *frugality*: in *all* classes in a *certain degree*, and in as far as current expenditure is concerned: but in a more special degree, in those

*Since the above was written, a passage has been discovered in *Pinto*, whereby it appears that at the date of his book (1771) a law to this effect existed in *Holland*, in respect of the interest bearing paper of that country, termed *Obligations*. (*De la Circulation et du Credit*, p. 81.) There is a great deal of good and a great deal of evil (he says) in the effects of this law: but the good appears to consist in the mode of *employing* the money as above: the evil to the *hands* in which the management is reposed, or in some other such *collateral* circumstance, as the forced sale of property, in whatever other shape it may be in, besides money, for the purpose of converting it into *this*.

humble, and at the same time most *numerous* walks of life, in which it is of most importance, to prudence, probity, and happiness.*

In the existing state of the money-market, the hoards of the *opulent* are prolific and accumulating: the hoards of the *poor* alone are dead and unproductive. By the proposed measure the condition of the *poor* in this respect would be raised to a level in the first instance *not much below*, and in process of time (as the price of stock annuities rose, and the rate of interest obtainable by the purchase of them diminished) *altogether upon a par with*, the condition of the *rich*.

A result not to be viewed without regret is, that, in every *period* after the *second*, and, in proportion as the rate of interest afforded by government annuities comes to be reduced, the encouragement thus given to frugality will thus be reduced likewise: for though, after the reduction, the *remainder* will be *gain*, as compared with the *present* period, yet the *difference* will be *loss*, in comparison of the period then *last in experience*. But in the mean time, the condition of the poor in this respect will, at any rate, have been raised to a level with that of the rich: and will so continue. The habit of frugality will have taken root: and, having so done, may derive strength rather than weakness from the encreased exertions it will have been called upon to make.

***Frugality*, itself a virtue, is an *auxiliary* to all the other virtues: to none more than to *generosity*, to which by the unthinking it is so apt to be regarded as an *adversary*. *The sacrifice of the present to the future* is the common basis of all the virtues:—frugality is among the most difficult and persevering exemplifications of that sacrifice. Important in all classes, it is more particularly so in those which most abound in uncultivated minds. In these, to promote frugality is to promote *sobriety*:—to curb that raging vice which in peaceful times outstrips all other moral causes of unhappiness put together. In the prospects opened by frugality, the wife and children have a principal share: they derive nothing but vexation and distress from the money spent at the *ginshop* or the *alehouse*. Compared with the *prodigal*, the hardest of *misers* is a man of virtue.

In the *"Outline of a Plan of Provision for the Poor"*, as printed in Young's Annals of Agriculture, among the *collateral uses* there mentioned, as derivable from the system of *Industry-Houses* there proposed, is that of their affording, each of them to its neighbourhood, a *bank*, for the reception and improvement of the produce of frugality on a *small scale*, under the name of a *Frugality Bank*. In the plan that was handed about of the then proposed *Globe Insurance Company*, since established by Act of Parliament, among the uses mentioned as proposed to be made of the stock of such company, is that of carrying on the business of such a *Frugality Bank;* with a reference to the suggestion given in relation to it in the above papers.

Were the proposed Annuity Note paper to be emitted, *"Every* poor *man might be his own banker:"* every poor man might, by throwing his little hoards into this shape, make banker's profit of his *own* money. Every country cottage—every little town tenement—might, with this degree of profit, and with a degree of security till now unknown, be a *Frugality Bank*.

CHAPTER XVII. CONSTITUTIONAL ADVANTAGES

Among the effects resulting from the national debt, in the *early* stages of its existence, was the security it afforded to the old established constitution, by engaging the *purses* and *affections* of the moneyed *interest* in the service and support of the new-established government. *That* was the *great* moneyed interest. In *other* points of view, the institution of that debt has found *many* disapprovers: in *this,* it has found *none*—among those, at least, by whom the existing constitution is regarded as fit to be preserved. The advantage resulting from the transmutation of that debt into the proposed form would be—the securing to the constitution and government now grown into one, the support of what may be called the *little moneyed* interest by the same powerful tie.

The body *politic,* not less than the body *natural,* is subject to its constitutional diseases. *Tyranny* was the grand disease in prospect *then: anarchy, now.* The danger *then was* from a single person: in respect of the sentiments of submission pointed to that person, and carried to excess: the danger *now is* from the great multitude: in respect of the disposition to unruliness which has been, and continues to be, propagated, with but too much success, among the lower orders—among those (let it never be out of mind) of whom is composed the vast majority of the people.

If the name of *great moneyed interest,* employed above for distinction sake, be well applied, it is with reference to *money,* and by reason of the greatness of the *shares*: but with reference to *men,* and even with reference to money, if the magnitude of the total be the object of consideration, it is the *little moneyed* interest that should be termed *great.*

As the disease changes its form, so should the remedy. *Stock,* in its large doses, served for the disorder of *that* time: *paper,* in its small doses, is the specific for the *present.**

Admirable are the remedies that have already been applied: admirable, not more for their efficiency than for their gentleness. There remains this one (and perhaps another that might be named)—remedies not less efficient, and still more gentle.

*To judge of the *steadiment* which an engine of this nature is capable of applying to established order, turn to France, and see the support it lends to *subversion.* The affections of the people ebbing fast into the old channel: but the revolution in property operating as a barrier against the return of *antient* monarchy, and as a sheet-anchor to the *name* of a commonwealth.

2. Turning to Ireland, the demand for the remedy will be found the same in kind, but much more urgent in degree. The proportion of petty to great money-holders much greater: the bias to turbulence and anarchy (not to speak of idleness and drunkenness) beyond comparison more prone.*

3. Turn, lastly, to British India: What a sheet-anchor to British dominion—to the mildest, the most upright, the steadiest of all governments—if, by insensible and voluntary steps, the population of that remote, most expanded, and most expansive branch of the British Empire should be led to repose the bulk of their fortunes and their hopes on a paper bearing the image and superscription of a British Governor! What a reduction in the rate of *interest* paid *there* by government! What a remedy to the risks and embarrassments attendant on the interchange of so many debaseable and incommensurable modifications of metallic currency! What an augmentation to the general mass of currency, capital, and wealth!

But all these are trifles, in comparison with the additional pledge of popular attachment, and the encreased assurance of internal peace. From the Zemindar to the Ryot, every Hindoo, every Mussulman, who possessed *this* money—every individual, in a word, who possessed money—might thus, by his own money, and to a great part of the amount of his own money—might thus, and without impeachment of probity be converted into a pensioner of the British government.† For a premium equal to the interest the paper yields.

**Irish Debentures*—price and value not less than £100—paper or parchment instruments as much out of the reach of the body of the people as Exchequer Bills—have, to this purpose, as little application as so much stock.

†Though the debt is in *loose* paper, it is in *large* paper, and in that respect on a footing with stock. There seems therefore no bar to the introduction of the proposed plan, unless it be from local circumstances, such as, without particular investigation and opportunities, it lies not in a man's way to be informed of.

Who can say but that the circulation of this paper might come to extend itself even beyond the sphere of British dominion, the value of this paper in exchange having been once established and certified by experience?

"The Narrainee is a base silver coin, [1]struck in Cooch Bahar, of the value of about ten pence, or one third of a sicca rupee. The commodiousness of this small piece, the profits the people of Bootan derive from their commerce with Cooch Bahar, and some local prejudices against the establishment of a Mint, have given the narrainee in these regions, as well as in those where it is struck, a common currency, though both countries are perfectly independent of each other, and totally different in their language and manner[2]."—*Turner's* [Account of an Embassy to the Court of the Teshoo Lama in] *Thibet*, 1800, 4to, p. 143.

The seal or other mark of the East India Company on their packages (I remember he would be underwriting—perpetually underwriting—to the amount of the principal, the security of the Empire.

Recapitulation and Conclusion

Upon the whole, the proposed measure, it is believed, will be found to promise, with some degree of assurance, the following connected, but perfectly distinct advantages:

1. The financial profit, by contributing in so many various [forms], and to such considerable amounts, to the redemption of the principal of the debt, as well as to the reduction of the rate of interest, and [by][1] affording an instrument more advantageous than any other for the application to that end of such means as are, or may be provided, from other sources.

2. The moral advantage, the encouragement to frugality, and thence to temperance, among the inferior and most numerous ranks of the community.

3. The constitutional advantage, the safeguard given to internal tranquillity.

4. The politico-economical advantage, the addition made to the mass of national productive capital, and thence to the mass of growing wealth.

Success the greater, the earlier: but sooner or later, and to a certain degree, infallible: even failure unattended with any loss.

Seldom has a measure been brought to view pregnant with such high advantages: none in which, in case of success, the degree of success has been so precisely ascertainable—none in which the deviation from the path of safety, as indicated by experience, has been so slight and imperceptible.

The [fact that] portions of government currency less than heretofore [in use, are to be] brought into the market: this is the only

hearing once from authority that appeared unquestionable) is received in *China*, at vast distances from the factories, as satisfactory evidence of the quantities and qualities of the contents, to the value perhaps of some hundreds of pounds. Is it a supposition altogether chimerical, that a similar confidence might be brought in process of time to extend itself to the exchangeable value of a piece of paper, value a few pounds or a few shillings? In Africa, in more places than one, Park (as he tells us)[3] made a paper money out of the Lord's Prayer. Might not commercial experience give *at length* a value which was thus given by mere superstition without experience?

[1] [2][In a Secretary's hand.]

[3][Cf. Mungo Park, *Travels in the Interior Districts of Africa*, 1799.]

[1][The MS reads "for".]

feature which, separately taken, can be called new: portions less than have yet [been] issued by government in this country, but not less than what have been issued by government in other countries, and in this country by individuals.

The other leading features collected altogether from established institutions: the annuity engaged for perpetual, but redeemable: the paper containing the evidence of sale, light and transferable: the produce of the sale appropriated to the extinction of the national debt.

Each of the above four masses of advantage appears sufficient to warrant an experiment attended with some risk. Shall not all of them together [be deemed sufficient to] give birth to an experiment pure from risk?

Were the proposal to be expressed in these words—Make your Exchequer Bills for small sums*—this, though not compleatly [nor]

---

*Supposing the general plan of the proposed Annuity Note currency to be discarded, an advantage upon a smaller scale might still be derivable from it, by applying some of the features of it to the improvement of the existing species of government currency called an Exchequer Bill, in such manner as to cause it to be accepted of at a lower rate of interest than it would otherwise be.

1. It might be made out for much smaller sums, say £10 or £5: that is to say, a part of the whole mass might be broken down with a view to general circulation, a competent portion being reserved in the present large sums for operations on a large scale.

2. It might be furnished with the proposed aids to computation, by proper tables printed on the front or back of it.

3. It might be made to receive those facilities for general circulation, which depend upon the physical qualities of the paper—viz. upon the size, form, texture, and thinness—and which are possessed by the notes which compose the currency of the Bank of England.

4. It might be put in possession of the new securities against forgery, which are here proposed.

5. Markets for the purchase of it might be opened all over the country, by the simple expedient of remitting it in such quantities and proportions as should be deemed advisable, [to][1] the several local offices already in the pay of government: for example, Post Offices, Stamp Offices, Excise Offices, Custom House Offices.

I mention this only by way of illustration. Compared with the proposed general plan, the sacrifice made by thus confining the application of it, would be a sacrifice without an object. Limited as it is in respect of its total amount—limited as it is in respect of the duration of the annuity conveyed by it, the Exchequer Bill currency is radically incapable of meeting the demand of the two classes of *petty hoarders*: and thus a proportionable part of the accommodation afforded to individuals would be lost. The utmost it could do would be the going a small part of the way towards meeting the demand for temporary interest on the part of the other great class—possessors of temporary sums—customers for *flying annuities*: and even to this portion of the demand it would become less and less suitable, as the time when the correctly expressive of the measure, would express all the innovation of it.

---

annuity would cease, and the trouble of carrying in the Bill for payment, and receiving the redemption money for it, approached.

The supposed modification and improvement of the Exchequer Bill currency would be productive of but a part, and that a very small part, of the advantages held out by the institution of the proposed Annuity Note currency. But by the institution of the proposed Annuity Note currency the advantages thus derivable from the supposed improvement of the Exchequer Note currency would be obtained in their full extent: obtained in the way of collateral result, and without any distinct measures directed to that end.

At an early period of the Exchequer currency, Bills were issued for sums as low as £10 or even £5. How it should have happened that the practice of issuing such small notes should have ceased, and the *minimum* note raised to and insensibly fixed at its present pitch of £100, is not difficult to conceive. The form of the security would naturally be adapted to the convenience of the *lenders*, more especially as the lenders were individuals acting on their own account, and the borrowers statesmen acting without any personal interest for the public at large. The lenders on this security have been, on the one part, and that the principal part, the immensely opulent Company, the Bank of England, partly the small but prodigiously opulent circle of moneyed men, known to each other and meeting one another continually at or in the neighbourhood of the Exchange. £100 was a magnitude quite small enough for persons of this class. The faculty of employing in the same way a smaller sum, suppose £50, would have been of no use to [them][2]: since even £100 is not so much as [they] would be under the necessity of keeping by [them] or at [their] bankers, for the purpose of current expences, and payments on a small scale. Bills of less magnitude would thus be attended with no advantage, and they would be attended with the disadvantage of making a proportionable addition to the trouble of computation. Another relative disadvantage, and a much more considerable one, is, that the effect of small bills—£10 and £5 bills for example—would be to open the market to a greater number of customers, thence to encrease the competition for it, and to raise the price—in other words, to lower the rate of interest upon this paper, and thence diminish the profit to be made by purchasing it.

Whether government were aware of this at the time, is a point which at this time of day it might perhaps be difficult to ascertain. They might see it, but not be able to profit by it. If in times such as those of King William or Queen Anne, the connected circle of London moneyed men concurred in insisting upon large sums in preference to small sums, it would be difficult for government to resist: pressed by the exigencies of the moment, it might have been hazardous and perhaps impracticable to wait for the success of an experiment upon the more extended scale. As to the moneyed men, some would be aware of this, others not: witness the Bank, who, guided it should seem rather by habit than reflection, forbore, for such a length of time, to give that extension to the circle of customers for their paper, which, when given at last, relieved them from their embarrassments, and seems to have proved that the scarcity which had produced these embarrassments might as properly be stiled a scarcity of *small notes*, as a scarcity of *cash*.

[1][The MS reads "in".]

[2][The MS reads here and in the following instances "him" or "he" and "his".]

Annuity Notes and National Wealth

[march 1800]

The addition made to the amount of national wealth of all sorts in the country by a given amount of the proposed paper within a given space of time, over and above that which comes in lieu of the existing paper, will be equal to the addition made to the amount of national wealth by an equal amount of hard cash: setting aside that addition which is made by the intrinsic value of the cash, considered in respect of its being convertible into bullion at any time without exchange, and thence capable of being made into utensils, without exchange.

The addition made by any extra influx of hard cash in the course of a year to the mass of national wealth, can never (exclusive of the value of the cash) be either greater or less than the *value* (or real price) of the extra quantity of labour of which such extra quantity of cash has been productive in the course of the year: that is, of the goods and improvements produced within that time by that labour, exclusive of the value of any goods that may have been purchased and imported from foreign countries by a part of such hard cash, and exclusive of the produce of the labour of any labouring hands, which, without being sent out of the country, it may have attracted into the country from foreign parts.*

*It is common to speak of the quantity of wealth as being proportioned to the quickness, [i.e.] the briskness, of circulation. This, in as far as it is true, is only a mode, and that but an inaccurate one, of expressing the proposition laid down in the text. What can be brisker than the circulation of a guinea at a gaming table? yet what addition does quickness of circulation, i.e. multitude of transferrs in a given time, make to the quantity of wealth? The same guinea might experience an equal number of transfers within a given time even in the Corn Exchange, without producing any greater addition to the quantity of national wealth, than if the transferrs were made at the gaming table: it is only in as far as [it] gives birth to productive labour, it is only at the moment that the receipt, or prospect of it, puts in motion some labouring hand, that money (even hard cash) adds any thing beyond its own amount—adds any thing in the way of circulation—to the general mass of national wealth.

Taking the commercial world together, it is only by an addition made to the quantity of actual labour that any addition can be made to the quantity of wealth: no transfer of money of any kind from hand to hand contributes any thing to the encrease of the quantity of wealth in the commercial world any further than it is either made in return for actual labour, or in return for goods so circumstanced as that the transfer thus made of them shall be a means of calling into act some portion of labour which, but for such transfer, would not have been exerted, viz. by creating a demand for the preparation of an equal quantity of goods, to replace the goods thus purchased and taken out of the trader's stock.

The ways in which the encrease thus produced in the quantity of money in circulation will operate in augmentation of the mass of national wealth, are as follows: viz.

1. By converting into actual labour (containing its proportion of productive labour) such part of the yet remaining fund of possible labour, [or] capacity of yielding labour, as is possessed by such hands as it finds altogether without employment.

2. Do. such part as belongs to the hands it finds already in employment, but not yet in full employment.

3. Do. by transferring into more advantageous and productive channels, a portion of that labour which it finds employed in channels less advantageous and productive.

4. By encreasing the quantity (as well as fertility) of land in culture: viz. of that species of subject matter which is of such a nature, that, taking permanency and certainty into account, a given quantity of labour bestowed upon it is employed with more advantage to the nation, than if employed on any other.

5. By promoting the introduction of primarily expensive, but ultimately profitable machinery: whereby a greater effect is obtained from a given quantity of labour: [1]and the price to the ultimate consumer of the article is proportionably reduced, and the enjoyment of this species of wealth communicated to the greater number of consumers.[2]

6. By adding to the number and serviceableness of roads, canals. harbours, docks, and all other channels of conveyance: thereby diminishing the expence of conveyance, and reducing, in favour of the ultimate consumer, such part of the price of goods of all sorts, as is occasioned by, and dependent on, the expences of conveyance.

7. By drawing into the country from foreign countries, hands already able and willing to yield an immediate stock of labour, and thereby to make a proportionable addition to the actual stock of national wealth.

8. By furnishing to parents and guardians the means of rearing, and training up to labour, children not yet fit for labour, but already in existence: and thereby adding in that way fresh and fresh supplies every day to the national stock of productive labour.

9. By furnishing to labouring persons as yet unmarried, the means of engaging in marriage: and thereby laying up an indispensable, though necessarily distant, fund of future labour. N.B. The accession

[1] [2][Later brackets.]

thus made to the population of the country, remains for many years incapable of furnishing any addition to the stock of national wealth, meaning absolute wealth: and in the mean time, so far from operating an addition, it operates a diminution in respect of the degree of relative wealth: i.e. the quantity of wealth *per head*.*

10. By adding to the number of capitalists of all sorts, [i.e.] proprietors of stock employed in the several branches of productive industry in the production of the several vendible articles of national wealth, and thereby, by encreasing the competition amongst them, in their capacities of vendors of such articles, reducing the rate of profit upon stock (including the rate of interest on money borrowed to be employed as stock), reducing the real as well as money prices of such articles, in as far as the profit upon stock constitutes a component part in the composition of such prices, and thus encreasing the quantity of vendible articles of each given kind brought to market by the employment of a given sum of money.

The ways in which the encrease thus produced in the quantity of money of all kinds in circulation will operate towards keeping down the augmentation of the mass of national wealth, are as follows: viz.

1. By encreasing the quantity of money ready to be given by different persons in the way of rent for the use of land, and by a proportionable encrease in the competition as between those persons, raising the rent of land, and thence the prices (viz. the real as well as money prices) of vendible articles, in as far as the rent of land, i.e. of the land on which the raw materials are raised, enters into the composition of such prices: and thereby, and in so far, diminishing the quantity [of] vendible articles of each given kind brought to market by the employment of a given sum of money.

2. By encreasing the quantity of money ready to be offered by different persons to able hands in general (and thereby unavoidably to hands already in full employment, as well as to others as yet unemployed, or but partially employed), thereby encreasing the competition amongst such employers, raising the wages of labour, and thence the prices of vendible articles, in so far as the wages of labour enter into the composition of such prices: and thereby again, and in so far, operating in diminution of the quantity of vendible

*Supposing wealth preferred to domestic comfort and political security, labouring hands already of a self-maintaining age, labourers ready made, should be imported from abroad: marriage and procreation discouraged. By a similar strain of economy, Cato the Elder sold off his slaves when arrived [at][1] a certain age.

[1][The MS reads "to".]

articles of each given kind brought to market by the employment of a given sum of money.

Besides raising the real price or wages of labour, the addition thus made to the quantity of money in circulation will produce an augmentation of the money or nominal price or wages of labour, and in so far of the nominal or money prices of goods.

The only way in which any additional quantity of money (whether in the shape of hard cash or in that of paper, which consists always of a promise of hard cash) can make any addition to the general mass of wealth in the country (without importation of goods or hands from foreign countries) is by being *offered* to able hands, already existing within the country, in exchange for such labour as they are able, and may thus be rendered willing, to bestow, in that line of productive industry, whatever it be, to which the new portion of capital thus flowing in is applied.

If it were possible that such offer could confine itself to hands as yet altogether without employ, it would, in as far as it were thus accepted, be productive of a real addition to the mass of wealth, without any corresponding addition, or any addition at all, to the price of labour, and therefore without any addition at all to such part of the prices of goods as is composed of the price of the labour employed in the production of these goods.*

If it were possible that such offer should confine itself to hands whose time was already fully employed, and employed to as much advantage (in respect of the amount of their contribution to the general mass of national wealth) as they would be were the supposed fresh offer to be accepted by them, it could not, although it were accepted, be productive of any the smallest addition whatever to the general mass of national wealth: it could have no other effect than that of raising the price of labour, and thence the prices of

*The case of a decrease in the quantity of gold and silver in the commercial world, accompanied with an encrease in the quantity of wealth of other kinds, is a case easily conceivable, and involving no contradiction, but which in fact does not appear to have ever yet been realized. The diminution from all causes taken together, wear and tear, shipwreck, loss by mislaying &c, is more than compensated every year by the supply from the mines. Supposing such a decrease to take place, it is evident that, if any encrease in the quantity of wealth of all sorts besides gold and silver were thenceforward to take place, it would necessarily be in virtue of some other cause than an addition to the quantity of gold and silver in the commercial world or even of paper money deriving its value from no other source than the gold and silver of which it contains a promise.

goods, in respect of such part of the price of goods as is composed of the price of the labour employed in the production of those goods.

If, being confined to hands neither altogether out of employ, nor yet in full employ, but as yet in incomplete employ, the quantity of time and degree of exertion bestowed on their respective employments being below the customary rate, it were to confine itself in the invitation given by it within the quantity of time and degree of exertion sufficient to make up such customary rate, the influence of it upon the quantum of national wealth, and upon the price of labour and thence of goods, would be the same as if the class of hands it were confined to, were the hands as yet altogether unemployed.

But the simplicity of operation thus for illustration sake supposed, is plainly ideal and impossible in all its branches. The offers of fresh employment produced by the influx and investment of a fresh mass of money, can make no such discrimination as that supposed. A sum per day or per week is offered to all such as are able, and may thus be rendered willing, to bestow the species of labour which is in demand: offered to all alike—whether altogether unoccupied, imperfectly occupied, or already compleatly occupied.

If the offer thus made went no higher than the amount of the wages already paid to, and received by, the class of hands in compleat occupation, the effect of it would be confined to the making an addition to the stock of real national wealth, without making any addition to the money price of labour, and thence, as before, to the money price of goods. But where the additional quantity of money thus applied within the compass of any given spot, is in any degree considerable, no such exact limitation of price as is thus supposed for illustration sake, will ever in fact take place. If the money is all in the hand of a single individual, it will be better worth his while[1] to add something to the amount of the established rate of wages, rather than to wait the time that would elapse before an offer confined within such strict limits would be able to produce the number of hands for which he has a demand: if it were in the hands of more individuals than one, the competition that would thus take place, would, with still greater certainty and celerity, be productive of the

[1][The MS in fact reads: "it will not be better worth his while . . ." but the sentence originally continued "to save the expence". This clause was crossed out and replaced by "to add some thing" as above. Bentham obviously forgot to change the first part of the sentence accordingly.]

enhancement which, for illustration sake, has been supposed not to take place.

Upon the whole therefore, no considerable and in any degree sudden influx of money (metallic or paper) can ever take place from any cause, without being productive in [some][1] proportion of both these effects at the same time: viz. making a clear addition to the mass of real national wealth, and making a clear addition to the money price of labour, and thence contributing in a certain way and in a certain proportion to the making a correspondent addition to the money prices of goods: and thereby contributing in the same degree to the diminution of the value of the mass of money of all sorts pre-existing before the supposed new influx.

In as far as it raises, upon the whole, the money prices of [2]labour and[3] goods, it will operate as an indirect tax upon all persons [by][4] whom no share in the influx in question is received: and even in the case of those by whom a share in such influx is received, it will still operate in the same way, in as far as the profit by the share in such influx falls short of the loss by such depretiation.

Operating as a tax upon income, not upon this or that branch of consumption—being therefore inevitable, [and] not optional, it will, in that respect, be a disadvantageous species of tax. It will fall with peculiar weight upon all persons subsisting on incomes not capable of being raised: such as annuities, fixed stipends, salaries, pensions, and even rents, where fixed by leases as yet remote from expiration: also upon all creditors, having fixed sums to receive by titles accruing at periods antecedent to the depretiation.

In all other respects, considered as a tax, it will be highly eligible. By being inevitable, it will be so far equal: not falling upon the contributor in a greater proportion than upon the evasive: and it will be free from all the expences and vexations by which the weight of impositions meant to operate as taxes, are inevitably more or less surcharged.

The inconvenient part of these effects, being no other than what result in the same proportion from an encrease to an equal amount in the mass of national wealth from what source so ever derived, are the result of the proposed measure no otherwise than in as far as it is

[1][The MS reads "one".]

[2] [3][Later brackets.]

[4][The MS reads "to".]

productive of an encrease in the amount of national wealth; and thence in the degree of national security as against dangers from foreign adversaries, in as far as national security is strengthened by national wealth.

No one, by the contemplation of the inconveniences attached to the encrease of the amount of national wealth, has ever by any such consideration been led to wish to see that encrease put a stop to altogether: few, if any, have, by that or any other consideration, been led so [far][1] as to wish to see the rate of that encrease so much as retarded in any degree.

These effects, good, and bad, are no other than what will be the unavoidable consequences of the progress made in the discharge of the national debt, whatever be the rate of that progress, and from whatever source the means of making it be derived. All that the proposed measure does, is to accelerate the arrival of the state of things of which that discharge will be productive. What otherwise would not have happened but at a later period, it causes to happen at an earlier period: and thereby at such earlier period causes that to happen, which would not have happened otherwise.

Nobody hesitates about paying off the debt. Nobody thinks it can be paid off too soon. Whatever may be the rate at which the discharge proceeds, nobody but would wish to see done whatever were possible, towards accelerating it.

Though, if issued to a certain amount within a certain time, (i.e. to the full amount of the quantity of possible labour capable of being converted into actual labour by employment), any surplus issued beyond that amount would cease to add any thing to the stock of national wealth, and would therefore cease in that point of view to be attended with any clear amount of national advantage, the issue of it would not cease to be so much as retarded at that mark, since the advantage which individuals, as fast as hard cash came into their hands, would derive from changing it into the proposed paper, would remain undiminished. Every sixpence thus sent in for paper would, it is true, add to the depretiation, and thence lessen to the note-holder the value of the paper he thus obtained. But the loss by the depretiation produced by the taking out of a fresh mass of paper to the amount of £100, would not be a hundredth, a thousandth, or a ten thousandth part so great as the profit by the interest thus gained

[1][The MS reads "much".]

upon that same £100: and, what is more, if instead of taking out paper with it, he kept it in the shape of cash, the depretiation would attach upon it all the same.

The effect results from the paper not as paper, but as money: it would be just the same, were it so much cash. Every penny saved and laid by, diminishes in fact the value of every other penny, as well as its own to boot. But although this effect of frugality were to be universally known and borne in mind, the inducement to lay up money would not be in the smallest degree diminished.

But though the issue would not be stopped by the depretiation, and the depretiation would go on for some time in proportion to the issue, yet the depretiation would, before it had run any considerable length, be arrested by other causes, and that without prejudice to the rapidity of the issue. In proportion as the issue is rapid, the period at which the price of stock annuities will be raised to par by the produce of it will be accelerated, and no sooner does that period arrive than, let the rapidity of the issue be what it will, the depretiation in question will be arrested. For as soon as stock annuities are become as dear as note annuities, note annuities will be hoarded, that is, kept in the same hand for a permanency as a source of permanent income, as stock annuities are at present: and so long as an annuity note is thus kept in the same hand, every annuity so kept and hoarded is kept back from entering into circulation, prevented from acting in the character of money, and kept back from producing any of the effects of which an augmentation to the national stock of money is productive. A Note is equally capable, it is true, of acting in either capacity: but [it][1] can not act in both at the same time: so long as it is kept in one and the same hand as a source of income, it does not act as money: and the moment it is employed by a man as money it ceases to serve him in the capacity of a source of income.

In as far as it raises the real price or wages of labour faster than it adds to the population (in other words, adds to the absolute quantity of wealth in the instance of the labouring classes faster than it takes away from the relative quantity), it adds to the relative wealth, and thence, as far as comfort and happiness depend upon wealth, to the comfort and happiness of the labouring classes—that is, of the bulk and great majority of the whole community.

[1][The MS reads "in".]

[SUMMER 1800]

The effects of the proposed currency with respect to the quantum of the mass of [real] national wealth, will be the same as if it were so much hard cash: it will operate in addition to the mass of national wealth, so far as so much hard cash would operate in addition to the mass of national wealth—so far paper as it is, would this same paper: the effects of it in this way will be the [same] as if, for example, a peace were to be made with Spain, and the price of that peace were so much gold and silver to be sent from Mexico and Peru, and lodged in the hands of government here, upon trust to convert [it] into guineas and shillings, and apply those guineas and those shillings in the same way as here proposed, in the discharge of the national debt.

Being exactly upon a par with so much hard cash, the introduction [of] it will be productive, consequently, of all the bad effects as well as all the good effects that would result from the introduction of so much hard cash: producing, to the same amount as so much hard cash would produce, an addition to the mass of national wealth, it will be productive of all the bad effects as well as all the good effects that would result from an addition to that amount made in any way to the mass of national wealth.

As a state of endless accumulation in regard to wealth is the necessary result of that security which is the result of the perfection to which all arts, and in particular the art of government, have arrived in this part of the world, and above all in this country, the effect produced by an accession of money and of wealth in this way, will, when considered in kind, and setting aside the consideration of time, be no other than what would equally have taken place without it: but inasmuch as it will accelerate the arrival of each degree of future opulence, and cause it to manifest itself in certain early periods of time, in certain years in which it would not otherwise have manifested itself, hence the question whether to adopt the proposed measure or not, is even in this point of view by no means a matter of indifference.

Introduced in time of peace, it will accelerate the accumulation of [the] blessings of peace, and the encrease of that *plethora* of the body politic which is an inconvenience inseparable from those blessings: in time of war, it will introduce into the body politic such a degree of repletion, as hitherto has never yet manifested itself in any other season than that of peace.

It will add to the mass of national wealth in two ways: in respect of the quantity of money it will introduce on the sudden an addition to the mass of wealth itself, independently of that more gradual addition which would be made by the continuation of industry and frugality: and it will, moreover, make another addition, and that an unceasing one, by the new encouragement which it will hold forth to frugality and thence to industry, and [?] by the additional extent which it will thus give to the exercise of those virtues. The addition made in the first mentioned direct way, has its limits, and those determinate and visible: the addition made by the encouragement to the virtues productive of wealth, has no such limits.

It begins now to be pretty well understood, that if industry and frugality are virtues, the virtue of each man operates as a tax upon every other man: and that whichever income does not receive an encrease, is doomed to a perpetual and inevitable reduction: that each penny produced and laid up, takes from the value of every other penny: that a man whose income is nominally fixed, finds it really reduced by a rise in the money price of goods; and that the man whose property consists in money, finds the value of it in time of peace exposed to a certain, however slow, reduction, not only by the rise in the money price of goods, but also by a reduction in the rate of interest, [i.e.] in the quantum of income obtainable for the use of that money, lent out in the shape of principal money or capital.

War time is the harvest of the moneyed man: it is then that, by the additional quantity of income he may obtain in return for his money or the use of it, he more than makes himself amends for the addition made to the price of the goods he buys with it.

Money, a mass of money added to the existing stock, if it found in each instance a quantity of capacity with regard to dormant labour in readiness to receive it and, as it were, absorb its power of enhancing prices, would add nothing to the nominal prices of things, nor in that respect detract from its own value: this is a case which can easily be conceived: but where the mass of it is considerable, it can never be compleatly realized. Offers of money for labour can not, if made to any considerable amount, be other than general: extending to those whose capacity of labour is already fully brought into action, as well as to those of whose capacity in regard [to] labour either a part only is as yet brought into action, or none at all.

Money, therefore, in as far as the offer and acceptance of it is confined to that portion of the capacity with regard to labour which as yet has not been brought into action, adds to the real quantity of wealth (according to the application made of that labour), and does not add to the nominal prices of goods: but in as far as the offer and acceptance of it extends itself to that portion of the capacity with regard to labour which has been brought into action, it can not make any addition to the quantity of wealth (independently of any casual advantage in the application of the labour), nor can it do otherwise than add to the nominal prices of goods.

The proposed paper, for a considerable length of time, would add nothing to the quantity of currency in circulation. Before it could make any such addition, it would have, in the first place, the existing Bank and banker's paper to drive out and replace: in the next place, it would have the demand on the part of customers for small annuities to satisfy. This done, if it extended itself in a certain [measure], it would produce the twofold effect abovementioned—viz. the bringing into action the remaining unemployed capacity with regard to labour (and thence encreasing the quantity of real wealth, the produce of that labour), and the raising the nominal or money prices of goods (and thence sinking the value of money of every kind, without any addition made to the mass of real wealth) at the same time. If it proceeded a certain still farther length, the additional quantity would thenceforward operate purely in augmentation of the prices of goods, without adding any thing to the quantity of real wealth, the whole of the once remaining stock of capacity with regard to labour being by the supposition expended by being brought into act. Taken by itself, the latter effect is rather undesirable than otherwise: but, then, on the other hand, it is what can not take place, but the former effect, which is generally regarded as a desirable one, must have taken place before it.

If among the effects of the measure were [in fact] that of producing such an addition to the currency as should exceed the amount necessary to call into action the national whole of the unemployed capacity with regard to labour, this effect, so far as it obtained, would be to set to the side of disadvantage in any account taken of the effects of the measure in respect of advantage and disadvantage. When money is to this degree more plenty, commodities are so much the more dear. If the same persons were enriched by the influx of money, and that in the same proportion, and at the same time, as are drained by the rise of price (viz. nominal or money price), there would be neither good nor harm in the change: but this is what never happens. The drain is shared alike by all classes: the influx is confined to certain classes. The possessors of unencreasable incomes are among the most obvious victims of the change. The sensation of gain is produced on one part, that of loss on the other: but, sum for sum, the enjoyment from gain is never an equivalent for the suffering from loss. If it were, the reason for the creation and preservation of property would cease.

Considerations like these, have never yet been uniformly brought forward in argument: though, on a thousand occasions, they are more or less distinctly felt by every body. At the worst, however, this effect, so far as it obtains, is no worse than that of a tax: nor is it so bad by a good deal, sum for sum, as that of a tax, since the obnoxious hand of the tax-gatherer is not discernible.

The extra-addition in question is an addition to the quantity of money in the country, but it is no addition to the quantity of wealth: it is an addition to the quantity of nominal wealth, but not to the quantity of real wealth. All wealth is the fruit of labour: take the world together, it is only in proportion as the quantity of [labour][1] is either encreased, or employed with more advantage and effect, that the quantity of wealth can receive any encrease. Suppose the whole quantity of capacity with regard to labour during a given period to be employed and employed to the best advantage, no further accession to wealth can within that period by any possibility accrue.

Take a particular country, Great Britain for example, to which the accession of currency is supposed to be confined, the case is no otherwise varied, than in respect of the possibility of encreasing the quantity of real wealth by the exportation of a quantity of hard cash which, if unexported, would have made an addition to the quantity of nominal wealth, without making any to the real. Call the quantity of hard cash in Great Britain, £40,000,000: the total quantity of money, hard cash and paper money taken together, £60,000,000: the quantity of capacity with regard to labour unemployed at the commencement of the year, but capable of being called forth in the course of the year, by an adequate accession of money, £5,000,000:—and the addition made to the quantity of money in the shape of the proposed currency, £10,000,000. Here, supposing no part of the currency exported, the quantity of nominal wealth in the shape of money would amount to £70,000,000: but as of this £70,000,000, £5,000,000 would have no other effect than that of

[1][The MS reads "wealth".]

sinking the value of the rest, the £70,000,000[1] nominal wealth, would amount to no more than £65,000,000[2] of real wealth: but of this £70,000,000, suppose the extra quantity of £5,000,000 of the hard cash to be exported (for it is only that part of the currency that foreigners would take of us), prices of commodities would not be raised by the influx of currency, and the whole £70,000,000 of money would be so much real wealth.

In political economy as in chemistry, results are scarce ever obtained pure: while part of the new influx is employing in producing the beneficial result of an encrease of real wealth through the medium of profitable labour, other part will be employing itself in the raising of prices of labour here and there, and thence of this and that class of goods: and, indeed, it is scarce possible that a new mass of dormant labour should be called forth into act without making some addition to the recompence given to the mass already in employment.

The addition that will be made by the proposed paper to the quantum of national wealth, in virtue of the addition that will be made by it to the quantum of the currency, is an additional benefit over and above the profit which, as we have seen, will be afforded to government. That an addition of this sort will be produced by it, and that this addition will be considerable, seems evident enough. But (to avoid exaggeration) the addition made to the quantum of national wealth will not be equal to the addition made to the quantum of the currency: nor will the quantum of the addition made to the currency rise so high by a great deal as the quantum of the issue.

To come at the portion constituting an addition to the quantum of the currency or money in circulation, we must deduct in the first place the amount of the existing mass of Bank and banker's paper existing at the commencement of the issue, in the next place the amount of the quantity of the annuity paper itself which, at the period in question, will be hoarded and kept out of the circulation, for the purpose of affording income, as stock annuities do at present. As the issue of this paper descends to lower and lower sums, Bank and banker's paper, as we have seen, will fly before it: and to fill up the gap made by the disappearance of the existing Bank and banker's paper, a mass of the proposed Annuity Note paper will be necessary,

[1] [The MS looks almost like "90,000,000".]
[2] [The MS looks almost like "£68,000,000".]

before any clear addition to the quantity of currency in circulation can begin to take place.

The effect of the proposed currency (I mean of that portion which is over and above the amount of Bank and banker's paper expelled by it), is precisely the same as that of so much hard cash would be: if paid by Spain, for example, as the price of peace, and applied to the same uses.

In this respect, it possesses [1]not any[2] advantage over the currency supposed to be expelled. Let it be twenty millions, for example—whether the 20 millions be in the shape of hard cash, of the proposed currency, or of Bank and banker's paper, whether the money be in any one or in any other of the three shapes, is a matter that, so long as the money *lasts* and continues current, makes no sort of difference. But the value of hard cash can never fail—the value of the proposed currency is equally exempt from failure—[while] the value of Bank and banker's paper is essentially exposed to failure, and it is but too often that we, who are now alive, have witnessed it.

In all three cases, its effect upon the mass of national wealth, is obviously to encrease it. I mean here not merely nominal wealth, but real wealth. In all those cases does the addition it makes, run to the exact amount which the sum would seem to import: it succeeds, in as far as the fresh influx of money gives birth to a fresh influx of labour, and thence of goods, the fruit of labour: it fails, in as far as, without giving birth to any fresh stock of labour, it operates to the enhancement of the price of labour and of goods.

The amount of the addition made to the quantity of money in circulation, will be the amount of the issue intervening between two periods: the period of the expulsion of the last parcel of Bank and banker's paper, and the period when the paying off stock annuities begins to take place of the buying it in. The stock holders thus paid off without their applying for it, being by the supposition desirous of retaining their property in the shape of annuities, become purchasers to the same amount of Annuity Notes, which being kept in the hands of the purchaser to yield the annuity required, remain in his hands so long as he keeps the annuity, without entering into circulation, and consequently without constituting any addition to the stock of *actual* currency, current at the time.

What space of time may intervene between these two periods, and what quantity of this currency may come into the circulation in this

[1] [2][These words are a later addition and replace "no" of the original text.]

TABLE I.

TABLE OF A PROPOSED ANNUITY NOTE CURRENCY;

EXHIBITING divers particulars relative to a proposed series of Notes, carrying the same rate of interest, and having for their values sums rising one above another in a series of terms, 19 in number with 2 for their *common measure*; of which magnitudes more or fewer may be employed as may be found convenient. Also another corresponding series of *principal sums*, which (they being raised in their amounts, while the corresponding amounts of *interest* continue unchanged) give an inferior or *reduced* rate of interest, with reference to the series first mentioned. The sums proposed are in columns V. VI. VII. VIII. IX. X. XIII.;—those used for illustration, in columns I. II. III. IV. XI. and XII.

I.	II.	III.	IV.	V.	VI.	VII.	VIII.	IX.	X.	XI.	XII.	XIII.
No. in the series	Ratio to the Unit or Standard Note.	Daily Interests, answering to a Farthing per Day on the Standard Note.	Principal Sums corresponding to those Daily Interests, at £3 per Cent precisely.	Principal Sums as proposed at £3 per Cent nearly for the sake of even Money.	Amounts of Interest, proposed to be allowed on the proposed Principal Sums for					Correct Amounts of yearly Interest on the proposed Principals.	Differences between the proposed and correct Amounts.	Principal Sums corresponding to the same daily Interests at the reduced rate of 2¾ per Cent nearly.
					One day.	One week nearly; viz.—Eight days.	One month nearly; viz.—32 days.	One half-year nearly; viz.—182 days.	One year nearly; viz.—364 days.			
		s. d. f.	£ s. d. f.	£ s. d.	s. d. f.	£ s. d. f.	£ s. d. f.	£ s. d. f.	£ s. d. f.	£ s. d. f.	£ s. d. f.	£ s. d. f.
1	512	10 8 0	6,488 17 9 1	6,553 12 0	10 8 0	4 5 4 0	17 1 4 0	97 1 4 0	194 2 8 0	196 5 4 0	2 2 8 0	8,192 0 0 0
2	256	5 4 0	3,244 8 10 2	3,276 16 0	5 4 0	2 2 8 0	8 10 8 0	48 10 8 0	97 1 4 0	98 2 8 0	1 1 4 0	4,096 0 0 0
3	128	2 8 0	1,622 4 5 1	1,638 8 0	2 8 0	1 1 4 0	4 5 4 0	24 5 4 0	48 10 8 0	49 1 4 0	0 10 8 0	2,048 0 0 0
4	64	1 4 0	811 2 2 2	819 4 0	1 4 0	0 10 8 0	2 2 8 0	12 2 8 0	24 5 4 0	24 10 8 0	0 5 4 0	1,024 0 0 0
5	32	0 8 0	405 11 1 1	409 12 0	0 8 0	0 5 4 0	1 1 4 0	6 1 4 0	12 2 8 0	12 5 4 0	0 2 8 0	512 0 0 0
6	16	0 4 0	202 15 6 2	204 16 0	0 4 0	0 2 8 0	0 10 8 0	3 0 8 0	6 1 4 0	6 2 8 0	0 1 4 0	256 0 0 0
7	8	0 2 0	101 7 9 1	102 8 0	0 2 0	0 1 4 0	0 5 4 0	1 10 4 0	3 0 8 0	3 1 4 0	0 0 8 0	128 0 0 0
8	4	0 1 0	50 13 10 2	51 4 0	0 1 0	0 0 8 0	0 2 8 0	0 15 2 0	1 10 4 0	1 10 8 0	0 0 4 0	64 0 0 0
9	2	0 0 2	25 6 11 1	25 12 0	0 0 2	0 0 4 0	0 1 4 0	0 7 7 0	0 15 2 0	0 15 4 0	0 0 2 0	32 0 0 0
10	1	0 0 1	12 13 5 2	12 16 0	0 0 1	0 0 2 0	0 0 8 0	0 3 9 2	0 7 7 0	0 7 8 0	0 0 1 0	16 0 0 0
11	$\frac{1}{2}$	0 0 0$\frac{1}{2}$	6 6 8 3	6 8 0	0 0 0$\frac{1}{2}$	0 0 1 0	0 0 4 0	0 1 10 3	0 3 9 2	0 3 10 0	0 0 0 2	8 0 0 0
12	$\frac{1}{4}$	0 0 0$\frac{1}{4}$	3 3 4 1	3 4 0	0 0 0$\frac{1}{4}$	0 0 0 2	0 0 2 0	0 0 11 1$\frac{256}{512}=\frac{1}{2}$	0 1 10 3	0 1 11 0	0 0 0 1	4 0 0 0
13	$\frac{1}{8}$	0 0 0$\frac{1}{8}$	1 11 8 0	1 12 0	0 0 0$\frac{1}{8}$	0 0 0 1	0 0 1 0	0 0 5 2$\frac{384}{512}=\frac{3}{4}$	0 0 11 1$\frac{256}{512}=\frac{1}{2}$	0 0 11 2	— — — —	2 0 0 0
14	$\frac{1}{16}$	0 0 0$\frac{1}{16}$	0 15 10 0	0 16 0	0 0 0$\frac{1}{16}$	— — — —	0 0 0 2	0 0 2 3$\frac{192}{512}=\frac{3}{8}$	0 0 5 2$\frac{384}{512}=\frac{3}{4}$	0 0 5 3	— — — —	1 0 0 0
15	$\frac{1}{32}$	0 0 0$\frac{1}{32}$	0 7 11 0	0 8 0	0 0 0$\frac{1}{32}$	— — — —	0 0 0 1	0 0 1 1$\frac{352}{512}=\frac{11}{16}$	0 0 2 3$\frac{192}{512}=\frac{3}{8}$	— — — —	— — — —	0 10 0 0
16	$\frac{1}{64}$	0 0 0$\frac{1}{64}$	0 3 11 2	0 4 0	0 0 0$\frac{1}{64}$	— — — —	— — — —	0 0 0 2$\frac{432}{512}=\frac{27}{32}$	0 0 1 1$\frac{352}{512}=\frac{11}{16}$	— — — —	— — — —	0 5 0 0
17	$\frac{1}{128}$	0 0 0$\frac{1}{128}$	0 1 11 3	0 2 0	0 0 0$\frac{1}{128}$	— — — —	— — — —	0 0 0 1$\frac{216}{512}=\frac{27}{64}$	0 0 0 2$\frac{432}{512}=\frac{27}{32}$	— — — —	— — — —	0 2 6 0
18	$\frac{1}{256}$	0 0 0$\frac{1}{256}$	0 0 11 3	0 1 0	0 0 0$\frac{1}{256}$	— — — —	— — — —	0 0 0 0$\frac{364}{512}=\frac{91}{128}$	0 0 0 1$\frac{216}{512}=\frac{27}{64}$	— — — —	— — — —	0 1 3 0
19	$\frac{1}{512}$	0 0 0$\frac{1}{512}$	0 0 5 3	0 0 6	0 0 0$\frac{1}{512}$	— — — —	— — — —	0 0 0 0$\frac{182}{512}=\frac{91}{256}$	0 0 0 0$\frac{364}{512}=\frac{91}{128}$	— — — —	— — — —	0 0 7 2

[NOTES TO TABLE II]

(1) The figures of reference refer to explanatory matter, the greater part of which has been thought not worth inserting in this *compressed view.*

(3) The wording of the engagement is grounded on that of an *Exchequer Bill.* The *size* may be exactly that of a *Bank Note.*

(4) The *yearly* form, having been the first framed, is here inserted, to show its comparative simplicity; but (for the reasons mentioned in the *Observations on the Plan*) it is not proposed to be employed. Placed as it is, it saves the two other compartments from being covered by the leaves of the book.

(5, 7, 8, 9, 10) These blanks cannot be filled up till the last hand is put to the official arrangement of the business. The filling up will depend on the number of Notes issued, the number of hands employed in the General Office, the number of office hours for each hand, and on the mechanism employed for giving dispatch to the operations.

(14, 22) The object most difficult of imitation, to an *ordinary* artist, is a portrait engraven by a *first rate* hand. Imitation being a capital offence, the form must be such as no artist could possibly adopt, but with criminal views. The Epigraph should be so placed as that, in case of imitation, the intention shall betray itself at the earliest stage possible. A single *plate,* if multiplied according to the method invented by Professor Wilson of Glasgow, as described in his paper reprinted in Nicholson's Philosophical Journal for May 1798, will serve for any number of impressions.

(24) The type (say) as *tall again* as the tallest ever employed, the dimensions to be fixed, and types more than half as tall again prohibited.

The great quantity of letter-press places the information where it is most useful; and, together with the variety of type employed, renders the task of the forger so much the heavier.

For trust purposes (such as settlements, &c.) where the magnitude of the sum renders it worth while, the form of the Note might be varied, so as to be divisible into three, four, or more parts. The expence of the plates might be defrayed by a small extra fee on each Note. An Exechequer Bill, though for £1000, affords no such security. A Bank Note, whether for £1 or £1000, is divisible into two parts; but, yielding no interest, is not the subject of a settlement. Settlements of stock require sometimes *journeys*, always expensive *formalities*.

(28) Insert here, "*To make up the value of the Note for any odd day* (i. e. *any day which is not in the Table*) *add a farthing for every day between such odd day, and the day next before it in the Table.*"

(29) Insert here, "*When the blanks in this Register are all filled up, this Note, if not paid off, will be exchanged for a fresh one* gratis."

The obliteration of the Register of the payments made, is the only profitable fraud of which these entries are susceptible; and that might easily be rendered impracticable. The number of years here inserted, is that, at the end of which the value of the Note will have doubled itself, at simple interest.

Another mode of indication might be furnished by the principle of the French *Coupons*. An edging composed of compartments similar to those exhibited in the Table. In the interior column, the compartments filled with the figures expressive of the several half-years; in the exterior, the compartments left blank; and, on making the payment in respect of each half-year, one to be stamped off, a few words being inserted, as in the Table, for the purpose of explaining the import of the defalcation.

space of time (which will be so much clear addition, since the hard cash will remain likewise, unless sent out of the country, which it will not be but for a profit), are questions which it is not possible to resolve. They depend (the two amounts) on the state of the country in regard to peace and war, and in case of war, upon the continuance of the war. The more war there is, within the space of time in question, the greater the quantity of stock annuities that will be brought to market, and the longer therefore the time which it will take for an influx of money to a given amount, to raise the price of them to par.

Thus much is apparent at any rate—viz. that if it is good for peace, it is still better for war. It operates in supply of the drain of war. Will the amount of it fall short of that drain? will it equal it? will it exceed it? Another string of questions to which the answer is impossible. It depends on events all of them equally inscrutable—the number of years which the war is destined to continue—the amount of the money raised for it in each year—the amount of the Annuity Note paper, the demand for which presents itself in each year. The amount of the good remains in darkness: but that it is good upon the whole, is clear enough—and that is enough for practice.

The unexampled ductility, if so it may be termed, of this species of property—of this money—is worth observing. At a moment's warning, it becomes income or capital—either the equivalent of stock, or the equivalent of the money which stock is bought with—and in both cases without loss. Not so either the money or the stock.

It is not enough [however] that the paper in question should be capable of being applied to both purposes: what is necessary besides is—that it should be applicable at all times to that one of the two services that has the greatest need of it: but even this requisite will be seen to be fulfilled by it.

The time in which it serves to make an addition to the currency, is the time at which currency [is] scarce: I mean *war time*—a time in which money being to be raised in large quantities for the service of government, must for a time be diverted from other channels, the channels it would otherwise have run in, and notwithstanding the quickness of government expenditure, locked up every now and then, in portions more or less considerable, and for portions of time more or less considerable, in some or other of the many and capacious offices of government.

The time at which it withdraws itself from the currency, by being hoarded for the purpose of yielding income, is on the other hand the very time and no other at which, were it not for such a drain, the quantity of currency might become too abundant, and by such superabundance productive of the inconveniences above spoken of. I mean the time of established *peace*—a time in which money has a tendency to accumulate faster than a correspondent portion of dormant labour can be found to be put in action by it, and in which the difficulty of making it yield a higher rate of interest elsewhere, renders the comparatively low rate of interest allowed by government on this paper a desirable resource.

From this convertibility it follows, that is can not on any supposition be ever existing in excess. The longer the drain of war continues, the greater the quantity which there will be of it, because the longer the drain continues, the more stock will have been created. which must have been all bought up, or paid off, and a proportionable quantity of Annuity Note paper issued, before the vibration of the cash between the two markets, by means of which the stock annuities are annihilated and the note annuities introduced in place of them, can have arrived at its termination.

I do not say that, with the benefit of this paper, it is the same thing to the country whether the war continues a shorter or a longer time. I do not give this paper as a specific against the evils of war, or even against that evil which consists in the augmentation of the mass of public burthens. I do not say that it is the same thing to the country whether a less or greater mass of annuities be created, whether a less or greater mass of annual burthen is to be borne by it. I admitt that the imposition of such burthens is an evil to the full extent of it—all I contend for is, that supposing the war to continue—supposing the money to be raised—supposing a given quantity of annual burthen to be imposed, the addition which such an addition will make to the quantity of this paper, is not, separately taken, an augmentation of the evil, but on the contrary, a most powerful palliative: and that under a given quantity of that burthen, the greater the quantity of this paper, the better on every account: since whatever inconvenience the plenty of it may be supposed for a moment to be productive of, carries along with it its own corrective: and the power of the corrective rises with the magnitude of the supposed cause of inconvenience. For suppose for a moment the quantity of this paper to be so great, as that in the shape of currency it overloads the market, outstrips the supply of employment seeking labour, and raises the prices of commodities. From this same *plethora* it follows that money being a drug, and unable to find opportunities of being placed out at interest in other markets, pours on to the government market, buys up existing stock, lies in wait for impending loans:—the greater the avidity for such loans, the less disadvantageous the terms at which government obtains them, and the less the mass of national burthen, which, on that account, it finds it necessary to impose.

That it is not in the power of the Annuity Note paper to produce any such inconvenient excess of currency as is above spoken of, may be thus proved: the quantity of Annuity Note paper issued in a given space of time, does not depend upon the quantum of the expence of the war [or] upon the quantity of stock annuities created, even within that time: it depends upon the quantity of hard cash in the country (which is what a state of war has certainly no tendency to encrease), and upon the quickness with which that cash finds its way into such hands as shall have found an adequate motive to carry it to the Annuity Note market, to make interest of it.

Nor (for the same reason) does any length of war—any continuance of the expence occasioned by the war [and] of the process of creating annuities for the defraying of that expence—contribute any thing to *accelerate* the rate at which the issue of Annuity Note paper shall go on. The longer the time during which the issue keeps going on at that rate, whatever it be, the greater, it is true, the quantity of this paper that, at the close of the war, will have been issued, and requires to be redeemed. But the quantity of the paper *existing at a time* will not encrease in proportion to or by reason of [the] encrease in the total amount of the issue: because what encreases the quantity issued is the length of the war, and the longer the continuance of the war, the greater on the one hand is the drain which the paper in question has to fill up; and on the other hand, the quantity of that (viz. the Annuity Note paper) which, supposing it to find itself in excess in the shape of currency, affords to the possessor at once the power and the inducement to rectify that excess, by applying it to the purpose of a stationary and uncirculating source of future income. For, once more—the greater the quantity of this paper in the country, the greater the quantity of *money* or currency (paper and cash together) in the country: and the greater the quantity of money in the country, the less the rate of interest to be made of it in the country at large; and the less the rate of interest capable of being made of it in the country at large, the better it is worth a man's while to accept from government such rate of interest as the paper itself affords.

The quicker the rate at which the issue goes on, the better, because the quicker this rate, the sooner it brings up stock annuities to par, and the sooner it brings them up to par, the sooner it brings them in a condition to be paid off and converted into note annuities: and the sooner it brings the stock annuities in a condition to be thus converted into note annuities, the sooner it brings the national debt into the condition in which the rate of interest payable on its nominal capital, that is to say, the annual amount of the burthen of it, may and will be reduced.

When this forced paying off comes to take place, then indeed will come the *plethora* above spoken of, and this *plethora* will be the greater, the greater the quantity of Annuity Note paper that had been issued. But this inconvenience, such as it is, has for its origin, not the Annuity Note paper as such, not the shape which the annuities which it was necessary to grant had been made to assume, but the magnitude of the mass of annuity which, in some shape or other, it had been found necessary to create.

The reduction of the rate of interest is what I, for my own part, admitt to be an *evil*, though it has never been mentioned as such that I know of: and the amount of this evil is the greater, the greater the mass of annuity thus subject to be reduced, that is, the greater the amount of the Annuity Note paper that has been issued: but still it is not the Annuity Note paper as such that has added any thing to the evil: on the contrary, as we have seen, it will have contributed, and contributed largely, to the reduction of the evil.

The evil of a *plethora*, such as it is, is an evil altogether inseparable from the universally wished for reduction of the national debt. It is an evil attendant on prosperity: and for which nothing but adversity can be a cure.

What is more—it is an evil which neither has the proposed Annuity paper (the palliative to the evil of the national debt), nor so much as the national debt itself, for its cause. The national debt, so far from being a cause, is an obstacle to its progress, and a reduction from its amount. It is the necessary effect of accumulated wealth, the result of industry and frugality combined. The expence of war, by lessening that accumulation, breaks a vein as it were, and lessens the *plethora*: the accumulation is an effect that would have taken place in still greater degree had there been no war, no extra expenditure, no debt to discharge: but in as much as the discharge of debt will bring it under observation, the discharge of debt will have the appearance of producing it.

What is more—it not only operates, as far as it goes, in supply of the waste of war, but promises to supply that waste to any extent. Being always preferable to hard cash, yet never expelling any hard cash, the whole quantity of hard cash keeps perpetually pouring into the Annuity Note market so long as that market continues open, which it will do so long as there is any stock to purchase. The more stock annuities are created, the more there is for the produce of the sale of Annuity Note paper to buy in or pay off, and thence the more stock annuities are created, the longer the Note Annuity market must be kept open, and the greater the quantity of Annuity Note paper that must be issued in the first instance, and will come afterwards to be paid off. But this paper, considered as an addition to the currency, is not a burthen but a relief. Considered as a security for annuities to be paid by government, it is indeed a burthen, and heavy in proportion to the extent of it. But the supply is the effect and produce of this paper: while the burthen is no other than what would equally have existed (and indeed in considerably larger proportion), had the paper never come into existence.

[SEPTEMBER 1800]

[1]The addition made by the proposed measure to the quantity of capital, and thence to the quantity of wealth in both shapes, income as well as capital, may be divided into two branches:

1. the addition made to the amount of currency capable of being employed at every transfer in the shape of capital according to the hand it passes into, and

2. the addition made to the amount of that mass of currency which goes immediately into the hands of capitalists as such, and is known to be destined [and] seen at the very first stage to be employed in the shape of capital. The first of these effects it produces in virtue of the circulating paper which it puts into the hands of customers of all sorts—hoarders and expenders—in return for the guineas they give for it to government: the other it produces in virtue of the application made of those guineas, in respect of the addition made by them to the amount of extra-prices paid to stock annuitants on their part-

[1][This page and most of the pages numbered in the MS 185-205 show question marks or the word "Quere".]

ing with their incomes in stock annuities for the purpose of receiving capital in exchange: meaning by *extra*-prices the difference between the prices they receive in consequence of the influx thus produced, and the prices they *would* have received without the benefit of such influx.

So much money as is employed in the redemption of the national debt constitutes an addition to the mass of national capital: being paid in capital sums to persons by whom it can not but be employed in the shape of capital, as a perennial source of income, to replace the income parted with in the shape of annuities so redeemed.

By a million taken from the existing Sinking Funds, and employed in buying in stock annuities, as great an addition would be made to the mass of national capital, as by a million obtained by the sale of Annuity Notes: but the difference is, that in the first case the addition made to the mass of capital, [i.e.] of money employed and laid out in permanent improvements, would be made at the expence of the mass of money, the whole of which would otherwise have been employed in the defraying of the current expenditure of the year, and in the purchase of articles mostly destined and applied to the purpose of quick consumption within the year, it being raised by taxes levied upon articles purchased in the course of, and for the purpose of, current expenditure within the year: whereas in other cases, the million's worth of guineas is made over to those who will employ them as capital, while the place of them is supplied by paper to the same amount, put into the hand of those who will employ it, as they would have done the guineas, in the way of current expenditure.

Among the effects of the Sinking Fund establishments, a not much talked of, nor perhaps much heeded, but incontestable result is, the addition of so much capital to the amount of productive capital in the country by the produce of taxes, i.e. by defalcations from the amount of current expenditure.*

*It is gold always, and not Annuity Note paper, that on the redemption of the national debt, is paid in the shape of capital to annuitants in exchange for their annuities. But if of the Annuity Note paper which is left in the hands of the purchasers in exchange for that gold, which they took in expectation of its answering all the purposes of that gold, there should be any part that should fail of answering that purpose, or should be a means of driving out of the circulation any other paper to the same amount, the amount of such part so failing would come to be deducted from the amount of the addition to the mass of capital above spoken of. But, million for million, the addition made to the mass of national wealth, by the amount of paper currency of any kind, taken at the price at which it is received, and for such length of time as it continues to be received, is just the same as that of so much gold.

The effects of the two distinguishable masses thus constitutive of an addition to the mass of national wealth are very different, and in respect of the quantum of the addition they make, sum for sum, are very difficult to be compared.

The effects of the addition made by £1000 put into the hands of capitalists on the score of redemption-money, is to make a clear addition to that amount by the first expenditure of it, after which it is returned into the general mass of money or circulating capital, and the effects of it are no longer separately returnable. The next expenditure of it must therefore be taken to be divided between current expenditure and expenditure in the way of improvement and accumulation, in the proportion in which the general mass of income is distributed between those two destinations.

The effect of an addition to the same amount made to the mass of circulating capital is very different. In one supposable case, it makes no addition at all to the mass of national wealth. In another supposable case, it makes an addition to a much greater amount than that made by the £1000 redemption-money.

Case 1. It comes in in circumstances that render it incapable of making any addition to the wealth of the country in any other shape. either in labour or goods: which will be the case, if the whole stock of capacity of labour in the population of the country is actually employed, and employed to the best possible advantage, at the same time that by the effect of wars, prohibitions, or any other conceivable causes, neither any supply of labouring hands nor any supply of goods is to be had from any other country. In this case, the whole effect of it is expended in raising prices—the prices of labour and goods.

Case 2. [It][1] finds in the country a quantity of capacity for labour to the whole amount unemployed, and is accordingly employed in producing so much labour, i.e. in producing goods and improvements as the result of so much labour, by bringing that quantity of capacity for labour into act. In this case, it makes a perpetual, and perpetually encreasing addition to the mass of national wealth. It makes every year an addition to the mass of capital in the ratio of the amount of national savings to that of national consumption: and the first year of its existence, the addition it makes is either simply in that ratio, if it be expended for the purpose of consumption, or to the whole

[1][The MS reads "If".]

amount of it, if expended in the shape of capital, on productive improvements.

It is evident that, to their full extent, neither of these opposite and extreme cases is ever realized: but that the truth always lies somewhere between both, and that, in proportions which are susceptible of infinite diversification, they are both realized at once.

Suppose, then, a million to be paid by the Spanish Government to the British Government in exchange for Gibraltar and Minorca, and by the latter coined into guineas and employed in the redemption of so much of the national debt. Being put into the hands of capitalists, it would for that turn [?] be spent, all of it, in giving birth to productive improvements after which it would mix with the rest of the circulating capital, and as to giving birth to any further stock of productive improvements, act only according to the general proportion between productive and unproductive expenditure.

Again—suppose another million to have been first taken from Spain in the way of capture: and, to simplify the case, taken, say, all at one time. The permanent addition it would make to national capital at large, by addition made to the mass of circulating capital, to the part of that mass in circulation, would be on the same footing as in the first case: but the addition made in respect of its first expenditure would be very different.

The shares of the superior officers would be mostly saved: saved, that is, employed in the shape of capital, coming in masses sufficient to constitute what is called a *fortune*. The shares of the petty officers and common men, falling into hands more prone to dissipation, would be mostly spent within the year: i.e. expended in the way of current expenditure, in the purchase of articles consumed within the year, not being regarded as sufficient for any such purpose. In respect to the half of it, therefore, there would be an encrease to the entire amount of that half, an encrease by the first expenditure, in addition to the permanent addition to current expenditure and savings taken together.

Excepting a portion which will be mentioned, every £100 of the money borrowed for war-expenditure, and employed in war-expenditure, is £100 defalcated from the mass of productive capital. If by capital we understand the capital of all nations taken together, in a word, the capital of the commercial world, every £100 so employed is so much defalcated from the capital of the globe.* *Per contra*, every £100 paid in redemption of the national debt of any nation is, without any exception, £100 added to the capital of the commercial world.

The portion alluded to as excepted is—

[The] amount of mercantile profit (say £15 per Cent) on the amount of the expenditure: viz. the profit made by those by whom the articles in which the expenditure consists, were furnished. If we suppose one third of the 15 per Cent, i.e. 5 per Cent, to be employed in the way of current expenditure, this will reduce the amount of the portion excepted to 10 per Cent of the war-expenditure.†

On the Sinking Fund plan, cases might be put in which war itself might be a source of clear wealth: and that, not by reason of conquests and captures, but by reason of expenditure: and, the progress of redemption given, the worse the terms of each loan, the greater the addition to the mass of national wealth.

Even in the actual state of things, it would be a source of wealth, were it not that the period of reimbursement is placed so much later in the order of time than the period of expenditure. For, say, for every £100 of money borrowed and received, £200 stock [is] created: this makes defalcation from productive capital £100 − £10 = £90: addition

*Of the £100 thus expended in the way of war-expenditure in the course of the year, it is not every part that is *consumed* in the course of the year: a considerable part is expended in articles of a durable nature, such as fortifications, ships, docks, and stock of different kinds, which are employed for such or such a number of years, without being consumed.

The money thus expended may be said to be added to the capital of the globe, but not to the productive capital of the globe.

†That 10 per Cent is not too large a proportion for the amount of the perpetual annual addition resulting from an addition to capital in any given year, may be inferred from hence.

The whole annual income of Great Britain from stock and labour does not, according to Dr Beeke, exceed ...	[£]217,000,000
Average annual amount of capital defalcated by loans for war expenditure for the last seven years of war, after deducting the average amount of capital added by the Sinking Fund (about 3,000,000), above ...	[£]22,000,000

On this supposition, the consumption alone of national capital, has for these seven years amounted to more than the tenth part of the national income.

If the addition made to national capital by savings had been no more than the defalcation made, as above, by war expenditure (rate of profit on capital not being encreased), there could have been no addition in that period to the annual average amount of trade. But notwithstanding this defalcation, the addition has been prodigious: upwards of £9,000,000 a year on an average for the less lucrative period of seven years ending with 1798 on the amount of foreign trade alone: while capital employed on land-improvements, instead of diminishing, has gone on encreasing

£200: profit, £110. Neglecting interest, such would be the account. But in a right estimate, instead of neglecting interest, interest upon interest would be computed: for this is what is made in the way of trade.

Be it observed that by *wealth* is not here meant happiness. Wealth to A compensates not for death, nor for wounds, nor for impovrishment to B.

Be it observed again, that it is by the reimbursement caused by the borrowing, as the borrowing is by the expenditure—it is by the reimbursement, and not by the *mode* of expenditure, that the profit here spoken of—the accession to wealth—is produced: if, instead of being spent in war, the £100 borrowed were employed as the £200 employed in payment is, the profit, the addition to capital and wealth, would be augmented by £100. It is not by the waste and destruction which it produces in the first instance, but by the forced economy which, under the institution of the Sinking Fund, it gives birth to and keeps alive, for so many years after the years of waste, that war is productive of the profit spoken of. If it is productive of economy and encrease of wealth upon the whole, it is because by reason of the pressures and alarms to which it gives birth, it reconciles men to privations, such as they would not submitt to otherwise.

Say (as before) for every £1,000,000 received, £2,000,000 stock created: number of years, at the end of which the £2,000,000 is paid off, 7. Amount

added to capital	[£]2,000,000
Taken from capital, the million with compound interest on it at 10 per Cent for the 7 years	[£]1,948,717
Profit by neat addition to capital	[£]51,283
Deducting 10 per Cent from the above £1,948,717 loss, this makes addition to profit	[£]194,871
	[£]246,154

likewise. Moreover, £217,000,000 is given as the amount of national income at the end of this period of rapid accumulation. How much less, then, must it have been at the commencement?

Moreover again, this £217,000,000 is given as the greatest amount of income from both sources, stock and labour put together, income from labour constituting the greater part of it, viz. £110,000. But it can not be supposed that upon the mass of income from labour—most of it, £100,000 of it at least, being the labour of the poorest classes,—the ratio of savings to income can amount to any thing like what it does in the case of income from profit of stock: to any thing like 10/15=2/3ds of the amount of income: one should scarcely expect to find it amount to 2/30.

This indeed supposes the £2,000,000 stock, though not redeemed sooner than at the end of a period of seven years, to have been all along redeemed at par: as was the practice before the establishment of the existing Sinking Funds.

Supposing it redeemed, as at present, by buying in, and the average price to be 75—then the redemption-money paid for the £2,000,000 of stock will amount to but £1,500,000. In this case, to yield profit as above, the reimbursement must have taken place by the end of five years.

Added to capital	[£]1,500,000
Taken from capital by loan of £1,000,000, with compound interest at 10 per Cent for 5 years, [£]1,610,510.	
Deduct from do, defalcation 10 per Cent thereupon, [£]161,051	
Remains taken from capital	[£]1,449,459
Ballance, being neat addition to capital	[£]50,541

Such would be the state of the account, supposing the whole of the £1,500,000 to be paid at once at the end of the last year of the five years. But upon the principle of the existing Sinking Funds, a certain portion of it would be paid every quarter of a year of the five years. The restitution to capital would therefore take place, only to less amount, in the same or the next quarter to the defalcation. Upon this state of the case, the term taken for the completion of the reimbursement with a profit might, it is evident enough, be longer than the five years: but how much longer, I stay not at present to enquire. [The solution of this question] depends upon a calculation that would cost more time than it would be worth to so unexperienced a hand.

[OCTOBER 1800]

At the end of each year, a community is the richer in the proportion between the wealth produced and imported, and the wealth consumed and exported in that same year.

As far, then, as money is concerned, a nation is the richer, not in proportion to the absolute quantity of money, but according to the proportion of the money spent in giving birth to articles of slow consumption, such as ground improvements, buildings, and furniture, to the money spent in giving birth to articles of quick consumption, such as the costly kinds of meat, drink, apparel, and the like.

In this way, wealth is capable of receiving a continual encrease without any encrease in the quantity of money, either cash or paper.

In no other way would paper money, or even cash, make any addition to the quantity of national wealth. But when either paper money or cash, i.e. circulating capital, is added, the natural course it takes is that of making an addition to the mass of fixed or uncirculating capital in the first instance. For it is by hands of the productive class that it is introduced, and for those productive purposes that, in the first instance, it is employed.

When national wealth receives an encrease by means of circulating capital, it is only because, and in so far as, that circulating capital is employed in the first instance in giving birth to an encrease of fixed capital.

Thus it is, that, at the first step, money adds to the mass of real national wealth: at the next step, it adds nothing to the mass of national wealth, but only degrades the value of the mass of money of which it forms a part, and produces a rise of prices: producing the sensation of an universal tax to the amount of the rise.

Excepting the comparatively small result of addition made by machinery, for example, to the effect of labour, no addition can be made to the mass of universal wealth, the wealth of the commercial world, but by an addition to the quantity of labour. No addition is ever made to the quantity of labour in any place, but by an addition made to the quantity of money in that place: since (excepting the narrow case of forced servitude)[1] no man is, or ought to be made to labour without money, nor otherwise than by or for money.

In this point of view, then, money, it should seem, is the cause, and the cause *sine qua non*, of labour and general wealth: and in proportion to the quantity of the cause should, therefore, be the quantity of the effect. It should seem, therefore, that no addition can be made to the quantity of wealth at large, than by a correspondent addition to the quantity of that particular species of wealth which is in the shape of money.

The truth of the matter is, that in regard to any particular species of wealth, no addition can be made (except as excepted) but by an addition to the quantity of money employed in giving birth to that particular species of wealth. But an addition may be made to the quantity of money employed in giving birth to any particular species

[1] [This second bracket is interpolated.]

of wealth, without any addition made to the whole quantity of money taken together.

An addition may therefore be made to the quantity of wealth at large, without any addition to the quantity of money, or even labour, in two ways: 1. by employing a portion of the money in giving birth to productive labour, instead of labour totally unproductive: 2. by employing it in giving birth to productive labour employed in the production of articles of slow consumption, instead of employing it in giving birth to labour applied to the production of articles of quick consumption.

In this way it may further appear, how it may happen, and how it actually does happen, that the quantity of real wealth in a nation may be encreased by taxes. It is encreased by taxes, in proportion as by being raised in taxes, and in virtue of the application made of the produce of those taxes, money is withdrawn from those applications of it, the effect of which would be to give birth to unproductive labour, or to less durably productive labour, and transferred to those applications, the effect of which is to give birth to productive, or more durably productive, labour.

A particular case *here* supposed, but elsewhere and often realized, will help to make these general positions clear.

Pressed by [an] encreasing weight of taxes, a country gentleman makes a reduction in his establishment. He keeps a couple of coach or saddle horses the less—a stable boy the less—a labouring gardener the less: he gives up his pinery, and converts a part of his pleasure ground into arable. He makes a ploughboy of the stable-boy, and [a] labourer in husbandry of the gardener, and builds a cottage for the gardener, who marries and takes possession of it accordingly. The expence of these improvements coming on the back of the encrease of taxes, requires a sum of money in addition to his income: this additional sum he obtains by the sale of a quantity of stock annuities he has, for which stock, by reason of the effect of that part of his share of the taxes which has been carried to the Sinking Fund, he obtains a better price by many per Cent than he would have obtained otherwise.

An influx of money which produces no addition to the mass of wealth not consisting of money, can not but produce a depretiation in the value of money, that is, a rise of prices.

An influx of money which gives birth [to] a[1] proportionable addi-

[1][The MS reads "an" because the first version had been "an equivalent addition".]

tion to the mass of wealth not consisting in money, can not produce a depretiation in the value of money—can not produce a rise of prices.

Money employed, i.e. expended, in the shape of capital, *does* produce, or at least *ought* to produce, a proportionable addition to the mass of wealth not pecuniary.

Money expended in the way of consumptive expenditure does not produce any addition, or at least does not produce a proportionable addition, to the mass of wealth not pecuniary.

Money is called *circulating capital*: certain articles of wealth that are not money, are called *fixed* capital. It is therefore true and not true, that an addition to capital produces [a] rise of prices.

Money, while it continues in the shape of money, does not itself *constitute* any portion, properly speaking, of the general mass of wealth in use: not of the mass of wealth other than gold and silver, for it *is* gold and silver: not of gold and silver plate, because, by the supposition, it is not employed as plate.

But though it does not *constitute* any portion of the general mass of wealth in use, it does not the less contribute to the keeping up and augmentation of that mass: since it is only in exchange and in return for *money* that, in the general way of trade, any addition to the mass of wealth intrinsically valuable is made.

The gold and silver that comes annually into the country, in consequence of the ballance of trade—what effect has it in regard to the rise of prices? Answer.—It comes in in the shape of capital, being received by merchants by whom it is employed in that capacity. But it is not as yet money: and till then [it has not the effect of money, but the counter-effect of vendible articles, so long as it remains uncoined].[1]

Circulating capital, then, makes no addition to wealth—no addition at least that is not productive of [a] rise of prices—any further than in as far as it gives birth to an addition to fixed capital, and such an addition as would not have been made otherwise.

An addition to fixed or productive capital may be productive of an addition to marketable wealth (as above), without any addition to circulating capital.

So far, then, as an addition to circulating capital, or money, makes no proportionable addition to fixed or productive capital, nor thence to marketable wealth, so far it does no more than produce a rise of prices.

[1][Filled in according to an autograph pencil note on the margin of the sheet.]

An influx of money must produce a degradation in the value of the old stock, i.e. a rise of prices, in proportion to its suddenness: because in proportion to its suddenness is the smallness of the time allowed for that addition to the mass of wealth not pecuniary which, as far as it goes, would serve as a counterpoise to the other addition, and prevent its *depressive* effect.

If the quantity of money were doubled in the year, the [level of the] prices of vendible articles in general would be nearly doubled:—it would be *exactly* doubled, if the addition to money gave birth to no corresponding addition to the quantity of vendible articles: it fails of being exactly doubled, by the amount of the extra mass of vendible articles thus produced by it.

Each million of guineas, on being put into the hands of an expelled annuitant, are employed by him in making an addition to the national capital (in all manner of shapes but that of circulating money) by the amount of the labour produced by their first expenditure: but after that one step returning into the mass of circulating capital, they add to the mass of capital, or to the mass of consumable goods for immediate consumption, minister to productive or unproductive expenditure, and the addition made in this shape to national capital is at an end.

As to [1]the additions to the mass of[2] circulating capital, each million's worth of Annuity Note paper put into the hands of purchasers in the room of the guineas they pay for it, distributes itself at the first disbursement between productive and unproductive expenditure, in the proportions which the two modes of expenditure bear to one another, and continues so to do, so long as it continues in circulation.

The one addition [—the addition to fixed capital by redemption—] goes not beyond the first step [and] is compleated by one expenditure. [It] goes, all of it, to capital [and] is made at the expence of consumption, from which it is taken by taxes: but admitts of no such abatement as will be mentioned in the other case, from its value.

The other addition [—the addition to circulating capital by Notes issued—] takes a number of steps in a year, ministering sometimes to accumulation, sometimes to unproductive consumption—is made at no expence—i.e. takes nothing from consumption: but is continually losing of its value, in proportion to what it contributes towards the rise of prices.

[1] [2][Put into brackets at a later date.]

It can not but contribute to this effect, to the whole of its amount, except in as far as it finds a counterpoise in one or other of three results: 1. import of goods, by being itself exported to that amount: 2. encrease of labour, by bringing into employment a quantity of capacity for labour as yet unemployed, on the part of the existing stock of hands: 3. encrease of labour by import of labouring hands.

A million's worth of dollars, received by government (from Spain, for example, as the price of Gibraltar or Trinidad), made current by government, and applied at the first step towards the redemption of the national debt, would be an example of both additions put together. This, and a great deal more that might be added, is not in Adam Smith—but it belongs not the less to the science so well taught by Adam Smith.

If the application of the new influx of money were confined altogether to the bringing into employment the quantity of capacity for labour as yet unemployed, it would contribute nothing to the rise of prices: an influx of fresh goods (the produce of the labour) would be produced by the money, equal to the value of the money, the new stock of goods bearing the same proportion to the new stock of money as the old stock of goods did to the old stock of money, and the proportion as between money and goods, and thence the prices of goods, and value of money as compared with goods, would remain unchanged.

But in a perfect degree, such supposed restriction never can take place: no considerable addition, therefore, can ever be made to the mass of money, without making a considerable addition to the rise of prices.

In proportion as any addition to the mass of money is attended with an addition to the prices of goods, no addition is made to the mass of real wealth. Thus it is that every addition to the mass of real wealth is attended with an addition, commonly to still greater amount, to nominal and unreal wealth.

Observe that the equivalent of a sum of money in vendible articles is—not simply the value, but about three times the value: because a million of money in the year, serves for the transfer of about three times its amount of goods in the year.

Price (nominal price) being the result of the proportion between goods and money, a natural supposition is, that inasmuch as encrease of money makes goods dear, decrease of money would make goods cheap, and that thus whatever inconveniences were produced by the first state of things, would be cured and made up for by the second.

Unfortunately, this is not altogether the case. A case may indeed be put, and has perhaps been even realized, in which by decrease of money, goods have become cheap: but so far from curing or making up the inconveniences of dearness, such cheapness can never take place without having been attended. or rather preceded, by mischiefs beyond comparison superior to any inconveniences produced by dearness. Take away money, you may make goods cheap: but cheapness in this case is not synonymous to plenty. Though you have emptied the country of half its goods, goods will be cheap [—they will] be perhaps at half price, if you have emptied it of three fourths of its money.

Particular sorts of goods, such as goods manufactured or manufacturable by machinery, may indeed grow cheaper, without diminution in the quantity of money, and therefore without distress: but goods in general never can, and in particular provisions, i.e. those sorts of goods on which subsistence depends much more than on all other sorts of goods put together, and to the production of which machinery can never be applied with any considerable encrease of effect.

A *fixed* income therefore, so called, is in effect essentially a *decreasing* one: and relief, if the distress admitts any, can no otherwise be administered than by a retardation in the rate of encrease, that is in the augmentation of general wealth and prosperity which is the cause of that decrease.

By taking off taxes, indeed, in as far as this can be done, a certain degree of relief may be administered: but the relief is as nothing to the burthen. The burthen amounts to the reduction of a fixed income to the half or the third of it in the compass of fifty years: whereas the amount of taxes capable of being taken off on the redemption of the debt,* viz. those which go to the payment of it, amount not to a tenth part of the national income.†

That in certain events, among the results produced by the proposed measure would be, besides the certain addition that we have seen coming on to fixed and other intrinsically productive capital, an addition to that part of the circulating capital which consists in money (paper and cash included)—that such an addition would actually take place, in proportion to the amount of the proposed

* £20,000,000.

† £217,000,[000].

Annuity Note paper issued and retained in the circulation, deducting such portion, if any, of the mass of money (paper and cash together) as should come to be driven out of the circulation by such proposed paper—and that such neat addition so made, whatever might be the *nominal* amount of it (one, ten, twenty, forty millions), would be as real as if made by so much gold and silver coin—are propositions, the truth of which will appear clear enough: *—but [whether][1] any such addition to money would be productive of an addition to the mass of real national wealth, to any such amount—or would be so much as an innocent, not to speak of a beneficial, result—will also appear with but too sufficient evidence. For, instead of an addition to the mass of real wealth, the effect of by far the greater part, if not the whole of such neat addition to the money part of capital, would be the degradation of its own value as well as that of the mass into which it flowed—in other words, a *rise of prices*.

To avoid loading with theoretical disquisitions a proposal thus practical in its design, and swelling it to an immeasurable bulk, I will content myself on the present occasion with stating the result in

*At the time that *Yorkshire* had a paper currency as low as sixpences, a house was built that cost £100, labour as well as materials paid for entirely in these sixpences: the house built, the issuers of this paper absconded, not paying a farthing in the pound. The paper thus lost the whole of its value: but the house did not tumble down, nor did it become of less value than if it had been paid for in gold and silver. The difference is—that had it been paid for in gold and silver, the *gold and silver*, so long as there was any of it left in the country, would have remained ready to have built *other* houses: whereas, in the case of the *paper*, so soon as it had built that *one* house, there was an end of it.

For twenty years together, a certain bank having for capital £100,000 worth of gold, kept circulating that gold, and by the help of it another £100,000 of paper, promising on demand, to the bearer, so much gold. At the end of the twenty years, gold to the amount of this £100,000 was shipped by the bank, and lost: the bank thereupon broke, and, paying nothing in the pound, its paper would not go for any thing. The addition made in the twenty years to the mass of national wealth by the paper, was here, it is evident, equal to the addition made by the gold.

The only advantage the gold possessed in all that time over the paper was—that, if gold plate had been wanted during that time, and had not been obtainable by any other means with equal advantage, the coined *gold* would have been capable of being melted, and thereby converted into *plate*: which is what the paper would not have been capable of. This might amount to a *real* advantage, in a *conceivable* state of things: but what does it amount to in the actual state of things?

The addition made to that mass by a nominal £100 worth of the most degraded paper—by a paper which ended in not being received on a footing with the smallest portion of gold and silver—by the French Assignats for example—was, so long as it continued to be received on a footing with a sixpenny piece of silver, as real an addition to the mass of circulating capital, as would have been made by an additional sixpenny piece.

[1][The MS reads "that"; the sense, however, demands "whether". Cf. what follows.]

question as *hypothetical*: reserving the proof of it, if necessary, for some other place.

Stating it thus in the way of admission and confession (for doubtless the proposal would have stood much clearer of difficulty and objection, had no such result been to be apprehended), I will proceed at once to state the course of proceeding by which all danger on this score may be kept from converting itself into the apprehended inconvenience.

In the mean time, the notions generally current on the subject[1] (though, I am inclined to suspect, neither perfectly clear, nor correct, nor even consistent with themselves) extend thus far at least as to present the proposition in question in a point of view not unfavourable to acceptance, viz. that too sudden an influx of money of any kind may do more harm than good—more harm by addition to prices, than good by addition to the mass of wealth.

What renders this topic of peculiar importance is, that the rise of prices has grown to be the subject of peculiar complaint of the period of time at which the last hand comes to be put to the present papers: and though this pressure has evidently for its cause, in part at least, the succession of an indifferent season to a bad one, a cause which, of course, is hoped and expected to be but a temporary one, yet in [an]other part it would be found to result from the influx of money and from other causes [?] of inconvenience, from which the indisputable encrease of general prosperity can not be kept altogether clear by the utmost exertions of human prudence.

Assuming, then, that things are come to such a pass that a rise of prices to a degree beyond what would otherwise have taken place appears about to ensue, unless prevented, in consequence of the operation of this paper, I shall proceed directly to enquire by what necessary, and proper and sufficient means, such prevention may be accomplished.

Labour, operating upon land and the produce of land, is the source, and only source, of wealth. No addition therefore—no real addition—can ever be made to the mass of wealth, but through the medium of a correspondent* addition, either to the *quantity*, or to the *efficiency* of labour.

[1][The bracket now following is interpolated.]

*By a *corresponding* addition to the mass of vendible articles I understand such an addition, whatever that be, as shall do as much towards lowering, or keeping down the price of such article, as the supposed addition of money does towards raising them. This I suppose to be—not an *equal* addition, but a *proportionable*

Taking the commercial world together, no real addition can be made within a given compass of time—say, a year—to the quantity of wealth of the commercial world, but by a correspondent addition to the quantity or efficiency of labour. To the quantity of labour no addition can be made in the year, but in so far as there exists in the world a quantity of *capacity* in regard to labour, as yet unemployed, but capable of being within the year employed and brought into act.

In the case of a particular country, Great Britain for example, the enriching powers of money have a less restricted range. Within the given compass of a year, it may add to wealth, not only by adding to the quantity or efficiency of labour on the part of the existing stock of hands, but also by adding to the stock of labouring hands, or of wealth ready produced, by imports made from foreign parts.

Taking into account both these extensions, it has still its limits: so that, notwithstanding all possible extensions, it may be pronounced, that whatever addition made to the mass of money in the compass of the year, is not attended in the same compass of time with a *correspondent* addition to the mass of vendible commodities within the country by means of a *correspondent* addition either to the mass of those commodities produced in the country, whether by native or imported hands, or to the mass of those commodities imported from foreign parts within the time, can make no further real addition to the mass of actual wealth—can make no other addition than a nominal one—can not do otherwise than produce a correspondent rise of prices.

During a given period—say, as before, a year—the price of vendible commodities of all sorts is determined by the proportion of the mass of vendible commodities of all sorts, to the mass of money of all sorts. Let the quantity of money be doubled, the quantity of vendible commodities remaining the same, the price of vendible commodities of all sorts taken together is made at least twice as great, and perhaps

---

one: i.e. an addition in vendible articles which shall be in the same proportion to the standard mass of vendible articles as the addition in money bears to the standard mass of money. The mass of circulating money, it has been stated in another place, may be considered as being about a third part of the mass of income. What precise proportion the mass of vendible commodities bought and sold within the year may bear to the total of income received in the compass of the year, is a point which it does not appear very easy to ascertain. If they be regarded as equal, the error does not seem likely to be very great. On these suppositions, the addition in vendible commodities corresponding to an addition in money to the amount of a million will be—not one million's-worth, but three millions'-worth.

much more. In what greater proportion, if any, is a point by no means easy to investigate.

If all incomes could be raised in the exact proportion of the rise of prices and at the same times, the rise of prices would not be attended with any positive inconvenience. So much only of the effect of the fresh influx of money as was productive of this result, so much would be to be deducted from the accession to real wealth. The misfortune is, that it is in but a very imperfect degree that this supposition can be ever realized. Incomes from salary remain without encrease [or at least] can not be raised but by an express act unpopular in its nature, and never obtainable till long after the demand, on the part of government. Incomes from rent of lands and houses must wait for their encrease at any rate till the expiration of whatever leases the property happens to be burthened with. Incomes from interest of money lent, so far from encrease, are exposed to decrease from the operation of the same causes. Incomes from trade or profit of stock are subject in this respect to an infinity of variations and contingencies. Incomes from profession are sometimes free to rise to the new level, but more frequently perhaps [held][1] down by the fixity of the prices of corn or masses of money customarily given in the way of fees. By a fortunate position, in some instances it may happen that a man shall be enabled to derive a positive profit, over and above an indemnity, from the loss: but in by far the greater number of instances this can not be done, and the difference remains as a burthen in the nature of a tax on income, but beyond comparison heavier than any that has been, or can be, imposed by government.

There are three cases, and but three, in which a given mass of money of the supposed fresh influx, say Annuity Note paper, will not be productive of any rise of prices:

1. If, within the same compass of time, it comes to be productive of a correspondent mass of vendible articles, whether by addition to the quantity of labour or to the efficiency of it.

2. If, within the same time, it has the effect of expelling out of the circulation other paper money to an equal amount.

3. If, within the same time, it has the effect of expelling out of the circulation cash to the same amount, whether by causing it to remain unemployed, or to be melted [2](viz. for conversion into bullion or plate)[3] or exported.

[1][The word is illegible.]

[2] [3][The brackets are of a later date.]

Exclude all these suppositions, the influx in question makes a clear unballanced addition to the mass of money in circulation:—admitt any one of them, it fails of doing so.

As to its expelling other paper, to the extent of its own quantity, which may swell to the amount of that of the existing mass of other paper and beyond—that the result of such a substitution would be of a beneficial nature to the community at large, is shewn [in another place; as likewise] that it is a natural consequence of the extension of the proposed paper: and that, should it not take place of itself, it is such as may, with little hardship and no injury, be brought about by positive law.

As to expelling cash—the word (which is used for shortness merely) points to *violence,* and thence to damage. But in the result itself, supposing it to take place, there would be nothing that was not advantageous. If in any degree it expelled cash, it could only be in as far as it was preferred to cash. If it expelled cash altogether, it could only be by being regarded by every body as preferable to cash. But to say that it is preferred by every body to cash, is to say, in other words, that it is of greater value than so much cash: the difference between the one value and the other would be so much profit, created by the proposed paper. What is thus true of the whole community, that is, of all its members taken collectively, could not be otherwise than true of each of them taken separately. Coercion being altogether out of the question, not a man would have parted with his share, without obtaining for it in exchange some thing that, with reference to his own interests or conceptions at least, was of superior value. The damage to the community by such expulsion would be no greater than the damage done to a baker by the expulsion that takes place every day as he sells off his bread—the expulsion of bread out of his shop. The cause would be the same, and so would the effect.

By the expulsion of the whole five and forty million's worth of cash, were it possible, not a particle would be taken from the mass of real *serviceable* national wealth; on the contrary, *more* than the whole five and forty million's worth, with a profit to boot, would be added to that mass: the five and forty millions, *plus* the 15 per Cent, or whatever may be the rate of profit on mercantile transactions in this instance.

Cash, while it remains in the form of cash—metallic money any more than the paper money which conveys the promise of it—is not of the smallest value in the way of *use.* What value it possesses, consists merely of value in the way of exchange: in respect of which value it is not merely equalled, but by the supposition even exceeded, by the paper which expelled it and has taken its place. By being melted into bullion, and thence made into plate, it regains, it is true, that value in the way of use to which alone it is indebted for its value in the way of exchange, [1]but then it is cash no longer in the shape of cash.

But by being expelled out of the circulation of this particular country, the cash is not driven out of the world: it remains in the shape of bullion or plate somewhere, and wherever it remains, it regains its value in the way of use, having its value in the way of exchange replaced, and with encrease, by the paper which has expelled it. If it remains unexported, then there is so much more bullion and plate in the country, in consequence of the proposed measure, than there would have been without it: if it goes out of the country, any part of it, so much the better still: for it is not, can not be, sent out of the country, but in exchange for other things, which, in the country into which they are thus imported, are of still superior value.*

---

[1][One single bracket of later date is inserted here.]

*That gold and silver are articles of transcendent value, is not to be disputed: that *in all ordinary cases,* by means of a certain quantity of them, you can have a proportionable quantity of any thing else at pleasure, which is what can not be said of any other sort of thing, is not less indisputable: it is to this universal exchangeability, and to the physical properties [to][2] which they are indebted [for][3] it, that gold and silver owe no small part of their value. But still their value, how transcendent soever, has its limits: and to say that a guinea's worth of *gold* is worth a farthing more than a guinea's worth of *dung,* would be, in *political economy,* as flagrant an absurdity, as in *physics* it would be to say that a pound of lead was heavier than a pound of feathers: in both it would be a contradiction in terms.

Though two millions' worth of gold and silver is not worth a farthing more than two millions' worth of any thing else, there is not on that account any absurdity in the exultation testified by public men at observing in how [great] a degree what is called the ballance of trade is in favour of this country. Gold and silver, though they do not constitute a larger share of wealth in general than a mass of other articles to the same value, serve as an index of the magnitude of the mass of general wealth: so that when we find the import of gold and silver for a length of time on the encrease, we may be sure enough that the mass of wealth of all kinds taken together is also on the encrease. Wealth of other kinds creates at the same time a demand for gold and silver and the means of satisfying it. As a nation gets rich in other things, it will naturally and invariably get rich in gold and silver. Of this or that individual, this may be more or less true, according to his individual tastes and fancies: but of a nation, it will be invariably so. As a man's stock of general wealth encreases, he naturally finds himself disposed to add to the quantity of gold and silver utensils that entered into the composition of his stock. In no other shape can he make a more eligible addition to it: in no other article are the qualities of beauty, utility, and durability, to be found united in a higher degree. Seduced by the pride of discovery, Adam Smith, by taking his words from the kitchen, has attempted to throw an ill grounded ridicule on the preference given to gold and

By the addition thus made to the mass of vendible commodities, the mass of money remaining without corresponding encrease, the mass of vendible commodities taken together, it may appear (considering the matter in this point of view), should be made cheaper.

But the effect of the addition thus made to the mass of vendible commodities by bullion, is different from the effect produced by the addition of any other sort of article: for bullion being convertible into money in the literal sense, and without exchange, an encrease in the quantity of bullion can scarcely take place to any considerable amount without producing a correspondent addition to the mass of money. Bullion, like any other article, is subject to the depretiation resulting from a glut. When therefore the supposed fresh influx of bullion has met with all the custom that can be afforded to it by the demand for plate, i.e. by that quantity of demand which the quantity of wealth of other kinds is adequate to the production of—a demand for that additional quantity which the circumstances of the inhabitants of the country taken together enable them to *afford*, and wherever it can not with a certain degree of profit be sent out of the country for the purchase of other goods, it must seek some other employment, or be kept to a loss.

But bullion, being the material of which metallic money consists, has a means of employment which no other vendible article possesses, and which, under any degree of glut, secures it against being disposed of to a loss beyond a certain mark. For by the regulations of

silver, as if it were the smallness of their quantity that was the sole or chief cause of that preference.[4] He forgets that there is scarce a use to which either copper, tin, or lead, are employed at present, to which gold or silver could not be substituted were there but enough of them, and in most cases with vast advantage.

Thus much, however, must be confessed, that supposing the encrease of general wealth to be clearly ascertained and as clearly held up to view by other means, the ballance of trade is a matter altogether of indifference, [and] of the most perfect insignificance. To suppose that the trade of that nation which exports more gold and silver than it imports, is a *losing* trade, or that [there] ever was, or can be, such a thing as a losing trade, is to fall into the absurdity—the contradiction in terms—above held up to view. One nation may gain more by its trade than another, because in exchange with produce of a given quantity of its own labour, it may obtain the produce of a greater quantity of the labour of another: but to suppose [that][5] either side the trade can be any other than a gainful one, is to suppose what is impossible. If the million of silver which Spain exports to England, costs less labour than the goods she receives from thence in return, England is, it is true, a gainer by the exchange, but Spain is a still greater.

[2][The MS reads "for".]

[3][The MS reads "to".]

[4][Wealth of Nations, bk. IV, ch. VII, pt. I.]

[5][The MS reads "than".]

the public Mint, he who is in possession of a certain quantity of bullion has it always at his command to obtain for it a certain quantity of coined money: it is thus an article, and the only article, the owner of which can at all times, and in any quantity and at a known price, command the sale. Therefore though bullion itself can not be forced upon people as cash may, nor are people in general disposed to accept of it as cash, it is however that sort of thing, the possessor of which to a sufficient amount can never be long in want of any thing that can be had for cash: since by conveying it to the Mint, he can at any time convert it into the corresponding quantity of cash.

When therefore the stock of bullion in the market happens to be so great that a man who wants to sell his bullion can not find a purchaser for it among individuals—can not get cash for it from an individual to superior or equal advantage—he takes it to the Mint, where, in a regulated proportion, he has it always in his power to get cash for it.

In this way it is, that an answer may be found to a question for which I have in vain endeavoured to find an answer in Adam Smith and other books—in what mode is it, under what circumstances, and by the operation of what causes, and in what quantities and proportions is it, that coined money in fresh and fresh quantities finds its way into the world. In this way it is, that a certain *ratio* or proportion will always be found subsisting in a country, between the quantity of vendible commodities exclusive of bullion, the quantity of bullion, and the quantity of coined money, or at least the quantity of money. In this way it is, that a glut of bullion will always have a tendency at least, to produce an encrease in the quantity of money of all sorts taken together, though a glut of any other sort of vendible commodity will not have that tendency in any degree.

In practice, though the addition to the stock of money in the course of the present reign has been so great, and though the quantity of bullion that has from time to time been experiencing the sort of glut above spoken of must accordingly have been so great, as also the number of individuals by whom it has been experienced, yet it has not been by individuals that the influx of money into the Mint has in general been supplied, but by the Bank of England. The reason is, that by reason of certain circumstances, particular to the situation of that great and opulent company, it is enabled to make purchases of bullion to advantage at a certain price, in circumstances in which individuals in general would not be able to make such purchases to equal advantage at that price. And thus it is, that although it can not have been but by and through the hands of individuals that those additions have, from time to time, been supplied, yet the supply has passed from the hands of the individual not immediately, but through the medium of the Bank.

In the way of objection, a case may be supposed as possible (for the probability of it will not be easily made out by the assignment of any specific adequate causes) that a sudden demand may come to present itself for cash, which the paper that had taken the place of the cash would not be able to satisfy. Five million's worth of cash is wanted—what is to be done, if not so much as a single million's worth is to be found?

Wanted—by whom, and for what purpose—and, in case of non-supply, of what kind and to what amount will be the damage? to all these questions, were it necessary, would answer be to be given, for the objection to stand its ground: but an observation or two will be enough to save that trouble. By the expulsion of the cash from the circulation, the quantity of bullion and plate in the country is not diminished but rather encreased, and bullion and plate are the very materials, and the only materials, of which cash is made, and made in very large quantities in a short time. But, by the supposition, the proposed paper has all along been preferred to cash on all occasions, as well in payment for bullion and plate, as in payment or every thing else: and of the proposed paper there neither is, nor can be any want. Therefore, although the whole quantity of cash in the country should be driven out of the circulation by the proposed paper, yet. by such expulsion, any inconvenience that could be supposed to take place for want of cash would, so far from being augmented, be obviated and averted.

If, then, the whole amount of the cash in the circulation were to be expelled out of it by the proposed paper, it would only be so much the better: and the greater the degree in which any such effect took place, the greater would be the advantage. In what degree it would actually take place, it does not seem possible to determine: but that, in spite of every thing which could be done by, or wished for in this way on the part of the proposed paper, a large proportion of the cash in circulation would remain unexpelled, will be evident enough.

1. An encrease in the quantity of the paper itself could not be

kept up but by the medium of [1]a certain quantity of cash—of the cash requisite to be paid for it by those who take it out in the way of issue.

2. Cash is the form in which the interest on the capital of the proposed paper would be to be paid and received, in so far as such interest is demanded of the public Offices. Paper, it is true, *might*, and probably, it should seem, *would*, be taken in payment of such interest at those very Offices in a certain quantity, and that probably enough not an inconsiderable one. But the proportion is matter of contingency, depending upon public taste and humour, and other causes equally out of the reach of calculation. In the eyes of the multitude more especially, metal—the original—is more attractive to sense than paper—the substitute: and in the former instance, the association between money, the type, and wealth of all kinds, the thing typified, is closer, than in the latter.

Whatever be the value set upon the paper, the value of cash can never be taken away. So long as the paper is to be had in any quantity for a quantity of cash of the same nominal value, that is, during the continuance of the first issue, the cash can never obtain any considerable preference: it can never obtain a preference beyond that which would be given by the trouble and time consumed in one case, saved in the other—the trouble of putting a letter for London into the post, and the time of waiting for an answer.

If from and after the opening of the second issue, the paper of the first issue should come to bear a premium, still the maximum amount of that premium would have *known*, and those not very ample, *limits*: and a nominal thousand pounds' worth of cash would as surely be worth a thousand pound without the premium, as the nominal thousand pounds' worth of the paper would be worth the thousand pound and the premium put together.

Cash, and cash alone, is the subject matter of all existing pecuniary contracts: cash, and cash alone, unless by virtue of a conceivable special stipulation in favour of the proposed paper, would continue to be the subject matter of all future pecuniary contracts. Except as just excepted, every man who owes a thousand pounds, will have it in his power to acquit himself of the debt, with or without the consent of the creditor, by payment or tender of a thousand [pounds][2] of cash: no man will have it in his power to acquit himself of any such obligation, without the consent of the creditor, by the payment of a

[1][One single bracket of later date is inserted here.]

[2][The MS reads "worths".]

thousand pound's worth, or any other quantity however so great, of the proposed paper.

In proposing the quantity of money of all sorts already in circulation as the standard of reference, in respect of the quantity to be suffered to exist after and in consequence of the introduction of the proposed paper, I would not be understood to mark out for prohibition that degree of extension which the mass in question would have received in the natural course of things, and laying out of the case the degree of extensive effect that, unless prevented in the manner proposed, might have resulted from the particular operation of the proposed measure. The proper object of endeavour is—not absolutely to prevent all rise of prices, since to prevent that might be to prevent that encrease of opulence and consequent national security of which, in a certain degree, the rise of prices seems to be an[1] inseparable accompaniment: but only that degree of rise, which, had it not been for the preventive precautions in question, might have had the proposed measure for its sole efficient cause.*

All this while, let it never be out of mind, that it is only the paper of the open issue that can contribute any thing in addition to the mass of money in circulation, and that no part of the paper, even of such open issue, can stay in the circulation, but upon the supposition that the rate of interest it yields is so low as to be rejected by all customers for government annuities for the purpose of permanent income: at the same time that there exists no other species of government security from which permanent income at a superior rate of interest can be obtained, and that the quantity of this only remaining species is diminishing every day, while the quantity of wealth capable of purchasing it is encreasing at a rate of similar rapidity.

---

[1][The word may also read "one".]

*In the main, the positions contained in these papers will be found accordant with the doctrine of Adam Smith. To a classic of such high and deserved repute, by a simple reference, could it have been given, a great deal of dry and obscure discussion might have been spared. Such reference would accordingly have been made, had the views given of the subject in that work appeared uniformly just, adequate, and intelligible.

For my own part, I must confess, I never was able to obtain what to me appeared a clear insight into this part of the subject from the instructions of Adam Smith. Metaphors taken from wheels and water seemed to take the place too often of definition and exemplification.[2] The *paradoxical,* though not at the expence of *truth,* seemed sometime to obtain the preference over the *simple* and *instructive.* Multiplicity of words appeared sometimes to have been employed in the course of the efforts produced, as it were, by distress, for want of the few words, which, had the views been perfectly clear, would have sufficed.

[2][Wealth of Nations, bk. II, ch. II.]

[Nicholas Vansittart's] Objections to the Annuity Note Plan with Answers

Objection 1st. *"We have already a larger proportion of paper circulation than is consistent with our security in times of public alarm."*

Answer. What the objection assumes is—that the *object* of the plan was—to make an addition to the mass of paper in circulation, or at least that such would necessarily be the *effect*. But this was certainly not the object of the plan, nor, if my view of the matter be correct, would it be comprized in the number of its effects: and, if I were mistaken in this point, the excess might be, and ought to be, repressed, by measures which, in my view of the matter, will be necessary, although no such measure as that proposed should be adopted.

In the first page of the Introduction, I state myself as aware of the superabundance of paper in circulation; and as relying upon the plan as a remedy, and such a remedy as cannot be matched by any other, for efficacy and security, to the superabundance. Since then, my suspicion of the existence of a superabundance, has every day received stronger and stronger confirmation from subsequent investigation, and the danger resulting from it has presented itself to me as so serious, that sooner or later, something, in my view of the matter, must be done to repress the growth of the excess, under pain of a most grievous and certain *rise of prices* (over and above the amount of any casual rise from bad seasons) with the addition, sooner or later, of general Bankruptcy.

By measures operating, in a *direct and declared* way, in repression of the excess in the mass of the existing papers, I do not doubt but that the repression might be effected: all I contend for under this head is, that the repression cannot be effected in so smooth and convenient a way without the proposed Government Paper, as with the help of it. The repression of the excess is a point of some delicacy: since Bankruptcy might equally ensue from a sudden *diminution*, as from too sudden an augmentation, of the quantity. Among the properties I ascribe to the proposed paper is that of possessing a sort of *amphibious* nature, in virtue of which, it will, of itself, and without any regulation on purpose, be *added* to the mass of the circulating medium, or withdrawn from it, from time to time, as the circumstances of the time may happen to require. This is argued in several passages not yet printed—I believe in the unprinted part of Ch. 4.

My notion is moreover that, as *this* paper *advances* in the circulation, at the same pace, and no greater, will the *other* papers *recede* and withdraw themselves out of it: that this effect is no more than what is likely to take place of itself, without any positive regulation for the purpose: but that if it should fail of taking place in a sufficient degree, measures, operating in a direct way in that view, may be taken with greater safety *after* the institution of the proposed paper, than *without* it. These points too I have argued at large.

It is among the properties of the proposed paper to be essentially *incapable* of excess: and that as well with reference to *rise of prices* as with reference to *Bankruptcy*: it is of the essence of the existing papers (legislative repression apart) to be perpetually running on in the career of excess, with reference to *both* these evils.

True it is, that, according to the proposed plan, the amount of the proposed paper is proposed and expected to swell in time, so as to be equal to, and give its form to, the whole amount of the National Debt: but were it (for argument sake) to swell to that amount in the compass of the first month, it would not on that account contribute any thing considerable to rise of prices, much less to the approach of Bankruptcy. True it is again, that at any given point of time it is in every part of it equally capable, of being kept in hand, like Stock Annuities, in the quality of a permanent source of Income, or passed from hand to hand like Bank paper in exchange for goods or Estates &c; and accordingly, so far as concerns its exchange for *goods*, of being employed in such a manner as to contribute to the *rise of prices*: but it cannot, any part of it, operate in *both* those capacities *together*: it cannot, any part of it, be *at the same time* kept in hand and parted with, *by the same person*. *After* the conversion of the whole mass of Stock Annuities into the proposed form of Note Annuities, men will not spend more of their capital in the way of *current expenditure* (in other words in the purchase of goods for consumption and other uses) than they do *now*: but it is only in proportion as the proposed Note Annuities are employed for the purpose of current expenditure that they can add any thing to the *rise of prices*.

As to the *existing* papers—*one* of the properties they have in common is—that, taken in the *aggregate*, the performance of the engagements entered into by them (viz: for the delivery of so much cash) is *physically* and *constantly* impossible.

Another is—that, in proportion as the amount of them swells, the amount of the *cash* so undertaken for swells likewise; and that, whether the amount of the cash capable of being delivered in pursuance of such undertaking *encreases, remains the same,* or *decreases.*

On the other hand, it is among the properties of the *proposed* paper, to make no *addition* whatever to (but on the contrary a *defalcation* from) the aggregate mass of the cash, the delivery of which is undertaken for by the party from whom it issues: *at present,* the money that government stands bound for the delivery of, on the score of the National Debt, is—the amount of the *interest* of it, and that payable in certain fixed proportions at certain fixed times of the year: and this is all it *would* stand bound for the delivery of, were the mass of the proposed paper to be equal to the whole amount of the *principal* of that same debt.

What the mass of *existing* papers undertakes for, is—the delivering, on any day, if demanded on that day, a certain mass of cash which, if demanded on any one day, would—most certainly, *not* be to be found: what the proposed paper undertakes for is—the delivering. at sundry prefixed and foreknown periods—two or four of them in a year—each consisting of a number of days and as distinct from one another as possible—a quantity of cash, which *cannot* be *greater,* but on the contrary, in proportion to the increase of the proposed paper, cannot *but* be continually *less and less,* than the quantity which Government is *already enabled* and *accustomed* (as above) to deliver on the same account.

In a word—what I *admitt* is—that the paper in circulation exists already in excess. What I am strongly inclined to think is—that the *insecurity* resulting from that excess, is—not merely *contingent*—depending upon *accidents* of a nature to bring on alarm—but *certain*: viz: though not certain of happening at any *near* point of time, yet certain of happening *sooner or later, if not prevented* by the application of some proper remedy.

What I maintain is—that the proposed paper is not of a nature to add to the excess.

What I am again inclined to think is—that the proposed paper *might of itself* be capable of operating as a sufficient remedy.

What I moreover maintain is—that, if other and more direct remedies should be thought fit to be applied, the proposed paper, so far from affording *obstruction* to their operation would be *auxiliary* to it.

I will conclude this head with giving an exemplification of its *amphibious nature* (as above mentioned) from whence results that *regulating power* in virtue of which it is alike calculated to correct any *excess* or *deficiency* in regard to the quantity of money of all sorts in circulation: observing however, that this supposes the whole, or a considerable part, of the existing mass of Stock Annuities to have been already converted into this shape, as per Art. 20.

1. Let money, on a sudden, become *scarce*. A Merchant, besides the capital he has invested in *trade*, has in Government Annuities, to the value of £10,000, in this *Paper*. The sum he wants is £5,000 for two Months. The scarcity is such, that he cannot raise it in the usual way by putting his name to Bills and getting them discounted. Were his Annuities in the form of *Stock* Annuities, as at present, he would then have to *sell* them, for less by perhaps ten or twenty per Cent, than what he *gave* for them. Being in Note Annuities which (it is shewn in Chap. 4) can never, at the supposed period, bear either *discount* or *premium*, to an amount worth regarding, he simply takes the £5,000 worth from his hoard, and *passes them* on in payment as he would so much cash, replacing the amount and recompleting his £10,000 worth of hoarded capital, at the *two* Month's end.—The result will of course be the same, in the case where, instead of his having the £5,000 of his own, a man meets with a *friend*, who is content to supply him with it on those same terms.

2. Next let the stock of money in circulation be swelling to *excess*: that is increasing at such a rate, as, were it not for the sort of drain afforded by the amphibious nature of this part of the mass *would be* productive of that inconvenience.

Now then, as the quantity of money, existing in *all* hands taken together swells, so does that *part* which is in the hands of those who are *laying up money*, i.e. for the purpose of deriving income from it, without bestowing their labour on the *management* of the fund, whether in the way of trade or otherwise. In this case in proportion as a man betakes himself to what is called *laying up money*, instead of *laying it out* in the way of his trade, (which *deprives* him of the interest) he *keeps it in hand* for the *sake* of the interest; which now comes in lieu of *profit* on Stock, and *pro tanto* constitutes his income. But so much of the mass of money as is thus *kept up* is, for *so long* as it *continues* to be so kept up, withdrawn from the aggregate amount of the mass of money in *circulation*.

At *present*, Government Annuities are said to be *"converted"* into ready money—and *vice versâ:* but at present the *conversion* is true in a *figurative* sense only; and in *each* instance the operation is liable to be attended with a *loss*: in the *proposed* state of the Government Annuities the conversion is *literally* true in both instances, and is *not* exposed to *loss* in *either* case.

The same *double function* is performed by *Exchequer Bills,* tho' with inferior advantage: *large,* even in their smallest sizes, they are incapable of serving for dealings on any but the largest scale: *limited* in their *duration,* they are incapable of securing a permanent mass of income: limited in their aggregate *amount,* they are incapable of carrying this species of accommodation to the *extent* in which it may sometimes be required.

For *illustration,* it was necessary to suppose—in the one case the *deficiency,* in the other the *excess,* already in *existence.* But the same cause which, according to that *supposition,* would operate as a corrective, would *in fact* operate as a *preventive*[1]: deficiency, and excess, would respectively be corrected, each in its *nascent* state: as they doubtless are already in a certain degree by *Exchequer Bills,* especially under the late encreased amount of that part of the floating Debt.

In the present state of things each one of the opposite evils receives, sooner or later, a remedy of the *corrective* kind. But *how*?—always by the operation of some *new* force: in case of *deficiency,* by a quantity of *fresh matter* of some kind or other, added to the *pre-existing* mass: as by the increased issues of Bank Notes; and, before that, by the increased amount of *Bills of exchange,* substituted (as according to Mr Henry Thornton's Evidence) to the *Cash notes* drawn out of the circulation, by the distrust that took place, at different periods, in regard to the paper of the Country Banks. In the *proposed* state of things, the correction[2] would take place *of itself,* without the aid of human reason, and without the application of any *new* force: In the *present* state of things, the evil *continues,* till the corrective[3] is applied: and how soon, if at all, it shall have been applied, and have produced a cure, depends upon a variety of contingencies: in the

[1][Bowring's text, *Works* X, 368, reads "promotive"—a particularly flagrant error.]
[2][Bowring's text reads "corrective".]
[3][Bowring's text reads "correction".]

proposed state of things, all *delays* and *uncertainties* are wiped away. In the present state of things, in the case of *deficiency,* during the operation as well as before the application, of the remedy, the price of Government Annuities, and other *sources of permanent income* remains more or less in a state of *depression;* and great *losses* are thus experienced: in the *proposed* state of things, this source of loss is absolutely dried up.

Objection 2d.—"*Any*[1] *subdivision of the Unit or Standard Note would be unadvisable: for any interest note is ill calculated to supply the place of metallic money in small payments as the variation of value would render it perplexing and unintelligible to the common people and expose them to imposition, notwithstanding any contrivance of Tables &c.*"

Answer. This seems to suppose—that the notes, of magnitudes inferior to the proposed standard note, are proposed all or a great part of them to be poured in at *once.* But (by Art. 10 & 11) this supposition is *expressly negatived. Two,* or at most *three* magnitudes are proposed to be issued by way of experiment: If *two* be deemed too many, then let the experiment be confined to *one.* Setting aside possible *speculation,* the paper will be taken out in the first instance by the owners of *petty hoards,* (as per Ch. 4 &c) for the sake of obtaining an *interest* for sums on which at present *no interest* is (as per Do) obtainable, on terms of any thing like equal *security* and *convenience.* Taking them then *one magnitude at a time,* I do not see how they are more liable to "*expose the common people to imposition*" than *Bank notes* are. A man who *cannot* read is liable to take a £1 note for a £2 note. Even a man who *can* read is exposed to a danger much more difficult to obviate—the danger of taking a £2 note or £5 note. of a hollow or tottering *Country* Bank, for a Do of the *Bank of England.* The man who can *not* read applies in such cases to some such person as the Country Shop-keeper or Ale-house keeper, whom he deals with. Such a person is seldom without a whole-sheet *Almanac* behind his door; which Almanac is never without *Tables,* is I should say itself composed of Tables—of a more complex nature than that proposed. If in a proposed note a man reads the *day of the month* wrong, or the *sum opposite* it wrong (all the error the Table is exposed to) the utmost of the loss is a *minute* sum on the score of *daily interest.* If a man receives a bad *one pound note* or a bad *Guinea,* the loss goes to the *whole.*

[1] [Bowring's text reads "My".]

TAB

FORM OF A PROPOSED ANNUITY NOTE (1) ON THE SI

BACK OF THE NOTE ON THE YEARLY PLAN.

By Statute Geo. III. c. , counterfeiting the Portrait of any Public Officer on an Annuity Note is Forgery. The having in one's possession, without special licence, any Drawing or Plate, &c. designed to represent such Head, is presumptive evidence of such Forgery: Punishment Death. (23) Like provision in respect of the counterfeiting this type. (24)

PORTRAIT

FROM AN ENGRAVING ON WOOD:

THE AUDITOR

OF THE

EXCHEQUER,

WITH THE

EPIGRAPH. (22)

I. *Daily Interest or Augmentation Table:* (25)

Shewing the Value of this Note for every Day in the Year, as the same is encreased by the addition of daily Interest. No Interest for the last day of any Year: (26) Nor for the 29th of February in a Leap Year: (27) Nor for the day on which the Note is passed. (28)

Day.	Value.	Day.	Value.	Day.	Value.	Day.	Value.
Jan. 8	£12 16 2	Apr. 14	£12 18 2	July 19	£13 0 2	Oct. 23	£13 2 2
16	12 16 4	22	12 18 4	27	13 0 4	31	13 2 4
24	12 16 6	30	12 18 6	Aug. 4	13 0 6	Nov. 8	13 2 6
Feb. 1	12 16 8	May 8	12 18 8	12	13 0 8	16	13 2 8
9	12 16 10	16	12 18 10	20	13 0 10	24	13 2 10
17	12 17 0	24	12 19 0	28	13 1 0	Dec. 2	13 3 0
25	12 17 2	June 1	12 19 2	Sept. 5	13 1 2	10	13 3 2
Mar 5	12 17 4	9	12 19 4	13	13 1 4	18	13 3 4
13	12 17 6	17	12 19 6	21	13 1 6	26	13 3 6
21	12 17 8	25	12 19 8	29	13 1 8	30	13 3 7
29	12 17 10	July 3	12 19 10	Oct. 7	13 1 10		
April 6	12 18 0	11	13 0 0	15	13 2 0		

II. Underneath is the *Register of Yearly Payments of Interest*. (29) In which are set down the several Years of our Lord (if any) for which Interest upon this Note has been paid by the Government:—

If upon the face of the above Register, the Interest on this Note, for any number of Years, appears to remain unpaid, to find the total value of it, add to its value for the Day, according to the above Table, the amount of the Interest for the aforesaid number of unpaid years, according to the following

III. *Yearly Interest or Augmentation Table.* (30)

Years.	Interest to add.	Years.	Interest to add.	Years.	Interest to add.	Years.	Interest to add.
1801	£0 7 7	1810	£3 15 10	1819	£7 4 1	1828	£10 12 4
—02	0 15 2	—11	4 3 5	—20	7 11 8	—29	10 19 11
—03	1 2 9	—12	4 11 0	—21	7 19 3	—30	11 7 6
—04	1 10 4	—13	4 18 7	—22	8 6 10	—31	11 15 1
—05	1 17 11	—14	5 6 2	—23	8 14 5	—32	12 2 8
—06	2 5 6	—15	5 13 9	—24	9 2 0	—33	12 10 3
—07	2 13 1	—16	6 1 4	—25	9 9 7	—34	12 17 10
—08	3 0 8	—17	6 8 11	—26	9 17 2		
—09	3 8 3	—18	6 16 6	—27	10 4 9		

FACE OF THE NOTE, NEAR

N° ______ (2) Price and Value, besides Interest, £12 : 16 : 0.	Daily Interest, One Farthing.	Yearly Interes £0 : 7 :

This Note, price and value *Twelve po* the Bearer (3) to a Farthing per day, from t solidated Fund; but subject to redemptio

The above interest is paid half-yearly; (ceived any time not earlier than (5) ( ) d the medium of any Local Annuity Note Of having been made at the same Office not les days before such last day, and such *conditi* Office.

The Fee to be paid at the Office on the pu on exchanging the same for a fresh Note, (

Issued at the General Annuity Note Office in St. Margaret's Street, Westminster, this ______ day of ______ 18 by order of me ______

______ Auditor (11) of his Majesty's Exchequer (12); and by the hands of me ______

______ Issuing Clerk. (13)

POR

FROM AN ENG

KING (

WI

EPI

O

SCE

" FOR SECU

FORG

N° ______

By Statute Geo. III. c. the faith o conveying a perpetual redeemable annuity price as to give a *higher* rate of *interest* th Annuity Note shall ever be *paid off* witho able stock annuities continue unredeemed

For security, in cases of *trust*, *conveya* may be separated from the body (20) by cutti of the uses and purposes of such division (21

By Statute Geo. III. c. *counterfeit* an Annuity Note is Forgery; the having in drawing or plate, &c. designed to represen forgery, — punishment Death. (23) Like type. (24)

LE II.

EVERAL PLANS OF HALF-YEARLY AND YEARLY INTEREST

LY THE SAME ON BOTH PLANS.

, t, 7.	Rate of Interest, 3 per Cent nearly.	Interest commences from 1st January A. D. 18 .	Issued to the Purchaser, A. D. 18 .

unds sixteen shillings, besides interest, entitles the first of January last for ever, out of the Con-n, on payment of the above sum, with interest.

(4) and the interest of each half year may be re-lays after the last day of such half year, through ffice (6) in town or country; previous application s than (7) (   ) days, nor more than (8) (   ) *ons* being observed as may be seen at every such

irchase of this Note, is (   ), (9) and no more; (   ). (10)

****

TRAIT

RAVING ON COPPER:

THE

CROWNED,

ITH AN

GRAPH

N THE

EPTRE,

URITY AGAINST

ERY." (14)

*********** (15)

Issued at my Local Annuity Note Office in ______ (16)

____

this __________ day

of ____________

One thousand eight hundred and ______ (17)

by me __________

____

____

Office-Keeper. (18)

____

f Parliament is pledged, that no Annuity Note, payable to bearer, shall ever be issued at such an is given by this Note; (19) and that no such ut the consent of the holder, while any redeem-

ance by post, &c., the *head-piece* of this Note ng it across through the *waved line*. An account) may be seen at the said several Offices.

ing, &c., the portrait of any public officer on n one's possession, without special licence, any it such head, is presumptive evidence of such provision in respect of the counterfeiting this

BACK OF THE NOTE ON THE HALF-YEARLY PLAN.

1. *Daily Interest* or

Shewing the Value of this Note for every Day in the Year, as the same is encreased by the addition of Daily Interest.

****

PORTRAIT

FROM AN ENGRAVING ON WOOD:

THE AUDITOR

OF THE

EXCHEQUER,

WITH THE

EPIGRAPH. (22)

****

Augmentation Table: (25)

No Interest for the last Day of any Year: (26) nor for the 29th of February in a Leap Year: (27) nor for the Day on which the Note is passed. (28)

First Half Year.		Second Half Year.		
		If the first be unpaid		If first be paid
Day.	Value.	Day.	Value.	Value.
Jan. 8	£12 16 2	July 3	£12 19 10	£12 16 0½
16	12 16 4	11	13 0 0	12 16 2½
24	12 16 6	19	13 0 2	12 16 4½
Feb. 1	12 16 8	27	13 0 4	12 16 6½
9	12 16 10	Aug. 4	13 0 6	12 16 8½
17	12 17 0	12	13 0 8	12 16 10½
25	12 17 2	20	13 0 10	12 17 0½
Mar. 5	12 17 4	28	13 1 0	12 17 2½
13	12 17 6	Sep. 5	13 1 2	12 17 4½
21	12 17 8	13	13 1 4	12 17 6½
29	12 17 10	21	13 1 6	12 17 8½
Apr. 6	12 18 0	29	13 1 8	12 17 10½
14	12 18 2	Oct. 7	13 1 10	12 18 0½
22	12 18 4	15	13 2 0	12 18 2½
30	12 18 6	23	13 2 2	12 18 4½
May 8	12 18 8	31	13 2 4	12 18 6½
16	12 18 10	Nov. 8	13 2 6	12 18 8½
24	12 19 0	16	13 2 8	12 18 10½
June 1	12 19 2	24	13 2 10	12 19 0½
9	12 19 4	Dec. 2	13 3 0	12 19 2½
17	12 19 6	10	13 3 2	12 19 4½
25	12 19 8	18	13 3 4	12 19 6½
July 1	12 19 9½	26	13 3 6	12 19 8½
		30	13 3 7	12 19 9½

II. *Register of Half-Yearly Payments of Interest*: (29)

In which are set down the several Years and Half-Years of our Lord (if any) for which Interest upon this Note has been paid by Government.

N.B.—The Figures 1 and 2 distinguish the First and Second Half-Years of each year.

1	2	1	2
2	1	2	1
1	2	1	2
2	1	2	1
1	2	1	2
2	1	2	1
1	2	1	2
2	1	2	1
1	2	1	2
2	1	2	1
1	2	1	2
2	1	2	1
1	2	1	2
2	1	2	1
1	2	1	2

III. If, upon the face of the above Register, the Interest on this Note, for any number of Half-years, appears to remain unpaid, to find the total value of it, add to its value for the Day, according to the above Table, the amount of the Interest for the aforesaid number of unpaid Half-years, according to the following

Half-Yearly Interest or Augmentation Table: (30)

Years.		Interest to add.	Years.		Interest to add.	Years.		Interest to add.	Years.		Interest to add.
1801	1	£0 3 9½	1809	2	3 8 3	1818	1	6 12 8½	1826	2	9 17 2
	2	0 7 7	1810	1	3 12 0½		2	6 16 6	1827	1	10 1 11½
1802	1	0 11 4½		2	3 15 10	1819	1	7 0 3½		2	10 4 9
	2	0 15 2	1811	1	3 19 7½		2	7 4 1	1828	1	10 8 6½
1803	1	0 18 11½		2	4 3 5	1820	1	7 7 10½		2	10 12 4
	2	1 2 9	1812	1	4 7 2½		2	7 11 8	1829	1	10 16 1½
1804	1	1 6 6½		2	4 11 0	1821	1	7 15 5½		2	10 19 11
	2	1 10 4	1813	1	4 14 9½		2	7 19 3	1830	1	11 3 8½
1805	1	1 14 1½		2	4 18 7	1822	1	8 3 0½		2	11 7 6
	2	1 17 11	1814	1	5 2 4½		2	8 6 10	1831	1	11 11 3½
1806	1	2 1 8½		2	5 6 2	1823	1	8 10 7½		2	11 15 1
	2	2 5 6	1815	1	5 9 11½		2	8 14 5	1832	1	11 18 10½
1807	1	2 9 3½		2	5 13 9	1824	1	8 18 2½		2	12 2 8
	2	2 13 1	1816	1	5 17 6½		2	9 2 0	1833	1	12 6 5½
1808	1	2 16 10½		2	6 1 4	1825	1	9 5 9½		2	12 10 3
	2	3 0 8	1817	1	6 5 1½		2	9 9 7	1834	1	12 14 0½
1809	1	3 4 5½		2	6 8 11	1826	1	9 13 4½		2	12 17 10

To the columns of which an almanac is composed at present (one for the day of the week another for the day of the month) a natural *addition*—in case of the emission of the proposed paper—would be—a *column* indicative of the *interest* due, on each day, on an Annuity Note.—Will it be seriously contended, that the additional column will be *unintelligible* to those by whom the original ones were *understood*?—As to this point, see further in the answer to the *next* objection.

Objection 3^{d}. "*It would be very difficult at any Office to make an actual payment of interest on the small notes on account of their dispersion and multiplicity.*"—

Answer. This objection, like the preceding one, seems to turn, in part at least, on the supposition of the *suddenness* of the introduction, instead of the *graduality* expressly recommended. So much as to "*multiplicity*". As to "*dispersion*", *that* is provided for by the dispersion of the *Offices*, at which it is proposed that the *sale* of the Notes, and *payment* of the interest, shall be made: viz: the *existing* Post Offices. The plan of payment is delineated in the Note to Articles 13, 14 and 15: which I am inclined to think had not yet met your eye: since, if it had, it would rather have been expressly *referred* to as insufficient, than passed by without reference.

In a word—wherever *preponderating inconvenience* presents itself, there of course will *extension* stop. The proposed paper is not proposed to be *forced* into the market, like Exchequer Bills &c &c: It will only be issued in proportion as it is *demanded;* and it will only be demanded in proportion as *all inconveniences* attending it are found by *experience* to be *outweighed* by the *convenience*. The dilemma seems impregnable: if inconvenience, no demand; if demand, no inconvenience.

I call every commodity *forced*, of which the quantity offered to sale is proportioned—not to the *demand* and *pleasure* of the *purchaser*, but to the *exigency* of the *seller*. All known Government Annuities and other Government engagements (securities for money payable *in future*) being of the *forced* kind, the mind has (I am sensible) no easy task in squaring itself to the conception of a *new* species, which, being *not* of the forced kind, is in its nature so essentially different from whatever else we have been used to see under the same name.

Applied indeed to the *small* notes the *objection* is a perfectly rational one and *prima facie* a conclusive one: especially if *all* the different magnitudes of the small Notes are taken into the account.

But the *answer* is such, as (I cannot but flatter myself) will be found ultimately conclusive on the other side. It is *referred* to, tho' not *given* (for every thing could not be given at once) in Note 14, to Article 16. Supposing the small notes established in the circulation (casual *whims* apart, which as such can be but rare) a man will never apply for interest at the *Offices*, because (as in the case of Exchequer Bills) in proportion as he circulates his notes, the interest will be allowed him in the circulation. It is contrary to the nature of *man* and *things*, that a man should take the *more* troublesome course for what he can obtain by one *less* troublesome.

Observations by Sir Frederick Morton Eden, (in form of a letter) on the Annuity Note Plan, as contained in the three first printed sheets with the two tables: with counter-observations by the author of the plan

1801

Contents

§ 1. OBSERVATIONS.

"Your ingenious correspondent's new currency, though, meant like *Shylock's* money, '*to breed as fast as ewes and lambs*', I fear would not answer *any* of the ends proposed by it, sufficiently to justify so *novel* an experiment in finance, as the issuing a *large* circulating mass of paper, representing capital as well as interest."

COUNTER-OBSERVATIONS.

These "ewes and lambs", foreign as they may appear to be to the subject, are not altogether without their use. Innocent as they are, they have betrayed at the very outset, the temper that brought them on the carpet, and the views and apprehensions, by which that temper was produced.

> "Ah silly I! more silly than my sheep,
> "Which on my flowery plains I once did keep!" . . .

Such is the couplet, which, to a man of the learned Critick's memory, might have served as a warning, not to introduce poetry (and such poetry!) into a grave and important question of finance.

For the mode in which the *Review* of a plan is conducted, the plan *itself* is certainly neither better nor worse. Features, such as the above, being so many irrelevancies in the Review, notices taken of them in a reply to it, may appear open to the same charge. So they unquestionably would, were direct *reason*—fair and naked reason the only force by which, in giving judgment on a proposed plan, the human mind was accustomed to be influenced. But such insensibility to all grounds of general presumption and other collateral considerations, neither is—nor, in the nature of men and things ever can be perfectly exemplified. *Authority* is a ground of decision, to which no man can altogether refuse to allow a certain degree of weight, however competent he may be, or appear to himself to be, in point of leisure, faculties, and all other requisites, to determine the question upon its own naked merits. In the present instance, this power presents itself as being alike adverse in its direction, and formidable in its force. It becomes proportionably necessary, to endeavour to take off whatever can be, and ought to be, taken off from that force: and, in this view, to point to the symptoms by which it appears, that the *understanding* thus occupied, is not in that state, in which, on other occasions, it would be found to be—unclouded unruffled free to follow the path of reason wherever it shews itself, but turned aside by a sinister bias, corrupted by subjection to the *will* itself, under the dominion of hostile passions, excited by personal apprehensions.

A clue of this sort, may afford a species of satisfaction, such as might not otherwise be obtainable:—a solution of a heap of inconsistencies, such as might otherwise appear inexplicable.—A professed experienced Reviewer, keeping his eyes shut throughout against the work that lies before him, or opening them but to spy out some difficulty, which after gleaning it from the work itself, he exhibits as a discovery of his own, taking care to say nothing of the solution that stands beside it*—a mind stored with real and extensive knowledge. reduced on the sudden (for so we shall find his at the very first step) to a state of profound and matchless ignorance:† a memory on other occasions so tenacious, bereft on a sudden, as it were, of all its powers:‡ a Judge, at the very moment of being consulted as such, descending to the station of an adversary, and of an adversary using poisoned weapons:||—a discernment, on other occasions so acute, heaping on the same object, contradictory imputations in the same breath:¶ A projector clinging with that fondness, which it is so natural for such parents to feel, to his ideal offspring, yet so blind in his fondness as to run this his own offspring through and through, in running amock at another's, which does not receive from him so much as a scratch:** these, together with others, that might perhaps have been adduced, are incongruities such as could not otherwise be accounted for, but of which the causes above indicated, will afford an explication but too natural, and in the course of human life, too frequently perceptible.

What then is the inference from all this preface? that because the review is bad—(supposing it to be so)—the plan reviewed must be a good one?—By no means. What the object of it?—to turn aside the eye that is to judge from the question proper for its cognizance? Nor that neither. What is aimed at—what is asked for—is simply this: that all collateral and irrelevant considerations may be dis-

*§ 8, § 9, §12, § 13, § 15, § 17.
†§ 1, see ‡.
‡§ 3, § 10, § 11, § 13.
||§ 1, § 6, § 21, § 23.
¶§ 1, § 7.
**§ 1, § 3, § 7.

carded on *both* sides—that the *review* may be attended to, in exact proportion to whatever it may be found to contain of *real* argument, and the *plan* thus reviewed be judged of by its own merits.

The word *"novel"*—*novel* applied in preference to new, is another symptomatic word—*novel* a sort of conjugate of *innovation*. Employing, and at this early stage. instead of words of impartial and undelusive import, one of those words (a tribe unhappily for the interests of truth and reason but too numerous) that are used only in what is called *a bad sense* (i.e. such as are never brought upon the carpet but on account of their bringing with them, as an inseparable concomitant, the idea of *disapprobation*)—plying the mind of the reader with such delusions, and thus seizing, as it were, upon his hand, to employ it, whether he will or no, in inflicting censure upon the subject to which the opprobrious attribute is applied—this is among those arts of verbal warfare, which may be termed *fighting with poisoned weapons*. To try our Reviewer, whether guilty or innocent of this charge, let us take a hint from *Solomon*, and make an experiment upon the paternal nerves. Reserving the neutral epithet, *new*, for the Annuity-Note plan thus assailed, let us apply the term *novel*, to what has been termed in a strain of congenial criticism *"The Portentous Globe"*: and, in the same strain, calling the former, simply a *novelty*, let us call the latter, an *innovation*. Will the paternal feelings consent to such a change?

If *words* like these are to pass for argument, behold an answer to it, an answer to it in kind—what? is he raising a hue and cry then against *novelty*?—There's a man for you!—a libeller of establishments!—of all establishments in the lump, past, present, and to come! For (as has been said, and not untruly said, by somebody): *whatever is now establishment, once was innovation*.

But—*novelty* or *innovation*—call it which he will—where is it to be found?—In the proposed experiment, according to *his* description of it, there is not a grain of novelty. *"Circulating masses"*—yes and *"large"* ones—*"representing capital as well as interest"*—exist *now* and have existed for ages—exist not *here* only, but *elsewhere*. What are *Exchequer Bills*? What are *India Bonds*? What are *Irish Debentures*? What *have been Navy Bills, Victualling Bills, Transport Bills*, and *Ordnance Debentures*? I will not here insist on any *Foreign* interest-bearing paper, such as *Dutch Obligations*, and *Austrian Government paper*: those (with others about which my enquiries have not yet been so successfull as I could have wished), exist not, it is true, in a shape precisely the same, as that which is here given as a supposed improvement upon every thing of the kind that has been before it: (if they did it would be no improvement) but they do not the less exist, and so exist, as to constitute, each of them *"a large mass of paper, circulating"*, with a degree of facility and rapidity governed necessarily by their bulk, and (to use the learned Baronet's own words) *"representing capital as well as interest"*.

In repelling thus the imputation of *novelty,* I must of course be understood to confine the vindication to that particular feature on which the imputation has thus been fixed. For, if no point of view could be found, in which the plan would bear the appellation of *new,* what would there be in it to propose?

An entire Chapter* of the Plan is employed, in shewing what features the proposed engagement has, *in common* with the several sorts of pecuniary engagements, the several securities, already known —and what other features are *peculiar* to it: *Eight* are reckoned up of those *common,* and *twelve* of those peculiar *features.* Among those, which, being thus *common,* are *not new,* is that of the *"principal's not being demandable"*; viz. at any certain time: the instances there given (besides *Stock* Annuities, which are not in *paper*) are *"Irish Debentures, India Bonds"*: also the lately disused *"Navy, Victualling,* and *Transport Bills* and *Ordnance Debentures"*: all of these "masses of paper" (in the learned Baronet's language) *"representing Capital as well as interest". Exchequer Bills* constitute another instance, that meets his eye in several places of the *same* Chapter. With such an indication (if he would have vouchsafed to look at it)—with such a refutation before him, it is—that he speaks of this as a *novel* feature.

Misunderstanding the plan—misunderstanding every thing else that touches upon it—misconceiving the whole subject thus compleatly and staunchly from the first, of what complexion will be the *further* views he gives of it?—we shall see as we advance.

But perhaps his reply might be that, though, of the masses of paper above exemplified, it *is* true that they *"represent capital as well as interest"*, yet it is *not* true, that they *"circulate"*: for something of this nature is actually insinuated (though in other words), in a passage we shall see. That, among the tribes which, in another passage,† he speaks of with a view to wear and tear—*"market women, turnpike*

*Chap. III.

†§ 14.

keepers, and publicans"—masses of paper like these do *not* circulate, is true enough. But, by the same argument, it might be proved that the existing paper of the Bank of England does not circulate: I would venture to offer him a £100 Exchequer Bill, or India Bond, at his choice, for every £100 Bank Note he finds *circulating* in such hands. When the Bank of England, in virtue of an Act of Parliament, receives a parcel of Exchequer Bills, what is it that, in appropriate language, it is said to do with them but "circulate" them? *Quickly* indeed, masses such as these cannot be expected to circulate; at least every where: though, in the great game played almost every day at the Exchequer, he will find the *Bills* changing hands not less quickly than the *Notes*: as between monies, and monies of different values, *velocity*—quickness of circulation—(as Adam Smith[1] has so well observed) is inversely as their magnitude. The Hour-hand in a *watch*, does not circulate so quickly as the *Second-hand,* nor yet as the *minute* hand: but, slow as the circulation of the hour-hand is, does any body ever say on this account, that it does *not* circulate? But of this further in its place.*

Another feature here impliedly ascribed to it—ascribed to it by the epithet *"large"*—is a feature which does *not* belong to it, and which is so far from belonging to it, that the *exemption* from this very feature is among the characteristic properties, and (as supposed) advantages, of which its essence is composed: among the properties ascribed to it as *new,* as well as among the properties relied upon as *advantageous.* Most, if not all, other species of paper money as yet known, may *really* be in large masses: i.e. in masses that are *too* large, for it is only for the purpose of suggesting the idea of *excess,* that the word *"large"* can have been introduced. Why *too* large?—because it is by the exigencies of Government that issues them, that the quantity of the mass thrown into the market is determined: thence the *glut*—the *depretiation*—the *excess.* In the case of the *proposed* paper, the quantity is determined—determined from *first* to *last*—by the number of purchasers that *call* for it at a *fixed price.* If a hundred millions worth of it should be *called for,* a hundred millions worth of it certainly would exist: but the mass of engagements, resting on the shoulders of government, is not the *greater* in proportion to that amount, but the *less*: viz. by the difference between the *lower* rate of interest it *gives,* and the *higher* it

[1][*Wealth of Nations,* bk II, ch. II.]

*§ 9.

supersedes. In what respect then is the *proposed* mass of engagements more liable to *excess* than the *existing* ones? the existing ones which it cannot be *added to,* without *diminishing their* amount? For this plainest of all reasons it is—(though, as will be seen, not for this reason alone)[1]—that the larger it is the better, and it is impossible it can be too large.

Here however the objection is—(for though not brought forward it is announced) the objection is—that it, the mass of paper, will be *too large.* Wait till the next sentence—the very *next* sentence—and what is *now too large* becomes *too small*: *"not great enough to be an object of finance"*.

§2. OBSERVATIONS CONTINUED.

"Of the two objects proposed by the scheme, viz. to render that mass of money, which by existing circumstances is either excluded from yielding interest, or which, by means of Bankers and otherwise, yields a rate of interest, inferior, all things considered, to what Government could allow, and so to furnish a new circulating medium of daily encreasing value, the first (I should apprehend) would only operate in the most numerous and least opulent classes, whose hoards are too small to bear the charge of investing in Stock or other interest yielding security. I should doubt however whether the aggregate of such sums is *great enough to become an object of finance.*"

COUNTER-OBSERVATIONS.

None:—none seem necessary—here at least: but see the next section.

§3. OBSERVATIONS CONTINUED.

"As to the benefit to individuals, it is not probable that the owner of a hoard of £12 16s (the amount of the Author's Standard Note) would feel disposed to *sink* it in the purchase of an Annuity (not equal to 3 days labour) of 7s 7d."

COUNTER-OBSERVATIONS.

This sentence—not a very long one—is yet long enough to contain two fallacies—

[1][Bentham here adds a marginal note: "§ . . . See Plan, Table of Contents", but it is difficult to guess which chapter of the pamphlet he has in mind.]

1. One is—the insinuation thus conveyed, that a sum, to the amount of £12 16s, or any other sum, invested in the way of purchase of one or more Annuity Notes—would be *sunk*: *absolutely sunk*. As to this point it is stated among the advantages possessed by the proposed paper, that, in every particle of it, it will, at all times, be alike susceptible of being *kept* in hand, as a source of interest, or *passed* from hand to hand as *money*:* a property by which amongst others it stands distinguished (in my view of the matter to its advantage) from such sources of interest as are in the shape of *Stock* Annuities: a species of property that can in no other sense be *converted* into money, than in the same *improper* sense, in which *land* and *houses* can be converted into money—viz. by being *sold*, and so made over in *exchange* for it. The learned Baronet, for the convenience of the argument, divides in his imagination the mass into two distinct and uncommunicating masses—the one, good for *hoarding*, if for any thing[,] and nothing else, the other, good for *circulating*, if for any thing, and nothing else. That, of the mass designed for circulation, there may be *some* part susceptible of circulating, he does not absolutely deny, provided it be but a *small* one. At the same time, let it not be altogether forgotten, that although, for argument sake, this aggregate should fail of being sufficient, *of itself*, to become an object of finance, it will not follow but that it may be raised to that amount (whatever it be) when *another* aggregate, especially if to an *equal* or *greater* amount, comes to be *added* to it. Such *another* aggregate (the demand created by persons seeking profitable employment without trouble or risk, for temporary sums *below* £100, and even in *some* cases *above* that mark) is pointed out and enlarged upon in the pages against which our Critic so resolutely shuts his eyes.†

In an interesting pamphlet, for which, perhaps the Globe, and at any rate the world, is recently indebted to the learned Baronet,[1] individuals, participating in the benefit which it is the object of Friendly Societies to administer—*these individuals*, to the number of 2,592,000, according to his calculation (not forgetting their *funds*) stand forth as an object, which has not appeared unworthy, either of his attention or his care: and, from the causes pointed out in some papers from which the learned Baronet (certainly not without reference, nor altogether without addition) did not disdain to borrow, even

*Ch. IV.

†Plan Ch. IV.

[1][Observations on Friendly Societies, London 1801.]

this number may appear scarcely superior to the number, which, by one untoward circumstance or another, are precluded from entering into associations upon such principles; though not excluded from participating in those rewards, which, by apposite institutions, might be held out, to the virtues of *industry* and *frugality*, when united in the breasts of unassociated heads of families or other individuals.

But if the *whole* of the mass—be it *great* or *small*—be "in *every part of it*" alike susceptible (as it really would be) of *circulation*, then whatever part may have been employed *"in the purchase of an Annuity"* (i.e. of *Interest;* so long as *Interest* was the thing wanted) *would* be susceptible of being put in circulation, in the shape of principal money; and *that*, at whatever time, should any such time arrive, at which *principal*, at the expence of *further* interest, came to be the thing wanted: of which mass, consequently, not *any* part would be *sunk*.

In what conceivable state of things would the supposition so lightly made be realized? If there were but *one* Annuity Note taken out, certainly: *not certainly*, if there were *two* Annuity Notes, taken out, at different times, by so many different individuals. If A° 1803, a whimsical man (whom we will call A) took a fancy to become possessor of an Annuity Note (say a Standard Note, price £12 16s) and took one out accordingly, nobody else ever taking out another,—*then* indeed would there be *hoarding without circulation*—and consequently there would be *"sinking"*: but if, in the year 1804—the same day of the same month happened to produce *another* whimsical man —an acquaintance of A's (whom we will call B), at the same time that A, being tired of his bargain, or wanting to spend the money, took a fancy to *part* with his note, then would the *same* piece of paper, which at *one* time was *hoarded*, be at *another* time *circulated;* in which case the money, employed in the original purchase of it, would *not* be *"sunk"*.

Thus would the matter stand, if the mass of notes taken out—whether with a view to hoarding, or to circulation, or to both—by *one* set of *individuals*—depended, for its actually getting into circulation—(so much of it as within a given period came to be brought to market for that purpose)—upon the *contingency*, of its meeting with *another* set of *individuals*, ready to accept of it with the same views. On this supposition, true it is, there *would* have been room for contingency to operate. But, by Art. 14 (if that article be allowed to stand as part of the plan) all *contingency* is at an end. The *Exchequer* with its branches, the subordinate local offices of receipt, spread over the whole Kingdom—afford a market at everybody's door—constantly open—and bound to receive this commodity—in whatever quantity it can be offered to them—and at market price. Where *now* is the money, which, to the imagination of the learned Baronet presented itself as "sunk"? What *could* be sunk, by such artillery as the learned Baronet's, is indeed sunk—viz. the mention of that article:—but nothing else is sunk, unless it be the *time* employed in counter-discussing such "discussions".

All this while, here am I (I confess it with regret) confounding the order fixed upon and announced by the learned Baronet. But why?—because he has so ingeniously, and compeatly, confounded it *himself*. First head of argument—probability and utility of getting the proposed paper *out* in the way of *issue*: second head of argument—probability and utility of getting it *on* in the way of *circulation*. Circulate, (according to him) it will *not*: moneys employed in the purchase of it will be *"sunk"*. Such is the proposition, set down for *argument* in his *second division*: but, in the mean time, *to be doing*, he *takes it for granted*, in the *first*.

2. The other fallacy consists in the holding up, as an object of scorn on account of its minuteness, the rate of interest proposed to be given upon this paper: *"an Annuity of 7s 7d, not equal to three days' labour."*

What is a man to make of such an argument? Of so many things—any one of which should have been enough to keep him of all men from making use of it—what is it that the learned Baronet does not forget?—what is it that he remembers? Does he remember *the rule of three*? Will he tell you, that the *ratio* of one to thirty three is *less* in *small* sums than in *large*? Does he remember, that it is possible out of a *number* of small sums to make a *large* one? out of a *proportionable* number to make one of *any* size? Does he remember, that there are such people in the world as the *poor*? Does he remember that there are *more* of them than of the *rich*? Let him look round among his acquaintance, and, for every man whom he finds *looking down* on so petty a profit, as an object not worth stooping for—a profit not worth earning by a twelvemonth's self-denial—for every such disdainful estimator—I will find him—I fear to say how many—who, *at present* at least—and untill, by some such mode of encouragement as we both of us join in recognizing the utility of, the habit of frugality shall have become extensively diffused and deeply rooted—

would *look up* to it, with hopeless regret, as a blessing above their reach. Does he remember what he himself is saying at the same time? Does he remember, that this profit, so *unacceptable*—so contemptible—is inferior, by no more than one sixtieth to what he himself, in his magnificence, allows to the *same people* on the *same score*? —nor that, but upon condition of *his* having the principal to sport with for six months; to be lent to, and employed all that time by, *any* body, *but* the poor man whose property it is, and who, having contrived to spare it in *one* state of things, may find himself in want of it in *another*.

In the case of *some* men, a want of sensibility to such microscopic objects, would be a sort of failing, at once natural and pardonable. That, to a man who handles the *public* money by millions and *his* own by thousands—that to a man (situated for example like the gentleman I found with you t'other day) the interest, of any thing less than an Exchequer Bill, should be an object as impalpable, as a double Moidore was to the hands of the great company, into which *Gulliver* in one of his Voyages found himself introduced—is altogether in the order of things: to an eye seated on so *peculiar* an *eminence*, the wonder is not great, if objects thus minute should, (at least when a man is taken by surprize, and without the benefit of effort and preparation) be invisible. An oversight of this kind has the same claim to indulgence as that of a late Minister, who, in a discussion with certain *sugar-bakers*, observing, with great truth, that no sugar, other than *trible-refined* made its appearance at any of the tables he was in the habit of sitting down to, could with difficulty bring himself to credit the existence, of any article of the same generic denomination, and of inferior purity. But that Sir Frederick Eden!—that a gentleman who has earnt such great and well merited celebrity by his attention to the poor! to *every thing* that characterizes their humble lot!—that Sir Frederick Eden!—the *historiographer*—the *teller*—the *caterer*—the *patron*—the *advocate*—and (if God and the Crown Lawyers permitt) the *Treasurer* and *Banker* of the Poor!—that *such* a man should thus forget *every thing about the poor—means—exigencies—numbers—proportions—every thing*—forget, for the purpose of the argument, and such an argument!—forgetfulness like this is absolutely past indurance! No: this advocate of the poor—this self-chosen—and not unretain'd advocate—shall not be permitted, thus to put off his sympathy with his robes.

§4. OBSERVATIONS CONTINUED.

"Perpetual Annuities may suit great capitalists: but they seem to be ill-calculated for furnishing an investment for the earnings of the lower classes:—"

COUNTER-OBSERVATIONS.

This proposition, being of the oracular cast, is, like other oracles, scarce worth hunting, through its possible meanings. Unapplied, it amounts to nothing: applied, it involves the same mistake that went *before*: it supposes the money to be *"sunk"*. The plain truth is—*some* exigencies there really are, for which it *is* necessary that capital *should* be sunk:* *others* there are, for which such sinking is *not* necessary.† Where it is *not* necessary, the institution of the proposed paper *would* be an adequate resource: where it *is* necessary, there comes in the necessity of some *further* institution, adapted to the purpose: of the *once* proposed system of *Industry Houses* (for example) in their proposed character of *Frugality Banks;* or the equally diffused system (for such I suppose he would not be sorry it should be) of *his* Frugality Banks, branching off from the General *Globe Insurance Office*: if a *project,* so little noticed as the former, may be mentioned in the same sentence with a *plan*—(with a *plan* I say—for the Baronet shall have his choice of words—the advantages from *good* and *bad senses* shall be all his own) with a *plan,* which, justly or unjustly, has some how or other, met with more notice than was wished.

§5. OBSERVATIONS CONTINUED.

"and of perpetual Annuities, that sort strikes me as the very *worst,* which will require no form of assignment, but what a man may carry about him as cash in his pocket (the *worst* of all *Banks* as Mr Bentham justly observes) and which (supposing these Annuity Notes would pass as money) might be *stolen* in a *crowd, lost* at a *gaming table,* or *spent* at an *alehouse.*"

COUNTER-OBSERVATIONS.

1. As to being *"lost at a gaming table,* or *spent at an alehouse,"*

*Examples taken from *Pauper Management improved*[1]; pp. 167. 168. 169. 189. 1. Superannuation provision.—2. Widow provision (i.e. superannuation provision).

†Examples taken from d°. 1. Failure of employment-provision. 2. Sickness d°. 3. Ostentatious burial d°. 4. Child maintenance d° in some cases. 5. Marriage fund d°.

[1][The reference is to a private reprint of Bentham's contribution to Young's "Annals of Agriculture", vols. 29-31: "Situation and Relief of the Poor".]

can the learned Baronet inform us of *any* species of property—*terra firma* not excepted—which stands *exempted* from such casualties?

2. As to being *"lost in a crowd"*, a principle of security against *that* accident constitutes one of the *express* features, of this *very* proposed species of property, to which the being *exposed* to such accidents is objected as *peculiar* to it.* *Exchequer Bills—India Bonds—Irish Debentures* (if I am rightly informed) are not susceptible of this safeguard. The lately disused Navy Bills *were*, whether by *design* or *accident*: because they could not be transferred, without an instrument of assignment; which instrument was on a separate paper. Bank of England Notes *are*, by *design*, as to those purposes, in respect of which a division *bipartite*, is sufficient to afford it: it was from *that* species of paper the idea was taken.

The security afforded by division, depends upon the precaution taken, to keep the *condivident* parts (to borrow a word from the logicians) in different *places*: either in the same *custody*, or in a *different* custody, according to the nature of the mischance meant to be guarded against. The security will be embraced, or not embraced, according as a man does or does not, look upon it as worth while; which will be according to the value of the Note: understand, to *him* —meaning—not the *absolute* value, but the *relative* value—relation being had to his own circumstances: a distinction which men, in the superior ranks of life, scarce ever bear in mind with sufficient constancy, but on which the effects of money, on the well-being and comfort of the individual, on *every* occasion depend, whether on the *coming in* of the money into his pocket, or the *going out* of it. From Government, the Note holders will receive, the means of affording themselves that security, wherever in their own estimate it is worth receiving, together with a memento to make use of it: which, in the way of safeguard, seems all that can be, or ought to be, done in such a case, for individuals by Government.

In *this* feature of it, the proposed paper, possesses a sort of safeguard, which (not to repeat what has already been said of other species of paper money) is not possessed by metallic money itself.

In the passage referred to by the learned Baronet, I held up the condition of the lower classes in this respect, in a light, which was certainly a *strong* one, and which, in the estimate of the learned Baronet—(of so good a judge as he is when he chooses to act in that

*See Table II Note (24) and see the Note to Ch. XVI Moral Advantages which Mr V. has seen (Quere whether Sir F. E.) in MS.

character) appeared a *just* one. On *that* occasion, I exhibited the *mischief*: on the *present*, it was no small satisfaction that, in the improvement of a useful hint already furnished, I looked upon myself as having found a *remedy*: a remedy, which, if not quite so perfect as could be wished, is at least too promising (I should think) to be despised. The learned Baronet (I conclude) has overlooked the Note which speaks of it: (Table II Note 24) but, after so many marks of such unreserved and *indiscriminate* reprobation, what regret must it not impress upon a generous mind, to find that any feature or passage, of a nature to require an *exception*, had been overlooked!

After the condemnation we have thus seen passed by the learned Baronet on property in general, it may be almost superfluous to turn back, and take notice of the stigma inflicted by him, on *this* or *that particular species* of property,* for the misfortune of possessing a feature of insecurity, *supposed* to be *also* possessed by the obnoxious paper, but which, where a man thinks it worth while, is (as we have seen) capable of being expunged from *this* paper, though not from *those*.

Literally speaking, *they* indeed are not—some of them, at least, are not—*perpetual* Annuities: but, as to the *spirit* of the remark. value being given, what difference does it make whether a species of security be or be not susceptible of that appellative? Not only *Stock* Annuities, but *Irish Debentures, India Bonds;* and even *Exchequer Bills,* are perpetual, till the period of payment comes; and, at that period, the perpetuity, even of *Stock* Annuities. as well as that of the proposed *Note* Annuities, is gone.

As to the dictum thus ascribed to *me*—viz. that *a man's pocket is the worst of all banks*—the idea of a *"Bank"*, and the superlative *"worst"* and the comparison which it supposes—are embellishments, for which it is indebted to the learned Baronet, who refers to it (I suppose) from memory: My words are—*"Pocket the only strong box and that an unsafe one"*.‖ At *that* time, the proposed Annuity Notes, with this their proposed *safeguard,* were offspring of the brain as yet unborn. What I *here* mention them for, is—that, at the next word, if it happened to be before the learned Baronet at the time

*Such as the 26 million of Exchequer Bills;† the I don't know how many million (seven million)‡ of Irish Debentures, the [2 to 3][1] million of India Bonds.

†Commons Accounts, 7 May, 1801, No. VII p. 5.

‡Commons Union Accounts, 2 April, 1800, p. 108.

[1][cf. William Fairman, An Account of the Public Funds, ed. 1824, p. 135.]

‖Paup[er] Manag[ement Improved], B.III. Ch. V. §3. p. 172.

(which I suppose it did not) at the next word, he would have found an observation by which the utility of this safeguard (though then unthought of) may stand exemplified. "2. *Difficulty*" (says the next article) "*of opposing a never-yielding resistance, to the temptations afforded by the instruments of sensual enjoyment, where the means of purchasing them are constantly at hand*".* Among the cases, to which the proposed paper money, with its proposed divisibility, may in this view be applied, is—that of a man's lodging one part of his hoarded note in the custody of some friend, some superior friend, whose opinion he stands in awe of, and looks up to, as a security against hasty and indefensible alienation; under the spur of a "*temptation*" of the nature of those alluded to, as above. A *Mentor* thus appointed, will be a sort of *Upper House,* with a power of putting a *temporary* negative, upon *all* applications of the money, and thereby a *peremptory* negative upon all *such* applications, as the proprietor would be restrained from *avowing* by a sense of salutary shame. If in the *Vestry Room* (for example) of each Parish, a box were to be kept for the reception of such duplicates, under appropriate custody, would there be any incongruity in applying that almost consecrated apartment, to a so truly *pious use*? With one part thus secured against all *unavowable* applications on the part of the *proprietor,* and against *all* applications *without exception,* on the part of every body else, a man ill-provided, or even unprovided, with any receptacles, such as "*strong boxes*" and chests of drawers by which masses of property, in a small compass, may be protected, against *observation* as well as *depredation*, may, with the less danger and solicitude, trust the duplicate, reserved by him for his *own* custody, to such otherwise inadequate means of security as his humble residence may afford.

§6. OBSERVATIONS CONTINUED.

"If this *project for making money breed in a drawer* could be realized, the *Legacy Tax* would not produce much, and a man's children, living with him at the time of his death, would, probably, often, be the *only* children who would share his fortune."

COUNTER-OBSERVATIONS.

Here the Baronet is at his ewes and lambs again—and the very idea of *giving or receiving interest,* is thus to be *twice* drowned in ridicule.

**ibid.* p. 173.

All borrowers, and all lenders—Bankers and their Customers—Grantors, and Receivers of Government Annuities—Governments, and Nations, all consigned to scorn, for the hope of involving the obnoxious institution in the common infamy!

As to the injury to the *Legacy-tax*, the argument bears with *equal* force or rather (as we have just seen) with *more* than equal force—not only against the *public* securities above mentioned—but against all *private* securities for money (such as Bonds, Notes of hand, Bills of Exchange) and against *money* itself; metallic money, and paper money payable to bearer, more particularly.

The injury, if it amounted to any thing, would be matter of *account*: *profit* by sale of Annuity Notes; per contra, *loss* by diminution of produce of *Legacy-tax*: *loss* on this score (I presume) would not do more than keep pace with *profit*: profit, at *its maximum*, and consequently at the *maximum* of the *loss*, would be worth—I cannot say how many *score* of Legacy-taxes. The division above spoken of will as far as it obtains, diminish the facility, and increase the danger, of concealing this species of property, where a contribution out of it is due; and thereby afford a security against evasion, beyond what obtains in several of those other cases: In regard to Notes rising to a certain magnitude (£100 Notes suppose or £50 Notes) would it be worth while, to require *evidence of transfer* in that view, such as indorsement at a Local Annuity-Note Office, with the attestation of the Office-keeper accompanied with registration by entry on a list? I will not at present pretend to say:—it might eventually be worth thinking of. Where any the least particle of useful instruction presents itself to view, no indication of hostility would render me less eager to pick it up, than if it came from the most strenuous friend and advocate.

The like observations apply, though with diminished force, to the case of *natural* representatives. The public, in consequence of a propensity but too natural and too active, the *public*, a forced and self-appointed representative, might be apt to suffer by the *contrivance* of the deceased: *individuals*, such as he might be inclined to favor, could only suffer by his *negligence*. A paper of *Instructions*, accompanying the issue of the higher denominations of these notes, might do something towards lessening the amount of this already existing inconvenience. With me, at any rate, the prevalence of an inconvenience in *other* instances, will never pass for a reason, for leaving it without remedy, in any instance in which a remedy may be applicable with advantage. Not the inconvenience, but the remedy, would thus be the fruit, of the plan on which the inconvenience—and *that* alone—is thus charged.

In regard to securities, of the several kinds actually in existence, in the instance of which the *division* of the instrument is not in use—*Exchequer Bills—India Bonds—Irish Debentures*—the absent representative is altogether without security against this danger: not to speak of *private* securities, in respect of which the necessary privity of the debtor operates *pro tanto* as a check. The proposed paper, by the division to which it is adapted, affords the contingent security of a *condivident bailer* or trustee, besides the clue that may be afforded by the Local Annuity-Note Office-keeper in a case where interest happens to have been recently received.

It is a real relief to the mind, when, after such arguments as we have seen above, others present themselves which, like the last, deserve that name: indications of *specific* inconvenience, as likely to ensue from the proposed measure.—Inconsiderable as they are, they tell as far as they go. This is reasoning, such as reasoning should be: objections—which, though they *admitt* of an answer, *require* it.—Had all been thus . . . but less [*sic*] us continue.

§7. OBSERVATIONS CONTINUED.

"I however admitt" (continues the learned Baronet) "for" (says he) "I have long ago made the remark that a market for yielding a reduced rate of interest to small hoards (now lying unproductive, exposed to temptations of the worst kind, and not forming, like Stock, a cement of attachment to the state) is a grand desideratum.

"With a view to remedy this inconvenience in some degree in the Metropolis or rather to *ascertain*, whether the lower classes would deem 3 per cent good interest, for their hoards deposited on good security; and likewise to induce them to form funds, for the purchase of widow hood, and other Annuities, more particularly suited to their exigencies, I inserted a clause in the *Globe* Act, to authorize the proposed Establishment, to receive deposits, not payable at a less period than *six* months, and to allow interest on them. If it is meant that the Charter shall be granted, the *experiment* may be fairly tried at our cost: and means may be provided, that, if it is eventually successful, Government may *participate* in the success."

COUNTER-OBSERVATIONS.

With reference to the proposed *Government* plan, these admissions, in relation to the *Globe Insurance* plan, proposed on *private* account, are certainly not without their value.

What is to become of the *"ewes and lambs"* now, and of the "project for *making money breed in a drawer*"? The securities, given by the *Globe Insurance Company* to their depositing customers, the petty hoarders that deposit money with them, are to breed 3 per cent; the Annuity Notes as much within a small fraction; but, for a particular reason, not *quite* so much by one sixtieth: if then the obnoxious *"project"* breeds *as fast* only as ewes and lambs, the favorite *plan* breeds thus much *faster.* From the *situation* or *size* of the *"drawer"*, no ground of difference is to be collected. In the one case, as in the other, the *situation* is that of the *cottage* or the *garret*: the drawer is one of the *little* old worm-eaten nest of drawers, which, if any, *such situation* may afford: for as to the money bred in the *ample* drawers of the *Globe Insurance Company,* with their gilt handles, little is said of it though perhaps not the less thought—*praefulget eo quod non visitur.* Yet money is certainly expected to *"breed"* in those *large* drawers (an odd 80 per cent or so)*—or probably there would not have been quite so much anxiety to send it a *"breeding"* in the little ones.†

As to the *"ascertaining whether the lower classes would deem 3 per* [*cent*] *good interest for their hoards deposited on good security"*—this, and more than this, if I do not egregiously misrecollect, upon a point easily enough ascertainable, had been pretty well ascertained

*Globe Insurance Act 39 G. 3. c. 83. §10.

†As to the time of the learned Baronet's having *"made"* the above *"remark"*, by which the set of experiments he is thus desirous of making was suggested, he speaks of it as being *"long ago"*. As to this point, if *priority* be the object glanced at, I refer it altogether to the recollection and testimony of the learned Baronet: the *truth* of it being admitted, neither the chronology, nor the genealogy of it, are of much consequence. But, if the period of making it was not *anterior* to the publication of the *"Hints"* (as they are called)[1] to which he has done the honor of copying them, and which constitute the whole of that matter which has either the merit of being *new,* or the demerit of being *"novel"* in his Insurance *plan,* or Insurance *project,* unless it be the picture displayed of the magnitude of the profit to be divided (for even the idea of dividing the profit with Government is to be found in those same hints) he might have saved himself the trouble of making it: inasmuch as among those *"Hints"* which, loose as they may have shewed themselves to a more commanding eye, cost the Author some trouble to put them into what appeared to him a *method*—among those same loose *hints* (I say) he might have found it *ready made.*

[1][The allusion is to Bentham's "Pauper Management Improved".]

by an experiment ready made. (In the year 1792 or thereabouts.) A Banking House—(*old-established,* or established for the purpose, I forget which) had been opened at the West end of the Metropolis, upon the terms of giving this very rate of interest for money, on condition of its not being called in till after a certain length of *notice.* Upon these terms, money came in—not from the *lower* classes probably, but from the *higher* classes: money seeking employment, in masses commensurate by their magnitude, to the circumstances of those higher classes: and this, notwithstanding that rivalry from *Exchequer Bills,* which we shall see relied on presently by the learned Baronet, as an insuperable bar to the circulation of the proposed Annuity Notes.* The great complaint was, in that instance[,] not that money did not come in *fast enough*—but that it came in *too fast*:—faster than the House could find the means of employing it on adequate *security,* and, at the same time, with a *profit* commensurate to the trouble and the risk.

This experiment did not (as I was observing) afford any *direct* proof (I should suppose) that the rate of interest in question (3 per cent) would be accepted of by the classes of persons in question—the *inferior* classes: For I should not suppose, that money, in sums commensurate by their smallness to the circumstances of those classes, would have been accepted of by any such Bank. But (as I was also observing) it proves a good deal *more*: for, if the superior classes, who, then as now[,] were in possession of so many sources of employment for money at a superior rate of interest—viz. those afforded by *Exchequer Bills—India Bonds*—and so many others that might be mentioned—affording 5 per cent or more—if these opulent classes, with all their resources, found their account notwithstanding in taking up with 3 per cent, in how much superior a degree must this be the case with [the] frugal poor, who to *this* purpose are as yet in a manner without resource?

This untried experiment however—this proposed experiment of the learned Baronet's—having been brought upon the carpet, the proposed Annuity Note institution ought not, according to him, to be set on foot, and that for two reasons:—because it *is not* itself competent to the purpose: and because another proposed institution—the *Globe Insurance Company*—destined by him (amongst other things) for the trying of this experiment, *is*:—which company, is ready and willing to make the experiment at their own *"cost"*—and

*Infrà § 9.

to let in Government for a share of the profit:—producing at the same time what he calls *"a cement of attachment to the state"*.

. . . . . No (says Government)—*we* want nothing of *you*: neither your *money*—nor your *security*—nor your *experiment*—nor your *"cement of attachment"*—nor any thing you can do for us.

1. *Not your money: present money* is *not* a thing wanted to enable a man to pay *future interest: ready money* is *not* the thing *taken from* the party charged with payment of interest—it is *put into* his hands.

2. *Not your security*. Our security (we hope) you will allow has at least *some* points about it superior to your's: were you ever more careful of your own that [*sic*] what you seem to be. It has the *whole property of the Nation* for its basis. It is of somewhat *longer standing* than yours: the people are somewhat better *acquainted* with it—rather more *used* to it than to yours. It has stood the test, *as long as it has been tried,* notwithstanding every thing that has been said about *"dying of the Doctor"*: it has stood the test, as long as it has been tried, and *it has been tried these hundred years.* Good as it ever has been, and is, it never could, nor ever can be made *so* good, by any *other* means, as it will be made by borrowing on these terms: good, in proportion to the *extent* in which they are accepted: because, till Stock 3 per cents have risen beyond par, not a penny can thus be *borrowed,* on the basis of this security, without *exonerating* it of a burthen of the same kind, to a *superior* amount.*

3. *Not your experiment*: Town—country—every where—it has been already tried—and the results sufficiently *"ascertained"* without you. In the country, according to your own admission under your next head:† in the Metropolis in an instance too well known surely to have escaped you.

4. *Not your "cement of attachment"*. Of attachment to the *state,* yes: but who are you? are you the state?

As to the share of profit you have the goodness to lay by for us if we thank you for it, it must be for nothing. *Half*‡ a loaf is better than no bread: but the whole loaf, which is our's whenever we please, the *whole* loaf is better still.

Our exigencies have forced us, from time to time, to borrow money

---

*Art. 8 & 9.

†§ 8.

‡A momentary misconception to the advantage of the Globe. Not a tenth part; but the exact amount baffles calculation.

upon terms of disadvantage—greater and greater disadvantage, according to the pressure of the times. If, by laying open the market to a greater number of lenders—to a greater number of customers for the fresh parcels of redeemable annuities, by the sale of which we borrow what we want to help us pay off the old ones—if by those, or any *other* fair and honorable means, it be in our power to ease ourselves of parts of our load of debt, by money borrowed upon terms of less disadvantage, is it for *you*—unborn embryos like *you*—creatures who wait for *our* nod to bring you into existence—is it for *you* to presume to throw yourselves in the way, and stand up to hinder us?

One word at closing this first head of the learned Baronet's discussion: one word, in the way of recapitulation, about the *rate of interest*, proposed by me to be allowed on the proposed Annuity Notes. It is ridiculously high: it is contemptibly low: and, within a sixtieth, it is the very rate the learned Baronet himself proposes.

§8. OBSERVATIONS CONTINUED.

II. "As to the new currency—The Grounds of expectation (p. 42)[1] appear to be very narrow. The circulation of Bankers paper bearing interest is mentioned as the principal one" (no such thing) "Country Bankers indeed allow interest on deposits at their Banks, and some few may issue notes bearing interest. But in what part of England do such Notes circulate to any considerable extent?"

COUNTER-OBSERVATIONS.

I know not, and I do not care. This question may be best answered by a string of other questions. In what part of England lives there a Banker, whose *security* is, all over England, looked upon as being upon a par with that of Government? 2. In how many parts of England are there Bankers, that give, secured in the shape of interest-bearing notes, an interest which amounts in reality to *so much as 3 per cent*? 3. In how many instances do these interest-bearing notes afford, like Exchequer Bills, *even sums*, or aliquot parts of even sums, for daily interest? 4. In how many instances are they adapted, by *diversity of magnitude*, to every diversity in the amount of the capacity for taking them, on the part of individuals borrowing them or taking them in payment? 5. In what instances is the glance of *inspection* substituted to the toil of *calculation*? 6. What Banker is

[1][Chapter IV.]

there, that could or would undertake, that the *continuance of the interest* thus allowed should be coeval with that of the National Debt? 7. and—what is more—how many Bankers are there, that can find their account in borrowing their money in driblets in this way, when they can get it in larger sums, or in sums of equal size secured by engagements not transferable to Bearer:—taking their profit by passing for value notes that cost them nothing—that run in even sums of convenient size—that, in regard to interest, require neither calculation nor so much as inspection—that subject them in a word to no interest—and the amount of which, is neither limited by the amount of the sums deposited with them on condition of paying interest, nor in short by any thing else, but their own prudence and the facility of those who take this paper off their hands? Where has the learned Baronet found—by what logic will he prove—that the circulation of Bankers paper bearing interest, is mentioned in my plan, as the "*principal*" ground of expectation I rely on, in respect of the circulation of the proposed Government Annuity Notes?—in this sense at least (which is the only apposite one) viz. that the amount of that private paper at present circulated, constitutes the principal part of the amount of that mass of Annuity Note Paper, which I should expect to see in circulation?—So many points of *distinction* as you have seen—(and I know not that they are all that might be seen) are they not altogether enough to constitute a *difference*? Is there any one of them that does not constitute an *advantage*? Some of these advantages—the principal ones—those which respect security—duration—rate of interest—facility of calculation—are in the very page and sentence he refers to, staring him in the face: but he fancies he annihilates them, when he shuts his eyes.

In mentioning the *rate of interest* allowed by some of the Country Bankers, on interest-bearing Notes issued by them, I mentioned, for the principal, if not sole purpose, of shewing that an interest so much inferior—not only to the five per cent (more or less) afforded by the *existing* Government securities, but even to the almost 3 per cent proposed to be allowed by Government on the proposed *new* securities, actually met with individuals to accept it. I might have gone further: for, to judge by what I have since learnt, the example of money lent to Bankers, at much less than a real 3 per cent or £2 19s per cent, and without the convenience of a security susceptible of circulation—of the security afforded by an instrument promising payment to Bearer—is still more in use. In Suffolk (I have it from Mr Arthur Young) the terms are these. For any sum under £100, no interest allowed: if, after £500 deposited, a single sixpence is drawn out, the interest of one of the hundreds is struck off by that single sixpence. I rather think too—but am not sure—that even in this case certain *conditions* are added—inconvenient to the Banker—inconvenient to the depositing Customer—and rendering the rate of interest less than what it seems: such as that of interest not *commencing* till after a certain time, or obligation of giving a certain length of *notice,* before principal is drawn out.

The case of the Bankers, as referred to in that part of my plan, was referred to only as an *example*—an example of the demand already existing, for this rate of interest, among the customers for *temporary* interest alone, in the present state of things, on terms of so much *less advantage* in comparison with mine. For a measure of the possible *amount* of such demand, on the part of that class of customers, under the proposed state of things, I took a much more extensive standard. In the very next page, commences, under 14 different heads, a list of masses of money, capable of being employed in the purchase of interest, as afforded by the proposed Annuity Notes, supposing the holders to find their account in it: the example of these Bankers Notes is brought to shew (and does it not shew?) that people *do* find their account in purchasing interest-bearing paper and *do* accordingly purchase and hold it, and pass it on from hand to hand, at terms of much less advantage. The true amplitude of the grounds of expectation with regard to the proposed paper is the amplitude—not of the existing mass of Banker's interest-bearing paper—but of the aggregate of the masses of money there enumerated.

The very admission made by the learned Baronet in this very passage—the admission that "Country Bankers allow interest on deposits at their Banks"—would have been sufficient to suppress the proposition it follows, had he but seen the force of it. If a man lends his money on a security (such as a *receipt*) unsusceptible of circulation, will he be less ready to lend it, other circumstances equal, on a security *possessing* that advantage? What the admission predicates, it predicates of Country Bankers in general: in this sense at least it is as capable of being understood, as in a more confined one. But if the proposed rate of interest (not to speak of inferior rates) meets with general acceptance, when proffered by an individual with no other security than that of the individual—on the security of a receipt or note, which binds nobody but that one individual, for payment of the sum so deposited; if interest, engaged for on a security thus slender, meets with acceptance every where—is it less likely to meet with acceptance, when the persons bound for acceptance, are as many of the Officers of Government, as the holder, or any of his acquaintance, have occasion to pay money to, on the score of *taxes*? Does not this circumstance give the paper some chance at least of circulation, even among *intermediate* hands? And *who* are these *intermediate* hands? all hands, into which money, to the amount of the Note in question, could have found its way.

§9. OBSERVATIONS CONTINUED.

"Exchequer Bills, which the author admitts (p. 17)[1] would rival his Notes of £50 and upwards, have never yet performed the functions of money: and I believe Sir Francis Baring in his answer to Boyd (but I have not his pamphlet at hand) gives several very substantial reasons why they cannot do so."

COUNTER-OBSERVATIONS.

"The author admitts"?—no, indeed—I admitt no such thing.—One would think there were a prize given for incorrectness, and that our Baronet was wishing for it. The notes I speak of—and speak of not merely as being *"rivalled"* in the market (the word is his own) but altogether thrown out of it—are "notes above the £51 4s Notes:"* because the next above the £51 4s Notes are £102 8s Notes: and Exchequer Bills, which at present yield upwards of 5 per cent, being within the purchase of those whose stock of money in hand would enable them to receive those notes, I durst not, *at that time,* promise myself, for these scarcely 3 per cent Notes, any purchasers upon terms of such comparative disadvantage. The difference between what he *supposes* me to admitt, and what I *do* admitt, is prodigious: look at Dr Beeke's Table† you will see it goes to million's worths—of—if it be too much to say *probable* custom—at any rate *possible* custom—for these Notes.

I was however too scrupulous: I erred against myself:—for, by the case just alluded to it is established, that people *will* accept of £3 per cent, even for sums much *more* than adequate to the purchase of Exchequer Bills.

[1][Chapter I, Art. 13, footnote.]
*Art. 13, Note 11.
†[Observations on the Produce of the Income Tax] p. 155, 2d Edit.

Observe, that though it should be *true,* that Exchequer Bills would, (to recurr to my own expression) draw off from the proposed Annuity Notes, all customers for NOTES above the sum spoken of—on that occasion viz. £51 4s Notes, yet is it neither true—nor there given by me as true—that they would throw out of the market all SUMS above that amount. They would neither shut the door of the market against Annuity Notes, nor so much as rival them, in respect of any sum less than £100:—because what is an offer, of £5 and upwards per cent for £100 good for, to a man who can raise but £99? He must content himself with the next best offer he can get.

As to *Exchequer Bills*—and the notion of their "never having yet performed the functions of money"—in the first place it is not true:—besides that, if it were true, it would prove nothing against Annuity Notes.

I. It is not true: at least if the conclusion I was led to draw from the nature of the case, and which has been confirmed to me by positive evidence, is a just one. Among Bankers at any rate, they do serve as a succedaneum to money (i.e. to Bank of England Notes) of such large sizes, in the composition of what I call (as Necker calls them)* their *Security Funds.* By means of these interest-bearing Bills, they are enabled to let go out of their hands, cash and Bank of England non-interest-bearing cash-paper; to an amount greater than they would venture to part with otherwise. This I call *"performing the functions of money"*, or I know not what is, in respect of pieces of that magnitude. The price of these securities is not altogether exempt from variation: from several circumstances (of which presently) it cannot be: but the *variation* it is subject to is comparatively so *small,* and the *market* for them, at a trifle below the price of the day, so *sure,* that a Banker need never fear a want of cash for answering drafts, so long as he has these Bills to the amount:—at least no more than he need with Bank of England Notes of the same magnitude.

But, in any case, for paper of that magnitude, what expectations would the learned Baronet entertain, in respect of its *"performing the functions of money"*? or what expectations did he conceive me as entertaining? Did he suppose that I expected to see it swelling out the pockets of the "market women", the "turnpike keepers", and the "publicans", whom he speaks of afterwards?† Did he suppose me not

*[De l'] Admin[istration des] Fin[ances de la France, 1784,] III, p. 277, *Fonds de précaution.*

†Infrà, § 14.

to be aware, that in the pecuniary world, the velocity of a mass must be inversely as its magnitude? Does he suppose my plan to be grounded on the expectation, that *wholesale sums* should be employed in *retail purchases* [?]

As to *opinions*—it is not (as he supposes) *Sir Francis Baring* in his answer to Mr Boyd, but Mr *Boyd* himself, in the pamphlet to which that of Sir Francis's is an answer, that combats the idea about Exchequer Bills—viz. that of their performing the functions of money; combats it, upon the strength of such *"reasons"*, as have passed upon our Baronet it seems for *"substantial"* ones.

These reasons are drawn from a *mechanical* theory of his, taken from Adam Smith, about *"wheels"* and *"circulators"* and *"objects of circulation"*.* Money (says he) is a sort of a *wheel*, which Smith has described; a sort of hollow wheel which I call a *circulator*:—*objects of circulation*, are all things which are bought with money or sold for money—that is almost *all other* things. To buy them, or to sell them, you put them into this wheel. But a thing (say an Exchequer Bill) put into a wheel, is one thing: the wheel itself, another: a thing, so different from a wheel as to be put into it, can never *pass* for the wheel itself: therefore an Exchequer Bill, is a sort of a thing that can never pass for money† Q.E.D.—N.B. By the same argument it may be proved, that no one sort of money is money: for there is no one sort of money, that is not made to go in change for—that is bought by and with money of every other sort.

It is a pity the learned Baronet had not this pamphlet with its theories at his elbow:—he should have it at his fingers ends: it would enable him, if possible, to misunderstand the subject more compleatly than he has done. It would teach him, if he wanted teaching, how to triumph—and at the very best time for triumphing—the time he has himself chosen—before the battle. For the Baronet with his *"ewes and lambs"* has not triumphed more unmercifully, over a little man, than the Banker, with his "wheels and circulators", over a great one.‡

As to Sir Francis's evidence, it is on my side. To prove that the currency once proposed by Mr Boyd would not run—(a currency in every feature of it different from the proposed Annuity Notes) what he says on the subject of Exchequer Bills is in these words.—

*[Walter Boyd, Letter on the Influence of the Stoppage of Issues in Specie on the Prices of Provisions, second ed. 1801,] pp. XXVI, 2, 17, 66, 86.

†[*Ibid.*] pp. 86, 66.

‡Mr. Pitt. Boyd [*l.c.*] 2d. Edit.: Postscript, pp. 83, 87.

..."Although Exchequer Bills carry an interest of 3½d per day, they never did serve the purpose of *general* circulation, for the sake of a daily interest: the foundation upon which the whole of Mr Boyd's plan rests."[1] The word *general* is in Italics. These Italics are decisive. They admitt the circulation, though they assert that it has its *limits*. It would be strange indeed, if it had *not* its limits. It would have its limits if it had no others than those which confine the circulation of Bank Notes for the same sums: and it has other limits.* The same thing might be said of Gold and Silver money, if there were pieces of it of that value. The same thing may *actually* be said of Guineas, in certain places: guineas do not serve the purpose of "general circulation" among beggars—scarcely among day-labourers.

Of sums like these, the *circulation* as contradistinguished from the *keeping in hand* for interest, will necessarily confine itself to the superior ranks of money'd men: such as Bankers and great Merchants: more particulary Bankers, and the London Bankers. Mr Boyd, having a *theory*, preferred it to his own experience. Sir Francis having no theory—or at least no *such* theory—spoke according to his own experience, and nothing else.

II. If it were true of Exchequer Bills, that they have never yet performed the functions of money[,] it would prove nothing against Annuity Notes.

1. Exchequer Bills have never yet (within time of memory) been for less sums than £100: Annuity Notes are commensurate to the pockets of all Customers.

2. The *mass* into the composition of which an Exchequer Bill enters, is a vast mass, poured into the market at once: its *magnitude*, proportioned to that of the *exigence* that gave it birth—not to that of the *previous demand*, as made known on the part of the customer in each separate instance. The quantity of Annuity Note paper issued, *follows* the demand in each instance—and never can *precede* it. From this difference, the price of the Exchequer Bill must be continually exposed to variation—that of the Annuity Note never.

3. The Annuity (if such it may be called) conveyed by an *Exchequer Bill*, is for an *uncertain* time, and that a *short* one. The value of it therefore cannot but be more or less dependant upon that uncertainty. The annuity afforded by an *Annuity Note* is, as far as it goes, as truly *perpetual* as a correspondent mass of Stock

[1] [Observations on the Publication of Walter Boyd, Esq., M.P., 1801, p. 28.]

*Infrà.

Annuities, besides being exactly commensurate to every *temporary* purpose.

4. Under an Exchequer Bill, the time of payment is never determined at the *issue* of it, nor for an uncertain time afterwards:—neither for principal, nor for *interest*: nor is interest paid, till principal is paid. Under an Annuity Note, the times for payment of *interest* are as much fixed as they are in the case of Stock Annuities. And as to principal, the Government Offices being always equally open for the reception of Annuity Notes, the faculty of obtaining value for them is not subject to contingencies.

5. In the case of an Exchequer Bill, a man must be upon the watch, for the advertisements by which *notices* are given in respect to times of payment: which if he overlooks after the time appointed, he *loses the interest* from that time. No such necessity of watching, nor danger of loss, in the case of Annuity Notes.

6. In the case of an Exchequer Bill, the same necessity of *watching*, if, after payment, a man wishes to *keep* his money employ'd in the same way: and then, till the advertisement comes, he knows not whether upon the same terms, or what other terms: and, if he lets slip the time appointed by Government for renewal, he has the fresh Bills to buy in the market at an uncertain price. In the case of an Annuity Note, a man keeps his money thus employed, without any such *trouble,* or any such *risk,* upon the *same terms,* for as *long,* or as *short,* a time, as he finds convenient.

To these I will add three or four features more, transcribed, with little addition, from the printed pages which the learned Critic had before him, when from the supposed non-currency of Exchequer Bills he inferred the non-currency of Annuity Notes.

7. *Annuity Notes. "Interest receivable* with scarce any trouble or expence; *wherever* letters are receivable". *Exchequer Bills,* only at *one* Office.

8. *Annuity Notes "purchasable* of Government, with scarce any trouble or expence, *wherever* letters are receivable". *Exchequer Bills.* only at one Office.*

9. *Annuity Notes*—"receivable of *Individuals,* in the course of circulation, if at all, without any *trouble* or *expence*". *Exchequer Bills,* not, unless by accident, without *expence of Brokerage,* and the *trouble* of applying to a *Broker*: to which is added, out of London,

*The effect of this single circumstance promises to be very great. It may be conjectured from the low interest accepted of from the *neighbouring* Bankers.

the expence of *Postage,* & professional Agency, or the *obligation* conferred by the *gratuitous* performance of such a service.

10. *Annuity Notes.—Security against depretiation*: the result principally of a property already mentioned—that of not being issued, but in *quantities proportioned* to, and *preceded* by, the *demand,* at the *price* set upon them: that demand *gradual,* and likely to *keep on* increasing, by the continuance of whatever causes gave it birth. No man need ever take an Annuity Note, at any thing *less* than its full price[,] in the way of *circulation,* while there are others paying that full price for them, on taking them out in the way of *issue.* The demand for them in the way of *issue* must have ceased *every* where, before a man need take less than the full price for them *any* where. That *Exchequer Bills* are subject to depretiation (though, for reasons obvious enough, not so much as Stock Annuities) is matter of every day's experience.

Of the above features of difference, some had been already pointed out, in the already existing pages against which the learned Baronet shuts his eyes:—these, and others, in those as yet unprinted ones, the intimation of which operated as a memento to him that it was time the "discussion" should be *"closed"*.* It is from these features put together, which perhaps are not all that might be adduced, that I have drawn the inference, that, although it *were* true of *Exchequer Bills* (which, according to me, it is *not*) that they have never yet *"performed the functions of money"*, the same thing would not follow of the proposed Annuity Notes.

§10. OBSERVATIONS CONTINUED.

"An essential quality of money" (continues o[u]r Critic) "is invariability in *nominal* value.

"This convenience" (he adds) "makes us readily take shillings as shillings (we know they will go as shillings) though they have lost a fourth of their original size; and would make us take them for shillings still, but for no more, though the magic of a great interest could increase them a 33*d*"

COUNTER-OBSERVATIONS.

"An essential quality" &c—Here we have another Oracle: and not less advantageously entrenched in obscurity than the former.†

*Infrà, § 23.

†§ 4.

I am really most sadly puzzled with this argument: if any thing is to be made out of it, I think it must be this—

Your money won't go (says he) and for this reason. Money won't go unless there be a *name* to call it by. Your paper shillings, so long as they have no interest due upon them, might go, if people would but take them, because there is a name—(shilling Annuity Notes)—to call them by:—that is—I mean, they might go, if there were nothing else to hinder them, inasmuch as they would derive no hindrance from this source. But the moment any interest became due upon them, there would be an end to their going:—because then there would no longer be any *name* to call them by. The *first* day of their existence they *would* be capable of going: because there *would* be a name to call them by: they would therefore be in no want of *"nominal value"* at least, however it were with them in regard to *real*. But the *second* day (and so every other day) they would *not* be capable of going any longer: because there would be *no* name to call them by. The *first* day, they would have been *called shilling notes,* being notes for shillings, and so *would* have been capable of going for shilling notes: but the *second* day, they could *not* be called *shilling Notes*—since now they are notes, each of them, not for a shilling *merely,* but for a shilling with a day's interest upon it; that is, for a shilling and something *more*:—in short there would no longer be any *name* to *call them by*: therefore they would not *go* any longer.

So far the learned Baronet's argument, according to the best it is in my power to make of it. My answer is—if this be all there is to prevent my paper shillings from going, I shall not have much to fear for them. I *admitt,* that, in this case as in any other, there might be some difficulty in getting a thing, if you could not contrive to make known, by some description or other, what it was you wanted to get. What I *deny* is—the existence of that difficulty in *this* case. If I wanted to *receive* or (what would come to the same thing) to *pass* off a shilling note the *first* day, I should call it a *shilling note*: the next day, if I made a point of receiving the interest upon it, I should call it *a shilling note with a day's interest*: and so for any number of days. But if I did *not* make a point of receiving the interest upon it (which I imagine would most commonly be the case—at least till the interest had risen to a farthing) I should call it a *shilling note* still: and, if there had been people disposed to take it of me, as and for a shilling, the *first* day, I cannot think that the number would be less of those that would be ready to take it from me, at any such supposed *subsequent* day, being a day on which, if it has acquired but little *encrease*, at any rate it has not suffered any *decrease* in *real* value.

Let us take which case the learned Baronet pleases—that of the person *by* whom the note is tendered, or that of the person *to* whom it is tendered; and let the tender be *accepted* or *refused*—in *no* case can there be any difficulty.

Let the note (a shilling note) have interest to the amount of a farthing due upon it. First let this shilling note be *mine*, and let the learned Baronet be the person to whom I tender it. If he *consents* to allow the farthing, then by the supposition there is no difficulty. If he *refuses* to allow the farthing, nor even then is there any difficulty. There is none, if, upon such his refusal, *I consent* to have credit for no more than a shilling—waving the farthing interest. Nor is there any, if I do *not* consent, to let it pass out of my hands upon those terms. It is no legal tender; neither for the shilling and the farthing, nor yet for the shilling alone: nor in short for any sum. Oh but (says he perhaps) then I make you *lose* your *interest*: and your plan of making these notes of your's carry interest in circulation is thus defeated. No—say I, you cannot make me thus lose my interest: you cannot defeat my plan for making these notes carry interest in circulation: (so far as the holders of them think it worth their while to receive it) *you*, nor all the strength you could *muster* for this purpose. At any of the Local Annuity Note Offices, when the time comes for receiving the interest, I can be sure of receiving it. I receive it there indeed without the principal—the farthing without the shilling: but the principal—the shilling—I can then receive at any rate in the course of *circulation*: for, by the supposition, the refusal to accept applies only to the *interest*. But (I hear him say again) it is not *worth your while* to apply to any one of these offices for this minutest of all sums: therefore you will *not* apply for it, and so you will lose it. That—(say I) depends—partly upon my disposition—partly upon my circumstances. In shops, there are still several articles of any one of which a quantity may be purchased by a farthing. In all these cases, there is a person—the shop-keeper—who so far from disdaining to receive a farthing in *entirety*, disdains not to receive the 15 per cent, or whatever other portion of *profit*, may be extracted from it. In the *Two-Penny Post Offices*, (at least while they were *Penny Post Offices*) no person who consented to have his shop employ'd in the character of such an Office, disdained the profit of the *tenth part of a penny*, on each letter taken in: a transaction which frequently involved taking payment for the money and giving change, besides *constantly* affixing a couple of *Stamps*, and keeping the *account* with the superior offices. It may therefore very well happen, that I should think it worth my while to receive a farthing for each of a *number* of shillings, if, at the time, I happened to have a number of shillings so circumstanced. But *another* circumstance, that renders this discussion superfluous, is—the *certainty* I have of getting this farthing allowed me, at any of the other *Government Offices*, in payment of my own, or any body else's *taxes*:* and that, as soon as the farthing's worth of interest has become due, according to the *day*: just as an *individual* would allow it me, if he chose to comply with my claim of interest (as in case of *Exchequer Bills*) without waiting for the arrival of the day of half yearly payment, at which it became *actually payable* at the Annuity Note Office. I therefore still maintain, that, after the minutest scrutiny that can be made, it is impossible to find any cause of dispute or difficulty about the value *real* or *"nominal"* of any such Note: much less any such difficulty as can operate as a bar to the circulation of it.

Once more, will *possibility* be proved by *fact*? The *difficulty*, such as it is, is as old as paper money: and it has never been an *obstacle*. Not to speak of *private* paper, such as *Bills of Exchange*, or *interest-bearing* Promissory Notes in respect of which the adjunct of *discount* or *interest* has never been productive of any such difficulty—the case of *Exchequer Bills* is more particularly in point: and whether on the occasion of *passing* or *receiving*, and whatever might be the amount of interest due upon it, who ever found any difficulty about the *"nominal value"* or denomination of an Exchequer Bill? A £100 Exchequer Bill, on the day of its issuing, is called simply *a £100 Exchequer Bill*, or *a £100 Exchequer Bill without interest*. An Exchequer Bill on any *other* day, is called an *Exchequer Bill with interest*: viz. *with so many days interest upon it*: making at 3d½ a day, *so much*. Who ever heard of either dispute or difficulty about the interest on an Exchequer Bill? The interest on an *Annuity Note* is the *aliquot part* of the interest on such a Bill.

Oh, but (says the learned Baronet) I wont allow it to be *"money"*. Well then (say I) be this as you please: call it however what you will, it is a sort of a thing that *passes from hand to hand*, now and then at

*Plan. Art. 14.

least, as *money* does. If then people *really* wanted to make use of it as money, would there be any more difficulty in finding a name to call it by than there is at present? Would *the mere want of a name* be an obstacle to its being received as such, if there were no other? No more then would it in the case of an Annuity Note.

It would be with these *farthings-worths of paper,* as it is with *copper* farthings. This of the copper farthings, is a case in point: though it is the converse of the other. Where there is a copper farthing to pay, it is sometimes paid, and sometimes not: because the party to whom it is due sometimes thinks it worth his while to receive it, sometimes not: but there is no dispute; because it is known, that the other party, if it be demanded of him, is *bound* to pay it. So, in the case of the farthing's-worth of interest. on a shilling note or any other *Annuity Note*: where the Note is offered to be passed, the farthing will sometimes be *added* to the shilling in the account, sometimes *not*: because sometimes a man will think of claiming it, and claim it accordingly; at other times he will *not* think of it, or not think it *worth while* to claim it. But at any rate there can be no dispute: because with or without this additional farthing, the other party is not bound to take the Note.

Many people I have known refuse farthings: some people I have known carry the refusal as far as halfpence: though most people I suppose take both. If this uncertainty, about acceptance or refusal, on the score of *smallness of value,* were to be insisted on as a *bar* to the circulation of *Annuity Notes,* by the same argument might it have been proved *a priori,* that a system of metallic money, which should have farthings in it, could not circulate.

The proposition adduced by the learned Baronet for illustration, and which runs so smoothly, is not (to my conception) quite so clear in its *application*—nor, in itself, altogether *true*. "This convenience" (viz. invariability in nominal value) "makes us readily take shillings" (says he) "as shillings (we know they will go as shillings) though they have lost a fourth of their original size". This proposition, if not *exactly* equivalent, seems at any rate to be pretty much of the complexion, of the following. *Whatever value a piece of money is* SAID *by its denomination to possess, people will give that value for it, although it wants five and twenty per cent of possessing it.* Whatsoever countenance the proposition may receive, from the example of *silver,* adduced as it were in proof of it, will hardly extend beyond *that* example: it will *not* extend to *gold*: people do not receive a light guinea, weighing but sixteen shillings, for a heavy one. I will not push the argument further: nor enter into any enquiry in regard to the limits of the sort of confidence thus spoken of. Governments (not to speak of malefactors) have acted in this respect but too often, as if they had had the learned Baronet for their Councillor: but the success of such operations has not in general been quite so great as on this occasion he represents it.

It is in the *application,* that this argument of the learned Baronet's breaks forth in its genuine lustre. The difference between *real* and *"nominal" value* in a piece of money, is *not* a [*sic*] impediment to its circulation (says he) *even* where the nominal value is *inferior* to the real value; inferior by as much as a fourth: therefore it *will* be an impediment, where the real value is *superior* to the nominal. So *easy* are people as to this point in regard to *bad shillings,* that, when a thing is *called a shilling,* they will take it for a shilling, though it be *worth* but *nine pence*: *therefore,* so *difficult* will they be in regard to *good Annuity Notes,* that, though they will take an Annuity Note for a shilling, when, being worth but a shilling, it is called only a *shilling Annuity Note,* they will *not* take it at all, when it is become worth a shilling and *more.*

As to *"magic"*—"shillings" . . . *"by the magic of a great interest . . . increased a* 33^d^"—here the learned Baronet is at his *"ewes & lambs"* again: but, what his quarrel with *three per cent* is *just now*—whether it is to be held up as *ridiculous* for its *excess*—or as *contemptible* for its *deficiency,* or both together, is more than I am sure of. One thing I am pretty clear about—which is, that, if I were a publican, and instead of the thirty three pieces of miserable trash I am so frequently losing by, under the *name* of shillings, I were to find myself, at the time when I had my *licences* to pay for, in possession of 34 shilling Annuity Notes, each with a year's interest due upon it, I should not be sorry to find, that, without any more *trouble* on my part, than *"magic"* on the part of any body, I had thus got out of these 34 shillings (many if not all of which I had taken for no more than *shillings*) an *additional* shilling to help pay my licences.

§11. OBSERVATIONS CONTINUED.

"Standard Annuity Notes, varying in 6 months from £12 16s value to £12 19s 9d½, would not answer the purposes of circulation, which requires quick and simple *computations.*"

COUNTER-OBSERVATIONS.

"Computations"—yes. Where computation is necessary, as in the case of an Exchequer Bill, or an India Bond, *there* indeed the *quicker* and more *simple* they are, certainly the better. The Exchequer Bill is in that respect better than the India Bond, because in the *Bill,* the *daily* interest is an exact aliquot or commensurable part of the *yearly* interest, which in the instance of the *Bond,* is not the case. But in the case of the *Annuity Note no* computation at all is necessary: *inspection* takes the place of it. Is not that better still?—Opposite the day of the month you see the value.

Oh but (it may be said) there are people that cant read at all—and what will *they* do, with your *paper* and your *table*?—I answer—they will do with *this* as they do with *other* paper: as they do *in England,* with Bank of England £1 and £2 Notes, and with Country Bankers one guinea and two guinea notes; not to speak of so many higher denominations: as they do in *Scotland,* with these and with 10s and 5s Notes: as they *did* in *America* with paper Notes of all denominations down to shilling Notes,* and as they did in Yorkshire with sixpenny Notes.† A man who can't read (though there is many a man who can't read things in *general,* that yet will read *particular* things, such as those in which he has a particular and frequently recurring interest)—a man however who can't read, will, if he has confidence enough in the man that tenders the note, take *his* account of it:—if not, he will *wait* before he takes it, untill he can take the account of *somebody else* in whom he has sufficient confidence. If he wont *take* any body's account or cannot, within the time he chooses to wait, meet with any body who is capable of *giving* him such account—what then?—why then he wont take the Note. Then there will be that *one* person who, on that *one* occasion, will not take *that* note. But what impediment—what restriction—will that be to the general circulation of such notes? Ask, as above—in England—Scotland—America—Yorkshire.

This brings me to the learned Baronet's word *"require"*—and the fallacy that lurks under it. *"Circulation"* (i.e. a mass of paper engagements designed to circulate as money) *"requires quick and simple computations"*. "Requires"?—in order to what?—in order to circulate at all? or only in order to its circulating in the greatest quantity

*A. Smith [Wealth of Nations] vol. 1. 8vo, p. 487 [Bk. II. ch. II.]
†*ibid.*

which the nature of the engagement in other respects admitts of? In the first sense, it is not true: Witness *Exchequer Bills* and *India Bonds**—each to the amount of so many millions. In the other sense, it may, for aught I know, be true, to a certain extent: but to an extent altogether undefinable, and altogether inadequate to the learned Baronet's purpose. A deficiency in this respect *might* operate so *far*, upon any paper—upon the proposed paper for example—as to render the *quantity* of it in circulation at any given time *less* than it would have been otherwise: it might act as an *impediment*: but this would not do for the learned Baronet: what *he* wants is a *bar*. In what *degree* the impediment would operate in *restriction* of that quantity—or at least in what *quantity the* paper would *circulate notwithstanding* the impediment —*experiment* and nothing else would shew: but *experiment* is the very thing *he* deprecates.†

Meantime let this be understood (and it may be understood without experiment) that the *obstruction* afforded *in the case in question* (the case of the proposed £12 16s Annuity Notes) would be much *less* than in those *other* cases, in which it does not appear to have operated even as a *restriction*—much less as a *bar*. This superiority it would derive from several circumstances:—the *occasions* for passing off the note, and consequently of its being exposed to the obstruction, would, by reason of the *inferior* magnitude of it, be so much the less *numerous*: the chances *against* its finding itself, on each occasion, in *illiterate* hands, in whose instance the complication in question would be a cause of obstruction—would also be the *more numerous* and the *trouble* of obtaining the requisite literary assistance, would be the less grudged, the greater the amount of the value at stake.

When *two* such Annuity Notes come to be added together, *then* indeed *simple inspection* (I must confess) is no longer sufficient: *then*

*Both require computation: but Exchequer Bills give daily interest—three pence halfpennies that require only to be multiplied by the number of days. On India Bonds a day's interest being an incommensurable sum between 3d and 3d½, the amount of interest each time of passing them requires to be puzzled out with the help of pen and ink or particular books to be hunted out for the purpose.

The India Company could not give 3½ if they would, it would be usury: though the interest they give is thus between a 1/16th and a 1/18th less than is given by Exchequer Bills the Bonds bear at least as high a price commonly as Exchequer Bills. Why? because of the permanence of the engagement in the case of the Bonds added to some other circumstances mentioned above in the parallel between Exchequer Bills and Annuity Notes.

†§ 1.

indeed *"computation"* is required. But then in this case, the *three* elements just mentioned, unfrequency of the occasion for circulation —improbability of the want of sufficient learning—and ratio of the value at stake to the trouble of enquiry—are, each of them, *doubled*: and now the value of the *principal* has *risen* to above a *quarter* of that of an *Exchequer Bill*, or *India Bond*.

Oh, but the sums thus to be added will be uneven sums. Be it so. But is there any such insurmountable difficulty, in the *addition* of uneven sums or of pieces of money passing for uneven sums? Is there any the poorest day-labourer who has not occasion to make such additions *frequently*, not to say continually: especially additions by which farthings are converted into pence and shillings, which are the conversions most *frequently* occurring to such accountants, and attended with the most *embarassment*.

Neither a *guinea*, nor a *half-guinea*, nor a *seven-shilling piece*, are for perfectly even sums, familiar as they are to us. Along with these, (except[in]g the 7s piece) as well as *with one another*, I remember the 36s—the 27s piece—the 18s *piece*—the 9s and (I believe) the 5s 3d: and I know of no inconvenience that the *variety* was ever attended with. In the case of those *foreign* pieces, there may have been a little difficulty—now and then—to some people at least—in the making out the value of them by their *looks*: there would be *no* such difficulty, in regard to *Annuity Notes*: since, beside their looks, by which the principal sums are distinguished, the *value*, by interest for each day, stands opposite the day in the Table.

In *France*, besides silver money more various than our's (*Crowns, Half-Crowns, Shillings, Sixpences,* and *Threepences*) I remember having, in inferior money, *five* different pieces in my pocket at the same time: *penny-pieces, three-farthing-pieces, half-penny* pieces, *farthing* pieces, and *half-farthing* pieces. *These* were embarassments, not mounted upon a *great mass* attended with *no* embarassment (as in the case of the shillings, pence, and farthings for *interest,* mounted upon a *principal* of £12 16s); but composing, frequently, the whole of the sum, to be transferred, on each occasion, from hand to hand; transferred and made up, out of such elements, by *"computation"*— among the poorest and most illiterate of the people.

In *America*, the *silver* paper monies, circulating under a continually varying *discount*, as compared with Silver *Metal* monies of the same denomination, must, in their mixture with those *undepretiated* monies, have given rise to *"computations"*, attended (I should think) with every degree of intricacy, that can be ascribed to the proposed Annuity Notes.

In *France* again, how much greater embarassment must there not have been, where *Assignats*—but more particularly where *Assignats* and *Mandats* both—were in circulation; under degrees of depretiation *varying* almost from day to day. *This* currency came, in no short space of time, to an end. True: but from what cause?—not from the *embarassment* attending the *computations* (this is pretty well established by the examples given already) but from the worthlessness—the absolute worthlessness of the *security*.

In a word—*uneven* sums, in all their varieties, come to be *paid*. Where is the *great* inconvenience, in having *monies* in a *correspondent* degree of variety, for paying them? By the addition of interest to principal, if, in *some* instances, "*computations*" will require to be made, more than would have been to be made otherwise, in *other* instances they will be saved. In the case supposed by the learned Baronet—the case of a £12 16*s* note, raised by a half-year's interest from that value to £12 19s 9d½, suppose £13 to be the sum to be paid: *with* this note, principal and interest together, the sum will be made up, by adding *five* halfpence to it. *Without* the Note, the very simplest possible mode of making up the sum would be by *twelve* Guineas and *eight* shillings: and, in proportion as *guineas* and *shillings* were deficient, the computation would increase in intricacy. How much greater the advantage in point of simplicity if the sum requisite to be paid happens to be the exact amount of the Annuity Note? a supposition that will as frequently be verified, as that of any *other* given sum approaching to the mark: such as, in the case of the £12 16s Annuity Note, the above supposed sum of £13.

§12. OBSERVATIONS CONTINUED.

"I think your best computor under the old regime of the Custom House, the most perfect adept in summing up nine or ten different subsidies and imports, would be puzzled if he were to attempt to give change for a £100 Bank Note, from a mass of Annuity Notes (part bearing nearly 3 per cent and part 2⅜ per cent interest p. 33)[1] consisting of Standard Notes, Halves and Quarters, with a few odd years, months and days, interest due on each, even with the assistance of small change i.e. Notes of 5/3 bearing an interest of 1/512 part of a farthing per diem."

[1][Ch. I, Art. 20.]

COUNTER-OBSERVATIONS.

On this head, what has been said already, may, I should hope, be found tolerably satisfactory in the character of a *defence* of the plan attacked. What remains to be said on the occasion of the present paragraph, concerns rather the *weakness* of the mode of the *attack,* than the *strength* of the *work* against which it is directed. The objection, like so many other of the learned Baronet's objections is borrowed, copied I may almost say, from the work objected to. To the objection, in starting it, I gave what seemed to me an answer in two places: the *objection,* the learned Baronet gives as a discovery of *his own,* leaving the *answer,* as usual. *without notice.*

The answer was 1. That the extension would be *gradual*: therefore the notes would not be presented to the public in *any degree* of variety, till it had been shewn by experience, that the *next preceding degree* of variety, had neither opposed any perceptible *impediment* to their *circulation,* nor been productive of any preponderating *collateral* inconvenience.* 2. That, as far as the *number* of magnitudes was concerned, the complication would be little, if any thing, greater than that which had been proved, by *experience,* not to be attended with inconvenience, in the instance of *Bank of England* Notes.† 3. That, in as far as the complication was the result of *fractions* (mere *addition* of the amounts as presented by inspection being all the "*computation*" that could ever occurr) it would be no material impediment to the *circulation,* because any fractions that might occurr would be allowed or not allowed, as people could *agree*: and there could be no fear about *agreement,* since, the paper not being proposed ever to be a legal tender, the *acceptance* of it, and consequently the *terms* of that acceptance, would depend altogether upon the *choice* of the *party,* to whom in each instance it came to be *offered.*‡

It is with these answers before his eyes, and without vouchsafing them a word of notice, though *referring to the very passage,* that the learned Baronet constructs his argument, consisting of a repetition of the objections thus made for him and thus answered, with a reference to the superseded system of *Custom House* computation, to which (except that figures are concerned in both cases) the system reprobated on this pretence bears not the smallest likeness. In the *Custom*

*Plan, Art. 11 Note 10.

†*ibid.*

‡Suprà, § 11.

House system, *all* the rules of arithmetic (*division* in particular, the most perplexing one) were continually called into action, and the *fractions* that were perpetually occurring, were of the most diversified and intricate nature:—in the *proposed* system of paper money, *addition*, the most simple of the rules of arithmetick, is the *only* rule ever called into action, and the fractions are of *one kind* only, and that likewise the *most simple;* viz. that which has the number 2 for the *common measure*.

The total number of the magnitudes which I speak of as *capable* of being introduced upon my plan is 19: of these I give 14, as the greatest number which I should *expect* to see capable of being introduced with *advantage*. The ground I have made, in point of experience, for supposing, that even *this* utmost degree of complication, would not be productive of *material* impediment to the circulation, has been already seen.* Nevertheless, *out* of this *utmost* number, the number which *I recommend*, in express terms,† as *proper* to be introduced in the first instance, is *one*, *two*, or at *most* but *three*. Setting aside this my plan, and substituting a plan of his own, *made* as *inconvenient* as possible, for the purpose of *inferring* the *impracticability* of it, the learned Baronet, for change for his supposed £100 Bank Note, supposes me to have issued my Standard Annuity Note of £12 16s of the *first* issue, with the 9 magnitudes *below* it, making me omitt the *two* magnitudes *next above* it (the £51 4s and the £25 12s) by which the complication might have been so much reduced.

What is more, to encrease (as he supposes) the impracticability, he supposes the system of the *second* issue (of which the magnitudes are for *much more even* sums, and, under which, change for his £100 Bank Note might, with the help of the two superior magnitudes, which he accordingly makes me discard, be given in the compass of *three* Annuity Notes) to have been already put into circulation at this *first* stage. At the very *beginning* of the measure, which the *Author* is so determined to make a gradual one, the *Critic* supposes it arrived at the *middle* of its career, if not almost at the end.

What answer will he give to this? will he *adhere* to the supposition I have made for him, or *disavow* it? If he disavows it, and says—no, I do not suppose this to be the state of things you would propose to *begin* with, but the state of things to which I suppose it *at length* to

*Suprà, § 11.

†Art. 10.

have arrived, for the purpose of my argument, in order to deduce my consequences from it—if such be the interpretation he puts upon this his own supposition, then mark the consequence. You suppose it then (say I) to have been *carried into practice,* to the *utmost* of its extent, and this is your way of proving it to be *impracticable.*

In vain would it be for him to say—This argument of mine is in the stile of some of Euclid's—putting a case in itself *impossible,* but the truth of which, would be the necessary consequence, if a false proposition, the falsity of which is thus to be demonstrated, were true. The state of things he supposes to be in existence (viz. the proposed system in the extent in which he is thus to prove it to be impracticable) has nothing of impossibility in it, but what is to be *proved* upon it by the medium of argument he thus employs to prove it:—viz. the degree of complication inseparably attendant on it. But the degree of *complication* attendant on the system in *this extent* of it, cannot exist, unless the *system itself* exists in *this extent*: and if the system itself exists in this extent, then, by the supposition, in this extent it is actually *in practice,* instead of being *impracticable.* Thus stands the argument, according to the only plan proposed by *me* for the introduction of the measure—viz. the plan of *gradual introduction*—one magnitude after another—each *subsequent* magnitude not being introduced, till after the convenience of the system, as composed of the several *preceding* magnitudes, has been established by *experience.*

Such is the paralogism—the self-contradiction—of the argument brought up by the learned Baronet, with so triumphant a solemnity. The only possible defalcation that could be made in point of extent from the self-contradictoriness of it (and it is a most insignificant one) is this.—Give me leave to suppose (says he) for the purpose of the argument, that there is a *certain extension,* place it where you will, in the instance of which the degree of complication the system would be attended with, *would* be a bar, to its taking place with advantage: say for instance at the fifth magnitude inclusive, from the Standard Note, reckoning downwards (viz. the 16s Note). Be it so, say I: but if this be the point at which, *for the first time,* the complication operates (or, if tried, *would* operate) as a *bar,* then, *till* the extension of the system has arrived *at* this point, neither the complication nor any thing else, can have proved a bar to it. In the extent given to it by the four first magnitudes, the argument thus brought to prove the impracticability of it, can do no otherwise than admitt it to have been carried into practice with advantage. *Practicable,* your argument *must* admitt the system to be, and not only so, but *actually in practice,* in every degree *prior* to that at which the supposed unsurmountable degree of complication, and the ulterior impracticability of it is supposed (supposed on no better ground than that of a vague presumption) to commence.

Thus must this argument, brought to prove the impracticability of the system, begin with admitting the practicability of it, if employ'd against any stage of it *beyond* the first; and *in* that first stage, the degree of complication is so slight, even in the opponent's own view of it, as not to be worth producing for the purpose.

According to the supposition actually made by him, for the purpose of proving the impracticability of its running any length at all—of its succeeding in any degree—he supposes it (and can do no otherwise than suppose it) to have *already* gone through *those* degrees of extent, which are attended with the *utmost* degree of complication it is susceptible of—with the exception, at the utmost, of only *one* degree, and that a degree altogether immaterial with regard to the success of it. I might therefore *admitt* the system to be impracticable, in the degree in which by this feeble presumption he endeavours to prove it so, and *still* the argument against the *putting it to trial*—(which is the aim and practical conclusion of all his argument) would amount to nothing.

When, under the security afforded by *gradual* extension, I ventured to bring to view the *possible* extension of the system downwards, to magnitudes so *small* as those which present themselves at the *bottom* of the Table, it was under the expectation therein expressed that the minuteness of the "small notes would be protected from *contempt* by their relation to the large ones". The contempt I had then in view, was, however, I must confess, no other than that natural, and unaffected, and therefore *placable* sort of contempt, which might be apt to be suggested by a *hasty* glance, to superficial but unbiassed minds: against the *studied,* and in no small degree *apparently affected* contempt, of which an example has just been seen, neither this, nor any other precaution, can be expected to afford any protection or resource.

The more closely this plan of gradual extension is scrutinized into, the more perfectly it will be seen to be exempt from every particle of possible *danger* or inconvenience: since, if, for supposition sake, it were carried to what might be thought *too advanced* a stage—a stage at which the complication attached to it would *begin* to operate as a *bar,* still no real inconvenience could ensue.—What would be the consequence? *Not,* that paper of the too small magnitude in question *would* get into circulation and be productive of inconvenience; but simply, that, beyond such or such an amount, it would *not* get into circulation. For, on the proposed plan—which is a plan of perfect *liberty*—no man *need,* and therefore no man *would,* accept of it—either in the way of *issue* or in the way of *circulation—to his own inconvenience.*

From these same considerations, when duly attended to, it will also appear—that—so pure from danger is the plan—that, even a *departure* from the above principle—(the principle of gradual extension)—could not be productive of any very material inconvenience. The magnitudes, for which the state of the public mind and public habits were not *as yet* ripe, would *not be taken out,* when offered: or, if *taken out,* to some small amount — the embarassment experienced in the course of the offers made of it in circulation would operate as a bar to the ulterior extension of it.

Whether upon the ground of the impediment expected from the complication, or on what other ground (for no explanation has ever yet been entered into on this point) persons—not affected towards the proposed system in the manner of the learned Baronet—but entertaining favourable expectations of it—have felt themselves disposed for prescribing this or that limit *before hand,* rejecting of course all ulterior extensions.[1] Upon second thoughts however, a fixation thus arbitrary and unnecessary, how naturally soever it may have presented itself to a first glance, would be given up. It would be preferring vague conjecture—and that without any particular use or reason that hath as yet been alledged—preferring *unfounded conjecture*—to the *experience* of future times. The advantage by giving to the *number* of magnitudes every degree of *extension downwards* (the ineligibility of which has not been testified by special indications, deduced from the experience of the magnitudes last in issue) is plain and palpable: because with every *such extension,* the extension of the *market,* and an addition to the *number* of the possible *customers* for this paper, and thence to the possible *amount* of it, would keep pace.

The utmost amount of the inconvenience capable of resulting from

[1][The allusion seems to be to Nicholas Vansittart. Cf. Bowring's *Works* X, 366, and above, p. 78.]

it, would be the inconsiderable *expence,* produced, on the score of engraving and printing, by the magnitudes thus offered without acceptance, or, after acceptance changed for others more convenient,* added to what little degree of disappointment might be the result and what little discredit might be supposed to be reflected by mis-calculation.

From the above suggestions, two *practical* recommendations may, in the present stage of the business, be deduced. The first is—not to mistake for an objection—much less a conclusive objection—to the system any suggestion that may present itself with regard to the proposed expediency of its stepping at this or that particular stage in its extension downwards: a suggestion of this sort how apposite soever it were in the character of an amendment would have no force whatever in the character of a peremptory objection to the measure.

The other is—not to be drawn aside, by the conception of any *supposed,* but *undefined* and *undemonstrated, necessity* or *inconvenience,* to depart from the system of *sums* and *rates of interest,* contrived, as this is, with a view to its being carried *both ways,* to a degree of *extent,* subjected altogether to the future decisions of *experience*: in a word not to committ the decision on this point to mere presumption and *caprice,* how imposing soever may be the authority that calls for it, while *reason* presents at once so *easy* and so *safe* a guide.

§13. OBSERVATIONS CONTINUED.

"Paper money never can answer as a substitute for copper money till copper is as valuable as gold."

COUNTER-OBSERVATIONS.

This is one way of asserting (or rather *more* than asserting—in a stile of greater confidence than can be expressed by *simple* assertion) —that no paper money has ever been employed as a substitute for *Silver Money*. So much for assertion: but how stands fact?—Is *possibility* sufficiently proved by *fact*? Once more, what has the learned Baronet done with his memory? Did he never hear of such a person as *Adam Smith*? Did he never hear of the *Yorkshire* paper *sixpences*? not to speak of the paper *shillings,* and so many *other* paper monies, spoken of by that Adam Smith[1]. Did he never hear of

*As per Art. 17.

[1] [Wealth of Nations, bk. II, ch. II.]

such a place as *America,* with its *Colonies* and their *currencies*? Did he never hear of such a place as *France,* with its Assignats of all *values,* from hundreds or thousands of livres, down to I know not what *minimum,* reduced in value at last down to a fraction of a farthing?—Did he never hear of such a place as *Scotland,* with its 5s Notes, or of such things as Acts of Parliament, sometimes *forbidding* those Notes, and sometimes *legalizing* them?—What is it he means by *"answering"*? Can it do otherwise than *"answer"* to a man, when he gets *sixpence,* or any thing else, for what costs him *nothing*? When *Assignats* perished, was it because it would not have *"answered"* to Government to issue them at their denominative value?

Paper money, be it made as cheap as it will, will *not* cost absolutely *nothing.* But does he look upon it as part of my plan, that it should be issued in sums in which it could *not* be issued but to a *loss*? In what page or line of those printed sheets, will he find a syllable, that can fix a suspicion on *me,* of ever harbouring any such absurdity? would he not find a *direct contradiction* to it, if he could prevail upon himself to look at it?

§14. OBSERVATIONS CONTINUED.

"The wear and tear would ruin the paper money mint. A month's circulation, among *market women, turnpike-keepers,* and *publicans,* would *obliterate* every *clause* of the portable contracts—every *receipt* for interest—every *table* of computation."

COUNTER-OBSERVATIONS.

Before, we had *assertion*—now, we have *argument*—against fact. Had *France*—had *America*—has *Scotland*—no *"market people"* nor *"publicans"*? Does he suppose that his own, or any other *hostile* powers, will be suffered to call for change *ad libitum* for the purpose of bringing on the ruin he predicts? let him look to Article 16,* he will find all such ingenuity anticipated and barred out.

In the picture he gives of the speedy *illegibility* of these instruments, one would think he had been speaking of a *manuscript,* and a manuscript *without a copy.* Instead of the *thinnest paper,* as in Bank Notes, he supposes a thickness, like that of *parchment,* or the

*Note.

paper of *Exchequer Bills;* in which the *pigment,* howsoever incorporated by impression, may be *worn off,* while the *ground* remains *entire.* He considers not, that in case of a doubt or a difference, respecting the tenor of an instrument, copies of which are continually passing through everybody's hands, the *window* of every *Local Annuity Note Office* (that is of every Town and Country Post-office) if not the *pocket* of the *next neighbour,* would present wherwithal to remove it. He does not consider, that so long as the *principal sum* (which of course will be in *great* letters) is discernible, all the rest, in any other view than that of *security against forgery* would be a matter of indifference. *Colour* alone—*form* alone—much more, colour and form *combined*—afford difference enough, to convey the difference between sum and sum, to the few eyes unable to comprehend numerical figures. He forgets (what is not our learned and really and eminently learned Baronet capable of forgetting for this purpose?) he forgets all those *devices,* the *efficiency* of which has been established by the experience of so many ages—all those expedients for producing the *effect of letters* on *unlettered eyes.* Did he ever see such a thing as a Coat of Arms? Did he ever see a sign-post with a *sign* to it? Does he suppose, the customers of the *Lion* would not be able to find the *house,* because a piece of the *tail,* or two or three of the *claws,* happened to have scaled off? But supposing this *proposition* of his were as true as it is erroneous, in what respect would his *argument* be the better for it?—Who would be the sufferer by the obliteration? Not the *public;* but the *individual,* who *chose* to be so by his *negligence.*

As to *copper* Notes, I point them out merely for *"consideration"*:* nor so much as for consideration for the *present* time; but only for the *future possible time,* in the state of things that would take place, supposing the line of currency to have been *already* extended downwards—and extended with success—to the level of the *lowest* rank of the *Silver* Notes.

When he speaks of obliterating *receipts,* he speaks, as usual, from imagination: had he looked at what was before him, he would have seen, that he might as well have talked of *wearing out the air.* The receipts are proposed to be given—as such receipts have *actually* been given—not by *adding words,* but by substracting paper.

*Art. 11.

§15. OBSERVATIONS CONTINUED.

"Of [£]400.000,000 of Annuity Notes—*supposing* them all as good as Bankers' Notes—*how much* would be wanted as a *circulating medium*? Would the *remainder* be any thing more than a mere security for an Annuity?—Its imperfections in this Office I have already noticed."

COUNTER-OBSERVATIONS.

And so its matter of *supposition* only—a sort of *concession* to be made for the *moment,* only for the purpose of *argument*—that a mass of Notes, issued on the security of the whole mass of national property—and of which, to the amount of 400 Millions worth, have, by this same supposition, met with purchasers—should be *"as good* as Bankers Notes"! But what does *"good"* mean here?—good in point of *security*?—good in point of *currency*? or *both*? What is the proposition, to which he vouchsafes to give this momentary consent? —That the whole property of the community, is *as* capable of fulfilling the mass of pecuniary engagements charged on *it,* as the aggregate property of the aggregate number of Note emitting Bankers, is of fulfilling the aggregate mass of pecuniary engagements charged upon *their* Banks?—*or,* that a species of property, which, by the supposition, has already found purchasers to the amount of £400,000,000, shall have as good a prospect of *continuing* to find purchasers, as a species of property which, by how much soever it may now be deemed excessive, will scarcely be supposed to have swollen beyond a tenth, or even so much as a twentieth part, of that sum.

I say nothing here of the *matter of fact* (for such it is) viz. that these 400 Mushrooms* (who are thus put by the learned Baronet in *one* scale, while the rest of the Nation, with his Globe (when created) in the middle of it, are, in the stile of Chinese Geography, crammed into the *other*) are of that sort, that, in the compass of a few months, have been known to die off, by a hundred at a time:†—nor of the *principle* (for such it is that ought never to be out of mind, when Banks and Bankers are on the carpet) viz. that it is of the *essence* of the trade, that, in an event which may happen at any time, the *ful*

*In the beginning of the year 399; according to the printed *List*.

†Chalmers's Estimate [of the Comparative Strength of Great Britain], edit. 1794, p. [XLVIII] Preface [or rather "Dedication"].

fillment of their engagements, *taken in the aggregate, is physically impossible*. The *concessions* which it would be the tendency of these observations to make *absolute*—the concessions which, in any other than an *hypothetical* form, the liberality of the learned Baronet cannot prevail upon itself to gratify me with—come in but in a parenthesis: questions such as these are rather too long to be settled in the compass of a comment on a parenthesis.

The learned Baronet has weighed the Annuity Note plan, and found it *light*: but behold the texture of his scales!

"Of this 400,000,000" (says he) "*how much* would be *wanted* as a *circulating medium*? would the *remainder* be any thing more than a mere security for an Annuity"?—How much would be "*wanted*"? The meaning of the word *wanted*, though it is so *familiar* a word, is not quite so *clear* as might be supposed: but of that elsewhere.*

*In one sense, money *will* always be *wanted*—wanted in a quantity which has no *limits*: *paper money* consequently, and in a quantity always alike unlimited—so long as it will pass for money: for what *individual* is there, that does not find himself the richer the more he has of it? Does it follow from hence that it is incapable of existing in *excess*? that it is impossible the *Country* should have too much of it? Most surely not. It seems a contradiction in terms, to say that money can be constantly *wanted*, in a quantity constantly *excessive*. The result is—that the proposition *money is wanted*—is true and false at the same time. It is evident therefore, that the sense in which it is *false* must be a *different* one, from that in which it is *true*.

Wanted is, on this occasion, exactly synonymous, to the more plausible and more frequent word *required*.† The solution of the question *whether the increase of money by paper money ought to be suffered to go on without restraint*, depends upon the distinction, between what is true, and what is false, in the *propositions* of which this word has been the characteristic *term*—upon the detection of the deep-rooted fallacy, of which it has very honestly been made the vehicle.

On examination of the opinions given, in the form of *evidence* to the two Houses, on the occasion of the *Stoppage of the Bank*, I find the more use of this word *required*, given and received as an equivalent for all information as to the nature and ground of the alledged demand. I have *numbered* the *occasions* on which, and noted the *persons* by whom, it has been thus employ'd: and it is but in *one* instance, that I find the idea attached to it, connected with any others that are more determinate.

The investigation of the above *practical* question, relative to the *stoppage* of paper money, resolves itself therefore in effect, into a comment on the word "*required*", when predicated, as it has been, of an *increase of money*.

Of the result of this investigation, the following is a statement compressed to the utmost point of condensation.

1. That every addition to the mass of money (over and above what corresponds to the addition made in the same time to the mass of consumable and other moveable and vendible commodities),[1] is productive of *rise of prices*.

2. That the additions made to the mass of money, have *hitherto* been all along productive of additions to the mass of real *wealth*, beyond what would have been made without the *added money*.

3. That however, even where the addition is made solely in the shape of *metallic* money, the *suffering* produced by the *rise of prices*, and its attendant pressure, is

In any sense thus much may be answered.—In *each* shape, sometimes *more*—sometimes *less*: the *proportion* depends upon the *times*. —In whichever of its two shapes each Note is *most* wanted, at *each* point of time—in *that* shape (we may venture to say without any

always *more* than an equivalent, for any *enjoyment* produced by the addition to the mass of wealth: and that, metaphysical as the case of the proposition may seem to be, the truth of it is capable of being made apparent, by considerations already familiar to the public eye.

4. That the disadvantage arising from the encrease of money, is not only *aggravated* in *degree*, but *doubled* in *kind*, when the encrease takes place by *paper* money of the sort actually in use: because in this case, not only the rise of prices receives an *augmentation without limit*, but a danger of *General Bankruptcy* is introduced: a danger, which, *sooner or later*, cannot fail of being realized, *unless* a remedy be applied.

5. That the effect of a *defalcation*, if *copious* and *sudden*, from the mass of money in circulation, would be productive of more *pressure*, as well as more *danger*, in respect of general Bankruptcy, than an excessive *addition* to the same amount: and, that, if such *addition* were to have the effect of bringing on such a catastrophe, a sudden and copious *defalcation* would be among the first *effects* of the addition, and immediate *causes* of the catastrophe.

6. That a *simple stoppage* of the encrease of money by *Bank* and *Bankers* paper money, would at once stop the rise of prices (taken in the aggregate) and dispell the danger of General Bankruptcy: nor would it be productive of any inconvenience, beyond the inconvenience, resulting from the stoppage of pernicious gains.

7. That as to the proposed *Government* Annuity Note paper, so far as, in the character of circulating money, it came *in lieu* of an equal quantity of the existing sorts of *private* paper, it would (besides the *profit* to Government by reduction of the National Debt and other items) contribute to *reduce the danger* in respect to particular Bankruptcies.

8. But that if, in any *sudden* and *considerable* quantity, it rises to constitute a *clear addition* to the mass of money in circulation, the *benefit* it would be of in *other* respects, would not be an equivalent for the *inconvenience* it would be productive of, in respect of *rise* of *prices*.

9. That therefore the *desirable* result would be—that, as this *Government* paper *encreased*, such *private* paper should *diminish*: that it seems probable enough, that such diminution on the *one* part would, of *itself*, keep pace with the encrease on the *other*, with a degree of exactness sufficient for the purpose: but that *if it did not*, the quantity of private paper should, from time to time, be subjected to *ulterior* retrenchments by *positive law*.

10. That the suffering individuals to *coin*, each for his *own* benefit, that which has in every respect the effect of *money*, was originally an *oversight* on the part of the *legislature:* and that the utmost *hardship* that can result to *individuals* from any *defalcation*, which for the good of the *whole* may *require* to be made, from time to time, from the quantity of such money, is no greater, than that which results from the endeavours all along employ'd, to prevent the mass of money from receiving additions, from *counterfeit metallic* money.

11. That, in proportion as the proposed *Government* paper money came to extend itself at the expence of *private* paper money, it would act partly as a preservative[,] partly as a *cure*, with respect to those occasional and sudden *scarcities* of money (i.e. of money actually employ'd in circulation) which have for their cause, in most, if not all instances, the *radical imbecillity* inherent in the constitution of the chief of the existing sorts of private paper money: viz. the conveying of a *promise*, importing

such nice scrutinizing into the import of the word *wanted*) in *that* very *shape* will it be employed, *at that time*.

And here comes a *second* occasion,* to notice a feature, as useful in itself as it is *peculiar* to the proposed system,† together with the pains taken by our Critic to avoid the sight of it. Here, as before, he is resolute in his efforts not to see, that each and every note, not excluded by its magnitude, is of an *amphibious* nature, alike applicable to *either* branch of service. To avoid this sight, here as before, he divides the aggregate of them, without mercy, into two *uncommunicating* masses, each applicable to *one* of the services alone, if to any, and never to the *other*. After such a division, what in the name of common sense can be done with questions that are thus grounded on it? What answer can be given to them? The distinction is altogether of the Critic's *own* imagining—the *"remainder"* he speaks of, is altogether of his own *creating*. In the *plan itself* among the Annuity Notes *themselves*—there is *no* distinction—*no remainder*: and this to any eye that will be pleased to see it, is one of their great uses and points of convenience. As to our Critic, if nothing will serve him but he must have *distinctions* and *"remainders"*, where the nature of things refuses them, let him try his hand upon a *Squadron of Seahorses*—let him divide them into troops—and say to one troop—mind me—*your* place is in the *water*—and you others—*your* place is on the *land*.—But, observe! you must stay, every one of you, where you are *put*: you must not ever think of changing places.

The force of this argument, such as it is, consists in the not seeing the difference between an *Annuity Note* and a parcel of Stock:—between a thing that *may* be passed from hand to hand *by mere delivery*, wherever there are two hands belonging to two bodies: and

---

a man to be *always ready*, for the payment of *metallic* money, in the shape of *ready money*, in *greater* quantities than it can be *always* had.

12. That, in proportion as it came to extend itself, in *Ireland* as well as in *Britain*, the *proposed currency* would constitute a *remedy*, to the inconvenience under which not Ireland only, but Britain likewise, labours, by the *high extra price*, which, in *Ireland*, a man is obliged to pay, for *money to be received in Britain*: and that this remedy, as far as it could be made to extend, would be more *direct* and *simple* and *lasting*, than any other that could be employ'd.

†Suprà, § 11.

[1][This second bracket is interpolated.]

---

*See above, § 3.

†Viz. as far as concerns paper money, in pieces, each of any thing less than £100 value.

a thing which *cannot* be transferred from hand to hand, but at *one* particular place, with a particular set of *formalities.* Of a parcel of *Stock,* it may *indeed* be said, with truth, that (in our Baronet's words) it is *"a mere security for an Annuity"*, and nothing more: but an *Annuity Note* is a security for an Annuity, and it is *a piece of money besides*: not both, indeed, to the *same person,* at the *same time* (the boy with his cake:—thought it was so good a cake—could not eat it up—and still have it untouched) not *both* at the *same time,* but *either* at *all times: each* at *that* time, at which it is *most* wanted.

In this latter of the two inseparable characters—that of a mere security for an Annuity—the *"imperfections"* of the species of paper in question are what (the learned Baronet informs us) he *"has already noticed"*. Noticed them—indeed he has—viz. the points which shewed themselves as *"imperfections"* in *his* eye: noticed them he has—so also have *his* notices been noticed. The *new* matter that *remains* to be noticed here, consists in the *fresh* supposition—the *newly supposed state of things,* in which by this reference he assures us that the self same imperfections would be found.

The imperfections *then were*—and now (according to him) still *are*—

1. That the proposed paper will not come into existence in any *quantity* worth regarding.*

2. That to *individuals,* considered as customers for it, in the character of a *source of income,* permanent or temporary, it will not be productive of any *benefit* worth regarding.†

3. That to *Government* it will produce more *loss,* by the defalcation it will make from the *legacy tax*‡ than it will produce *profit* from *all* sources taken together.

4. That the mischief it will be productive of, *at the death* of the head of a family, by the opportunity it will afford to one member of the family to *steal* the property of another, will, together with its other bad effects, be more than an equivalent for any benefits it seems likely to produce: || at least in the character of a source of permanent income.

Such (according to him) were its *"imperfections"*, in what (according to him) would be the most *probable* state of things.

---

*§ 2.
†§ 3, 4, 5.
‡§ 6.
||§ 6.

Now for the re-appearance of the *same imperfections* in this *different* state of things, which, for the purpose of the argument only, but however for the purpose of the argument, is to be *supposed* a true one.

1. *New state of things*—£400,000,000 of Annuity Notes out in issue. *Concomitant imperfection the 1st. This* a quantity not worth regarding.
2. *New state of things,* as before. £400,000,000 of Annuity Notes out in issue. *Concomitant imperfection the 2d.* The benefit to individuals a quantity not worth regarding. *Proof*—Purchases one after another to *this* amount, without *benefit* and without motive: *effects* to *this* amount, produced without a *cause.*
3. *New state of things,* as before. £400,000,000 of Annuity Notes out in issue. *Concomitant imperfection*—more *loss* to Government, by defalcation from the *legacy tax,* than *profit* from *all* sources: Proof—Interest upon £400,000,000 capital of Annuities taking the whole at no more than 3 per cent per annum 12,000,000

Profit by conversion of 3 per cent Stock Annuities into £2 19s Note Annuities (supposing Annuity Notes to be issued all of them when Stock Annuities were at par instead of being issued when Stock Annuities are at 60, 61, and so on respectively) 1/60 of the £12,000,000: this alone makes £200,000

Deduct total present amount of the legacy tax for the year ending 5th Jan. 1801* supposing it were *all* lost—

England†	135,095
Scotland‡	2,890
	137,985

Neat profit from this source alone, and in a state of

*Commons Accounts, 2 June, 1801, No. 1.

†*ibid,* p.26.

‡*ibid,* p.30.

things, in which, according to our Baronet,* there can be no profit at all	£62,015
Add profit *in money,* by difference between £400,000,000 of Annuity Notes sold at £100 and Stock Annuities bought upon an average at 85, viz. 15 per cent being the supposition made by Mr Secretary Rose in his Finance Pamphlet of 1799-1800:† supposing 3 per cent Stock Annuities to have risen to par by the end, or in the course of, this conversion: (if they have not, the profit will be greater)	£60,000,000
Quantity of Stock Annuities bought in or paid off with this £60,000,000 of money, at 85 as above	£70,588,235
Besides profit by *reduction* of 5 per cent and 4 per cent *Stock* Annuities to 3 per cent *Note* Annuities: (profit, by the difference between £3 per cent and £2 19s per cent, being already reckoned:) of which profit the Annuity Note system would either have been the *causa sine quâ non,* or a *concurrent* cause to an indeterminable degree.	
Two per cent per annum upon £48,250,427‡ of 5 per cents (subject to correction from the *Loyalty loan*) is per annum	£965,008
One per cent per annum upon £45,269,669‖ of 4 per cents is per annum	£452,696
Making together, per annum	£1,417,704

Besides 5 or 6 other inferior sources of profit, not worth particularizing in this view. The amount however would be more than the deduction, for the over estimate of the profit in the Loyalty loan 5 per cents, convertible optionally into 4 per cents. Sixty million of principal money—added to about 1½ million a year in Annuities—such is the *profit, over* which, in this estimate of the learned Baronet's, a supposed *possible loss* — not *of,* but *upon,* a sum of £134,000 a year (of which supposed loss not a penny might come to be realized)—would, upon this supposition, preponderate.

---

*Infrà, § 18.

†Brief Examination &c, p. 26, 6th Edit.

‡Commons Account No. VI, 17 April, 1801, p. 9.

‖*ibid.*

§16. OBSERVATIONS CONTINUED.

"If *hoarders* should prefer Annuity Notes to *Banker's paper* and Banker's tills, will not the 4 or 500 Bankers in Great Britain be injured and entitled to compensation? If *Circulators* should prefer Annuity Notes to *B[an]k of England paper,* will not *that* public body be a sufferer?"

COUNTER-OBSERVATIONS.

Bankers sufferers? the Bank a sufferer?—Well and what then? As a man, I might feel—as an advocate for the public—preferring the superior interest to the inferior—the more extensive to the less extensive—I neither know nor care. What? shall not the public be allowed to borrow its own money upon the *best* terms?—upon any terms which, without fraud or force, it can get the lenders to accept? These are among the topics, which I have discussed at large—as our Critic might have *seen* already in the Table of Chapters; and as he might well have *imagined* without seeing it. The effect of the measure, will not be *all* damage to them, if it be *any* damage: but if it *were* all damage, what damage was ever more pure from *injury*?

By this argument—if there were any thing in it—his own *"plan"* or *"project"* would be struck through and through. His own company is a phantom yet *waiting for existence*: Can that be said of the *public,* or of *Government*? The recoil [?] upon self and Co he does not see: in "the zeal to destroy", *self-destruction* is no object with him. I will save him from the blow. His question is worth nothing: *not* even against *himself* . . . If another *man's-mercer* were to set up in Bond Street, would not the existing man's-mercers *"be intitled to compensation"*?

Any body that pleases, issues paper, *without interest,* and *with* or *without security*. Government must not issue it, even *on payment of interest*—and on the *very best security*: a security made better and better still, by every piece of paper issued on these terms.

§17. OBSERVATIONS CONTINUED.

"Till however the Stocks are near par, there seems little probability that a 3 per cent Note will rival a 3 per cent consol."

COUNTER-OBSERVATIONS.

More blindness, similar to what we have seen manifested above in the case of *Exchequer Bills,** but still more determinate. The features of advantage possessed by *Annuity Notes,* in comparison with *Exchequer Bills,* might, without much difficulty, have been collected by the learned Baronet from the sheets he had before him, in some such form as that in which they are exhibited above.† The features of advantage, possessed by Annuity Notes, in comparison with the object *now* upon the carpet—*Stock Annuities*—were and are *ready collected* to his hands.‡ In regard to *purchase,* 7; during *custody,* 4; in regard to *transfer,* 8. They were staring him in the face: for he quotes one of them *in terminis*: he controverts not one of them: unless it be the one about the facility afforded for making *settlements in trust* (which is the one he quotes)|| and that no otherwise than by representing it as unintelligible, because the explanation given of it was in one of the Tables he had before him (Table II), instead of the printed pages. He controverts *not one* of them: but, shutting his eyes against them *all,* he keeps on his train, as if he had reduced them to non-existence.

I have shewn that for *temporary* sums to *any amount,* and for *permanent* sums to any less amount than about £100,¶ a *nominal* and *apparent* 5 per cent in Stock Annuities, is not so much as a *real* 3 per cent: is not so much as the £2 19s per cent, afforded by the proposed Note Annuities: that accordingly, at the hands of *Bankers,* in Town as well as in Country, a 3 per cent, and even that but *apparent*—wanting considerably of being a *real* 3 per cent—has been, and is, *preferred* to the nominal 5 per cent given by Stock Annuities: meaning what, if *risks* and *expences* were thrown out of the account, the 3 per cents *would* give *at present.* But, as *three* per cent Stock Annuities rise towards *par,* the *now* nominal 5 per cent becomes *less and less,* till their arrival at par; when it is reduced to an *equally nominal* 3 per cent. *Real* 3 per cents rival *already* these *nominal* 5 per cents: *Note Annuities are* (within 1/60th) *real* 3 per cents: and yet they *will* not (according to him) rival these *nominal 5 per cents,* till the nominal 5 per cent is nearly reduced to an equally nominal 3 per cent!

On the advantage that *Note* Annuities will have over *Stock* Annuities, in respect of *superiority of duration,* I will not insist, on the

*Suprà, § 9.
†*ib.*
‡Plan [ch. IV.]
||Infrà, § 20.
¶Plan [ch. IV.]

present occasion: because, by the supposition (as he *now* words it) at the period he supposes, Stocks are *not* yet *"near par"*[—]are *not yet* at the period, at which (if there be any such thing at that time as the proposed Annuity Notes) the universal *redemption* of Stock Annuities, either by *extinction* or *conversion* into such *Note* Annuities, cannot but take place: a proposition demonstrated (I had thought) in the printed sheets that were before him yet denied by him, with his usual decision; as will be seen presently,* and upon what grounds. But this period being by the supposition not *"near"*, may be supposed not to be as yet *in prospect*: for if it *were*, the advantages which the *Note*-Annuities would hold out, in point of *permanency*, while the *fall*, as soon as it took place, would be from almost £3, to not quite 2⅜ per cent, would surely form no inconsiderable item in the catalogue of their attractions.

§18. OBSERVATIONS CONTINUED.

"When they (3 per cent Stocks) are at par, the public will derive no benefit from this scheme, unless they can issue Annuity Notes yielding only 2⅜ per cent interest."

"The extension of the plan to paying off public Annuitants would in no case be practicable."

COUNTER-OBSERVATIONS.

Of this mass of argument, with the sweeping denial that crowns it, the substance, if I understand it right, will be found to be contained in the two following propositions.

Position.—When Stocks (3 per cents) *"are at par"*, Government will *not* be able *"to issue Annuity Notes yielding only 2⅜ per cent interest"*.

Inference. Therefore, when Stocks (3 per cents) *are at par, "the public will derive no benefit from this scheme"*; viz. the issuing of Annuity Notes.

As to the *position*—taking it as it stands on paper—and as it appears to have been standing in the learned Baronet's mind—it is indisputably true; but his argument will not be much the better for it.

According to the *plan* itself, while there are *any* Stocks at all—(any redeemable Annuities remaining in the form of Stock—unredeemed

*§ 18.

by Annuity Notes of the first issue—by Annuity Notes bearing £2 19s per cent)—no Annuity Notes of the second issue *can* be issued: for, by the terms of the Article,* it is only *"upon the redemption of the last parcel of redeemable Stock Annuities"*, and not before—that *"the Offices are to be opened for the emission of a second issue, at a reduced rate of interest"*.

Taking it strictly then, the case he mentions, as a case in which *"the public will derive no benefit from the plan"*—viz. the case of Government's trying whether *"they can issue Annuity Notes yielding only 2⅜ per cent interest"*, and finding it impracticable—is a case which, under the plan against which he is urging this argument, can never happen.

A case which under and according to the plan cannot *but* happen, is—that of the extinction of the *whole* mass of *redeemable Stock* Annuities: the place, of such of them as have not been bought in or paid off, being occupied by a proportionable quantity of *Note Annuities,* viz. Note Annuities of the *first* issue—the mass of redeemable Annuities then remaining, having been converted in point of form into Note Annuities.

As soon as Stock Annuities (3 per cents) *"are at par"*, *then* it is, that, with the help of the existing *Sinking Funds,* such conversion (according to my view of the matter) cannot fail to *begin* to take place: and, almost as soon as it has *begun* to take place, *then* it is that (according to my view of the matter) it can *scarcely* fail to be compleated.

In the *course* of the process, and naturally (on account of the profit) at the *earliest* stage of it, different parcels of redeemable Stock Annuities—5 per cent—4 per cent—3 per cent—will all of them have been *paid off,* and the rates of interest respectively borne by them, reduced to the rate borne by the *Note* Annuities: viz. £2 19s.

When, with all this before his eyes, the learned Baronet asserts—and asserts with so much composure—that *"the extension of the plan to paying off public Annuitants would in no case be practicable"*. I am altogether at a loss to conceive, what could be the ideas that, in his mind, presented themselves in company with those words. *Paying off,* is the word *I* used: † *paying off,* is the word he uses. *Buying in,* I mention as the first stage of the plan: ‡ *buying in, he* (by implication

*Art. 20.

†Art. 19, 20.

‡*ibid.*

at least) considers as that first stage. *Paying off,* I speak of as an extension* from that first stage: *paying off, he* speaks of as an *"extension"* likewise. The practicability of the plan as to the *buying in,* he does not directly controvert: on the contrary, by an implication which I am almost bold enough to state as tantamount to a necessary one, he even admitts it: yes, in a certain quantity, he certainly *does* admitt it: in short in *any* quantity, *"not great enough to be an object of finance"*.†

Well then: during the existence of the Annuity Note plan, viz. between the opening of the issue and the arrival of Stock 3 per cents at par, *some* part of the mass of Stock Annuities *has,* according to him, been *bought in,* by money produced by the sale of Note Annuities. From the arrival of Stock 3 per cents at par, the *conversion* in question (the conversion of them (as above explained) into Note Annuities) will be *going on* till it is *compleated*: which conversion, consists in the expelled Annuitants, buying Note Annuities with the money put into their hands, in the paying off their Stock Annuities. Yet according to him, "the *extension* of the plan to paying off public Annuitants would *in no case* be practicable".

The difference between *buying in* Stock Annuities, and *paying* them *off,* is simply this. *Buying* them *in,* requires the concurrence of the Annuitant: *paying* them *off,* requires *no* such concurrence. It is where the purchase depends upon the *Annuitant* as well as Government, that according to the learned Baronet, it is *practicable*: when it depends *altogether* upon Government, then, according to him, it is no longer practicable.

Without *money,* it certainly is not practicable in *either* case. But the Annuity Note plan, how small soever may have been the mass of money it has *put into* the hands of Government, at the worst has not taken any *out.* But, at this *present* time, the Sinking Fund is already putting into the hands of Government above 5 Million a year, for that purpose: and the increase in the price of Stocks must have been rapid indeed, if, by the time they are at par, those 5 Millions have not received a very considerable *increase.* The Annuitants, thus forcibly expelled out of the *Stock* Annuities, will have no other Government Annuities to resort to for the employment of their money than the *Note* Annuities. At a time when Note Annuities were not to be bought but at a *sacrifice* of two per cent, out of the

*Art. 19.

†Suprà, § 2.

5 per cent which they might have made of their money by buying 3 per cent Stock Annuities, at the price they bear at present—notwithstanding this prodigious sacrifice, these Note Annuities according to the Baronet's own admission* had at any rate *some* purchasers: now that *these* Annuities are to be had without *any* sacrifice—now that Government Annuities are not to be had in any *other* shape—now that the quantity of Government Annuities capable of being had is *lessening* every day—now that the quantity of *money,* capable of being laid out in the purchase of Government Annuities, is *encreasing* every day—*now* it is that, according to the learned Baronet—(who has not the smallest doubt about it)—Annuity Notes will no longer obtain a single purchaser.

From the time that *Stock* 3 per cents are arrived at par, let the money raised by the emission of *Note* Annuities have contributed ever so much, or ever so *little,* to the rise, from that time, if any Stock Annuities are paid off, and any Note Annuities bought in, with the money received in exchange for the Stock Annuities so paid off, the *conversion* has *commenced,* and (to use the learned Baronet's own words) *"the extension of the plan to paying off public Annuitants"* has commenced. At the *completion* of such conversion, i.e., when *no* part of the mass of redeemable Stock Annuities remains, ["]the extension of the plan to paying off public Annuitants" has been *compleated.* This completion will *equally* have taken place—and that in virtue of "the extension of the plan"—whether any part of the money employed in the paying off the Stock Annuities, be over and above what has been raised by the paying off of prior masses of the same sort of Annuities: that is, whether any *fresh* money has been brought in for the purchase of Note Annuities, *besides* that which had been previously obtained, by the sale, forced or spontaneous, of Stock Annuities. If any fresh parcels of money *have* during the time been brought into the market for the purchase of Note Annuities, the conversion will have gone on so much the *quicker*: but *without* any such import of fresh money, so long as there are Annuity Notes to sell, the quantity of money furnished by the Sinking Funds will have been amply sufficient, not only to *set* the conversion a going, but to *keep* it going at a rapid pace: so that *"the extension of the plan to paying off public Annuitants"* by means of these Note Annuities, may be compleated, even without any preference given by purchasers to this *new proposed* form, in comparison of the *existing* form

*Suprà §2.

of *Stock* Annuities.* It is under these circumstances that it is, according to him, "*in no case practicable*".

§19. OBSERVATIONS CONTINUED.

"The extension of the plan to paying off public Annuitants would in no case be practicable. How could my *Trustees* convert Consols into Annuity Notes, and give me authority to receive the annual interest, without, at the same time[,] giving me the Annuity Notes, which, being payable to bearer, would enable me to spend the principal?"

COUNTER-OBSERVATIONS.

I repeat the *proposition*, to preserve the connection between that and the *demonstration*. The *demonstration* I call it, for, if to serve in that character be *not* the intention of it, then is the *proposition* a mere crude assertion without proof. If the naked word of the learned Baronet were to be taken, in respect of this the most *important part* of the obnoxious project, as well might he have proposed it being taken as to the *whole*: nor is this the first time of its occurring to me, that a method thus short and easy, would not have been less prudential, than the more troublesome course he has pursued.

On more occasions than one it has appeared to me (not to say on every occasion) that his assertions would have gained much in force, by being disencumbered of his arguments. If what we have seen be really meant for argument, and for argument in support of the otherwise unsupported proposition that stands next before it, let us try the experiment upon it and see whether the present occasion, may not at any rate serve as an example.

*During the period *previous* to the commencement of the conversion, the amount, of the *profit* made by the Annuity Note plan, will indeed depend, upon the quantity of fresh money brought into the Government Annuity Market, for the purchase of these Note Annuities. The *price* of Stock Annuities purchased with such monies being *given*, the amount of the profit will be in exact proportion to the *quantity* of *fresh money* so imported. But *during the conversion*, the amount of profit will *not* depend upon the quantity of such fresh imported money in any degree, any otherwise than in as far as the conversion of the higher rates of interest into this lowest rate is *accelerated* by that means: and if the whole conversion should be effected at once by *subscription* (as explained in the Note to Art. 20) *then*, there being no room for such acceleration, no fresh profit can be derived on that account from *this* source. The only profit produced in this case by such fresh money, will be that which depends on the *acceleration* of the arrival of the respective periods of the *subsequent* reductions (from £2 19s to £2 7s 5d per cent & so on) by so many successive issues.

"A great part of the Funds belongs" (says he) "to *Trustees*"; and then comes the difficulty about Trustees. Let this difficulty (for the argument sake) be unsurmountable: and now let us observe the use he makes of it. You cannot pay off Funds belonging to Trustees: therefore you cannot pay off Funds *not* belonging to Trustees. Paying off is not practicable in this *one* case—therefore it is not practicable in *any* case.

The learned Baronet's *law* here matches with his *logic*. In what law book—in what book of Statute Law—of Common Law—or of Equity Law—or even of morals—has our lawyer made the discovery that the Trustee of a Creditor *cannot* be made, or *ought not* to be made, to receive his debt? In what part of the *Reports of the Committee of Finance* has he read, that the *redeemable* part of the Government Annuities consists of two portions — one *redeemable* — the other *irredeemable*? — and that the *irredeemable* portion is *any* part of the *redeemable* portion, that the proprietors may, at any time, by the contrivance of a *trust*, choose to *save* from being redeemed?

But "how could my Trustees" (says our man of law) "convert consols into Annuity Notes and give me authority to receive the annual interest, without at the same time giving me the Annuity Notes, which being payable to bearer would enable me to spend the principal?"

Before I give a direct answer to this question, I will trouble him with a few more. Has he ever (I must ask him once more) heard of such a place as *Ireland*? Does he know (or not know) that in that Country there is a *public debt*? Does he know (or not know) that in that Country, till a few years ago, their debt had no other form than that of separate and portable notes called Debentures? that so *late* at any rate as the 2nd of April 1800 (and (for aught I know) to the present day) above a fourth part of it was in that form*—issued, some, if not all of them, for £100—a sort of thing like India Bonds? Does he suppose that in Ireland there are no such persons as *Trustees*? or that the debt of that Country—to the amount of so many millions —could have existed for such a length of time, and no part of it have become the subject matter of a *trust*? When he has found an answer to these questions, he will have found, that even in this narrow part of the case—this narrow portion which in his mind had

*Commons Union Accounts, 2 April, 1800, p. 108. Total Debt 25,662,640. Whereof Debentures 7,172,740.

passed itself for the whole—the objection, even before discussion, will have dwindled into nothing.

Without staying for any answer to my questions, I will now satisfy the curiosity testified by his. His Trustees may be as many as he pleases: he paying, if it please him to have *more than two,* the very moderate recompence I shall require of him for the extra expence and trouble. For the purpose of explanation—to save the trouble he might otherwise have to bestow in understanding or misunderstanding me—for the purpose of explanation, I will suppose *but two.* His Note (as I had already had the honour of observing to him,* though he was too much engaged to listen to me) may be divisible in *three* or *four* or even *more* parts: but say here *two* parts. When the time for payment of interest is come, his Trustees (having put each of them his own name and direction on his own part) deliver or send, each of them his own part, to the *Local Annuity Office nearest* to him (that is to the nearest Post Office) or any other that may be more *convenient* to him:—each using the *same* Office, or, if it be more convenient, a *different* one. The Office-keeper, or Office-keepers, respectively transmitt the part, or respective parts, to the *General* Annuity Office, from which place the clerk, whose business it is, remitts back each part-Note to that one of the two Local Offices from which it came: with the addition of the *rouleau* or *packet* containing the amount of such interest money, to *one* of those local offices: at which place it will be sealed up, and directed, for one of the Trustees, or for the learned Baronet himself, according to such appointment as shall have been made in that behalf by such Trustees:—where it is,[1] till the person who is to receive it, by himself or *order, calls* or *sends* for it; with the other part of the note: the time being pre-ascertainable by the course of the post. *Printed forms* expressive of such *words* as appeared to be of a *general* nature in the several instruments—with *blanks* for such as were of a *particular* nature, would have been provided by his humble servant—the fly upon the wheels. *Receipts—Orders—Letters*—none of them larger in size, nor more complicated in phraseology than the *printed forms* we see for receipts—or the *engraved* forms we see for *promissory* Notes. The process (I am sorry to say it) would be to be repeated *toties quoties*: just as it would be, if he were to set his *Attorney* to receive the money, charging 6s 8d for it; with or without other attendancies, journies, letters,

*Table II, Note 24.

[1][The MS reads "where it his".]

parcels, and *etceteras*. As for me—not meaning to make a profit by him, I should do the business for him upon my own frugal plan:* charging no more for it than the very small portion of time, necessarily bestowed upon it, and paid for on that plan, would require. A few pence for business done as it were by *steam*: a few pence[—] considering the scale I work upon—would satisfy me.

.... A pretty piece of work! (exclaims the Baronet here as before)† a pretty piece of work "for the interest of a note of 5d¾ bearing an interest of 1/512 part of a farthing per diem"! to which I reply—(out of one of the thousand passages he has been so careful not to see)—that, according to such human probabilities as human creatures find it necessary on ordinary occasions to be governed by, people will not be at this trouble and expence, in other than *such* cases "where *the magnitude of the sum*"‡ (and he has my leave for adding the relative magnitude relation being had to the peculiar circumstances of the parties) *"renders it worth while."*

Two parts (a head piece and a tail piece) capable of *division* and *reunion*—every note, made out according to the form exhibited in Table II, (where it courts the honour of his glance, if he would be pleased to look at it) contains *already*.

After this specimen, I don't know whether I may be fortunate enough to obtain credit with the learned Baronet, for the very small degree of ingenuity that would be requisite, for the framing of a Note to the like effect, according to a form which should render it divisible into *three, four,* or even *more* parts.

Where the necessity of the concurrence of *two* parties is not deemed a sufficient safeguard—so that the concurrence of a *third* party—and thence a Note of the *tripartite* form—is thought necessary to be required—I should hope and expect, that, for the protection of a mass of interest, to less than some such amount for example as £3 0s 8d (the year's interest on a note or mass of Notes of the amount of £102 8s principal money) this *extra* degree of complication would not be thought requisite. But this would be matter for experiment *at the time*.||

---

*Art. 15, Note 13.

†§ 12.

‡Table II Note 24.

||A process like *this*, takes no small portion of time to *describe*: it might take ever so much *less* to *practice*.

Of the degree of *time* or *trouble*, requisite to the performing of this or that set of operations (especially if it include any thing of the *mechanical* cast) the *measure*

The learned Baronet has heard or not heard, of such things as chests, each with *two* or *three* different *locks,* and as many different keys, for keeping documents, or other valuables, under joint custody, for *corporation* or other purposes. Opening such *three* locks, requires the possession of the three corresponding keys, to be assembled and met together, in *person* or by *proxy,* all of them at the same *time,* and at that same *place.* For, a loaded chest, with three locks, would not travel by the post or otherwise, with quite so much convenience, especially to and from two or three places at once, as three little slips of paper would each to its respective place. Yet had it not been for the *fact*—or even *notwithstanding* the fact (for *facts* do not afford much obstruction to the learned Baronet) how much better a game would he have had to play (if such had been my plan—I should have said my project) in proving the impracticability of keeping trust money or trust documents in a chest furnished with three such locks.

He has heard and seen, in no small numbers—things called *Indentures*—*bi*partite—*tri*partite—*alias*-partite and *pluries*-partite—being parchments with *notches* in them, now serving no other purpose but that of occasionally vitiating deeds by their absence, but originally destined and applied to purposes of the sort here in view; though the adaptation of the article to those purposes be now disused for reasons neither unsubstantial nor very difficult to divine.

He has seen or not seen, the pieces of wood called *Tallies* furnished with corresponding sets of *notches*: contrivances, which, whether better or worse imagined than the notches in paper or parchment, were directed to the same general object, and will hardly be regarded as contemptible ones, at least in the Office in which they are still in use. In *this* instance, one of the correspondent pieces goes on its travels, while the other, designed as a check to it, stays at home. If both were to travel, while the payment of the money depended upon their *reunion* at the Office from whence the money was to *issue,* the case would, in principle, be more apposite, than that of the actual

afforded by the *number of words* employed, with or without necessity, in the description of it, would, though a *natural* measure enough, be in many instances a very *fallacious one.* Were an Anatomist to set about describing the mode, in which the performance of a *capriccio* on the *piano-forte* was produced, by a detail of the different *muscles,* or distinct bundles of muscular fibres, with the bones and so forth of the hand, and arm, by which the several *strings* were made to sound, with or without a designation of the respective shares possessed by the several portions of *inanimate* matter (*keys, picks* and so forth) in the production of the effect, when would he have done! The *tune* [?] would be finished, before our historiographer had finished the *first note.*

practice, in that office, to the case of the proposed Annuity Notes.

These *split sticks* with correspondent notches, may be considered as a contrivance of no small ingenuity for the age that gave them birth: and, for aught I can pretend to say, may be at least upon a par with any other, for the particular purpose for which they are in use: but, to the purpose of the *proposed* currency, the *transfers* it is destined to undergo, and the *dangers* it will have to combat, a system of checks, embracing the arts of *engraving, paper-making* and *letter-founding*—each in its most delicate and difficulty-imitated forms—(a system of which the learned Baronet has given so exquisite a mis-representation in a passage we shall come to presently) will perhaps be deemed still better adapted than the parts of a split stick—as well as to the lights and usages of the present age.

§20. OBSERVATIONS CONTINUED.

"I do not *comprehend* how (p. 46)[1] *settlements of money* could be made by this scheme without *trouble or expence.*"

COUNTER-OBSERVATIONS.

I will try what I can do (which to judge from experience will be very little) towards prevailing upon the comprehensive faculties of the learned Baronet to atchieve [*sic*] this enterprize.

If I had said that ALL *settlements of money may thus be made without trouble or expence,* I should have said what I did not mean. Contingencies, with conditions, limitations, and restrictions, depending on such contingencies, such as are sometimes found in settlements, cannot be expressed, but by a deed containing words. adapted to *each* respective purpose. Settlements, the object of which confines itself to the preventing *one* certain person, from receiving money without the consent and participation of *another* (the *husband* for example without that of the wife or of the trustee for the wife) may *really* thus be made, "without any trouble or expence" worth regarding in such a case, and at any rate, with a degree of each very inconsiderable indeed, in comparison of what is necessary, in regard to the species of property in question, in its *present* form of *Stock* Annuities.*

[1][Chapter IV.]

*The learned Baronet, mentions it among the obstacles to industry and frugality among the lower classes‡, that the hoards of an industrious and frugal wife lie so compleatly at the mercy of a dissipated and ungenerous husband. To this mischief the divisibility of the proposed Annuity Notes might perhaps do what consistently with the matrimonial engagement can be done towards supplying a remedy.

‡Observations on Friendly Societies, p. 22.

Nor is saving of trouble and expence the only benefit: in point of security also there is some advantage. In the case of Stock Annuities, in the way in which settlements of that species of property are generally arranged, though the concurrence of *two* or *more trustees* is made necessary to the alienation of the *principal*, the receipt and application of the *interest* is commonly confided to the probity and punctuality of a single person. As to so much (if I do not at this moment misrecollect) unless special precautions are taken to the contrary,* an encrease of the *number* of Trustees rather *encreases* than *diminishes* the danger; since any *one* of a number of Trustees —the *first* that happens to apply—may receive and dispose of the money, without the consent or privity of the *rest*. A survivor might at any rate;—as also of the principal.

Upon the plan of my Annuity Notes, in the case put (as above) by the learned Baronet, neither should *he* (the *cestuy que trust*) without the concurrence of his *Trustees "spend the principal"* nor should his Trustees, all or any of them, be they ever such knaves, have it in their power to spend so much as the *interest*. The *interest*, if received at all, should be received upon such *terms*, as should ensure the immediate coming of it into *his* hands.

§[21.][1] OBSERVATIONS CONTINUED.

"I don't think the Author's plan of types twice as *large* as those on the wall facing the Treasury, would prevent forgery."

COUNTER-OBSERVATIONS.

Proportion (is it necessary for me to say?) is the circumstance *I* trusted to, not *size*: proportion, with the view that was explained, and which he was so resolute not to see. *Tall* was my word:—the *principle* being *argument* proof—a *joke* there was to be, at any price: and the word *tall* was unfortunately not "large" enough to let it in. What was to be done?—out, with *tall*—in, with *large*:—and now—head and ears—comes in the joke. Large types *my* expedient against Forgery! as if the *tallness*, or even the *largeness* was all *I* trusted to against forgery! That *my* views were not quite so narrow—my confidence not quite so blind—might have been seen by any body that

*This, I should suppose, must depend upon the concurrence of the *Bank*: whose usage to that effect, howsoever it might be sanctioned in Equity, would not be warranted at Common Law.

[1][The MS reads in fact "20".]

had not determined not to see it, in the notes on that subject in the Table;* in one of these two Tables, into *both* of which the eye of the learned Reviewer could carry so close a scrutiny, when a triumph, on the *pre-occupied*† ground of *complication* was to be the fruit of it.

A plan for putting types by *hundreds,* into a *space* not capable of holding a *dozen* of them! This *"the Author's plan"* too! 'so declared *in terminis*'—No, indeed; not the *Author's,* but the *Critic's. His* stamp it bears—in characters not quite so large indeed *"as those on the Wall facing the Treasury,"* but yet quite large enough to be *read.*

§22. OBSERVATIONS CONTINUED.

"He supposes possible cases in which his Notes would bear a premium p. 32.[1]

Other possible cases may be supposed, in which, like Exchequer Bills, they would bear a discount.

As to the probability of any state of things so extraordinary as to produce a Discount he refers to a Chapter not printed.[2]

I shall therefore close the discussion . . ."

COUNTER-OBSERVATIONS.

The sort of *smoke,* in which so hot a fire thus evaporates, is not the least extraordinary part of this *review.* To judge from every thing that has gone before, these three observations could not (it is plain enough) but have been designed to point, some how or other, against the plan in the character of *objections.* Is it so, then? But how can this be? Of themselves they point at nothing. *"He supposes possible cases in which his Notes would bear a premium".* Do I so? Well, and what then? *"Other possible cases"* (says he) *"may be supposed, in which, like Exchequer Bills, they would bear a Discount"*—may they so? Well, and what then? *"As to the probability of any such state of things so extraordinary as to produce a discount, he refers"* (concludes the Critic) *"to a Chapter not printed".* Well, and what then?—What would he have had me do? Are not sheets printed one after another? can *every* thing be put into the same sheet

*Table II, Notes 14, 22, 24, 29.

†Suprà, § 11, 12.

[1][Chapter I, Art. 20.]

[2][Chapter III, point 20.]

or the same page?—Will the sale of Annuity Notes be less *probable* or less *lucrative,* for any thing of all this?

The turn of the argument (as far as I can make any thing of it) seems to be as follows: urged by the necessity of the case, I will venture to take the place of my learned opponent, and speak, to the best of my inadequate ability, as *he* might be supposed to speak, in explanation.

[1]"Here you see this projector, notwithstanding all his pretensions, and overweaning confidence, about the *steadiness* of this paper money of his, in regard to its current value—here you see him notwithstanding, speaking of cases in which *it would bear a premium.* His eagerness to gain credit to his wares, for every valuable property that he thinks may help to recommend them, has betrayed him into the inconsistency of thus ascribing incompatible properties to the same subject.

"This (it is true) is what of itself would not much affect him: for, so long as the alternative, lies only between being always at par, and being sometimes *at* par and sometimes *above* it, the supposition of a *premium,* true or false, will give his paper so much the better a complexion than it would wear otherwise.

"Meantime, what his propensity to self-delusion will not suffer him to be aware of, and what it is therefore necessary for *me,* who am *proof* against self-delusion, to remind him of, is—that whatever article is observed at *times* to bear a *premium,* is observed at other *times* to bear a *discount.* Hope of premium, and danger of discount. go uniformly together: and, by thus imprudently bringing forward the supposition *favourable* to his views, he has unawares given me a right, and an equal right, a right which he is *estopped* from disputing, to advance the opposite *unfavourable* one.

"In one place to be sure, he *does* bring himself, to admitt a discount upon this paper of his, as an event *just "possible".* But the colours in which he paints this possibility are so *faint,* that the words he employs on this occasion, are worth quoting, for the purpose of shewing the strength of the delusion that has got possession of his mind. "As to the probability of any state of things so extraordinary as to produce a discount (these are his very words) he refers to a Chapter not printed".—After such an opinion, can there be any

[1][It is obvious that the whole passage put into inverted commas here, should have been in inverted commas in the MS, but Bentham's copyist was not very conscientious in this respect.]

reasonable hope of seeing, in this or any thing else that is to come, any argument by which the decision ought to be affected?—No certainly. It is therefore already time to *"close the discussion"*; and to express my "hope" (the hope to the consummation of which this discussion has, on *my* part, from first to last been directed) "viz. that *'public credit' will not be permitted"* to be destroyed, by this pretended *'medicine'*."

Such is the *spirit* and *tendency* of my learned opponent's argument, *as it strikes me*: now comes my answer to it.

1st. As to *bearing a premium*, the cases termed by him *"possible cases"*, and spoken of as if this were *all* the *probability* I could venture to attribute to them, I gave, and still give, as *certain* ones:* as certain of taking place, sooner or later, in regard to Annuity Notes. supposing them to be in existence. *I* averred the certainty: I exhibited the *grounds* of it: *he* has looked at them, and found them impregnable. This *certainty* is no particular result of the *proposed paper*: it is not given as such. It depends upon the *times*: upon the proportion between National *hoarding* and National *expenditure, at the time*: it depends upon the demand for Government Annuities *in any form*, rather than upon the particular form proposed to be given to them by the proposed Annuity Notes.

2. As to their *bearing a discount* in *"possible cases"* which (the learned Baronet says) "may be *supposed"*; but by suppositions, none of which he has ventured to produce; I leave his argument in possession of all the advantage, derivable to it from such *"cases"* and such *"suppositions"*, with all the *"possibility"* that belongs to them. The *possibility* will, at any rate, never rise in *my* mind to a *probability*, so long as it rests upon no better foundation, than the *"likeness"* he has found in them to *"Exchequer Bills"*. What the *causes* are, by the operation of which *Exchequer Bills* are made to bear a discount, I have shewn above:† in the same statement in which it is shewn, that not one of these causes apply to the case of *Annuity Notes*.

All depends upon *epochs*: distinctions, which he is as resolute to keep out of sight or confound, as I have been studious to discriminate them. During a certain period (viz. till Stock 3 per cents are about par) I give it as altogether *impossible*, that these securities *should* bear a premium. *From and after* that period, I *do* look upon it as scarcely possible, that they should *not* bear a premium; in any event

*Art. 20, Note 17.

†Suprà, § 9.

other than the event contemplated and spoken of in this view*—viz. the event of a supervening *war,* with a fresh and *copious* creation of Stock Annuities, for the expence of it.

"As to the probability of any state of things so extraordinary as to produce a discount",† the states of things I had in view, are—1. the case of a demand for the *materials of Gold and Silver money* for exportation, so copious and so urgent, as to have exhausted the *whole amount* of the stock existing in the state of *bullion*: 2.—that of a *generally prevailing* doubt, in respect either of the *solvency* or the *stability* of that Government, on which the fulfillment of the engagements conveyed by this species of paper depends.

The first case exhibits a state of things, to the production of which I cannot conceive any adequate cause, distinct from those of which the second case would be productive: viz. such a scene of general calamity, whether by foreign invasion or intestine war, as—by reducing the value—not merely of future *money,* but of *wealth of all kinds* expected *in future*—would produce a general eagerness to possess that species of *money* (metallic money) which does *not* depend upon futurity for its value.

"Possible cases" like *these,* I do not consider however as constituting *any* objection to the proposed currency:—1st because I have the satisfaction of not seeing any reason for considering them as wearing any face of *probability,* proper for acting upon, or worth regarding with a view to action, in the present state of things: 2ly because, if they applied at all, in disrecommendation of the *proposed paper,* it would not be till after all paper of *weaker texture*—that is all sorts of existing *private cash paper* (Bank of England paper not excepted) were utterly suppressed:—3ly because the dependency of a species of currency on the stability of the *existing Government* (even were it a much less *good* one, than it is) is a property that, in my view of it, pleads in *favor,* rather than in *disfavor,* of the measure.

OBSERVATIONS CONCLUDED.

"I shall therefore close the discussion; with a hope, that if public credit wants *medicine,* it will not be permitted (to use Hume's expression) *to die of the Doctor.*"

---

*Art. 23.

†Plan, ch. III.

COUNTER-OBSERVATIONS.

What can he mean by *"public credit wanting medicine?" Who* supposes it to be in want of medicine? In *any* sense, howsoever *figurative,* what has the case to do with medicine? Government. according to circumstances, borrows, sometimes at one rate of interest, sometimes at another. What has *one* rate more than *another* to do with *medicine*? Does the argument run for example in this vein[?]? "Whatever has any thing *new* in it, is *quackery,* and quackery consists in *the abuse of medicine. Annuity Notes* have some points *new* about them: therefore, the issuing of them would be *quackery—vending of quack medicines."* What if the *Attorney General,* in a judgment he is to give, were to take for a precedent, *this* judgment of this our[?] Judge? *Globes* (he might say) are *round,* and so are *bolus's.* Go—you are no better than a *quack;*—we want none of your Bolus's: away then with your Globe. The two judgments—the supposed and the real—might, I think, be shaken in a bag.

If public credit must needs be made a *patient* of, the only thing that can be called *medicine* is *the Sinking Fund.* So far then from the patient's *"dying of the Doctor"* it is only by the Doctor that he *lives.* In the *formula* I have ventured to propose, has this our *Censor* been able to find any thing like a reason, for supposing that the *virtue* of the *medicine* will be improved by it?

But enough of *Death and the Doctor;* and all such figures and such jokes.—If *public credit*—if the capacity of the public, in regard to the fulfillment of its engagements, be *lessened,* it must be in one or other of two ways: by an *encrease,* in the amount of those *engagements,* or by a *decrease,* in the quantity of the *matter applicable to the fulfillment* of them. The proposed paper does *not* make any *decrease* in the quantity of the *matter applicable to the fulfillment* of those engagements: it does *not* make any *encrease* in the *amount of them.* On the contrary, the leading property of it—and that an inseparable one—is—the making a *decrease* in that *amount.* Not a *note* can ever be issued, but *some part* of the mass of those engagements is *cut off.* This is what the *"project"* does, *so far* and *so long* as it does *any* thing. It is matter of *intention*: and even the learned Baronet, who disputes every thing, has not been able to dispute it. —If public credit be *injured* by *this,* by what then is it to be served?

I cannot conclude, without taking serious notice of an attempt thus to convey the most impressive of imputations, without the shadow of a ground for it:—nay—or so much as an endeavour to support it.

The arguments we have seen, were they ever so much stronger than they are, do not so much as glance that way: what they point to, is—so far as *public credit* at least (the object of this charge) is concerned—mere *impracticability*—not *dangerousness*.—Danger?—In the whole field of political history, what plan was ever more pure from it?—If the paper *does* sell, the public will be proportionably *served* by it: if it does *not* sell, it will do at any rate no *harm*: the public will *not* be *injured* by it.

Impracticability is to be made matter of *proof*: but dangerousness—an objection beyond comparison more conclusive—is to be taken for granted *without* proof—without *attempt* at proof—and *against* proof—taken for granted upon the strength of a joke—and such a joke!—And now I take my leave of the learned Baronet with his jokes.

PAPER MISCHIEF [EXPOSED]

PAPER MISCHIEF [EXPOSED]

[BEING AN INDICATION OF THE UNDESIRABLE RESULTS FLOWING FROM THE UNLIMITED ISSUE OF PROMISSORY NOTES BY COUNTRY BANKERS]

1800-01

[TABLE OF CONTENTS]

[Preface]

The position here submitted to the judgment of the public is the accidental and collateral result of a train of investigation I was led into by the pursuit of a different object. In the course of that enquiry I soon saw that prices were raised by paper money, and that the rise of prices was an evil—but, seeing at the same time that the addition made to wealth by paper was not less real, sum for sum, than if made by gold, I was led to regard the evil as among those which are to be regretted without being combated, as being inseparably attached to masses of greater good. In this persuasion [at one] with Sir W[illiam] Pulteney[1] and so many other distinguished statesmen, whose countenance may well serve to screen against every imputation of temerity, I was actually occupying myself with contrivances for adding to the existing mass of the circulating medium. When, as the enquiry advanced, I came to examine into the supposed connection, and taking measure of the evil, great was my surprize to find the connection purely imaginary, and the evil swelling to a most enormous magnitude, swelling to such a magnitude as to eclipse those which, among evils of the same kind, have hitherto been felt as inflicting the severest pressure.

I had thus recognised my error and spread out before me the mass of argument that had led me to conviction, when, on seeing in an advertisement a pamphlet bearing for its title *"The Iniquity of Banking"*,[2] I was curious to observe the train of reflection that had been brought forward by another on the same side.

What led me to this anonymous pamphlet was another pamphlet, *"The Cause of the present threatened Famine"*,[3] which I saw advertised at the same time, and as issuing from the same shop, as Mr.

[1][Cf. Substance of the Speech of Sir W. Pulteney . . . for shortening the time during which the Bank of England should be restrained from issuing cash for its debts and demands. London, 1797.]

[2][The Iniquity of Banking: or, Bank Notes proved to be injurious to the Public, and the Real Cause of the present exorbitant Price of Provisions. London, Part 1, 1797, pp. 47; Part II, 1800, pp. 64. Author probably W. Anderson.]

[3][The Cause of the present threatened Famine traced to its real Source, viz. an actual Depreciation on our Circulating Medium, occasioned by the Paper Currency. London, 1800, pp. X, 32.]

Fox's speech of the 10. Oct. 1800.[1] In this pamphlet, what share of reason presented itself to my view seemed to be included in the compass of the title, mixed up and confounded with a larger quantity of matter to which the same term of approbation could not, as it seemed, without great impropriety be applied.

In the course of the speech thus ascribed to Mr. Fox, that illustrious statesman is made to speak of the "encrease in the amount of the *circulating medium*" as what "must, of necessity, have greatly depretiated the value of money": and to the words *circulating medium* is subjoined a reference in form of a note, saying "Vide Iniquity of Banking, Parts I, and II. Published by J. S. Jordan". Sending accordingly for the two pamphlets I found that, if the title page may be believed, Part I had arrived at the 4th edition, and Part II[2] at the second.

Turning to Part I and hastening to the practical conclusion, the remedy proposed for the indicated grievance, I found it consisted in an universal refusal of "Bank Notes". The system of the Bank of England is there accused of being a bubble, and as being "in every respect as great an imposition, and resting upon as sandy a foundation" as "the South-Sea Bubble" [p. 45]. The mischief of a bubble consists in its bursting: and the author, forgetting that his object was to prevent mischief, recommends measures for the express and declared purpose of bringing about the mischief—of causing this bubble of a hundred and six years standing to burst.

In the course of it I also found [the opinion] that, in regard to the country bankers, one of the classes thus endeavoured to be consigned to perdition, not only their mode of traffick produced the joint effect of oppression, fabrication of counterfeit, and robbery "by force of arms" (a proposition, the truth of which as to a certain part, but no farther, it is also the object of these pages likewise to bring to view), but that the conscience of all these his Majesty's subjects harbours moreover the whole mass of guilt attached to that congeries of crimes. For not only the terms of *combination—depredation—robbery*—and, lest that should not be strong and plain enough,

[1] [Cf. Mr. Fox's Celebrated Speech, with the Proceedings at the Shakespeare Tavern, on Friday, October 10, 1800, being the Anniversary of his First Election for the City of Westminster. Wherein he shews the improper Conduct of Ministers in continuing an unjust War, that has spilt our Blood; squandered our Treasure; contracted a Load of National Debt we are unable to bear, and reduced the People to their present deplorable Situation. London, 1800, p. 12.]

[2] [The MS reads "2d".]

robbery *by force of arms*—are all along applied to them without reserve, without a word in any part to cover them from the odium attached to these crimes, but with unremitted endeavours to fix it upon them in its utmost force: and as to the "depriving the labourer of a part of his wages", it is not only declared that such is the effect of their conduct, but we are given to understand, though in terms of not inconvenient ambiguity, that such is their very object and end in view. "What words, for example (says he, p. 40), could we find sufficient to express our indignation at the conduct of a set of men who should deprive the labourer of a part of his wages?—Yet this the bankers have positively done"—i.e. simply produced that effect, or combined in the view of producing that effect, as you choose to understand it.—"For" &c—"therefore the bankers, by issuing their notes, have as effectually robbed him of one third of his wages, as if they had put their hands into his pocket and stolen it, or formed a combination in order to reduce his wages".

As I read on, I found not only a considerable part of the arguments which had then already occurred to me, and which the reader will here see employed in substance, but the main proposition, the same which is the object of these pages, made out in such a manner as, I make no doubt, would have made a convert of me, had they come across me at a time when my leaning towards the opposite opinion was at the strongest.

Finding the cause in such able hands, for the clearness of statement and closeness as well as strength of argument were such as seemed capable of doing honour to any cause, I felt myself much inclined at first on several accounts to trust it there and withdraw from it. Several considerations, however, concurred in producing a contrary result. Though the arguments that had occurred [to me] were in part anticipated, this was by no means the case as to the whole: though the body of argument therein contained was sufficient, to my own apprehension, to prove the point, and that in a sufficient degree for practice, yet to the apprehension of others that might not be the case. The prejudice to be surmounted was such, that the utmost force capable of being brought against it by human reason might still prove insufficient after all, and different modes of reasoning are suited to the conception of different minds. The school of politics. [with][1] which this publication appeared from different circumstances to be connected, was such to which a numerous class of readers, and

[1][The MS reads "to."]

those not among the least respectable, might never be able to persuade themselves to look for any useful truth: and since, as to the main question, the view I had taken of the subject was similar in so many points to that which had been given [by the anonymous author], whose declared object in writing was to bring on a state of things which I knew not how to distinguish from universal bankruptcy (immediate bankruptcy for the sake of averting the distant possibility of it), it seemed to present a means of removing some degree of prepossession, and smoothing the way for the reception of what appeared to me in the character of useful truth, to let it be seen that the same opinion could be entertained and manifested by an individual who had no end in view but what was diametrically the reverse of the one just mentioned, and who feared not to make himself responsible for it by his name.

Mr. Fox (I mean always the Mr. Fox of the real or pretended speech), Mr. Fox, in speaking of the astonishing encrease of the circulating medium as having of necessity greatly depretiated the value of money, speaks of the vast addition to our national debt as the cause, or at least a cause (I will not take upon me to say which), of that astonishing encrease:—"the vast addition . . and the consequent astonishing encrease" [&c]. To the Mr. Fox of the pamphlet this, it appears, must be evident to every one: to me, I must confess, the contrary seems evident, as evident as in such a case a negative can be. Taxes are one pressure, rise of prices another: two pressures connected or unconnected are felt more than one: there is the only connection I can see. Taking, as the custom is, and without further enquiry, concomitance for causality, with much more colour of reason might it be advanced that the effect of the war has been to diminish the amount of the other grievance. Just before the war it was at the highest pitch of which we have any account, viz. at 90. Came the war, with the commencement of the really consequent encrease of the debt, and the amount sunk to 63: which fall is thus universally regarded and indeed felt as a grievance—of which grievance the war, one may venture to assert without enquiring, had the credit in the minds of the bulk of those by whom the war was ascribed to government as a matter of guilt as well as to the country as a misfortune. During the war it got up again as far as 78: then sunk again to 40: at which it was by the last determinate accounts, though its having risen[1] much higher since is as generally

[1][The MS reads "of its having risen."]

known as it is unknown to what pitch. So much for the Mr. Fox of the pamphlet: to whom that consequence appears evident to every one, in support of which not the shadow of an argument is adduced, and of which the contrary is in proof, on an occasion too memorable, one should have thought, to have escaped notice.

In the mere idea—the idea simply taken—that the universally acknowledged rise of prices has [the unrestricted issue of paper money] for one of its causes, or even for its principal cause (such part of the effect as is not accounted for by the state of the agriculture of the country), there is nothing new. It is an idea that has been long ago started and from quarters too numerous to be counted [—an idea that] has been repeatedly held up to view.

What there is new in the following pages is confined to what regards such questions as the following, viz. in what proportion that cause has contributed to the effect; of the evil, which can not be denied to be attendant on it, what the magnitude may be; in what, if in any, degree the evil may be attended with a degree of good capable of being considered as affording a compensation for it, [i.e.] accompanied with any good effects flowing from the same cause: whether the ballance, if on the side of evil, be of a magnitude considerable enough to call for legislative interference; what may be the measures, and the most eligible measures, to be adopted in the view of applying a remedy to the evil; and what the course of proceeding best adapted to that purpose.

[INTRODUCTION]

We are now at a crisis which seems to call for contributions of all sorts, and for the sacrifice of personal considerations of all sorts, from the well-wishers to mankind: contributions in wealth, where there is wealth to spare: contributions in time and intellectual effort, where the education has been suitable [so that] habits of attention and reflection have been formed, and directed either to the particular subject on the carpet, or [employed] in any other track so near to that ground as to be capable of being made to bear upon it with any degree of advantage.

Had reputation been my object, or even that sort of personal satisfaction which results from the consciousness of success in the pursuit of important truths, of a successful exertion of intellectual powers, I should either have turned aside altogether from the field of this enquiry, or delayed the completion of it and [the] publication of [its] result to I know not how much more distant [a] period. But besides that the chance of being useful depends in so great a degree upon time, there is another circumstance that may help to encrease the utility of an even precipitated effort. In a work that contains a certain degree of useful truth, one error or two may help to excite a degree of attention which a work of more uniform perfection would have missed. Errors, real or apparent, may serve to draw in antagonists, by presenting to their view the matter of triumph and the means of refutation.

Connection with the grievances of the day will sometimes procure for a political topic of a permanent nature a degree of public attention which its intrinsic importance, how real soever, would not have been sufficient to excite. The case of *paper money* may be mentioned as an example.

To me it presents itself as the principal of the permanent causes of that *rise of prices* which, now that the amount happens to have been swelled by causes of a temporary and accidental nature, has made up that accumulation of inconvenience which is the cause of suffering, and subject of complaint and lamentation, to all classes.

To the opposite opinion I can not consistently annex any very considerable degree of contempt: since, till within these few months, it was that to which I felt myself most inclined, so far as a man can be said to entertain an opinion on a point to which he had never had occasion to apply the powers of his mind.

Still less can I attach any moral blame in my own to the exercise of that profession from which the mischief, if such it really be, results as from its immediate and indisputable efficient cause.

I consider the country bankers (in number, or at least in number of partnerships, between 2 and 300) as a set of men who, without the smallest particle of guilt, have for such a length of years been levying for their own benefit a tax upon a great part of the community, and upon that part of all others which is least able to endure such pressure—the aged, the infirm, the fatherless, and the widow: upon those on whom, in respect of their rank in life, and habits and sentiments assorted to that rank, the demand for expence presses with a degree of urgency unknown to others: a set of men who, from the exuberance of their opulence, have derived the means of imposing a tax on indigence: and whose profit, abundant as it is, bears yet but a small proportion even to the pecuniary amount of the loss by which it has been purchased—the loss to those already but too severely pinched and distressed classes.

I consider them—still without the smallest particle of blame—as usurpers in effect of another attribute of sovereignty—the right of coining money, in practising on a vast scale, and with perfect impunity and security, and even universal respect and applause, that sort of act which, in them, is not high treason, but which produces to the actors a profit, and to the rest of the community a loss, superior in degree, but similar in effect and mode of operation, to what is produced by a species [?] of forgery inaptly included in that formidable name.

The rise of prices, so universally felt and complained of, has its source in a variety of causes, some temporary, others permanent—some affecting vendible commodities in general, some attaching in a particular degree on certain species of vendible commodities—some prominent and universally acknowledged, others deep-seated and generally unperceived.

It affects *vendible commodities* in general—it affects in a particular and superior degree those particular classes of vendible commodities which are comprized under the denomination of *provisions*: and, among provisions, it affects, in a degree still superior, those species of grain which, in proportion to the poverty of the individual, constitute the larger share in the composition of his food and maintenance.

What concerns grain in general, and wheat in particular, belongs not to the purpose of the present enquiry. The pressure, so far as confined to these articles, is sufficiently understood to be the result of the joint influence of two causes: the one *occasional,* the unfavourableness of two successive seasons:* the other *habitual,* a deficiency in the quantity of land employed in the production of the article in question, regard being had to the continually encreasing numbers of the mouths that call for it.

Among the causes to which the rise of prices in the article of provisions, and more particularly in the article of bread corn, has been ascribed, is one however, which bears an unquestionable relation to the subject of the present enquiry: and that is the assistance sup-

*I speak not here of the grievance, real or supposed, of *engrossers, forestallers, regraters* &c—of the supposed encreased, and (as supposed) more successfully than ever encreased, exertions of dealers in these necessary articles, to augment the rate of their own profits. This cause, in whatsoever degree it may have operated, is but of a secondary nature, deriving itself from the real or supposed scarcity of the article, as resulting from those other primary and independent causes.

posed by some to be derived from country bankers. The allegation is —that by money, and of course more or less of it paper money, supplied by the country bankers, the growers of corn and other provisions obtain a respite from that necessity, by which they would otherwise have been obliged to send in their commodities to market for sale, while the dealers in those same commodities are not only assisted in the same way, but enabled at the same time to extend the amount of their purchases. What ground there may be for reckoning this among the mischievous effects produced by paper money will be considered in its place.

[AMOUNT OF THE MISCHIEF]

The value of money is now (in the beginning of the year 1801) no more than half what it was 40 years ago: 40 years hence (in the beginning of the year 1841) it will be no more than half what it is at present.

Such are the two propositions which constitute the basis of the ensuing pages: and of the proposed measure to which they lead. Such are the propositions which, in a form more commodious for discussion than any that would be more accurate, and with a degree of accuracy sufficient for practice, express the [1]best[2] estimate I have seen reason to form of the amount of that depretiation, the existence of which in a considerable degree is not a matter of doubt with any body.

I say sufficient for practice: for although, for argument sake, the depretiation, instead of amounting, as above, to 50 per Cent, should not prove to amount to more than 25 per Cent, the demand for remedial measures would not by an aberration even of this magnitude be found, I conceive, to be taken away, nor the propriety of the measures recommended in that view disproved.

But it will appear, I am inclined to think, that the depretiation, if it be not quite so much as 50 per Cent, is at any rate much nearer the 50 per Cent than the 25.

I speak of the past depretiation. But what is past is matter of curiosity rather than value, otherwise than with reference to the future. It is with a view [to][3] forming an estimate of what the depretiation is likely to amount to in an equal future period—it is for that purpose, and that only, that I should have thought it worth the

[1] [2][Put into brackets at a later date.]

[3][The MS reads "of".]

enquiry what it has amounted to in the period just past: and if my view of the matter be right, then, whatever the amount of the depreciation may want of being equal to 50 per Cent[1] with reference to the state of things at the commencement of the past period of 40 years ending with the end of the year 1800, I believe it will appear but too probable that, at the end of the current period of 40 years ending at the end of the year 1841, it will be more likely to exceed than to fall short of the same rate of 50 per Cent with reference to the state of things at the commencement of this current period: insomuch that, though, with reference to the end of the year 1760, it should not be found to have amounted at the end of 1800 to quite so much as 50 per Cent, yet at the end of 1840 it will be found to amount, with reference to that same year 1760, to not less than 75 per Cent.

Prices have *risen* to such a degree as to be double to what they were 40 years ago: or, even though this should not be exactly true, they will at the end of another 40 years be at least quadruple what they were 40 years ago, and thereby either exactly double, or more than double, what they are at present.

These propositions, which are but the same as the two former, come nearer the mark of clear and explicit language than they do: but still not, as yet, near enough for the purpose. Familiar as they are, the texture of them is general in the extreme, and proportionably vague and inexplicit: nor will any sufficiently accurate conception of the import of them be obtainable without unfolding them, and displaying one by one the more particular propositions of which they are composed.

In the developping of these propositions, and the first of them in particular, two things will require to be brought to view: the nature of the matter of fact announced by it: and the nature of the evidence from which the existence of the matters of fact so announced is inferred, [and] the truth of the proposition announced by it collected.

Prices being a general term (meaning the sums of money given for vendible things in general), and no words importing restriction being added to it, by saying: *Prices have risen so much in such a time*—is meant, in strictness of speech, that this same ratio of encrease has taken place in regard to vendible articles of all sorts without exception:—but, the degree of uniformity thus indicated being contrary to all experience, the utmost that can ever be really understood by it is that, supposing the quantities and qualities of the vendible articles

[1][The figure of the MS looks like "80".]

sold at the two periods had been the same, it would have been found that the sum of the moneys with which they were purchased in the later period was in the ratio in question (the ratio of 2 to 1)[1] to the sum total of the moneys with which they were purchased in the earlier period: and accordingly, that in some instances the encrease was to less than to that amount, in others it was as much greater.

Prices were in this country (meaning Great Britain) in 1800 *double what they were in* 1760. In this extremely general proposition the following subordinate and less general propositions are virtually included—

1. That, supposing the total aggregate of vendible articles sold in 1800 in the whole island to have been exactly equal (in quality as well as quantity) to the total mass of vendible articles sold in 1760, the sum total of the sums of money employed in the several purchases made in 1800 was exactly double the sum total of the sums of money employed in the several purchases made in 1760: and that, accordingly, if in 1760 the amount of that sum total was 100 millions, in 1800 it was 200 millions.

2. That, supposing the total mass of vendible articles sold in the whole island in 1800 was double the total mass of vendible articles sold in the year 1760, then the sum total of the sums of money employed in the several purchases made in 1800 was exactly four times as great as the sum total of the sums of money employed in the several purchases made in 1760: and that, accordingly, if in 1760 the amount of that sum total was 100 millions, then in 1800, on this latter supposition, it was 400 millions.

Or, if instead of being double, i.e. as 4 to 2, the total mass of vendible articles sold in 1800 was to the total mass of vendible articles sold in 1760 as 3 only to 2, then, if in 1760 the amount of the sum total of the sums of money employed in the purchases made in 1760 was 100 millions, then in 1800 it was 300 millions.

A consequence respecting the value of incomes is—that, supposing the sums of money employed in purchases made out of income, in the way of expenditure of income, to have been in the two different years in the same ratio to the sums employed in all other purchases, the sums of money employed in purchases made out of income for a given quantity of goods of the same quality must have been double in 1800 to what they were in 1760: consequently, that, after allowance made for accidental variations of price as between day and day,

[1] [The second bracket is interpolated.]

article and article, place and place, and customer and customer, the utmost quantity of goods [that] could have been purchased with an income of £100 a year in the year 1800 was no more than half the quantity of goods of the same sort that could have been purchased with an income of £100 a year in the year 1760, unless [and] in as far as an abatement in *quality* was submitted to, for the purpose of escaping a proportional deficiency in quantity.

By the total of the sums employed in purchases made in the years 1800 and 1760 respectively is to be understood the total of the sums employed in the purchases made, meaning the *ultimate* purchases of all the several *individual* articles of all the several *sorts* in all the *days* of the year in all the *places* in Great Britain.

On the present occasion the object of enquiry being such purchases, and such purchases alone, by the terms of which the effective [?] value of the sums of money, received on the score of income, is affected—i.e. such purchases alone as, if made, are made in the way of current expenditure out of income; it follows that all other purchases may be thrown out of the account: and so ought to be, if and as far as such [purchases][1] may have the effect of varying the influence which any addition to, or deduction from, the amount of the money in circulation, that is the total mass employed in transferrs of all sorts, may have upon the effective value of it in respect of such purchases as are made (as above) in the way of current expenditure out of income.

The total number of transfers of all sorts remaining the same, as also the proportion between the number of transferrs affecting the real value of income and of the number of transferrs not affecting the real value of income, as also the quantities and qualities of vendible articles transferred at each of the respective transferrs, it is evident that by any addition made to the sum total of the money employed in the making of such transferrs as are made in the way of purchase within the year, the amount of the several sums employed in such respective purchases, some or all of them, can not but be augmented: and if [the] distribution of the mass of money thus added be in any other than the exact proportion of the several incomes, it follows that by any expenditure made of the totals of the respective incomes after such addition, the proportion[2] between the real value[s], quantity and quality included, of the goods respectively purchased by the possessors

[1][The MS reads "such deduction".]
[2][The MS reads "proportions".]

of those incomes can not have been the same as it was before such addition: but that in some instances it must be greater, in others less: and that, accordingly, in proportion as the effective power of the incomes so augmented taken together has been encreased by the augmentation, that of the unaugmented incomes taken together must have been diminished.

In looking for a point of time, from whence commencement of so much of the mischief as can be conveniently subjected to calculation shall take its date, I fix with pleasure on the commencement of the present reign. It is in every point of view entitled to be considered in one unbroken and uncompounded mass, as well as in preference to all preceding ones. It presents of itself a portion of time of sufficient magnitude for the purpose. It presents a reign of almost unexampled length, and [is] in point of prosperity, as well as copiousness of political lights, altogether without example. On the one hand, we know the exported surplus of our wealth, and the wealth imported in other shapes in return for it. On the other hand we know the amount of our annual burthens, of the mass of debt charged upon that wealth—the amount of the annual burthens imposed for the discharge of it [and] the produce of the different branches of revenue appropriated to the purpose, all with a degree of precision and minuteness and publicity without example in the history of this or any other state.

In looking for the amount of the rise, in casting about for the least incorrect as well as sanest[?] formed approximation that can be made use of for the purpose, I have been fortunate enough to meet with an estimate already framed, as if it had been on purpose. I mean the *Table of the Rise of Prices*, compiled and digested by Sir George Shuckburgh Evelyn, printed in the *Philosophical Transactions of the Royal Society* for 1798,[1] and reprinted in *Nicholson's Philosophical Journal* for the month of September in that same year. Framed without suspicion of the application now made of it, it is, on the score of impartiality at least, altogether above reproach. Another circum-

[1]["A Table exhibiting the Prices of various Necessaries of Life, together with that of Day Labour, in sterling Money, and also in Decimals, at different Periods, from the Conquest to the present Time, derived from respectable Authorities; with the Depreciation of the Value of Money inferred therefrom. To which is added, the Mean Appreciation of Money, according to a Series of Intervals of 50 Years, for the first 600 Years; and, during the present Century, at shorter Periods, deduced by Interpolation". This is an appendix to a paper entitled "An Account of some Endeavours to ascertain a Standard of Weight and Measure". It faces p. 176 of the volume indicated in the text.]

stance of peculiar felicity attending it is, that, being framed at and for a time when the existing century wanted a few years of its completion, it is carried down notwithstanding—carried down by analogy and proportion—to the end. It by that means presents the result of the gradual and regular encrease, cleared from those casual causes of disturbance which have swelled beyond all proportion the actual amount of the encrease for this last and the preceding year [i.e. 1799 and 1800].

Another circumstance of remarkable felicity is, that the rate of encrease or rise exhibited by it quadrates, with a degree of apparent correctness as singular as it is convenient for calculation, with what. in the irremediable darkness in which the subject is involved, seems to present as just pretensions as any other that could have been named to be received as the amount of paper money at present in circulation. By this means the amount of paper money, [or rather] the addition made to the total mass of money in this form, presents itself as exactly adequate to the production of the obnoxious effect. I make no scruple of confessing that the assumed amount of paper money has been fixed, in the midst of this darkness, with a special view to the attainment of the accomodation afforded by this coincidence. But this affords no objection to the choice. The assumption has been adapted, but not perverted to this purpose. No sacrifice of supposed accuracy was made for the attainment of it: in point of chance of accuracy, it presented itself as being at least upon a par with any other that could have been substituted to it: and after this confession, and the declaration that illustration and facility of conception are the points principally aimed at by it, it may be allowed to pass without the imputation of any deceptive tendency.

[Now, the computations of Sir George Shuckburgh Evelyn are based on four series of figures: 1. the price of wheat, per bushel; 2. the price of meat, beef and mutton, per lb; 3. the price of labour in husbandry, per day; and, lastly, 4. a compound of the prices of 12 miscellaneous articles, including five species of cattle, three species of poultry, butter and cheese, per lb., and ale and small beer, per gallon. From these data it appears that the same parcel of commodities which, in 1550, it cost £100 to buy, could not be had in 1760 but for £342, and in 1795 for £531. Had the secular tendency of monetary depretiation remained unaltered, the aggregate price would have risen by 1800 to nearly £562. The depretiation of money, then, between 1760 and 1795 is expressed by the ratio of the figures 342 to 531; it is somewhat more than 50 per Cent. This ratio, however, in which prices have encreased, is, as has been mentioned before, and will be shewn hereafter, roughly the same as that between the total amount of metallic money in the country, and the mass of paper money added to it of late years.]

[Exposition of the Mischief]

[The mischievous effects of an encrease in the amount of paper money, relative to the aggregate of vendible commodities, may be digested and exhibited under three separate heads: 1. General enhancement of prices, leading to a correspondent reduction of certain incomes, without promoting the encrease of national wealth; 2. Undue enhancement of prices, viz. of particular commodities, by engrossing; 3. Occasional shocks given to commercial security by this species of money, by reason of superabundance in the quantity of it. These several effects come now in turn to be subjected to closer consideration.]

[*First head of mischief:*[1] *General enhancement of prices, leading to a correspondent reduction of certain incomes, without promoting the encrease of national wealth.*]

1. First as to the *rise of prices.* In an aggregate view, the alledged evil may appear an imaginary one. But an aggregate view is an indiscriminate view, and an indiscriminate view is liable to be a false one. It would be found particularly so in the present instance.

Vendible commodities require now an additional quantity of money to pay for them:—true—this would indeed be a misfortune, if the additional quantity of money did not exist. But it does exist, it existed even before the rise—for it was the sole cause of the rise: then where is the mischief? The remedy, instead of treading tardily, as usual, upon the steps of the disease, precedes it: or rather precedes the result which otherwise would be a disease, and prevents it from becoming so.

First then comes the encrease of wealth—for is not money wealth? It is not indeed the only species of wealth: a man can neither be fed, cloathed, lodged, conveyed, nor warmed by it. But it is not the less a species of wealth: were it not, it would not be received, as it is, in exchange for every other. An encrease of wealth upon the whole is therefore not only a necessary concomitant, but the very cause of

[1][At the head of this page is an autograph remark of Bentham's: "Superseded", followed, however, by a question-mark.]

the alledged evil. Admitt it to be attended with diminution of wealth in the instance of individuals, still, being attended with encrease of wealth upon the whole, the loss is more than covered by the profit, and any conclusion that should be formed by dwelling upon particular instances of loss would be no otherwise than erroneous.

To this I answer:

Although it were an inseparable result of an encrease of wealth, it would not follow that it might not be an evil. Wealth is but a means: comfort is the end: shew but a loss in comfort, all encrease in wealth, be it what it may, loses all its value.

Follow it up, apply it to the several classes of parties interested, in point of comfort we shall find it productive of an indisputable loss.

[1]Three such classes may be distinguished:

1. The first is composed of those whose incomes are commonly called *fixed*—more aptly *unencreasable.*

2. The second is composed of those whose incomes are not in their nature unencreasable, but in point of fact do not receive an encrease in quantity of money proportionable, or more than proportionable, to the decrease in the marketable value of it.

3. The third is composed of those who, whether as proprietors of the supposed extra influx of money, or on any other account, do receive by means of it an encrease in money more than proportionable to the rise of prices, [i.e.] to the decrease in the marketable value of it, as above.[2]

To those comprized in the first class, the rise in question is, as to the whole amount of it, a *tax.* I mean as far as hardship is concerned: for the benefit of a tax—that benefit, the obtainment of which is the final cause and sole justification of this burthensome class of measures —is altogether wanting. It is a tax of which the produce is squandered and lost, no part of it coming into the Exchequer.

From a very instructive document in my possession, I am inclined to look upon 50 per Cent as being in round numbers as likely to fall short of as to exceed the average addition that[3] has accrued to the expence of living [and consequently, as indicating] the average depretiation of the value of money [or, what comes to the same] the average amount of the rise of prices that has taken place within the compass of what has already elapsed of the present reign. This at any rate is what I will assume for simplicity of conception and calculation:

[1] [2][Crossed out at a later date.]

[3][May also read "which".]

should it upon an accurate examination be found erroneous, and requiring correction, it will serve at any rate as a standard of comparison to which the corrections may be applied.

How grievous is the burthen of a tax on income to no more than 10 per Cent, is but too universally felt: a tax not to be endured without abatement, it was supposed, by an income less than £200 a year, and therefore softened down as low as 1/120th till it comes to incomes of £60 a year, at which mark it stops altogether. Of this indirect and unproductive tax by *rise of prices,* the burthen stops absolutely no where: though on the very lowest class in point of pecuniary circumstances—those whose food consists of little besides corn—the burthen is happily not quite so heavy as on the meat-eating classes. On those included in the income tax it amounts to five times the amount of the tax where it falls lightest, and no less than 60 times the amount where it falls heaviest.

Comparing the aggregate of its effect on the aggregate of income, with the aggregate of income (£217 millions*), we shall find it amount to £72 millions: while the total annual pressure of the taxes drawn down upon us on account of the national debt, payment of interest and redemption of principal together, but just exceeds 20 millions: and the total of all taxes to no more than about 27[1] millions.

Yet the pressure of the debt is matter of universal and continual lamentation, while the pressure from rise of prices, unless when encreased, as at present, by accidental and temporary causes, scarce provokes a word!

The reason however is not difficult to assign. In the case of debt and taxes, the efficient cause is known: the hand of the legislator—the human legislator—is visible. Lamentation has not only its object to look back to, but a rational end in view to look forward to: since, though it can not remove the evil, it may help to keep it within bounds. In the case of rise of prices, the root of the evil is in a great measure out of sight: it is supposed to be in the nature of things [and] ranked with sickness, old age and death: it is referred to causes over which the hand of man is supposed to have no power.

[2]This, it is true, only concerns the rate of its pressure on those on whom it presses altogether without relief. But who are those? At the

*Beeke [H., B.D., Observations on the Produce of the Income Tax, and on its Proportion to the whole Income of Great Britain. New and corrected ed., 1800, p. 136.]

[1][Bentham later put a question-mark behind this figure.]

[2] [2][Crossed out later.]

head of the list stand those who, by way of distinction, may be termed the distressed classes: the widow, the orphan, the aged, the infirm.

II. If then the rise of prices were a result inseparably connected with the encrease of wealth, and although it were no more than in proportion to that encrease, it would still be an evil, and an evil of the first magnitude. What shall we say then if, as far as the influence of the assigned cause is concerned, we find the desirable result connected only by mere accident with the undesirable—and therefore, which is the point of real importance, that a check may be given to the undesirable result, without any diminution in the amount of the desirable one?

In the production of this head of mischief, it is true, [we][1] shall not find the instrument here particularly in question (paper money) the only agent, the operation of metallic money in the same line being powerful and indubitable. But in the case of metallic money, though the amount of the mischievous agency may in this particular point of view [be] as great or greater, yet the mischief, if remediable in any degree, admitts not of so sure or safe a remedy.

Call the gold coin, with Mr. Secretary Rose, about £44 millions:[2] or, with Dr. Beeke, but about £40 millions[3]: call the silver and copper coin* two or three millions more: but, for simplicity of calculation, raise the amount too high (the excess being in prejudice of the position contended for), and call the whole amount of the metallic money in the country £50 millions. Call the whole amount of paper money 25 millions.† On this statement, in a gross view, the proportion of [the] addition to the mass of money [made] by paper money [—that is to say] to the mass of metallic money to which it is added —will be exactly equal to that of the addition made to the price of goods: and the amount of the assigned cause in question is exactly equal to the whole amount of the effect.

Such then is the mischief considered as to this branch: and such

[1][The MS reads "which".]

[2][George Rose, A Brief Examination into the Increase of the Revenue, Commerce. and Manufacturers, of Great Britain, from 1792 to 1799. 6th ed., 1799. Appendix No. 4.]

[3][l.c. p. 184.]

*According to the value it passes for, which is the true value to this purpose, how inferior soever to its intrinsic value if melted.

†Of [this sum-total][4] allott half to the Bank of England, the other half to the country banks.

[4][The MS reads "which".]

the quantity and proportion of the influence of the thing pointed to as the cause of it. But the same cause has been supposed to have been, and probably in proportion to the amount of it, the cause of the undisputed addition that has been made in the same interval to the mass of wealth.

The very fact of a rise of prices, when rightly considered, furnishes a proof—a summary, but sufficiently conclusive proof—that it is not the encrease of money that has been productive of any encrease in the quantity of other wealth. Prices have risen 50 per Cent: that is, the same quantity of wealth that before the rise would have been sold for no more than £150 million, now sells for £225 million. Take away then the nominal addition produced by the encrease of money to the nominal amount of the mass of other wealth: there remains the real amount, the same and no more as if the money had never come into the circulation.

In the course of my enquiry into the truth of this supposition, I shall exhibit the reasons that present themselves for thinking

1. that a different cause is the true cause of the addition to the mass of wealth,

2. that the cause in question contributes little or nothing to the same effect, and

3. supposing the error to exist—supposing the opinion [above characterized] to be entertained, and supposing it to be erroneous, I shall endeavour to find out to what source it is to be ascribed.

Meantime, before I speak of the true cause and measure of every encrease in the quantity [of] non-pecuniary wealth, I can not [forbear] indicating a source of illusion by which, unless the illusion be dissipated, or at least a clue given to the deception, any statement that might be made for the purpose of pointing out the true cause and measure [of economic][1] progress would remain exposed to suspicion, and be rejected as theoretical and fanciful.

Money is the instrument, from the operation of which every addition that is made to the mass of non-pecuniary wealth is seen manifestly to flow. The effect being (according to the familiar, but obscure and frequently questionable maxim) proportionable to the cause, hence the more money, the greater the quantity of other kinds of wealth. No wealth that is not produced by labour: no labour (to any amount worth considering for the present purpose) but what is produced by money: what is more—the more money a man has, the

[1][The MS reads "and".]

more labour he commands. What argument to appearance more conclusive, to prove that the quantity of wealth, existing in any community at any given time, will be in proportion to the quantity of money that has been employed in the production of it?—All this is true: yet, after all, it will be no less so, that the quantity of labour produced is not, unless by accident, in proportion to, [and] does not depend upon, the quantity of money employed in producing it.

Any quantity of wealth may be produced without any addition to the quantity of money.

Any addition may be made to the quantity of money in a country, without making any addition to the quantity of other wealth.

In that one of two periods which has most money, true it is that, in general, there will be most wealth: and so as between country and country in the same period. But in this case it is not the encrease in the quantity of money that is the cause of the encrease in the quantity of other wealth; but it is the encrease in the quantity of other wealth that is the cause of the encrease in the quantity of money. As a country without mines encreases in its wealth, it encreases the amount of those masses of wealth which, being collected each into a [?] single hand, afford the owner a surplus by which he is enabled to procure foreign commodities, together [with] masses of foreign money wherewith to procure more.

First then an encrease in the quantity of wealth to any amount may be made at any time without any addition to the quantity of money. This, when applied to the whole commercial world taken together, will be understood, or at least assented to, more readily than if confined in its application to any one country in particular.

In the case of each individual article, wealth is produced by labour—labour by money. But the quantity of wealth produced—the quantity of labour bestowed—has no fixed nor necessary dependence on the quantity of money given for it. Now, in 1800, a day's labour is hardly to be had for as much silver as is contained in 1s 6d. 650 years ago, it was to be had for 2d.* Upon quantity of provisions and other necessaries it does depend—in this sort, viz. that without provisions &c sufficient to keep a man throughout the year, the labour of a man for a year is never to be obtained. But the same quantity of provisions for which a given sum of money has been to be paid at a

*See Table of prices by Sir George Shuckburgh Evelyn, reprinted in Nicholson['s] Journal for September, 1798, from *Philosoph[ical] Transactions* for 1798, p. 176.

later period, has been to be had for less than a tenth part of the money at an earlier.

A given quantity of labour and thence of wealth is produced at all times by any quantity of money, however great or small, for which the quantity of recompense in provisions &c which the labouring hand finds himself enabled to require, happens at that time to be exchanged.

[*Second head of mischief*][1]: *Undue enhancement of prices: viz. of particular commodities, by engrossing.*

My business is here with general tendencies, not [with] particular facts Against the country bankers I have heard it observed, and from the purest sources as far as calumny through personal interest or antipathy is concerned, that in fact it has been a common practice among the trade to engage in what is called *speculation,* for the purpose of raising prices to an undue pitch for their own emolument. Of this practice, considered as a matter of fact, I must acknowledge myself not to have the smallest proof. In the station of an individual I could not be competent to offer any beyond the opinion of impartial and respectable men well acquainted with trade. Not a single instance in proof of such an opinion has ever come within my own cognizance. If any had, it would not be competent to my situation to mention them. Imputed to any individual in particular, it would be a libel upon that individual: attributed to the trade in general, i.e. to the 2 or 300 partnerships engaged in it, it would be a libel on the individuals composing those 2 or 300 partnerships. But to point out tendencies, as arising from situations, is competent to every one, and is what may be done by any individual without fear of incurring any imputation on the score of calumny or injustice.

The situation of a country banker leads him to give into this track of profit in any one of three ways—1. By affording to farmers, manufacturers, and other persons concerned in the production of commodities, such pecuniary supplies as shall enable them to keep back goods from market longer than is necessary or had been customary. and by that means to make to their own profit an undue enhancement to the price paid by the consumer.

2. By enabling dealers to buy up commodities, each of them in [a] larger proportion than he could have done otherwise, and by that

[1][The MS reads "Mischief 2".]

means, where the quantity of the commodity within a certain extent of space favours the design, to combine together in numbers rendered by their smallness susceptible of such a combination, and by agreement with one another impose an exorbitant price upon the consumer.

3. By engaging on their own bottom in transactions of the one sort or the other, more particularly the latter, to which the nature of their funds is better adapted than to the other.

As to this point, what seems plain enough at first sight is, that the facilities for engaging in a traffick of this kind are the greater in a country, the greater its degree of opulence. On a second glance, the matter does not appear quite so clear. If, on the [one][1] hand, in a more wealthy country there is more capital to buy up and keep up goods with than in a less wealthy one, on the other hand there are more goods to be bought up with the money. On the other hand again, in proportion as the country is more and more wealthy, the proportion of the quantity of capital capable of being employed in the buying up of goods, to the quantity of goods, will be great and encreasing: for such encreasing ratio is the characteristic and test, and the indication of it the definition, of growing opulence.

If the danger from enterprizes of this sort on the part of the banking trade depended merely on the quantity of wealth embarked in that trade, it would scarcely form ground for any article of charge: it would be a charge against wealth itself: and would involve the absurdity of bringing into view a retail evil, for the purpose of engaging men to quarrel with a wholesale good.

But the true gi[s]t of the charge is, that the banking trade stands peculiarly exposed to the temptation of injuring the public in this way by their wealth, in a degree more than proportioned to the quantity of that wealth: because it enables them for that particular purpose to create a species of wealth which to them is real, to the rest of the community imaginary, and would not have been created but for this purpose, and which has not the effect of wealth when applied to any other purpose.

The notes are issued—they are distributed in payment of the goods meant to be engrossed—distributed among the farmers or manufacturers by whom they were produced—the goods are got up into the confederated kind [?] of hands—the price to the consumer or retail dealer is raised in consequence, according to the discretion of the

[1] [The MS in fact reads "other".]

confederates—the money is received [back]—the original price replaced in the shape of notes issued as above, or in the shape of cash, and the profit pocketed—and immediately, with the addition of such profit, the banking house is in readiness for another such adventure on a still more extended scale.

Here then comes a tax upon a tax: the tax by the creation of the money, and the tax by the application of it: the tax upon uncommercial men in particular, by the reduction in the value of their incomes, and the tax upon the community in general, in respect of the part each person may happen to take in the consumption of the particular sorts of goods thus made the subject matter of the operation, [that is to say] engrossed.

It is the tendency and property of what may be called naturally formed capital, to lower prices in a variety of ways, in proportion to its encrease: to lower the cost of production in respect of labour, by division of labour, introduction of machinery and so forth, as per Adam Smith; to lower the rate of profit on stock, to wit by competition, as again per Adam Smith. If this beneficial property were shared in an equal degree by this artificial species of capital, as it may be called, if it were equally well adapted to the good purpose as to the bad one, the regret occasioned by the view of this unobserved tax, and blameless usurpation, would be the less considerable.

Unfortunately the mischief has not this palliative: the reverse is the case. This forced, this fabricated species of capital is particularly ill adapted to the encrease of real wealth, to the encrease of the efficient cause of wealth—productive industry. Capital employed in giving birth to productive stock must be capable of abiding, by the duration of its investment, [i.e.] the slowness of return to which investment in that shape is doomed by the nature of things. The capital thus employed in enriching the community—the whole community without any exception—must wait according to the computation full six years before it is returned without encrease, and more than twice that time before it is returned with a *profitable* encrease, with such an encrease as is equal to the ordinary rate of profit on capital embarked in trade.

The capital thus created and employed for the empovrishment of the community—of the whole community together, with the single exception of the creators and their associates—need not wait so much as six months, and, I am inclined to think, would not, upon enquiry, turn out in general to wait a period of that length. But to wait any such period as is adequate to the replacing of capital embarked in the improvement of land or establishment of manufactures, in a word to the giving birth to produce, has been proved by fatal and notorious experience to be incompatible with the nature of the capital created by the issuing of promissory notes. It is a capital therefore fit for nothing but mischief: mischief is the beginning of it and the end: mischief in one shape attends the creation of it, mischief in another shape the application of it: not to speak at present [of][1] what the enquiry is not yet come to, the mischief attendant on a but too frequent result—the annihilation of it.

In speaking of association, I have hitherto confined myself to those associations which, in a trade of that nature, may naturally be supposed to take place between individual banking houses and particular individuals among their respective customers. But another species or degree of association the trade lies open to, which places the mischief from this source in a still more extensive point of view: I mean the associations of these houses one with another. The associations now in view are not the associations as between tens of thousands and tens of thousands, but associations as between millions and millions.

I speak not now of tendencies and probabilities. I speak of established and undisputed facts. In one vast and almost universal association by far the greatest part of these 2, 3, or 400 houses, of these 10, or 15, or 20, or 25 millions, are already linked and have been so for some years. In March and April 1797 the gentleman who manages their affairs declares as much in the Committee of the House of Lords—the declared object, and, for aught I ever heard or suspected, the sole object, such as no set of men need scruple to avow: such as[2] touches not their probity, and does honour to their wisdom.

In a less accumulated and subordinate, but perhaps not much less extensive, system of association, they are known to coalesce in masses, for the extent and composition of which no public voucher can be produced. Here, if the groupes are few, the number of million[s] collected in any one groupe can not be very large. As to the object of these particular associations, I mean the known and only known, and certainly the only universal and constant object, [it] is no less irreproachable, no less laudable, than the other. It is the defending one another, and thereby the community at large, against those dangers

[1][Two words illegible.]
[2][The MS reads "has".]

to which (as we shall have more particular occasion to observe) it is of the essence of the trade to be everlastingly exposed. Whether to this main and constant object *speculation,* as above described, attaches itself as an accidental and collateral object, is a question, the answer to which must be left to rest on the same ground of inference and general probability, as before: but, be this as it may, in regard to associations directed avowedly and by the declared consent of all the several parties, what admitts of no doubt is, that, without any such express consent, an association of this nature affords the means [to] an enterprize of that kind embarked in by any one member of such an association [by the encreased security which it] derives from all the rest.

To support an enterprize that depends on money, it is not by any means necessary that the nature of the enterprize should be known by those by whom the money is supplied. In proportion to the mass of associated capital [?] by which he feels himself backed, is the confidence with which, and the abundance in which, a speculator of this kind issues his notes.

Third head of mischief: Occasional shocks given to commercial security by this species of money, by reason of superabundance in the quantity of it.

By excess it is well enough understood by this time that I can not mean excess with reference to the interests of the community at large. In that point of view, every penny of it is superabundant, any the smallest quantity of it is excessive. I mean that portion of the mass which, from time to time, proves excessive with reference to the interest of the issuers themselves.

[Excess in this sense of the word, it has been said, cannot arise where common prudence is observed. The bankers, we are told, know how far they may extend their note-issue without incurring undue risk: they know how much paper money is at any time likely to be presented to them for exchange against cash, and regulate their business accordingly.] But there is no certain proportion, there can not in the nature of things be any certain proportion, between the quantity of paper and the quantity of cash capable of supporting it: it all depends upon opinion, and opinion is liable to be turned against it, at any time, by all sorts of apprehensions, well or ill founded.

The only standard for the supposed natural proportion is

experience: the natural proportion is then the habitual, the experienced proportion. But inasmuch as this experienced proportion has, during the whole course of the experience, been dependent on opinion, so it must ever continue to be.

The natural and habitual proportion may be considered as the proportion that has generally obtained, bating particular causes of discredit. But though these particular causes of discredit should not rise [?] again, yet a general and permanent cause of discredit, a prevailing suspicion of the solidity of this sort of money, may obtain at any time, and, if so, might be mortal to it. Particular causes of discredit are like diseases, in the intervals of which the patient is restored to health: but this general discredit would be death.

The credit of paper money in some parts of the Kingdom may have derived occasional support from the *cash* in other parts of the Kingdom, where paper had not introduced itself in equal quantity: when therefore it has introduced itself into *these*, that support fails.

OF THE MONEY-HOARDING SYSTEM

Things are illustrated by their contraries. To take the benefit of this observation, let us bestow a glance upon what may be termed the system of thesaurization: the system of laying up hoards of money on the part of government, in reserve for casual exigencies. As the introduction of paper money makes, in the first instance at least, an addition to the mass of money in circulation, so does the hoarding system produce, in the first instance at least, a defalcation from that same mass.

If by paper money no addition is made to the mass of other wealth, by the hoarding system no defalcation (it may be said) will be made from it. The advantages resulting from the hoarding system are great and obvious: they have hitherto been looked upon as not clear, but bought at the expence of the addition that might otherwise have been made to the mass of national wealth. If that addition is illusory, the policy of the hoarding system will shine in added lustre.

Defalcation, like addition—defalcation from the source in question as from any other, defalcation as well as addition—may be considered, as before, with reference to addition to wealth, addition to prices, and influence on commercial credit. Let us begin with wealth.

[I.] 1. That a defalcation, made in this or any other way, from the mass of money in circulation should in any case be productive of any addition to the mass of wealth, is seen to be impossible at the first word.

2. If, at the commencement of the hoarding plan, the national stock of, [and] capacity for, labour happens to be fully employed, and employed to the best advantage, in respect of the encrease of wealth, or if, though not employed to the best advantage, things are so circumstanced that no addition to the mass of money, or no addition to the mass of money employed in the shape of productive capital, could have the effect of causing the stock of [or] capacity for labour to be employed to any greater advantage, and if at this time the ratio of money to wealth, and consequently the amount of prices, is on the encrease, a defalcation to any amount not exceeding that of the supposed encrease of the stock of money can not be productive of any defalcation from the growing mass of wealth.

3. In any other than this last-supposed case, the defalcation thus made from the mass of money will be productive of a defalcation to a certain degree from the mass of wealth. Of the amount of this latter defalcation let us endeavour to form an estimate according to the different modifications of which the case is susceptible.

Let us suppose that there exists in the country a quantity of unemployed capacity for labour adequate to the whole quantity of money that would have been employed in the shape of productive capital, had it not been for the supposed defalcation. In this case the defalcation from the mass of money is really productive of a correspondent, though not equal, defalcation from the mass of wealth. The money hoarded by government, and hence defalcated from the stock of money in circulation, is parcel of the money raised by taxes: the taxes are imposts laid, for the most part at least, if not exclusively, on expenditure. Of the money taken by the tax, part, and by far the greater part, would have been spent in a way not to make any addition, or not to make an addition to so large a proportionable amount as that in which it might have been employed to make an addition to the mass of wealth: [an]other part would have been spent in the most advantageous way in respect of the making addition to the amount of growing wealth: in a word, [the one] part would have been spent in the way of consumption, in the way of present enjoyment—the other part in the way of accumulation, in adding to the amount of the sources of future enjoyment and subsistence.

To afford the mind the relief that may be afforded by the use of figures, suppose the account to stand as follows:

Annual amount of money hoarded and thence taken out of the circulation—say	£1,000,000
Of this, if not taken from individuals by taxes, there would have been employed and expended in the way of accumulation, say 1/10th	[£]100,000
Of the remaining £900,000 spent in the way of enjoyment, there would have been expended in the purchase of labour so employed as not to leave behind it any produce whatsoever, such as that of domestic servants of all descriptions, actors, dancers, musicians, kept mistresses &c, say	[£]100,000
Of d° £900,000, there would have been spent in the purchase of labour employed in the production of commodities which, when sold, are sold for a mass of money, a part of which, say 15 per Cent, is returned in the shape of profit by the persons employed as cultivators, master manufacturers, merchants or shop-keepers, or carriers in the production or distribution of them	£800,000
Profit upon the above £800,000, at 15 per Cent ...	£120,000
Whereof saved up and added to stock, i.e. employed in the purchase of such labour and materials, the produce of former labour, whereby additions are made to the mass of productive stock or capital, say 5 per Cent	£40,000

On the face of this account, the result of the hoarding every year a quantity of money to a given amount is a loss to productive capital to the amount of about ⅙th part of the money hoarded: to which may be added [the] loss of the addition that would have been [made] in the way of interest, in each succeeding year.

The effects of hoarding metallic [money] have very little resemblance to the effects of those diminutions to which the stock of paper money is subject, though defalcation be the result in both cases. In the case of hoarding, the defalcation is gradual and comparatively inconsiderable: too much so to have any perceptible effect, it may well be supposed, in respect of the lowering of prices. The effects of a shock to paper credit, though the defalcation may be very copious and sudden, may also be incapable of producing any sensible effect in the way of lowering prices. But in this case it is from a very different cause. The same state of things which raised the stock of paper money to the height from which it was beaten down by the force of the supposed shock would, in no great length of time, be sufficient to raise it up again to that same level: and as this restitution would naturally take place before the time when prices might have adjusted themselves to the level of the reduced mass of money, any determinate fall of prices does not appear to be among the consequences naturally to be expected from shocks to which paper money in a country circumstanced like Britain is exposed.

But though there appears to be no period in which a defalcation from money to any such amount as is likely to be made by the money hoarding system appears likely to be productive of any very sensible effect in the way of lowering prices, a practice of this supposes the existence of a period at which a considerable effect will naturally be produced in the way of raising prices. I mean the period, whatever it be, at which the hoarded money may come to be disbursed. This period is that of war. War is that state of things, with a view to which, and for the sake of which, hoards of this sort are laid up. When the war comes, then comes the disbursement: and of this disbursement it may naturally be expected that it will [be] at the same time copious enough, and of sufficiently long continuance, to produce a very perceptible rise of prices.

A circumstance that helps to diminish the effect that the defalcation produced by hoarding would otherwise have in the way of lowering prices, is the defalcation produced by the same cause from what would otherwise have been the amount of the mass of wealth. By intercepting the addition that would otherwise have been made immediately to the mass of productive capital, it intercepts the additions that would otherwise have been made to the growing mass of vendible commodities, in the way of interest upon the principal of which that capital would have been composed.

II. Secondly in regard to prices—

Like the effects of addition, those of defalcation may in this view be beneficial, prejudicial, or indifferent, according to circumstances.

If the ratio of money to wealth be on the encrease, and to such a degree upon the encrease, as to produce a rise of prices, the operation of the defalcation in question will be in that respect beneficial, so far as the effect of it is to check the rise, or stop it altogether, without producing any such fall as shall be productive of a sensible inconvenience.

If the ratio of money to wealth be not on the encrease, still more if it be on the decrease, the effect of the defalcation in question will be to produce a fall of prices more or less sensible according to the proportion of the money defalcated to the mass from which it was defalcated.

[III.] In respect of commercial credit it can have no effect analogous to that with which paper money is apt to be attended by reason of the sudden, though temporary, defalcations to which the mass of it is exposed. In the case of thesaurization, the defalcation from the mass in circulation is always gradual, nor can ever be otherwise. It has a tendency to bear hard upon those classes whose incomes are subject to deductions to a fixed pecuniary amount, such as persons holding land or houses on long leases, but its real effect in this way can never be very considerable: especially since before the fall of prices, if any, can have had time enough to be very considerable, an occasion for disbursing the hoard may well be expected to take place, and then, whatever other effects, good or bad, may result from the overthrow, a proportionally great, and at any rate a sudden rise of prices will be an inseparable effect.

Of the money-hoarding system, the only example worth considering in this view that has been presented in modern times, in times of which the circumstances are at all analogous to those in which our country is now placed, is that which was afforded by [the] conquering King, the most celebrated of the Kings of Prussia. In his instance, in the circumstances in which he had placed himself, it was a matter rather of necessity than choice. The injustice and violence of his conduct and character had given him for an irreconciliable enemy the most powerful of his neighbours. Violating the laws of justice and good faith, habitually and even without a mask, he had precluded himself from all hope of seeing them observed by others to his benefit. With the prospect of a demand for money constantly before his eyes, a demand sudden in point of occasion, and unlimited in its amount, he found himself under a constant obligation, on pain of instant destruction, of straining every nerve for the purpose of laying in the largest stock of that instrument of defence which it was in his power to raise. The funding [or] borrowing system was not open to his choice. Reputation of probity [and] apparent solidity of power were both wanting on the one part: confidence and even money were wanting on the other. Neither his own dominions, nor even any part of the surrounding states,[1] especially when those parts were excluded which were either under the government or the influence of those whom he had made his irreconciliable enemies, furnished a stock of lendable money adequate to any such purpose.

But though in Frederick's situation, Frederick's line of conduct in this respect was an unavoidable one, it can not absolutely be inferred from thence, but that, independently of such necessity, it may have been the best that could have been pursued, not only in his circumstances [but in general]. It is by no means without example, especially in state affairs, that a man has been driven by necessity into measures, into which, had he possessed a just conception of his own interests, he would [never] have been led by choice.

To Great Britain, the adoption of the money hoarding system is not, nor ever has been, a matter of necessity: [nor does there seem to be][2] any sufficient reason in favour of its becoming an object of choice.

[Indication of the Remedies]

Besides bad seasons, the temporary cause, and the remediable deficiency [of land devoted to the production] of the articles composing the principal part of the subsistence of the community there are two permanent causes of reduction of income—diminution of the rate of profit on stock, whence also in the general rate of interest, and encrease in the relative quantity of money, cash and paper taken together. Of these two causes, the former is the inseparable concomitant of general opulence and prosperity, and is altogether unsusceptible of any thing that can be termed a remedy: since [?] the only thing by which the inconvenience, such as it is, could be prevented, would be a diminution in the relative quantity of stock, in other words, the substituting to a state of general opulence and prosperity, a state of general impovrishment and adversity.

The latter is within the reach of cure. The cure will consist—1. in the restraining the encrease of paper money: and 2. in the restraining, or at least forbearing to encourage, the encrease of cash.

[1] [The MS reads "in his dominions" and "in any other part".]

[2] [The MS which here breaks off, in fact reads "let us see whether there be . . .". The interpolation anticipates the result at which Bentham's argument, had it been worked out, would certainly have been driving.]

For Product Safety Concerns and Information please contact our EU representative GPSR@taylorandfrancis.com
Taylor & Francis Verlag GmbH, Kaufingerstraße 24, 80331 München, Germany

www.ingramcontent.com/pod-product-compliance
Lightning Source LLC
Chambersburg PA
CBHW060515220326
41599CB00022B/3333